Faizi

Faizi the undergraduate, 1929

Faizi

by

May Faizi-Moore

George Ronald
Oxford

George Ronald, *Publisher*
Oxford
www.grbooks.com

© May Faizi-Moore 2013
All Rights Reserved

reprinted 2015, 2024

*A catalogue record for this book is available
from the British Library*

ISBN 978–0–85398–568–6

Cover design: Naysán Faizi

Contents

Introduction	vii
Acknowledgements	xv
Prologue	xix

1	Childhood	1
2	Tehran – Tarbíyat School – Youth	40
3	Beirut	54
4	Return Home	71
5	Najafábád	78
6	Qazvín	120
7	Preparing to Leave Iran	132
8	Baghdad	136
9	Bahrain: The Lonely Years	140
10	Bahrain: Beginnings of a Community	160
11	The Road of No Return	225
12	The Holy Land: A Change of Direction	229
13	The End of an Era	259
14	'I Do It Because I Must'	291
15	No Time for Rest	297
16	Anecdotes and Insights	304
17	The Indomitable Spirit	330
18	A Quiet Year	334
19	Twilight	339
20	Vignettes	351

Appendix I: Passion Plays	375
Appendix II: *Zúrkhánih*	378
Appendix III: Record of Faizi's Travels	381
Appendix IV: Major Publications	388

Bibliography	391
References and Notes	393
Index	399

Introduction

My mother, Gloria Faizi, had begun work on my father's biography several months before she passed away. She had translated some of the accounts my father had himself written of his early years and recorded a few of her own recollections of their life together before her untimely death in June 2004.

This is the introduction she wrote to the book she was to have written:

> I was hoping that the story of the life of Faizi would not be written by one person. I have, therefore, over the years, tried to persuade some of his friends who had associated with him at different periods of his life to send me what they remember of those days. My intention was to put together these recollections in such a way as to portray a full picture of Faizi's life, filling in the gaps myself. Unfortunately this has proved to be impractical, and I find I am obliged to write this biography as best I can, drawing on my own notes for the most part . . . I feel I must, however, put on record that there are many inaccuracies in what has come out in print about the events in the life of Faizi. Most of these are stories that have passed from mouth to mouth and become completely distorted. Others are pure speculations and have no source whatsoever.

Wherever possible I have incorporated what my mother had translated; however, whilst drawing heavily on the documents she had collated, as well as my father's letters and diaries and the recollections of those who had responded to her request to send her their memories and anecdotes, the biography, inevitably, lacks information only my mother could have provided.

I have not gone into any detail about my father's travels, talks and the courses he conducted, as these are well recorded elsewhere, nor have I delved into his scholastic works – which I am sure those more able than I will one day address – but have rather concentrated on giving the reader some insight into his character and his personal relationships with family, friends and all with whom he came into contact.

My father's use of the Persian language in his written work and many of his letters is exquisite; but I must put on record that, although he loved poetry and knew many poems off by heart, he never wrote any himself. As for his English, he had his own, individual way of putting words together, which I have kept when quoting him directly. To have 'corrected' his English would have removed its charm and romantic quality.

For those not familiar with the Bahá'í Faith, I thought it would be useful to provide some information to enable a better understanding not only of the backdrop to this biography but also of some of the terminology used and the significance of some of the names mentioned.

☙

The Founder of the Bahá'í Faith was a Persian nobleman, Bahá'u'lláh, meaning 'the Glory of God'. Believers in the Bahá'í Faith are called Bahá'ís and within the Bahá'í community are sometimes referred to as 'believers', 'fellow believers' or 'friends'.

The Forerunner to Bahá'u'lláh was the Báb (also a Persian) who, in the mid-19th century, foretold the coming of Bahá'u'lláh and whose followers were called Bábís. From the beginning of their history the Bábís faced severe opposition in Iran. Over twenty thousand men, women and children were killed in the space of a few years and the Báb Himself was executed at the age of 30. His remains are buried on the slopes of Mount Carmel and the memorial is referred to as the Shrine of the Báb.

INTRODUCTION

Like the Báb, Bahá'u'lláh was persecuted by the authorities in Iran and was eventually exiled to the prison-city of 'Akká, which was at the time under Ottoman rule. He passed away in 1892 while still a prisoner, although under more relaxed conditions, and is buried in the vicinity, which is why the World Centre of the Bahá'í Faith is in the Holy Land. Bahá'ís visiting the resting places of Bahá'u'lláh and the Báb and places associated with them are referred to as 'pilgrims'.

Bahá'ís are now the largest religious minority in Iran but continue to be persecuted in their homeland.

༄

Bahá'ís accept the Founders of all the major world religions and believe that Bahá'u'lláh is the latest in a long line of Messengers sent by God to guide humanity.

In His Will, Bahá'u'lláh appointed His son, 'Abdu'l-Bahá (also known as the Master), as the Centre of His Covenant and as the person Bahá'ís should turn to after His death. When 'Abdu'l-Bahá passed away, His Will appointed His grandson, Shoghi Effendi, as the Guardian of the Bahá'í Faith. Bahá'ís refer to him either by name or by his title.

༄

The Bahá'í Faith has no clergy but does have an Administrative Order. Elections for the institutions that administer and coordinate the activities of the Bahá'í communities at every level are by secret ballot. Bahá'ís have a strong ethos of consultation in all their meetings and, indeed, in all their affairs.

While Bahá'ís are enjoined to share the message of Bahá'u'lláh with everyone, proselytizing is forbidden.

Through the Plans he gave to the Bahá'í world, Shoghi Effendi encouraged Bahá'ís to spread to different parts of the world and guided them in developing and strengthening Bahá'í institutions and the Administrative Order of Bahá'u'lláh. This included electing Local Assemblies in localities where Bahá'ís resided and National Assemblies in each country. In time, these would elect the world governing body of the Bahá'ís, the Universal House of Justice.

☙

Hands of the Cause of God were men and women who were chosen because of their outstanding qualities and abilities to assist in propagating and protecting the Bahá'í Faith internationally. Although both Bahá'u'lláh and 'Abdu'l-Bahá appointed Hands of the Cause, it was during Shoghi Effendi's ministry that most of them were appointed. The last Hand of the Cause passed away in 2007.

Shoghi Effendi did not appoint a successor after his death in 1957. The 26 Hands of the Cause at the time steered the Bahá'í world through the remaining five years of a Ten Year Plan which had been launched by Shoghi Effendi in 1953 and took the decision that the Universal House of Justice should be elected at the end of the Plan in 1963. The Hands of the Cause passed the reins of the Bahá'í Faith to the Universal House of Justice as soon as it was elected.

☙

By 'the writings' is generally meant Bahá'í scripture, which are the writings of Bahá'u'lláh, the Báb and 'Abdu'l-Bahá.

Among the teachings of the Bahá'í Faith are that humankind's spiritual development, as with its material civilization, should be progressive, that the moral teachings of the Founders of all the world's religions are essentially the same and that the reason why their social teachings differ is because they had to address the needs of the era in which they were revealed.

Unity is the hallmark of the Bahá'í Faith. Attempts have been made by individuals at every turn to bring about schism but none have succeeded. Bahá'ís who set out to bring about disunity,

INTRODUCTION

division and faction within the community, who persist with their intention and actively work against the Faith while claiming to be Bahá'ís, are expelled from the Bahá'í community and are referred to as 'Covenant-breakers'.

The Bahá'í Faith continues to progress under the protection of its institutions elected by its followers – Local and National Assemblies annually and the Universal House of Justice once every five years – and by the Counsellors (appointed by the Universal House of Justice), and their Auxiliary Board Members who continue the work of the Hands of the Cause.

ɷ

Some principles of the Bahá'í Faith:
- The oneness of humankind
- Universal peace upheld by a world government
- Independent investigation of truth
- The common foundation of all religions
- The essential harmony of science and religion
- Equality of men and women
- Elimination of prejudice of all kinds
- Universal compulsory education
- A spiritual solution to the economic problem
- A universal auxiliary language

ɷ

Bahá'ís have a calendar of 19 months of 19 days each within the solar calendar. The remaining days of the Gregorian calendar, which in the Bahá'í calendar occur at the end of February and beginning of March, are referred to as Intercalary Days.

Naw-Rúz, the Bahá'í new year, begins at the moment of the vernal equinox in the northern hemisphere on either 20 or 21 March. The beginning of every Bahá'í month and the holy days are adjusted accordingly, with the exception of the birthdays of the Báb and Bahá'u'lláh which fall on consecutive days approximately eight months after Naw-Rúz.

20 or 21 March – Naw-Rúz (New Year) and the first day of the Bahá'í calendar

20 or 21, 28 or 29 April and 1 or 2 May – A period when Bahá'u'lláh publically declared His mission, called Ridván

23 or 24 May – The day the Báb declared His mission

28 or 29 – The Ascension of Bahá'u'lláh, the day of Bahá'u'lláh's passing

9 or 10 July – The martyrdom of the Báb

2 consecutive days in the months of October or November celebrating the birthdays of the Báb and Bahá'u'lláh

☙

19 Day Feast: A gathering at the beginning of every Bahá'í month where Bahá'ís pray together, discuss the affairs of the community and socialize.

Abhá Kingdom: The afterlife.

Ancient Beauty/Blessed Beauty: Titles of Bahá'u'lláh.

Auxiliary Board Member: Assistants to Hands of the Cause and now to the Counsellors.

Continental Counsellors: Men and women appointed to assist in propagating and protecting the Bahá'í Faith in designated

INTRODUCTION

continents. (Both the Counsellors and Auxiliary Board Members are appointed for a limited term.)

Covenant: The instrument provided by Bahá'u'lláh to ensure the protection of the unity of the Bahá'í Faith after His passing, by the appointment in His signed and sealed Will of 'Abdu'l-Bahá as His successor, by 'Abdu'l-Bahá's appointment in His Will of Shoghi Effendi as the Guardian of the Bahá'í Faith and by the establishment of the Universal House of Justice as stipulated in the Kitáb-i-Aqdas (the Book of Laws).

Firesides: Common name for a gathering where the Bahá'í Faith is discussed with enquirers.

Heroic Age: The first period of Bahá'í history which ended with the passing of 'Abdu'l-Bahá.

International Teaching Centre: The body comprising Counsellors that continues the work of the Hands of the Cause into the future. The International Teaching Centre is based at the Bahá'í World Centre.

Pioneer/Pioneering: Leaving one's homeland to settle in another location.

The Remover of Difficulties: A special prayer revealed by the Báb to be used in time of difficulty.

Síyáh-Chál: The underground dungeon where Bahá'u'lláh was imprisoned for four months before being exiled from Iran.

For further information: www.bahai.org/

May Faizi-Moore
Cyprus
Autumn 2012

Acknowledgements

Foremost in this acknowledgement must be those who responded to my mother's request for anecdotes and memories of my father. Without the information provided by them it would have been impossible for me to give the reader a reasonably well-rounded account of my father's life. I list their names below with my deep gratitude.

No less credit goes to my father himself for not only recording his memories of the most important milestones in his life but also for leaving behind his written works and vast correspondence, much of which give insights into his daily life; and to my mother who collated almost all the documents referred to in this book and translated a good portion of my father's memories in the first chapter.

I want to thank, on my mother's behalf, Ruhi Nooreyesdan and Vafa Fakhri: Ruhi Nooreyesdan for typing some of my mother's translations and Vafa Fakhri for the immense help he gave her in categorizing many of the letters and documents in preparation for her writing of the biography.

I am indebted to the Research Department at the Bahá'í World Centre for answering my questions and sending me the information I needed.

There are a number of other individuals whose part in helping bring this biography to life I would like to acknowledge:

Drs Robert and Nazila Hercock-Ghanea for their encouragement and practical support.

Shapoor Vazirzadeh, who patiently spent many days with me going through the more difficult to decipher Persian documents and letters and without whose meticulous rewriting of the complex words and passages I would have found any progress impossible.

Shiva Ashrafi, who also helped me with the Persian documents and who was at the end of my frequent telephone calls to explain the use of certain Persian words.

Dr Masoud Afnan for helping clarify the diagnosis of my father's heart condition.

My 'sister' Lynnie Moore for reading the manuscript and giving me her opinion from the perspective of someone who is not a Bahá'í.

As for my family, I undertook to write this biography partly for them. For Hooshang and Naysán – who has been with me in spirit throughout this project – Zohreh, Chehreh and Árám. For my sons, Paul-Faizi and Thomas, who have supported me with the interest they have shown in the progress of the biography.

My editor, Dr Wendi Momen, has not only been a pleasure to work with but also invaluable with her astute and sympathetic editing.

Finally, my boundless thanks goes to Hushmand Fatheazam and 'Alí Nakhjavání: Mr Fatheazam, who from the very beginning gave me the impetus by telling me that if I wrote the biography he would translate it into Persian and has, throughout, offered me guidance; and Mr Nakhjavání who has been equally supportive and, together with Mr Fatheazam, given me sound advice.

The one person for whom I have no adequate words to express my gratitude is my husband, Peter. From singlehandedly converting half his precious workshop space into a study for me, to drawing up a reference system for recording every document I read, to pushing me to buckle down to writing when he felt I was being slack and negligent, to reading through every chapter and giving me his frank opinion, he has been my constant pillar of support. This biography would not have been completed without his unflagging encouragement and love.

ACKNOWLEDGEMENTS

Contributors

Ḥasan 'Abdu'l-Raḥímzádih
'Abdu'lláh Abízádih
George Adams
Abu'l-Qásim Afnán
Shomais Afnan
Mahnaz Afshin
Manouchehr Ágáhí
Rúḥu'lláh Ágáhí Najafábádí
Fu'ád Aḥmadpúr
'Ináyat Akhaván
Fazlollah Akhtarkhavari
Farhang 'Alá'í
Homa 'Alá'í
Shahab 'Alá'í
Aminu'lláh Anvari
A. Ashraf
Fu'ád Ashraf
Masíḥu'lláh Asadiyán
Maḥmúd 'Aṭṭár
Florence Avis
Khusraw Ázurdigán

Najla Baghdadi
Alan G. Bell
Paul Bellamy
Mark Benatar
Brett Breneman
Foster M. Buckner

Margaret Carey

Ellen Catherine Dekker-McMiles

Massoud Derakhshani
Ḥabíbu'lláh Dhabíḥiyán

Ralph Elberg

Muhammad Ali Faizi
Faramarz Farid
Amír Faráhí
'Atá'u'lláh Furútan

A. Ghalili
Kathy Gilbert
Amínih Gulmuḥammadí
Dhabíbu'lláh Gulmuḥammadí
U Ko Gyi

Mr and Mrs Hakiman
A. Hariri
Violet Hoehnke
Elizabeth D. Hollinger
Larry Hosack
Rouhi Huddleston

Ismá'íl 'Ináyatí

Lisa Janti
Reza Jahangiri
H. Jalili
Gulrukh Javánmardí
Shápúr Javánmardí
Amín and Nishát Jazzáb

Mr Junaydí

Shirin Khadem-Missagh
Jane Khamsi
Mas'úd Khamsí
Farah Samimi Khamsi
Samin Khamsi
Mr Khudádúst
'Abdu'l-Karím Khushábí
John Kolstoe
Arthur L. Krummell

Shirley Macias
Hassan Madjid
Amínu'lláh Mandigárí
Naṣru'lláh Mavadat
Mr Mawlavínizhád
Margaret Maytan
Iain McDonald
R. Mehrábkhání
Jalál Míthágí
Rúḥá Míthágí
Behjat Mokhless
Mr Mokhless
Gloria Momen
Moojan Momen
Touran Mottahed
Mr Mowzoon
Mr Mubidzádih
Aḥmad and Lami'ih Muḥsiní
Rúḥu'lláh Mumtází
Mitra Murray

FAIZI

Scott Murray
Saʻíd Muʻtamid

Faizollah and Ursula Namdar
National Spiritual Assembly of United Arab Emirates
Rúḥuʼlláh Nátiq
Soraya Nátiq
Margaret Nelson
Shaydá Nírú
Mehmet Niyazi
Salim Noonoo
Lea Nys

Joseph Peter
Shirin Podger
Winifred Pratley
Baháʼí Pústchí

Ḥusayn Rafíʻí
Yaduʼlláh Rafʻat
ʻAbuʼl-Faḍl Raḥmání
Hadi Rahmani
ʻAtá Rawḥání
Ḥasan Rawḥání
Marḍiyyih Rawḥání

Hishmatuʼlláh Rayḥání
Naʻím Rayḥání
Alexander Reid
Blanche Rudnick
Rafʻat Rustamí

E. Sádiqiyán
Maliḥih Safájú
Fariborz Sahba
Manouchehr Salmanpour
Valiullah Samadani
Badiullah Samadani
Jacques André Schweitzer
Ian Semple
Manzur Shah
Ṭúbá Shamsí
Kaykhusraw Sifídvash
Barbara Sims
Leilani Smith
Mohi Sobhani
René A. Steiner
Manúchihr Ṣubḥání
Mr Sulaymání
Kay Sullivan

Teresa Taffa
Vahid Tehrani
ʻAbbás Thábit (Sabet)
ʻAtáʼuʼlláh Thábit
Catherine Thompson
Adam Thorne

Mahin Vaḥdat
Qudratuʼlláh Vaḥíd
Fereydoun Vahman
Anthony Vaykovic
Katherine Villiers-Stuart

Qudsiyyih Wahid
Edna Warren
Bill Washington
Ngar Whiteford (Mohseni)
O. Z. Whitehead
Isobel Wilson

Daryúsh Yazdání

Ehsan Zahrai
Shahab Zahrai

Prologue

Although it is many years since his death in 1980 at the age of 73, the memory of my father remains fresh. But it is invariably the image of him as a youth that filters through my mind's eye. It is that of a relaxed, handsome man in his late twenties; his jaw line is gently angular; his chin firm but not aggressive; his lips well-proportioned, with humour playing at each corner; his eyes dark and pensive, and yet with a direct gaze reflecting the pure passion in his inner being. A slight questioning frown between his well-defined eyebrows leads to his broad brow, and from that brow is swept back his dark, luxuriant hair. His able hands rest on a pile of books on his lap.

Who was this man who from his youth to his dying day lodged such warm, sweet affection in the hearts of nearly all the men, women and children with whom he came in contact? What was the source of his inimitable charisma, his extraordinary capacity to love his fellow man, his unwavering, clear and totally focused aim in life?

In the Bahá'í world he was known as A. Q. Faizi, Hand of the Cause of God. To those who met him he was referred to as Mr Faizi, and to his closest friends as Faizi. To my brothers and me, he was our father.

My brothers and I adored our father and, quite naturally, thought that there was no other father like ours. As I grew in years I began to realize that others, too, felt intense love for him. It was, however, only after his death when his friends from around the world reminisced about him – not so much about his services, which we all knew about, but about his wisdom when his advice was sought, about the quiet, unobtrusive ways in which he helped the needy and about the courage and fortitude he instilled in believers, particularly in pioneers living in arduous conditions – when my private conviction that he was no ordinary man was reinforced.

This unique man was one of the spiritual giants of our age. He was one of the heroes of the Cause which had captivated his soul and to which he had, like a lover to his beloved, given his all to his very last breath before rising, phoenix-like, from his exhausted, burnt-up body to soar into realms of infinite joy towards the presence of those noble souls who were his heroes.

1
Childhood

Naw-Rúz had come and gone over the land of Iran and left spring in its wake. Wild flowers carpeted the countryside around the city of Qum. Fruit trees were bursting into blossom. The air shook off the chill of winter with every movement of the temperate breeze. The inhabitants of the city warmed themselves under the gentle rays of the sun with hopes of a good year to come.

In the home of one of the leading families of the city an expectant mother waited patiently for the imminent birth of her fourth child. As her time approached the woman willed her unborn to enter this world with the good fortune of a long life. Her firstborn, Muḥammad 'Alí was now a healthy seven year old boy and the apple of his parents' eyes but she had lost two infants after him and could not bear the thought of going through the heartache of losing another child.

In time the young mother gave birth to a son and as she held him in her arms the strong bond she already had with him grew even stronger. Little did she know what the future of her newborn would be as she gazed into his tender face. All she wanted to do was to hold him, to care for and protect him, to love him and his brother and to bring them up to be good men.

The child was named Abu'l-Qásim. And so Faizi's life began.

ଏ

Setting the Scene

Faizi was born in Qum in 1906 or 1907. The exact date of his birth is unknown, as most people in Iran at that time did not attach much importance to birthdays. The custom was that the date of a child's birth would be recorded on a page of the family Qur'án or the book of Ḥáfiẓ[1] and then forgotten. Faizi himself did not find celebrating birthdays important, nor did he care to find out when he was born but he once told me that he believed it was in the first week or two of April.

The city of Qum, not far from the capital, Tehran, is the second most sacred city in Iran. It is still considered to be the most conservative and fanatical of all the Muslim strongholds in the country with the rich, golden dome of the shrine of Ma'ṣúmih, the sister of one of the important Imáms in Islam, dominating the town and attracting pilgrims from all over the country. The turbaned priests of the city held the reins of all affairs in their hands and no one was permitted to utter a word contrary to their wishes – even in the privacy of their homes husbands and wives did not dare to speak their minds to each other, fearing that their words might reach the ears of the district priest and provoke his anger and severe punishment.

During Faizi's childhood the visiting pilgrims crowded the shrine of Ma'ṣúmih and the surrounding streets. Hovering nearby were the priests who offered to recite the right prayers for the pilgrims for a nominal fee and the Siyyids who pestered the pilgrims to pay their dues.[2] From the moment of their arrival until they left, the pilgrims were harangued by these men who would ruthlessly insist on receiving their money. The predicament of the pilgrims who were poor upset the young, tender-hearted Faizi so much that he would be reduced to inconsolable sobbing in the street and his grandmother had to spend a long time comforting and calming him down.

Adjacent to the shrine where the men came together was a large courtyard and a smaller one reserved for the women where they gathered in great numbers in the evenings to breathe a breath of fresh air and allow their smaller children, who had been confined to cramped houses during the day, to run around and play. On one of the graves in this area was a stone lion with an engraving of an Indian club and the bow-shaped iron that is used in Persian gymnastics. Little Faizi's favourite game was to ride on this stone lion. One day his grandmother told him that the grave belonged to Pahlaván³ Ḥusayn. 'God rest his soul in peace,' she said. 'He was like a strong pillar. When a loaded donkey fell in the stream he straddled the stream and pulled out the donkey and its load.' Her words created such great excitement in the child's vivid imagination that he pictured himself as Pahlaván Ḥusayn and wished that he could have known him. To the end of his life Faizi was drawn to *pahlaváns* and tried to spend some time in their company wherever he came across them.

The Family

Faizi's parents, 'Abdu'l Ḥusayn K͟hán and Siddíqih K͟hánum (Mádar-jún,⁴ as we knew her) were cousins and descendants of the well-known scholar and commentator of the Qur'án Mullá Muhsin-i-Fayz-i-Kás͟hání, in whose name the famous theological college in Qum, the Fayḍiyyih, was founded. His maternal uncle was Mullá Muḥammad Fayḍ, a powerful and influential Muslim scholar. (Faizi remembered going to this uncle's house as a child and described it as being very large with upper floor living accommodation, enclosed gardens and open grounds where carpets were spread under the trees. Priceless *termeh*⁵ hung over the branches of these trees and servants continuously served tea to the crowd of never-ending visitors.) Through his maternal grandmother Faizi was also a descendant of the much-loved 18th-century benevolent ruler of Iran Karím K͟hán-i-Zand, whose short dynasty was overthrown by the Qájárs.

'Abdu'l Ḥusayn K͟hán was a dignified person and respected by all who knew him. Faizi, who addressed his father as 'K͟hán' (as did everyone else), described him as being 'tall, good-looking and with a penetrating gaze'. Although K͟hán loved his sons, his relationship with them was rather formal and distant and, as was the custom of the time, he left their upbringing to his wife. By contrast, Mádar-jún's relationship with her sons was close, warm, affectionate and gentle, but firm when necessary. It was she who had the greatest influence in developing their characters and both spoke of the debt they owed her for instilling in them compassion for their fellow humans and teaching them endurance in the face of difficulties. They described her as being kind, generous and pure in spirit. My own memory of Mádar-jún is that she was quietly strong-willed but at the same time an even-tempered and loving lady who always seemed to be helping some disadvantaged soul. She was an extremely generous woman and did not think twice about giving what she had to someone who was needier than herself.

An example of her compassionate and charitable heart happened in Qum during a period of famine and left a lasting impression on her youngest son. One day during this time Faizi and his mother went to one of her sisters, who was a well-to-do woman, where Mádar-jún spent the whole day helping the family bake bread. Towards evening they returned home with a few loaves which Mádar-jún carried under her *chádur*.[6] On their way they passed a small group of poverty-stricken people leaning against a wall. As they approached the group one of the starving men who had caught a whiff of the freshly-baked bread moaned with hunger.

'Oh, what a good smell of bread!'

Without a second's thought or any hesitation in her walk Mádar-jún let all the loaves she was carrying drop in front of the poor people and continued on her way. She and Faizi returned home empty-handed.

Another of Mádar-jún's qualities was that she would not tolerate negative comments being made about anyone and would cut short any backbiter, saying that they did not really know what the person's circumstances were or what was in his or her heart. She was loved by all who crossed her path but remained an unassuming woman to the end of her life.

Khán had two brothers and two sisters. The three brothers were all civil servants working for the telegraph office but it was

Khán who was, as the head of the telegraph office of his area, posted to different cities. Rather than take his wife and young sons around the country every time he was sent to a different post, he left them in the care of his brothers and sisters in Qum, where his two brothers and one of his sisters and their families lived together in a large house. Faizi was seven years old when Khán was posted to Maláyir and decided to take his eldest son with him. (Faizi recalled that when they told him where his father and brother had gone he thought that Maláyir was in one of the distant lands of Asia and felt the other children in school, having heard the news, looked at him guardedly, so fantastic was the event.) A year later when Khán was posted to Hamadán, he decided to enrol Muḥammad 'Alí in the best school of the area, a Bahá'í school. It was there that my uncle first heard the message of Bahá'u'lláh. Khán started going to Bahá'í meetings at night but he never spoke about the Faith to his son. However, my uncle was certain that his father had known about the Bahá'í Faith for some time and was a believer at heart, otherwise he would never have sent him to a Bahá'í school.

My uncle soon became acquainted with the Bahá'í students in the school and he closely observed their manners and behaviour, which he found to be completely contrary to what he had heard from some of his relatives and other Muslims. What he learned about the message of Bahá'u'lláh during this time changed his heart and, as he put it, woke him from his slumber. Several years later he approached his maternal uncle, the *mujtahid*, and without letting him know openly that he had become a Bahá'í, told him that he had been associating with Bahá'ís, had attended their meetings, observed their character, behaviour and manners and found that all the rumours about them were unfounded lies. He questioned his uncle, asking him where he had heard the stories and whether he had read any books on the beliefs of the Bahá'ís. After some discussion the *mujtahid* retorted that there was no reason for him to accept the claims of this Faith. He then became a little more reasonable, telling his nephew that if the claims and teachings of the Bahá'ís were acceptable, he would believe and asked my uncle to prove the truth of the Faith to him. The two had a lengthy discussion at the end of which the *mujtahid* accepted that he had to investigate the claims of the Faith before passing judgement. He asked for a book on the teachings but he died before my uncle was able to give it to him.

Faizi believed that his father and paternal uncles knew about the Bahá'í Faith and had respect for its teachings. Although Khán and his brothers never declared themselves as believers, no one in the fanatical circles they moved in dared say a word against the Faith in their presence. Faizi was of the view that the reason why his father did not become a Bahá'í was because he could not give up his use of alcohol and hashish (cannabis), the use of which was widespread in Iran at the time and a common social activity for men. Faizi had memories of going to see him but just standing by the door because Khán was in a world of his own smoking the hubble-bubble.[7] All three brothers died quite young.

Early Childhood

Faizi's earliest childhood memory was of sitting on his paternal grandmother's lap in the courtyard at a very young age (perhaps two years old), when a bright light suddenly shone on a corner wall in front of him and mesmerized him with its brightness. The light disappeared as quickly as it had come but it left such an impression on his young mind that he never forgot it.

Faizi was a 'sensitive' and 'sickly child'. He suffered from tonsillitis, which inflamed with the slightest cold and meant that he had to endure not only the fever and sore throat but also the various treatments of the day. One of his aunts would be called for to carry out the most common of the many treatments. She would put two fingers down Faizi's inflamed throat while he was held down, squeeze his tonsils to the sides of his throat and then say, 'You will now get better.' The black wet-nurse of the family would then continue this treatment on a daily basis. In answer to his excruciating pain, she would say, 'It will now end', after which his grandmother would comfort him, saying, 'It has now ended.' The memory of what he went through as a child every time he became ill remained with him and he found it very difficult to deal with any of our childhood, or indeed adult, illnesses. He would fret and worry whenever my brother or I became ill, hold us close in his arms and repeatedly say, 'Give me your fever – let me suffer instead of you.' When I developed tonsillitis at the age of six he immediately arranged to have my tonsils out under general anaesthetic, saying that there was no way he was going to allow me to go through what he had as a child.

Family, Home and Daily Routines

The front of the Faizis' family home was distinguished from the other dwellings by a decorative brick design above the front door which many people came to admire. The entrance to the house was a cool hallway leading into a large courtyard which was divided into four gardens with grape vines, fig and other fruit trees, all dominated by an ancient mulberry tree. Hundreds of sparrows roosted in this tree at night – so many that one of the uncles would sometimes hold Faizi up to the tree for the little lad to cautiously catch a few birds and drop them one by one into the bag his uncle held up to him. What the uncle did with the birds remains a mystery.

The family had their breakfast underneath the mulberry tree in the summertime. Later in the morning the samovar[8] would be prepared in expectation of the women from the neighbouring houses coming with their tea and sugar. Faizi's grandmother would preside over them, serving tea to everyone. Their conversation, as Faizi remembered, was 'muddled, with all the women talking at once, responding to each other and agreeing with what was said without any one of them ceasing to chatter.'

The mulberry tree also served another purpose. It often happened that young men who had tried to commit suicide by swallowing opium[9] would be brought to the house, no matter what hour of day or night. A swing would be tied onto the mulberry tree and the afflicted young man would be made to sit on it. He would then be spun around until he grew quite dizzy and vomited. One unfortunate young man who was brought in the middle of the night was not only swung round but also hit with a belt to prevent him from falling asleep.

The household had a set routine which, as far as Faizi could remember, never changed: during the summer months they spent the nights on the roof of the house and the day in the cool of the underground cellar (where watermelons, honeydew melons and a variety of other fruit were stored) or in a special room built in-between two floors and which was cooler than the rest of the house. Winter was spent in the room with the *korsi*[10] and most of spring and autumn under the mulberry tree. In summer, as soon as the heat of the day subsided, the family's bedding would be spread out on the roof of the house. Faizi recalled that when he went to lie down on his mattress later in the evening he would 'feel strangely cool and rested', especially when the sky above his head was 'bright with the moon and stars' and 'the Milky Way passed over the house and stretched down towards the pomegranate and fig trees'. But there was one thing that terrified him: the scorpions in the neighbourhood. He had such a fear of them that even the word 'scorpion' frightened him. When the adults pointed out the various stars in the sky on these clear, star-studded nights, each choosing a star for themselves, the moment the scorpion of the skies was identified Faizi would stop listening and looking and 'pay no attention'.

As a child Faizi found it difficult to get up in the mornings. The maidservant of the household would shout up at him, 'Get up! Everyone has gone on an outing! Grandma, wait, he is just coming!' Faizi would jump up from his mattress and run down to see morning tea being prepared as usual in the corner of the courtyard and no sign of anyone going anywhere. Faizi never forgot that this maidservant made up a different story every morning in an effort to get him up.

During the winter season the family and any visitors would gather round the *korsí* for the evening. One of the uncles played the *tár*,[11] someone else played the hand drum and most of the women were able to play the tambourine. Many evenings would be spent in musical entertainment during which one of the young girls had to get up and dance, and if she acted coy she would not be left alone until she was obliged to obey. In revenge, the dancing girl would then twirl around the room behind everyone sitting round the *korsí*, swaying from side to side and deliberately deliver well-aimed kicks to whomever she wanted. At the end of the evening's entertainment the musical instruments would be put out of sight in case the critical eyes of one of the many *mujtahids* of the family fell upon them on one of their occasional impromptu visits. Those who had remained till late would sleep where they were for the night. Faizi's grandmother and the wet-nurse of the family found it difficult to sleep and would stay up most of the night reminiscing, their quietly murmured conversation lulling the young Faizi to sleep.

Naw-Rúz was an occasion for special celebration. The *korsí* would be stored away and there would be a thorough spring-cleaning of every part of the house and everything in it. A complete transformation would take place. The children, all excited and impatient for Naw-Rúz day 'were like chicks that had come out of their shells', jumping around and playing games.

The Neighbourhood

There were two other houses in the street where the Faizis and their extended family lived. One of the houses belonged to a man who was known as a Bábí and therefore no one spoke to him. Faizi did not know who he was or what he did but whenever the man appeared in the street Faizi and the rest of the children would run away in fear.

The other house belonged to the black wet-nurse of the household and her six, huge, strong sons. As a little boy Faizi would always make a point of being in this house when they were about to eat because he found the scene of the family gathered round a very large pot of stew eating, 'their arms going back and forth like the arms of a engine', spellbinding.

In the same street was a grocer, a spice shop where dried fruits were also sold, and the water reservoir. It was the shop selling dried fruits, with its large trays of raisins, almonds and dried mulberries, that interested Faizi and the rest of the children of the neighbourhood the most. The owner of this shop was an amusing man and made everyone laugh. The grocer had a fine voice and sang out, inviting people to come and buy his wares of yoghurt, cheese, watermelons and other produce. And then there were the men who would sit around and spend their time betting on various challenges such as eating a pomegranate without dropping a single seed or consuming fresh red mulberries without staining any of their clothing. The loser had to buy *chelo kabáb*[12] for everyone. Faizi could never understand how these men, who never worked to earn a living, found the money to have so many bets with one another and to eat so much.

Unusual and strange people would occasionally appear in the neighbourhood and their ways and manners made such an impression on Faizi's young mind that he could recall them in later life as clearly as if they were standing in front of him. One such individual was a slim, dark-complexioned Siyyid with large eyes and a green turban on his head. He would stand still every few steps as he walked in bare feet, lips moving as if in communion with spirits. The number of children following him increased as he wended his way through the lanes, but no matter what they did and however much they taunted him, he paid no attention and continued his slow stroll. The women used to talk about him in their gatherings, as did the men, and one of Faizi's aunts believed that the devil had tied his tongue. He carried a brass bowl in his hand in which those who wanted to give alms would put whatever they wanted. He never protested, never said a word, never gave anything away about himself.

When he grew old enough to go into the street on his own, the highlight of Faizi's day, after spending the afternoon in the courtyard of the shrine, was to watch the three street lamps in their lane being lit. He and a few other boys would wait for Ahmad, the man responsible for lighting the lamps, to arrive. Ahmad spent his days preparing opium, putting varying portions into matchboxes to send to his customers and smoking large quantities of the drug himself. Lighting the street lamps of the district was the only job he had. He would turn up half asleep a little before dark, carrying a ladder on his bent back and a dirty rag slung over his left shoulder. Leaning the ladder against the wall, he would climb the first three rungs to reach the lantern and take the lamp from inside its glass cover. He would clean the funnel, shake the container close to his ear to make sure it had enough oil, put the lamp back in its place and light it with a match. Faizi and two or three other children would continue standing under the lamp long after it was lit, feeling quite important that they were witnesses to such advanced apparatus. To them these street lights were true marks of civilization, as they had heard the adults say, and a clear proof of the great progress their country had made under a just and powerful government.

School Days

Faizi recalled the morning atmosphere in their courtyard as being very pleasant and that he was always in a soporific and dreamy state wanting to spend his whole day there. But he was growing up and soon reached an age when he had to start going to school, probably about seven years old.

As a small child, Faizi went to a *maktab*.[13] The lessons were held in a single room, where boys of various ages sat with a teacher who taught them to read and write and recite verses from the Qur'án. Faizi attended the *maktab* very reluctantly and would occasionally simply refuse to go. Later he was sent to a newly-established school adjacent to the shrine and which had a few more classes.

If any child was absent from the *maktab* the school caretaker, Háj Áqá, would be sent after him. As Háj Áqá walked down the street bellowing out, one by one, the absent pupils' names, the children's hearts would sink because they knew that they were going to be dragged back to the *maktab*. The young Faizi, however, would hide himself in the garden, leaving his grandmother, who always indulged her beloved grandson, standing by the door of the house in wait for Háj Áqá. When he appeared she begged him to leave the boy alone and made up different excuses such as, 'He is sick in bed', 'He cannot move', until the man gave up and left. As soon as news of Háj Áqá's departure from their street reached Faizi in his hideout he would relax and feel 'an incomparable joy take over' his whole being.

Faizi himself described a boy's first day at the *maktab* vividly and the following are freely translated extracts from his copious notes on his early life in Qum.[14]

Lessons, Chastisements, Injustices and Disappointments

> On the first day a boy starts school, a servant goes before him, carrying a large round tray on his head with sweetmeats for the teacher. The father then follows, holding his son by the hand. The boy, although dressed in new clothes, is far from happy and sobs and cries aloud, dreading the ordeal which awaits him. Fear of the *maktab* had been instilled in him for a long time because whenever he made a wrong move which displeased any of his elders, he was told, 'You just wait till you go to the *maktab*. The teacher there knows how to punish children and make them behave themselves. He has a well in which he keeps naughty children.' Even the servants of the house did not fail to remind the child of the punishment that awaited him. God knows what went on in the mind of the poor, tormented child as he was taken to the *maktab*. Perhaps he thought that he would never be able to go back to his home, that he had said his last farewell to his mother and the familiar rooms and trees in the

garden of their house. The unsympathetic father has no patience with his son and does not talk to him on the way except when, losing his temper because of the boy's continuous wailing, he shouts at him to shut up.

On entering the *maktab*, the boy sees the feet of one of the children in the bastinado[15] and another child standing in a corner wearing a ridiculous, tall paper hat on which was written the word 'Donkey'. The skinny, bad-tempered teacher with a black beard and moustache and bulging eyes, who sits in another corner of the room, pays no attention either to the tray of sweets that has been brought for him or to the boy who has come to him for the first time. The father of the child addresses the teacher respectfully, saying, 'I have brought this humble servant's son to your presence so that he may be trained under your guidance.' Then, leaving the poor boy to sit among children he does not know, in a strange place he has never seen before, he departs hurriedly. The miserable child sobs all the while.

After the father has left, the teacher approaches the new boy and speaks to him in a harsh tone.

'What on earth is the matter with you? Do you want to remain a donkey all your life? Don't you want to become the head of the Finance Department and ride in a carriage? Stop your stupid wailing and behave like all the other children! . . .'

The children attending the *maktab* are not dressed alike. The sons of Siyyids wear black skullcaps and long gowns that are open in front, and they sometimes tied green shawls round their waists. These children are treated with respect.[16] The sons of clergy wear white skullcaps and white clothes. The sons of merchants wear gowns which overlap in front and have deep pockets over which they wear a tightly wound shawl. The sons of civil servants wear a coat and trousers, but they are not many. The rest of the boys are dressed in whatever they can afford. Very few of the children have socks and the shoes they wear are an assortment of all kinds of footwear.

At the age of 14 or 15 years, the sons of the Siyyids and clergy are allowed to wear turbans. This is considered to be an important matter and a special ceremony is held to which the eldest man of the family invites all his relatives and some of his friends to witness the festive occasion. The boy, who has first been taken to the public bath where his hands and feet were dyed with henna, receives his green or white turban from the hands of the family elder who blesses him after the recitation of prayers and invocations. Thereon the boy considers himself to be a man: he walks with a rigid gait for some days before he gets used to the weight of the turban on his head and also has to get used to the fact that he now has to pay every now and again for his turban to be wound professionally.

Faizi then goes on to remember his own first day at the *maktab*, moving up to school and his experiences there.

You cannot imagine where they took us and called it a school. It was an old building with a damp basement and only three rooms which caught the sun. One of these was set aside for the teachers, another belonged to the caretaker who lived there and also had a shop where he kept things to sell to the children. The third room was for the older boys . . . The rest of us sat on the damp floor in the basement where a ray of sunlight came in from one corner. There was a single chair for the teacher. I have no recollection of what he taught us. All I remember is that we all sat around listlessly and gradually fell asleep. Our teacher, too, would go to sleep on his chair. I believe there was only one among the teachers who was somewhat educated, having studied Arabic grammar.

One day it rained heavily and we could not sit in the basement, so we were taken up to the room of the older boys where we all huddled together in one corner, a sorry sight of pale, sickly-looking children . . . One of the older boys asked our teacher what brought on the thunder and lightning. Our teacher threw a meaningful glance at us as if to say we should not think he could only teach the lower classes of the school, for even the older students could benefit by his knowledge. It must be said that he had a very pleasant voice, and though his words were displeasing to us and nothing he said was of any benefit, the tone of his voice remains in the memory. The answer he gave to the question asked of him that day is clearly engraved on my mind and I would like to write it down for the benefit of those who are misled by current scientific ideas . . . He said, 'An angel that is smaller than a bee but larger than a fly comes down from the sky to chase away evil spirits. This lightning is the angel's whip, and the thunder is the noise of his whip.' Having said this, our teacher waxed eloquent and remarked, 'If an angel as small as this can express such fierce anger, imagine the terrible wrath of the Angel of Hell, whose body stretches from the sky to the ground and who comes with clubs of fire with which to strike people and with red-hot pokers to pierce their bodies.' We were so terrified by these words that we came to consider God, who is called the Compassionate and the Merciful in the Qur'án, as the source of absolute tyranny, oppression and cruelty, and we were not on good terms with Him anymore . . .

There was no physical exercise or any kind of amusement in the school . . . We had no paper to write on, only a piece of wood on which we practised writing. We would wash this by the pond after the morning session to use again in the afternoon. I was quite content with this piece of wood until one day the teacher got angry and broke it on the head of one of the children. He then put the two pieces in front of me without a word of apology and with utter disregard for my feelings. I think the great love I now have for paper is because of the deprivation of those days. Even if I have one coin left in my pocket, when I pass a stationery shop and see a new type of paper on display, I involuntarily am pulled towards it and will buy it. Right now, as I am writing this I have a variety of papers – white sheets, coloured ones, with lines, without lines, flowers on the margins

– which I have either bought or ordered, but none of them give me the pleasure of even a single page of the old paper. Actually, I have some of that old, starched paper, coloured ones too, but I love them so much that I have not written anything on them and am waiting for my calligraphy to improve before penning a few historic lines on them.

One day a sophisticated boy came to join us at the school. His father had come to Qum on some kind of errand and he sent his son to our school during his stay. This boy was cleaner and better dressed than the rest of us children and we admired everything about him – the way he sat, walked and spoke to the teacher. The new boy was a little older than we were, so apart from being sophisticated, he was also looked upon as a leader.

Among his school things there was a pencil which was white but wrote in red from one end and blue from the other. This pencil took our attention away from everything else. We all wanted to look at it, to touch it and, if permitted, to test the red and blue colours on anything we could find . . . When my turn came to handle the pencil, I found a bit of paper and drew a red line and a blue line on it. I was fascinated by those colours as if I were looking at the moving waves of two seas of red and blue. Despite being an awkward and bashful child, I mustered enough courage to ask the boy about the price of the pencil. It cost 30 *sháhís*.[17] I asked whether he would buy one for me if I gave him 30 *sháhís* and he said he would. As much as I wanted that pencil, to buy it I would have to save my pocket money for 30 to 40 days! I would have to deprive myself of so many good things that were sold in the shops nearby: golden-coloured sweets that rolled on the tongue and made the teeth stick together, roasted nuts and raisins, sweet dried mulberry and almonds. How could I do it? But I finally decided to forgo all these pleasures.

I had a money-pot into which I started dropping my coins from the next day. It was a little easier the first few days, but after that, every time I wanted to drop a *sháhí* into the money-pot, I would hold it over the pot for a long time while different thoughts went through my mind before I could persuade myself to drop the coin in and hasten the day when I could own the pencil. What difficult days I went through! With what envy I watched other children suck their sweets or heard them chew mulberries and crack almonds with their teeth! One day a nut fell from the hand of one of the children and rolled towards me. I kept my eye on it and when no one was looking picked it up and put it in my mouth. First I enjoyed the salty taste and then chewed it for ages until there was nothing left to chew, but the memory of the taste made me happy.

I shook my money-pot every evening and calculated the weeks since I had started saving until I knew I had enough money to buy the pencil. I immediately took it to the home of the boy, who said he would bring the two-coloured pencil to the school the next morning. What a long night went by and what a bright morning dawned! I hurried to the school and stood waiting by the door. As soon as I saw the boy, I ran to him and asked for my pencil. He said he had not been able to buy it that day but would bring it the next morning.

Days and weeks, months and years went by and there was no sign of the coloured pencil. When the boy was leaving Qum he swore by the promised Qá'im and the holy shrine that he would send me the pencil and I, despite what I had experienced, still believed him . . . I now have dozens of coloured pencils on my desk but none of them can take the place of that magical red and blue pencil.

༄

A fiery event which took place in our school almost every day was the punishment of the bastinado. One day a shopkeeper came to the school and said to the headmaster, 'Sir, this boy, Asghar, does a lot of mischief on the road.' Poor Asghar was made to lie down and be bastinadoed. He was beaten with such savagery that he could not walk on the bruised soles of his feet for days after that. No one asked the shopkeeper whether he was a relative of As<u>gh</u>ar or why he thought he had the right to get the child punished. The headmaster, who had a passion for beating the students, satisfied his sadistic nature by torturing a poor boy who had no one to complain to. He might have also hoped that, by pleasing the shopkeeper, he would get a discount on the tea and sugar he bought . . .

Sometimes the matter was so important that we all had to line up to hear the headmaster read out the orders for the punishment and witness the victim being bastinadoed. It was a frightening experience and our knees shook as we stood there . . . I shall recount one of many such occasions that is engraved on my memory.

The headmaster walked up and down the rows of children while we all trembled with fear. He then pounced on one of the boys and pushed him towards the bastinado. This boy, Ibráhím, was extremely naughty and was always getting into trouble. As he was often punished with the bastinado, he had put pieces of felt inside his socks but on this particular day the headmaster ordered his socks to be removed. The pieces of felt were discovered and this made his punishment even more severe.

There was a notorious servant in the school who wore a thick moustache and was a real tyrant. Every time he appeared on the scene we knew the matter was unusually serious. Now he stood ready with a whip, holding it with both hands. Ibráhím was made to lie down on his back with his feet in the bastinado loop and held up by a servant on either side. The tyrant then began to whip the boy's soles with all his might. Ibráhím did not shed tears, only kept on crying out, 'What did I do, sir? Tell me what I have done, sir.' The headmaster said, 'Keep on whipping him; he will soon find out what he has done.'

The maths teacher felt sorry for the boy. He threw his *'abá* over Ibráhím's feet and asked the headmaster to forgive him. The headmaster said, 'I shall forgive him for your sake, otherwise I would have had him whipped this time till his nails dropped off.'

Ibráhím got up but the extreme pain he was made to suffer had emboldened him to such an extent that he dared to demand the reason for which he had been punished.

'Would you please tell me why I was bastinadoed, sir?' he asked once more.

'You don't need to ask,' he was told.

'I do need to ask!' the boy retorted.

The maths teacher said to him, 'Never mind now, go away.'

'No!' the boy answered back, 'I must know why I was punished.'

'Go, I tell you! Go!' the teacher yelled.

But the boy was adamant. 'I refuse to go until I am told why I was punished.'

Ibráhím became a hero in our estimation. He had actually dared to confront the school authorities! He was brave enough to ask 'Why?' But we were also terrified lest he might now be whipped again until his toe nails really dropped off!

In response to Ibráhím's vehement insistence, the headmaster finally gave in and said with an ugly smile, 'Go and look at the school's water-pot. At noon, when the children are all thirsty, you start throwing stones about and have broken the pot.'

Ibráhím shouted at the top of his voice and said, 'How could I have broken the pot, sir, when I was not in school? I went home for lunch and have just come back!'

Ibráhím had not cried up to this point. He had only shouted out, demanding to know what he was being punished for. Now he suddenly burst into tears, and sobbed in a way that effected all of us children. It was the tears of one who had been wronged that touched our hearts.

The headmaster was cornered and realized what he had done. Yet in order not to lose face, he said, 'You, mischief-maker, are so wicked that you must have arranged for the pot to be broken before you left the school at noon.'

That day the maths teacher did not ask Ibráhím the lesson he had had to prepare. The Arabic teacher, too, was kind to him and he went home in a somewhat happier mood.

The next day the school was in a state of utter confusion. No one rang the bell. The teachers did not seem to care and the children went wild. We afterwards learned that the headmaster had fallen down a few steps the night before and had sustained injuries which would keep him at home for a long time until he could walk again. Everyone said he had been cursed because of the injustice Ibráhím had suffered at his hands.

I don't know why it was but the class with the tutor for calligraphy was constantly noisy and without much discipline. The tutor always had coloured starched paper in his pockets and a piece of leather on which he would place a sheet of paper. He would first place a dot on the sheet and then write a line for the pupils to copy underneath. Sometimes he rubbed a finger along the side of his nose and then on the paper before writing so that the reed pen would run smoothly when writing the elongated letters. He would also sharpen our reed pens and in cutting them, much to our amusement, used such pressure, puffing his cheeks with the effort and slitting his eyes. He was slightly lame in one leg and was the only teacher who did not shave his head. Whenever he saw a woman approaching in the street he would slow his pace, take off his hat, smooth down his hair and replace his hat. He was on the whole a harmless teacher because, unlike the others, although the children messed around in his class, he never used uncivil language to get them to learn from him.

The School Photograph

One of the governors who had come from a nearby town had a photographer with him. The photographer was a black man and people said he placed a magnifying glass in front of a box with which he could take people's pictures on counting up to seven. They said only black people could become photographers because they would have to spend hours doing things like witchcraft and magic in a dark room to produce the picture.

The governors decided to take a picture of our school but this angered the clergy, who threatened to close the school altogether . . . Such matters, they said, were against the rules of religion and corrupted the character of Muslim children. It was clear that the clergy were emphatically against the least step taken to bring about any form of change in the lives of the people . . . In this instance, however, their wishes were ignored and the black man arrived at the school with his magic box. Benches were brought forward, rugs spread out and banners held up. The children sat on the ground, the teachers sat on the benches and the rest stood on steps behind them.

As soon as the photographer put the black cloth over his head and disappeared behind the camera, a few of the smaller children burst into tears and left the gathering. The older ones looked down but the teachers, to show that they were well-acquainted with such scientific matters, held their heads high. The Arabic teacher's head was held so high that only the lump of his throat faced the camera, but the maths teacher, who held fast to his walking stick with both hands, was visibly shaking. Our tall headmaster with a small turban sat up stiffly in his seat, looking straight at the camera with wide open eyes, and did not make a single movement all the time the photographer was adjusting his camera. The two servants who were on either side of him brought their hands out of their *'abás* to hold up the banners and one of the boys fetched the signboard of the school.

It was a strange sight that met the eye, with the group wearing an assortment of clothes – *'abás*, old-fashioned garments with shawls round the waist, skull caps and tall hats, short pasteboard hats with flat tops and felt hats with rounded tops. Some wore shoes, others were barefooted. A couple of the children were saluting in army fashion, a few were offering flowers to each other, but the rest were behaving as polite children should, with their heads bowed and their eyes avoiding the camera. For me, this photograph became the cause of continuous suffering because, together with one or two others, I had not only looked straight at the camera, but had even smiled! Everyone I came across rebuked me for my undignified behaviour. Worst of all were my elder cousins and other members of the family who felt greatly embarrassed and kept on scolding me for having smiled in the picture. Children with good manners, they reminded me, never smiled in the presence of their teachers. Why could I not have behaved like the son of Áqá Abú-Tálib, who was a picture of modesty, they wanted to know. What would the custodian of the shrine and the Governor say when they saw the photograph? The family reputation was at stake! I still have that photograph and whenever I look at it the same feeling of anxiety wells up within me.

A School Outing

I don't recollect what the occasion was, but they were holding a celebration in the house of the Governor and it was decided that the schoolchildren should attend it. We had to do a great deal of preparation before we went, practising when to say the special formula of praise and greetings to the Prophet Muhammad and His descendants and when to say 'Long live the King' and 'Long live the Governor'. While practising, we had no problem with the praise and greetings part as we were in the habit of repeating it often. Every time Ḥasan Áqá said, 'The Source of Wisdom, the Seal of the Prophets, His Holiness Muhammad, son of 'Abdu'lláh' we would all respond with great zest and gusto, 'Praise and greetings to Muhammad and His descendants!' But when it came to 'Long live the King' and 'Long live the Governor' we were in disgrace. We could never get the timing right because we were not sure when we were expected to say these words. First one child would start on it, then another, then a few, and finally a loud chorus of voices

CHILDHOOD

would be heard, all starting the phrase at different times and none managing to say it when it was supposed to be said. The reason for this was that the King and the Governor were given so many long titles before their names that we were completely confused. The headmaster slapped us, hit us with his stick, but never thought of telling us the names of the King and the Governor so that we could say 'Long live' after their names and not in the middle of their titles.

On the eve of the celebration we each had to take a candle to light and carry with us all the way from the school to the Governor's place. The headmaster's last injunction before we set out was addressed to Maḥmúd, a boy with a very loud, thick voice.

'Maḥmúd,' he said, 'remember to keep your voice down.'

We made an extraordinary spectacle as we walked along with our candles and dressed in every type of clothing, from *'abá* and turban to coat and trousers, from fur hat to a handkerchief tied round the head . . . We walked along with trembling hearts, not because we were excited about the celebration, but through the fear of coming face to face with the awesome personage we were about to meet. This was no joke. He was the Governor and had come from Tehran! The government had sent him and he lived in a big house! He got up late in the mornings and was surrounded by servants. He would not go walking to any place; if he ever did, he walked very slowly with people respectfully walking behind him. This was the kind of personage to whose house we were going and we felt as if we were being taken to the slaughterhouse. One of the students could not bear the ordeal. His legs began to shake so badly on the way that he could not continue walking, so he was sent home . . .

When we reached the Governor's house we saw wick lamps burning in every nook and cranny – an attractive sight from a distance – and there were lots of lighted lamps, candles and mirrors placed on a table. All the important people and noted merchants of the town were already seated with the Governor but no one spoke. Our headmaster went forward and asked permission of the Governor, then we all went and stood around the pool, facing the guests with bowed heads and shaking legs. We were terrified that we might not be able to say 'Long live' at the right time.

Ḥasan Áqá started reciting the homily and when he pronounced the name of the Prophet we all responded properly. Maḥmúd – with the loud voice – had difficulty with the candle he was holding and was frantically trying to adjust it. He suddenly came to himself when we had just finished saying 'Praise and greetings to Muhammad and the descendants of Muhammad', when his thick voice rang out in solo, 'And the descendants of Muhammad!' One of the merchants, known to be a swindler and of frivolous character, could not control his laughter – though he tried hard to keep his laughter down – and we saw the green shawl he had tied round his middle bob up and down on his fat belly for a long time. The homily continued till it reached the long titles of the King. Our timing was wrong again and Maḥmúd's voice rang out, loud and clear, right in the middle of the string of titles that preceded the actual name . . .

We stood round that pool for many hours, not knowing for what reason we had come . . . We saw the honoured guests seated on comfortable chairs, helping themselves to all kinds of sweetmeats and fruit, beautifully arranged on tables placed in front of them. Some were filling their handkerchiefs from the platters on the tables and stuffing them into their pockets but we, like polite children, did not lift our heads to stare at them in case they might think that we, too, would have liked to be offered some of the refreshments. When the headmaster finally said we could leave, we went to our homes utterly exhausted, with many questions in our minds regarding the celebration for which we had done so much preparation.

End of Year Examinations

The teachers spent some days preparing us for our examinations. They taught us the answers to questions which would be put to us at a celebration held by the school at the beginning of summer each year. All persons of distinction in the town were invited to this function and we had come to know them by now. They were the Governor, the custodian of the shrine, the heads of government departments, the merchants and businessmen and the learned clergy. We were told that each boy should bring a present for himself which would be given back to him at the celebration as a prize on behalf of the school. One year I took a calligraphy which was written by my grandfather and mounted on a red cardboard. The headmaster slapped it on my head and said mockingly, 'You should have brought your grandmother's photograph,' and all the children laughed.[18] I felt quite ashamed when I saw what the other children had brought . . . one of them was a large watch with a thick golden chain. We all gathered to admire it and the boy who had brought the watch said, 'My father does something to make it ring at night!'

When the day came the teacher called out the name of each child and asked him the question to which he would, of course, give the perfect answer, having already memorized it. Shouts of 'Bravo, bravo' would then be heard from every side and the teacher would tell the respected audience how he had worked with the students till late at night to make sure they knew their lessons well. It happened one year that the teacher made the unfortunate mistake of asking Rajab the question he was supposed to ask from Ḥusayn. The question referred to the definition of clean water according to Islamic law but Rajab, who did not understand the meaning of either the question or the quote he had been told to memorize, raised his voice and loudly recited the line of a tender poem he had learned by heart. He was proceeding to analyse it when the teacher's angry shout silenced him.

'You shameless idiot, is this how you have prepared your lesson?!' It was only through the kind intervention of the Governor that the poor boy escaped punishment. Ḥusayn, in the meantime, afraid that he might be called upon to give the correct answer to Rajab's question, hid himself and sneaked away, taking with him the present he had brought from home.

Despite all the rehearsals we had had, the boy who had brought the watch with the golden chain could not give a proper answer to the question put to him at the examination but when it was time for the distribution of the prizes and his name was called out, his father quickly came forward, caressed his face, then burned incense in an incense-holder and went around his son with it to avoid the evil eye. After that he put some money in the boy's palm and, turning to the Governor, said, 'He is an only child, Your Honour.'

The guests were getting tired and starting to go away when my turn came to take my prize, and I was happy that they did not take much notice of the insignificant thing I was given.

The important guests who came to our school's yearly celebration all knew their places and seated themselves accordingly. But the clergy always tried to outdo each other in occupying the more respectable seat among themselves. To show his superiority, a clergyman would squeeze himself between two others in a tight seat just to show that the place he occupied was more worthy of respect than where his rival sat. Such insignificant matters caused resentment and enmity, sometimes even resulting in fights and bloodshed between some of the men from two districts of the town. These men would come out onto the streets and attack each other with sticks, whips and leather belts. The curses and abuses they hurled at each other are too shameful to be repeated. The account of their wild encounters became the source of stories and discussions in the two districts for many days until another such fight took place. Unfortunately, this savagery which went on during the year was carried on in the month of Muḥarram[19] . . . Instead of concentrating on the tragedy they should be mourning, they engaged in the worst type of barbarism. They went completely wild and committed atrocities which struck such terror into the hearts of all the inhabitants of the town that mourning for Imám Ḥusayn was forgotten. When it was time for them to enter the courtyard of the shrine, each group tried to go in before the others and this was when the fiercest confrontations took place, the participants utterly unashamed of the lack of respect they were showing towards the holy personage buried there.

There was one group of mourners, however, that was always allowed to go in first. This was the group that led the whole procession of mourners and was headed by the well-known *pahlaván* of our town. This man was not only greatly feared because of his extraordinary strength but highly respected for his nobility of character and the fact that he was a Siyyid. When the group led by him arrived at the shrine everyone cleared the way for the group to enter the courtyard . . .

No one among the religious leaders and authorities spoke against the savagery that was perpetrated on the day of the martyrdom of Imám Ḥusayn. None asked his congregation to spend its time recounting the events of the life of Imám Ḥusayn and reflecting on how that holy personage and the members of his noble family willingly sacrificed their lives in the path of God . . . All these leaders wished for was to dominate an ignorant mass of people who blindly accepted the strange ideas advanced by the clergy and never questioned their authority. And how well they succeeded!

Faizi was always very interested in history, literature and the arts. Apart from writing, he loved sketching and was a good and enthusiastic amateur actor. As a child he was fascinated by the passion plays and recorded in detail events leading to the commemoration of the martyrdom of Imám Ḥusayn. Some of the actors of the passion plays made such a lasting impression on him that the tragedy continued to haunt him for a long time. In later life he wrote a booklet on the tragedy of Imám Ḥusayn.

Childhood Superstitions

I heard some of the ridiculous superstitions advanced by the clergy in those years and would witness how eagerly their followers listened to every word they uttered. One day a priest was telling a group of people that there is a verse in the Qur'án which, if dissolved in water and poured over the head of a patient, would reveal all the ailing parts of the body, thereby facilitating the work of the physician. This piece of information was received with great surprise and tremendous joy by the ignorant audience who, no doubt, imagined that now crowds of heathens would come to them begging for the miraculous verse that could help in curing every disease in the world.

One of the clergy who held a high position among the rest and who ascended to the highest step of the pulpit[20] after the others had spoken, spoke a lot of nonsense and, among other things, attacked the Bábís[21] in his sermon. He said, 'These people have a drug made of dates which they feed to all who come their way. For those who take this drug, everything becomes exaggerated: a brazier of coal-fire seems to them like the eternal fires of Hell and a bouquet of flowers like the garden of Paradise. They put their leader in a basket and pull him up towards the ceiling. Then they consider him to be God and start praying to him.'

The clergyman looked quite pleased with himself as he gave out this important information, while his audience, considering him to be a most knowledgeable person, loudly cursed the detestable Bábís.

Coming of Age

An event which occurred in every household with a son was the day they arranged for the boy's circumcision . . . In the morning when the boy woke up he would see that the household was unusually busy. The person in charge would come to his bedside and say, 'Get up, everyone is ready. They're bringing the donkeys to go on an outing. There are no lessons today and no school.'

The boy would jump out of bed with enthusiasm and be taken to a room where fresh bedding had been spread and only then would he realize what was afoot.

After the circumcision the boy's parents and other relatives would come to see him and give him money. He would collect the coins in a bag and spend the rest of the day taking them out, counting them and then putting them back into the bag, all the while musing on what he was going to spend the money on. However, invariably a relative, usually the grandmother, would come and with excuses such as, 'You will lose the money. I will keep it for you', or 'You will waste the money', take the money from the boy . . . The money was not that much but by taking it away from the boy they also took away the chance for the child to develop any sense of self-control and responsibility, as well as shatter all the hopes he had of what he was going to spend it on.

I remember the first time I had three coins which were mine. They were like diamonds to me. I could not sleep at night in anticipation of what I was going to do with them the next morning. Then one of our neighbours came and said that they wanted to go to visit the shrine but had no money and asked to borrow the money I had, so I gave it to him. I still remember the wicked smile on the neighbour's face, how I fell apart and how I did not have the strength to move till noon, feeling that all doors were closed to me. The shop where pencils were sold and the ice shop were now shut in my face. I had planned on first buying and eating some sweet ice and then buying a pencil and paper and keeping what was left of the money for later. But it all went. That neighbour never repaid the loan. He went from our house and from this world but I never forgot.

Faizi involved himself more and more in the family's activities as he grew up. He had a strong sense of curiosity, an impressionable, intelligent mind and took in everything that was going on around him. These early childhood experiences had a profound effect on his sensitive nature and on his development as a man and in later years he resolved that he would never treat any child the way he and his fellow pupils had been treated.

Growing Up

It was the custom of a group of dignitaries of the neighbourhood during Faizi's childhood to gather regularly in each other's houses to socialize, exchange views and spend the day together. All of them appeared huge men in the eyes of the young Faizi and 'their assortment of thick voices' frightened him so much that he was afraid to enter the room they were in. As he grew a little older the women in the household insisted that he join the men, so one day when it was his uncle's turn to host the gathering, Faizi mustered up enough courage to do so. Cautiously opening the door of the room, he slid in, greeted everyone in a quiet voice and sat kneeling on the carpet by the door. No one responded to his greeting. He noticed that the men were in groups. Some were sitting around the brazier talking, a few were playing backgammon and two or three were napping. Of all of them Faizi liked the colonel best – he was a huge man who inhaled deeply when smoking and then exhaled and talked at the same time with an unusual tremor to his voice. It was only when a member of the group started reading the newspaper aloud that everyone abandoned what they were doing, shook themselves from their dozing and listened intently to what was being read.

    Once, one of Faizi's uncles took him to another of these gatherings. Faizi sat kneeling on the floor from morning till noon. There was no one his age there and he did not enjoy the morning, especially as he did not dare change his position and sit cross legged in case he was seen to be disrespectful to his elders. However, he did manage to alleviate his discomfort somewhat by wriggling closer to a cushion against the wall and with some relief gingerly leaning against it. Lunch, which was an elaborate affair, did not come soon enough for the cramped young boy. Even at that young age Faizi was impressed with the artistic way the women of the house presented their mouth-watering dishes. 'They had created a pattern on the bowl of yoghurt and spinach, on the rice pudding were decorated the words '*bon appetit*' and the delicious smell of rice and meat filled the whole air.'

Modern Technology Arrives in Qum

One day after finishing his lunch and preparing to return to school Faizi was, to his utter astonishment, told that he could stay at home but on condition he did not utter a squeak. Very soon some of the family's close acquaintances and relatives started to arrive and sit silently in one of the rooms. Faizi, who was by now burning with curiosity, went to one of the servants busily washing the dishes by the pond and asked her what was happening. She told him she did not know, although she did know that something was going to happen after lunch.

After an hour or so one of the men of the household arrived carrying something underneath the cloak thrown over his shoulder. Establishing that there were no strangers among those present, he placed the box he was carrying in the centre of the room. Everyone pulled themselves up, sat respectfully and kept completely quiet while staring at the box. Some minutes later another person entered the room with a large horn and attached it to the box. Everyone started whispering as the champions of the moment did something to the box and suddenly scratching noises came out of it followed by music and singing. The audience 'were a sight to behold!'

This was Faizi's first encounter with recorded music and the beginning of his passion for the radio, the record player and music.

The Fire Carriage

One morning as the children arrived at school they saw one of the teachers standing by the door telling everyone to return home. At this point the still half-asleep Faizi noticed that some of the shops were closed and sensed the atmosphere around him was far from normal. He decided to make his way to the cemetery behind the shrine, a popular meeting point, where he saw most of the people of the district gathered. Milling among them he heard talk about a fire carriage which was going to arrive in Qum. No one had ever seen such a carriage and could therefore not tell the others what it looked like, so all eyes were glued in anticipation on the road leading into the city.

After some time a number of the old men who had brought their small children decided that the event was not suitable for such young minds and returned home with them. It was late afternoon when at last a cloud of dust was seen on the horizon. A strange object making a frightening noise and sounding an extremely loud horn appeared before their eyes. How fast it moved! One of the men looking on in disbelief commented that none of his mules could match its speed. Within seconds the great crowd of onlookers was reduced to a small number as people panicked and fled in all directions from this terrifying scene, 'expecting divine chastisement to descend from the sky and calling upon God to have mercy on them'.

The 'object' finally stopped in front of the shrine and the dust settled for all to see the horseless carriage. A man emerged from this amazing vehicle, yawned, beat his chest a few times with his fist, rolled his shoulders and walked round the carriage, looking underneath and over it. He then removed his hat and beat the dust out of it. All eyes were pinned on him to see what he would do next. 'This was a serious matter! Only a lion-hearted man could have the courage to endanger his life by travelling round the earth in such an unpredictable creation', and it seemed that he himself was aware of the greatness and importance of his own station.

The man then wanted to enter the shrine but was prevented from doing so. He had some water, washed his hands and face and, without saying another word to anyone, 'like a brave champion, few of words and dignified', he opened the door of the vehicle and resumed his seat. Smoke spewed out of the machine, there was a loud explosion and everyone ran away in terror. By the time they gathered enough courage to return to see what had happened there was nothing but a disappointing cloud of dust in the distance.

The Wedding

Sakinih was a young girl who worked in the home of a priest in Faizi's district helping with errands in the house and shopping for bread and food. She was of marriageable age but no one could be found who would marry her until one day someone from another district of the town asked for her hand. The two districts joined forces to celebrate the occasion. The days leading up to the wedding day were such an exciting time for Faizi and the other children as they tried to join in the activities of the adults preparing for the marriage feast. The special day happened to be in the middle of the month when the full moon lit up the whole town. A group from each of the two districts came together to play music and sing through the night. The young men who had undertaken to do most of the work carried large heavy trays of fruit and sweetmeats on their heads in a procession around the district, followed by a crowd carrying lanterns, lamps and candles to the newlyweds. As the procession wended its way through the lanes people brought sweets and sherbet for them from their houses and added gifts of sweets, fruit and small coins to the already laden trays. The sound of fun and laughter filled the air and everyone joined in the merriment. In Faizi's estimation 'it was the very best wedding anyone had seen and nothing like it was ever seen again'.

Zúrkhánih

In later years Faizi seldom spoke about Qum. He found the place stifling but one of the few real pleasures he seemed to have had was when he visited the local *zúrkhánih*.

The *zúrkhánih* is a traditional Persian gymnasium where young men come to practise ancient forms of Persian body-building under the guidance of a seasoned *pahlaván*. Apart from the rigorous physical exercises they undertake, those who attend the *zúrkhánih* are expected to develop such virtues as courage, generosity, truthfulness and humility.

The leader of the *zúrkhánih* in Qum at the time was a man with a pleasant personality and a rich, powerful voice. He used a rhythmic chant of verses from famous epics recounting the feats and bravery of ancient heroes to inspire his audience and to guide the *pahlaváns* in their various performances, accompanying himself all the while on a small hand drum with which he measured the pace for the different exercises. Whenever a revered person, such as a noted *pahlaván*, entered the *zúrkhánih* he would ring the small bell hanging in front of him to announce the personage's arrival.

The man who trained and guided the men at the *zúrkhánih* in Qum was a famous *pahlaván*, a wonderful person, Pahlaván Ḥusayn. Not only was he considered to be the strongest man in Qum, he was also well known for his fine character. He was shown special respect because he was a Siyyid. This man was Faizi's childhood hero.

Faizi's famous and influential maternal uncle, the *mujtahid*, did not approve of the *zúrkhánih* because of its use of the drum,[22] so Faizi had to make sure that his uncle did not find out about his frequent visits to the forbidden place. As an adult Faizi would sometimes exercise with Indian clubs as he had seen the men practise in the *zúrkhánih* and accompany himself with the special chants. I remember him twirling his clubs and impressing us as children by throwing them up in the air one at a time and catching them. As a little boy my brother, Naysán, would often stand next to him whenever he exercised and, with his encouragement, try to follow his lead with the little clubs and weights my father had made for him.

Given the stifling education he received as a young child, an education that did nothing to develop his latent talents, it is no wonder that Faizi, who had an innate liking for sports and physical exercise, would find places such as the *zúrkhánih* so interesting. About his clandestine visits to the *zúrkhánih* he wrote, 'My greatest love in life was the *zúrkhánih*, and every hour of my spare time was spent there. Sometimes I would even run away from school, risking the consequences, to sit in a corner of the *zúrkhánih* and watch what was going on. The atmosphere intoxicated me like pure wine.'

At the end of the *pahlaváns*' exercises one of the *pahlaváns* would hold open a long cloth and go round the men, who threw coins into it. Faizi, too, if he had a coin to spare, would throw one in and be rewarded by a glance from Pahlaván Ḥusayn, which was 'worth more than the whole world' to him. The *pahlaván* would then knot the cloth and hand it to the leader saying, 'May it be as blessed as your mother's milk.' When Pahlaván Ḥusayn was about to leave Faizi would dash out so that he could greet him as he passed by and the *pahlaván*, aware of the boy's admiration, would smile at Faizi and ask him how he was faring, which made the young lad's day.

Years later, remembering his escapades, Faizi wrote inside one of his French books on traditional Persian gymnastics, 'Happy the days when, as swift as an arrow with shoes on feet and cap on head, I was able to escape from my home in the early morning and hide myself in an inconspicuous corner of the *zúrkhánih* in wait for Pahlaván Ḥusayn. As the leader of the *zúrkhánih* started to play with great spirit on the drum and begin chanting in honour of the *pahlaván*, I knew the great *pahlaván* of our town had entered the *zúrkhánih*.'

Last Months in Qum

Faizi's life in Qum was, all in all, not an unhappy one. He lived in a comfortably-off household with his mother, beloved paternal grandmother and extended family. Although he had friends, he comes across in his memoirs as being quite happy to keep his own company. But he was a bright boy and as he approached secondary school age one of his paternal uncles insisted that he should be sent to Tehran for his education. The rest of the family were completely against this idea, saying that as soon as he learned a little of the Qur'án and some more reading and writing he should be put under the tutelage of one of the religious teachers. Above all, the religious leaders on the maternal side of the family completely forbad his move to Tehran, believing if he went to the city he would leave Islam and considered that it was best if he stayed in Qum. The paternal uncle who initiated the move to send Faizi to Tehran was, however, a single-minded man and his determination to shape his nephew's future was strengthened when Faizi's father was posted to Tehran.

Going to Tehran was 'a very weighty matter in those days as anyone who went was either very important or well-to-do'. Therefore, almost everyone who came to say goodbye to Faizi gave him a list of things they wanted from him – socks, clothes, handkerchiefs, etc. Faizi, who was at the time quite naive in these matters, felt honour-bound to carry out all of these requests and began to wonder how on earth he could afford all he had been asked to bring back when he returned to Qum.

Although initially excited about his imminent departure to Tehran – which to him was 'a different country and its people a different breed of human beings' – his enthusiasm was quickly overshadowed by the realization that it meant separation from his grandmother, his relatives and the family evening gatherings and camaraderie. Suddenly 'the lessons and living in the damp, cockroach-infested classroom, the bad-tempered, long-toothed principal and the bastinado' became dear to him – even the boys who because of their fathers' wealth were regarded as being better than him and would for no reason beat him. He roamed around looking more intently at all he knew and with a more favourable eye but was sad at heart because he knew he was going to leave it all behind.

The day before leaving Qum Faizi went to say goodbye to his relatives and even went to their *mujtahid* and kissed his hand in farewell. He then went to his school, the grocer and the spice shop and cast his eyes for the last time over the dried nuts, raisins and sweets he loved so much. He was feeling so sad, emotional and tearful at the prospect of his separation from all that was familiar to him that he found sleeping that night very difficult. Probably as a way of taking his mind off his distress one of his maternal aunts sat by him and started telling him a story. It was a long story and Faizi's eyelids soon became heavier and heavier. He was nearly asleep when his aunt asked him, 'Are you still awake?' To Faizi's drowsy response, and in reference to the story she had just told him, she said, 'Now that you are going away you, too, have to bring lots of things when you return', but Faizi fell asleep and never heard what the moral of his aunt's tale was.

The first thing Faizi did when he got up early on his last morning in Qum was to go to the mulberry tree and stare intently at the other trees in the garden in an effort to imprint them on his memory. He then remembered that there were two other things in the house which he had to check before leaving. He had heard the adults in his family discuss some of the items in their house and say that in time they would become antiques and could be sold at high prices. With this in mind he had some time previously taken a broken china plate and a glazed plate and hidden them in a section of the wall of the house. He now went to double check that these were still in place, re-secured the hiding place and thought to himself that by the time he returned from Tehran these plates would have become valuable – he would then be able to sell them and fulfil his aunt's wish to buy something for everyone.

The other item he had to see before leaving was 'a very thick book with many pictures and writing in a European language'. Everyone in the family wanted to have a page of this book, particularly in wintertime when they would come to Faizi's grandmother and she would tear the selected page from the book and give it to them. He found the book and once more flicked through the remaining pages. There was one particular picture which had lodged in his memory: a group of black men, each carrying a large box on his head, and a European with a gun walking in front of them. Faizi then went to the cupboard in which he used to play. Someone had given him a few pictures of miniatures which he had stuck on the inside of this cupboard. To him 'no other pictures as beautiful as these pictures could be found in the world'.

Custom dictated that a traveller, once ready to leave, walk under a mirror, put his hand into flour then pass under the Qur'án three times to be blessed with a safe journey. As he was with the men, Faizi held himself 'amazingly like an adult' and controlled his emotions during this ritual but as soon as he stepped into the street to leave his home tears began welling up in his eyes. He looked up and down the street, the arena of all the games with his friends – their ball games, chase, leap-frog, the games he had yet to learn from the older boys – and wondered again how he could bear to leave all that he had grown up with. At that point his uncle broke his reverie and called out to him to go to the coach. He said he wanted to see the *zúrkhánih* one more time but his uncle replied, 'Forget it! Why do you want to go there? Go to Tehran and see the strong men of the capital!'

He obeyed with a heavy heart.

Faizi remembered his day of departure from Qum as being an early spring morning because he was not suffering from hay fever and was 'wide awake'. The weather was good, the luggage loaded onto the coach and the women of the house had all come to bid him and his mother goodbye. They hugged and embraced him and cried because they didn't know when they would next see this gentle child again. The poignancy of the moment as the young Faizi climbed into the coach was intensified by the sound of the hand drum from the *zúrkhánih* rising, beckoning the *pahlaváns* to exercise. It was as if it was also signalling the beginning of a new life for him, a life which would not only open his eyes and ears to the many wonders of the world and give him the chance to receive an education that fed his intellect and thirst for knowledge, but one which would also lead him to the shores of an ocean into which he would plunge and swim forever.

He never looked back.

2

Tehran – Tarbíyat School – Youth

Journey to Tehran

Mádar-jún and Faizi's fellow passengers were a motley group of 40 travellers seated 20 on either side of the carriage, most of them men smoking their pipes. The coachman, who was a young man with a good voice, started singing as soon as they left the city and were on the open road. He was a good coachman and stopped at every rest house on the way for his passengers to stretch their legs and have some refreshment, and to change the horses. One night they stopped at a fort for the night where they were served a simple fare of tea, bread and fried eggs. Faizi found this meal to be absolutely delicious and savoured the memory of the pure air and beautiful moonlit night for a long time.

As they approached Tehran a new passenger joined the group at the last stop before the city and struck up a conversation with all the passengers. When they reached the gates of Tehran it became apparent that he was an official who was working under cover because he inspected everyone's luggage and, having got to know his fellow passengers and their business, was able to catch those carrying opium.

After an exhausting few days mother and son finally reached Tehran and were reunited with Khán.

It took the young Faizi nearly a year to get used to being away from his beloved grandmother. He spent many a night crying for her and thinking that the pain of separation would be with him forever. However, before the year was out the excitement of his new life and what it had to offer him eased his longing and he was quite surprised at how quickly his intense feelings had ebbed away and been replaced with so much zest for life and thirst for knowledge.

The family settled well in Tehran and it was not long before they were joined by Faizi's newly married brother and his wife. My uncle soon became aware that his brother was studying on his own at home and was concerned that he had not been registered in any school because their father was worried about his young son getting lost in the big and busy city. However, he had no difficulty persuading Khán that it was better for his brother's education that he go to school. Having already sent his eldest son to a school run by Bahá'ís, Khán agreed to send Faizi to the Bahá'í Tarbíyat School for boys – which was near where they lived so there was no danger of him getting lost. My uncle therefore arranged for his brother to be interviewed by the principal of the school.

A Quickening Breeze

Early one morning the two brothers set off to Tarbíyat School, the younger one in trepidation of what awaited him, the older one happy that he was going to entrust his dear brother to the daily care of a benevolent institution. The classes were all in session when they arrived and the principal, 'Azíz Miṣbáḥ, was waiting for them in his office. How different the young Faizi's reception at this school was to the one he had received at the *maktab* in Qum, how genial and kindly Jináb-i[1] Miṣbáḥ was compared to the so-called teachers in his hometown. No wonder that as soon as Faizi met this much-loved principal he was immediately drawn to him. After welcoming the two brothers Jináb-i Miṣbáḥ asked the quiet younger one a few questions to try and establish his level of literacy and decided to place his new pupil in the fifth class.

Tarbíyat School, which was the first of several schools throughout the land established by the Bahá'ís of Iran in 1898 (separate ones for boys and girls), was considered to be the best and most respected school of the capital. Many well-known Muslim families as well as almost all the Bahá'ís of Tehran sent their boys to it. Most of the teachers were Bahá'ís and the ethos of the school was based on nurturing the latent talents of its pupils, encouraging them to have high moral standards and fostering in them a love for and desire to be of service to humanity.

Faizi's first day at Tarbíyat arrived. Gone was his reluctance to get up and go to school as he jumped out of bed early in the morning. He excitedly ate a hasty breakfast, put on the clean clothes Mádar-jún had laid out for him and dashed enthusiastically to his new school. He followed the other children when the bell for the start of the day rang and was guided to stand in line with the rest of the pupils in a respectful manner, each row in front of the door to their own class. There was order and calm and the new pupil immersed himself in the quiet and peaceful atmosphere. He lifted his head up to 'the tall cypress trees in the grounds of the school gently swaying in the breeze', feasted his eyes on 'the riot of bright flowers planted everywhere' and was absorbing the natural beauty around him when he was suddenly jolted out of his daydream by the voice of one of the students rising in sweet melody with the daily prayer chanted at the beginning of every school day:

> O Thou kind Lord! We are poor children, needy and insignificant, yet we are plants which have sprouted by Thy heavenly stream and saplings bursting into bloom in Thy divine springtime. Make us fresh and verdant by the outpourings of the clouds of Thy mercy; help us to grow and develop through the rays of the sun of Thy goodly gifts and cause us to be refreshed by the quickening breeze wafting from the meadows of Truth. Grant that we may become flourishing trees laden with fruit in the orchard of knowledge, brilliant stars shining above the horizon of eternal happiness and radiant lamps shedding light upon the assemblage of mankind.
>
> O Lord! Should Thy tender care be vouchsafed unto us,

each one of us would, even as an eagle, soar to the pinnacle of knowledge, but were we left to ourselves we would be consumed away and would fall into loss and frustration. Whatever we are, from Thee do we proceed and before Thy threshold do we seek refuge.
Thou art the Bestower, the Bountiful, the All-Loving.

'Abdu'l-Bahá[2]

Faizi stood riveted. Since his arrival in the city his senses had been bombarded with sights and sounds which were alien, strange and amazing to him. He had a lot to learn and to cope with in his new life but this was beyond all his expectations. After his introduction to 'education' in the *maktab* in Qum under the guidance of tutors who seemed to have had little interest in whether the children learned anything, let alone had any regard for their feelings or spiritual development, one can only imagine the effect of this beautiful prayer on the young boy. He now stood on the shores of an ocean of knowledge and experience that even he with his vivid imagination could not foresee.

First Bahá'í Class

Faizi very quickly became so attached to all his newly-found friends that he wanted to spend his whole time in school. During the course of the week he heard some of his friends talk about their Friday class, so as soon as Friday (which is the day of rest in Islamic countries) arrived he got up at the crack of dawn to make sure he did not miss following them. Unaware that these were Bahá'í classes, Faizi joined his friends, who happily took him along with them without question. When they reached the house where the class was to be held they all sat down on the floor of a carpeted room. Faizi felt a little lost but was happy to be in the company of his friends. As soon as they were all settled the owner of the house entered the room with a tray of tea and, as the children took their glass from his tray, lovingly greeted every child individually. They had finished drinking their tea when a tall, well-dressed young man entered the room and sat down in a corner. Faizi remembered that the young man wore a red cravat, that he was extraordinarily radiant and that he felt an instant deep affection for him. He was the teacher and his name was Núru'd-Dín Fatḥ-i-A'ẓam.[3]

The class began and the students started reciting in turn the quotations they had been given to learn the previous week. One quoted from the sayings of Muhammad, another from Christ, another from Moses and so on, leaving the new student in a state of total astonishment. Sinking deep in thought, the confused boy wondered, 'Oh my God! What is happening here? Where have they gathered these words from?' He was shaken from these thoughts by the realization that it would soon be his turn and he had no idea what to say. It had, of course, not escaped the attention of the kindly teacher that he had a new student in his class so he did not ask anything of Faizi. Instead he gave him a quotation from the Bahá'í writings to learn for the following week and explained to him that the words were not only to be memorized but to be understood, pondered and put into practice.

The words Faizi heard in that class had a deep effect on him and were the inspiration for the man he was to become. He was so fascinated by what he learned that day that thereafter he waited impatiently for the Friday Bahá'í classes. Mádar-jún, who soon became aware of what he was learning in these classes, always gave him clean clothes to wear on Fridays. She also continued to 'nip any bad behaviour or language in the bud by saying that it was contrary to her wishes' and would 'seriously prevent any repetition' of unseemly conduct.

To the end of his life Faizi never stopped thanking God for having guided him to Núru'd-Dín Fatḥ-i-A'ẓam's Bahá'í class. Even as an adult he could not bring himself to regard him as a friend but rather as the respected tutor to that child from Qum who first heard of the teachings of Bahá'u'lláh from him.

Faizi's paternal grandmother

Siddídih Khánum, Faizi's mother, 'Mádar-jún'

Khán, Faizi's father

Pahlaváns exercising in their zúrkhánih

Left: Jináb-i 'Azíz Miṣbáḥ

Right: Faizi aged 18

Left: Tarbíyat students with teacher. Faizi is standing in the middle of middle row.

Below: Bahá'í undergraduates with Gloria, *centre front*, at Beirut University, 1928. Faizi, *far left, second row*; Hasan Balyuzi, *far left, third row*.

Faizi's tutorial group with Professor Seeley, Beirut

Faizi tutoring Gloria in Beirut

Hasan Balyuzi and Faizi acting in one of their plays, Beirut

Photograph Faizi had taken while in Beirut to send to his mother for Naw-Rúz

Above: Faizi in an acting role, Beirut

Left: In the mountains of Lebanon during undergraduate days

Faizi the military officer, 1933–4

The new bearded teacher for Najafábád, 1936

Faizi the oil company employee

Faizi holding the sword of Mullá Ḥusayn, which is now in the International Bahá'í Archives in Haifa

Faizi with some of his students in Najafábád

Above: Faizi exercising with some of the children in Najafábád, Hooshang, *front left,* with a tin bowl on his head

Right: Rolling rocks down the mountain to use in building the public showers, Najafábád

Donkeys ready to collect the rocks, Najafábád

Faizi and Gloria, taken on Gloria's visit to Najafábád before their marriage

Faizi and Gloria's wedding, Tehran, 26 September 1939

The newly married couple, Najafábád

Mádar-jún, Gloria and Faizi, Najafábád

Some of the Bahá'í women of Najafábád

Gloria dances with the children in Najafábád as Faizi sits, watching, in the background

A teacher with a sense of humour – note size of Faizi's book – Najafábád

The Faizi brothers with their wives, children and relatives; Hooshang, *far right, second row*

The Popular Boy

As he began his secondary education Faizi threw himself into all the activities available to him. When he was old enough he joined the Scouts and spent time helping and instructing children in the junior classes. He appears to have had his very special power of attraction from an early age. His school friends remember that he was a popular, 'good natured', 'polite' and 'dignified' boy and that he was friends with everyone throughout his years at Tarbíyat – Muslims, Jews, Zoroastrians, Armenians as well as Bahá'ís – and that they all had great affection for him and always sought his company. One of his old school friends remembers Faizi standing in front of the row for his class during morning prayers, 'always with a smile on his lips and exuding the exuberance of youth'.

Faizi excelled in all his academic subjects, as well as in sports, and was invariably among those who received prizes and certificates of excellence at the end of each month. His fellow students have recorded that he never paid much attention to the fact that he was continually receiving recognition for his achievements and would walk to the top of the class to receive his prize or certificate with an air of mixed embarrassment and humility. He studied for the sake of studying and played sports for the love of the games, not because he wanted to show off or be recognized as being better than everyone else. It happened, however, that a few of the students started taunting him by telling the other students, in front of Faizi himself, that 'Faizi is now filled with pride because he has received a prize and is at the top of the class'. One of them went as far as to say that he was going to do his best to 'topple Faizi off his pedestal'. Faizi was an exceptionally sensitive youth and these snide and unkind remarks upset him to such an extent that he felt as if they had physically, as he said himself, beaten the soles of his feet so that he could not walk properly or take part in any sports activities. Just to 'keep the tormentors quiet' and off his back he refused to jump over the hurdles in races and only did so on the insistence of the sports master. Of the lasting effect of this experience Faizi wrote, 'The wound of their tongue, as if inflicted by a sword and dagger plunged into my shoulder and sides, still gives me anguish. The injury caused by the tongue is more bitter and lasts longer than any physical injury.'

Apart from this one negative experience Faizi's memories of his years at Tarbíyat were fond and happy – memories of lots of play and laughter and never being stopped by the teachers from having fun because they knew that all the students would study when necessary and would deliver their homework when the time came for them to do so.

Some School Day Memories

The religious knowledge class was always noisy with lots of laughter. One day in the midst of the boisterous behaviour one of the students stood up and complained to the teacher saying, 'Sir! Muhájir is calling me a donkey!' Instead of telling off the students the teacher calmly turned to Muhájir and asked him, 'Muhájir, why don't you know the difference between humans and animals?' which sent the whole class into peals of laughter. Notwithstanding this bantering the pupils were all good friends, went to Bahá'í class together and spent the summer holidays in each other's company.

ఌ

One winter's day the weather was so cold that the students in Faizi's class found it difficult to settle down and concentrate on their lessons. Their principal, Jináb-i Misbáh, was to take one of the classes but when he entered the classroom he said, 'My dear students, it is very cold today and as we still have not installed the stove in your room it will be difficult for you to write what I say. So put your hands into your pockets and listen to my story.'

The boys shoved their freezing hands deep into their pockets and were all ears as they huddled next to each other, waiting for their teacher to begin. Jináb-i Miṣbáḥ told them the following tale.

A great magician once stood in a big square of a certain city in order to display his magical talents to the people who gathered around him . . . He kept the crowd amused for a long time and his many magical tricks filled the onlookers with joy and excitement.

Among the onlookers was a five year old boy who could not see the magician because of all the adults standing around him. His father put him on his shoulders and the boy was filled with awe at every magic trick. He became so excited that he bounced up and down with joy on his father's shoulders and shouted down to him, 'Father, why don't you laugh and cheer like me and the others?' A man who was in the front row turned round and said to the boy, 'The reason you are enjoying the show is because you are sitting on your father's shoulders and can see what is going on.'

Jináb-i Miṣbáḥ paused at this point to give the moral of the story.

'My dear sons, you, also, are standing on the shoulders of your fathers, mothers, teachers and great ones. Please appreciate your parents and all those on whose shoulders you are standing.'

Faizi was so impressed by this story that he narrated it on several occasions during his life to demonstrate the debt Bahá'ís owe to the early believers of the Faith. The most significant occasion on which he recalled his respected principal's story was at the World Congress held at the Royal Albert Hall in London in 1963 in one of his most moving addresses.

☙

Faizi continued to attend Bahá'í classes every Friday. As he grew older he naturally and without any formality became part of the group of Bahá'í youth and it gradually become evident to Mádar-jún that her son had become one of them. Far from showing antagonism towards the Faith, as the rest of her relatives did, she encouraged her son to keep to the principles and observe the teachings. A devout Muslim herself, she would rise at dawn during the Bahá'í month of fasting to prepare Faizi's breakfast and make sure that he woke up on time. By this time she knew that her older son had also embraced this new Faith.

Among Faizi's friends during his school days were the identical twins 'Atá'u'lláh and 'Ináyat T͟hábit, Íraj Mírzá, Dáni͟sh, K͟háliqí and Saní'í with whom at the age of about 15 he attended Naṣru'lláh Mavadat's Bahá'í class.

Mr Mavadat encouraged the youth to attend regularly and not miss any of his classes. If ever one of them was absent, he would send Faizi to fetch him. 'Atá'u'lláh T͟hábit seldom attended because it was the day he helped his father but his twin, 'Ináyat, was present at every class without fail. As he had a good chanting voice, 'Ináyat was always asked to chant the first and last prayer. One Friday 'Ináyat was ill and not up to attending the Bahá'í class but, being keen to keep his record of attendance, he asked his twin, 'Atá'u'lláh, to go in his place. He told 'Atá'u'lláh to ask Faizi to help him disguise the fact that he was the other twin so that Mr Mavadat would not notice his absence. 'Atá'u'lláh agreed to help his brother and was one of the first to turn up at the class. As soon as he was put in the picture, Faizi approached the other students and asked them to keep quiet about the fact that this was not 'Ináyat so that the teacher would not question 'Atá'u'lláh about his perpetual absence from Bahá'í class. Mr Mavadat arrived and, as usual, began taking the class register. Everyone acknowledged his presence. When he reached 'Atá'u'lláh he looked straight at him and said, 'You are always present, unlike your brother who is always absent.' 'Atá'u'lláh did not blink an eye and remained silent and the class, which for a second was about to erupt into laugher, froze as soon as they caught the look on Faizi's face, which said, 'Control yourselves!' They all sat quietly and, with great difficulty, pretended nothing unusual had happened and prepared to continue with their lesson. Mr Mavadat then turned to

'Atá'u'lláh and asked him to chant the first prayer. Faizi knew 'Atá'u'lláh had a dreadful chanting voice so he immediately piped up, 'Sir, 'Ináyat is not feeling well today. Please allow me to chant the prayer.' Without suspecting anything the teacher agreed and when the class finished another student chanted the last prayer. As soon as Mr Mavadat left the house the students tumbled out into the street and fell about laughing at what had happened and applauded Faizi for having saved 'Atá'u'lláh from chanting and giving himself away. This kind of deception was not exactly in accordance with the high standards and principles they were learning in their Bahá'í classes but they were young, carefree and fun-loving.

Summer Holidays

During the summer holidays a group of ten to twelve friends would meet at an agreed place and go together to a well-known inland waterway named Áb-i Mangul. The first to arrive would stand around waiting impatiently for the rest of the group but it was only when they saw Faizi, the unspoken 'leader' of the group, appear round the corner of the street walking towards them that they felt the fun of the day had really begun. As soon as they were all gathered the friends would set off walking to Áb-i Mangul where they spent the whole day under the trees and swimming in the pool to keep cool. As evening approached those who had a long way to return home would leave but the rest, especially on moonlit nights, would move further north of the waterway where a stream meandered through the trees, and settle down to an evening of reciting poetry and singing songs.

Faizi loved the mountains north of Tehran and would sometimes persuade his friends to walk to them with him. He was 'the most nimble' among his friends and seemed to have more energy than the rest of them. If one of the friends got too tired and could not go any further in their adventures it was Faizi who would help and accompany him back to his house. One of the friends recalls that Faizi would come to his house at the crack of dawn during the school holidays, walk into his bedroom without much ceremony and drag him and his brother out of bed to go to the countryside together. Their parents, who were very fond of Faizi, never worried about their whereabouts, trusting that if Faizi was in the group their sons would be safe.

Sometimes the group of friends would set off at early dawn and spend the whole day together in the countryside, sharing their food. If they were too far away from home when night fell they would lie down to sleep on the dried grass out in the fields. Many of their friends who were not Bahá'ís were attracted to this healthy way of spending time and would join them in their adventures. Eventually they asked the youth about their beliefs and many of them became Bahá'ís.

എ

Faizi was interested in the arts from an early age. He would spend hours in the early mornings of the three summer months of school holidays in the two areas of Tehran famous as centres of gilding and illuminating, moving quietly from stall to stall, keenly observing each craftsman's workmanship. The craftsman he spent most of his time with was an illuminator who was a Bahá'í. The man never spoke to him, nor did the shy Faizi impose himself on him. He would just stand by his stall for hours watching with total fascination the skill with which the master illuminated the writings. In later years Faizi regretted that, despite the great interest he had shown in this art, none of the adults in his family had thought of giving him a paintbrush, nor did the master, 'not even once', ask him if he wanted to learn from him.

എ

Apart from the excellent education he received at Tarbíyat School, what affected Faizi most was the behaviour of the teachers towards their pupils. Some of the teachers in the school at the time were 'Azíz Miṣbáḥ, Fáḍil S͟hírází, Naṣru'lláh Mavadat and Fu'ád Ashraf, all well-known, highly educated and erudite men who, rather than pursue any personal ambition, had devoted themselves to the education of children during the day and to teaching the Faith in the evenings. To the end of his life Faizi remembered their gentle manner, their kindness, their politeness, their encouragement and the love they showed towards every child and youth and he mentioned their names with great reverence.

As years went by the group of school friends graduated. Some went on to higher education, some entered into employment and eventually many of them settled in various countries around the world. Faizi never forgot his years in Tarbíyat, nor did he forget his friends. Whenever the opportunity arose in his many travels and some of the old students found themselves gathered together, having come to see Faizi, they would set time aside to reminisce about their school days, their teachers and their youthful adventures. Faizi would, 'for the short duration of such occasions, be able to put down his workload, relax and laugh from the bottom of his heart in enjoyment of recalling one of the happiest periods of his life'.

End of School Days

After completing his education at Tarbíyat, which at that time had only nine grades, Faizi continued his education at the American College in Tehran. He also attended the private English classes of Miss Qudsíyyih Ashraf to build on the basic English he had learned during his years at Tarbíyat where he had, in addition, been taught some French as well. By the time he was 19 years old there was no way of avoiding the dreaded military service any longer so his father decided to send him to study abroad rather than waste his time in the army. This decision must have been based on K͟hán's recognition of his son's talents and abilities and, no doubt, with persuasion from his older son, who had been the one to keep a close eye on his brother's education and signed his school reports as the responsible adult.

At the time Shoghi Effendi[4] encouraged the Persian students who wanted to go on to higher education to first go to Beirut for their studies rather than to any of the European centres of learning. It was therefore arranged for Faizi to enter the American University of Beirut, which was a well-known and respected university. Khán, however, did not have much money to spare for his son's education, and although my uncle contributed financially, Faizi had difficulty making ends meet throughout the years he was away from home.

The last time Faizi attended his English class with Miss Ashraf he was presented with an autograph book in which he himself wrote that it had been given to him by his dear teacher and friends. He invited them to write a few lines for him in memory of their friendship. Miss Ashraf, almost prophetically, wrote the following:

> So nigh is grandeur to our dust,
> So near is God to man,
> When Duty whispers low, *Thou must*,
> The youth replies, *I can*.
> Ralph Waldo Emerson, 'Voluntaries'

༄

Faizi was accepted at the American University of Beirut, not only on the basis of his academic ability but also because he was good at football (his love of football remained with him and in later years Pelé[5] became his favourite footballer). His intention was to study education and then return to Tehran to teach at the Tarbíyat School. He was, no doubt, excited at the prospect of going yet further afield in pursuit of knowledge, seeing new sights, finding out what else life had to offer him. But he was equally anxious at the prospect of a second major separation: it was the first time he was going to be away from his mother for any length of time. He never liked goodbyes and found them difficult to cope with but this was also going to be his first attempt at living the life of an independent young man, shouldering all his own responsibilities.

In the last few days leading to her younger son's departure Mádar-jún started to pack his clothing with a heavy heart. She had expected her handsome young son to marry and have children she could help to raise, but she was an intelligent woman and was not going to stand in his way. As she neatly folded and placed his clothing in a suitcase she could not help but wonder why her life was changing so rapidly and presenting her with situations she was neither used to nor liked. Her final gesture of maternal love was to scour the shops in her neighbourhood until she found what she felt her son should have now that he had to take care of himself. Faizi spoke with great tenderness on several occasions about the toothbrush he found nestled amongst his shirts when he unpacked his suitcase in Beirut.

3
Beirut

There is no record of how Faizi travelled from Tehran to Beirut in 1927 but in all likelihood it was by car with several other passengers, probably students like himself. On arrival at the University of Beirut he was allocated accommodation in Bliss Hall and later moved to College Hall.

As always, Faizi quickly adapted to another way of life and soon had a new circle of friends to add to those he had left behind. There were in the same years many young Persian men and women studying in Beirut. In general the men studied at the university and the women undertook nursing courses at the hospital. Most of them knew each other and they were all good friends.

Distinguished Friend

Of all of Faizi's new-found friends one stood head and shoulders above the others: Hasan Balyuzi. Hasan Balyuzi was a Bahá'í and already a student at the university when Faizi arrived. Their first encounter was on a spring afternoon in the university library. Faizi was studying when he was distracted by the entrance of 'a smiling, medium height young man wearing a snow white shirt and black suit with a black fur hat on his head'; he had 'an air of dignity' about him and, after spending some time searching for a book, sat down in a corner of the library to read. Hasan Balyuzi so held Faizi's attention that Faizi instinctively moved to sit near him. When the lights were turned off at dinner time and the students went to the dining hall Faizi noticed that Hasan Balyuzi was seated at the top table with the more senior students, deep in discussion and every now and again laughing out loud.

Faizi and Hasan Balyuzi became 'everlasting friends' and Faizi referred to this friendship as 'a brotherhood created by the blessing of Bahá'u'lláh'. He regarded his friend as above him in 'the ladder of scholarship' and looked upon him as his mentor. Hasan Balyuzi's relationship with all of his friends was 'exemplary' and 'he played the role of a true brother to all'. Although they always sought Balyuzi's company, if any of his friends ever saw him talking to a student with his hand in his waistcoat pocket, they kept their distance because they knew it meant that the student's allowance had not arrived from Iran and that Hasan was giving him enough money to survive until it did.

When reminiscing about his undergraduate days Faizi always said that it was Hasan Balyuzi who kept him and many of the other Bahá'í students 'on the straight and narrow', and that it was Hasan Balyuzi who encouraged them to serve the Cause. In describing his friend's character he said, 'Hasan Balyuzi assumed no rank and title but he was a candle whose light would show us the true path to success . . . his own life, manner and words shone light on all the paths that we had eventually to tread.' He would say that as long as they had Hasan Balyuzi amongst them they were 'safe and sound'. Late into his life he wrote, 'After many years I still hear the warm, penetrating voice of Hasan Balyuzi and still feel guided by his love and protective measures which he always surrounded us with.'

Gloria

My mother was sent to Beirut for her schooling the same year Faizi started his studies there. Raḥmat 'Alá'í, my maternal grandfather, had for years been the black sheep of a large, well-known Bahá'í family in Iran. He was not involved in any Bahá'í activities and was the cause of much consternation to his family because of the reckless way he led his life. The lowest point came when his wife left him and he found himself responsible for the care of his adored six year old daughter, Gloria. But his acrimonious divorce had left him in no mental state to carry out his duties as a father.

Rather than leave Gloria in the care of one of his brothers or sisters, he decided to remove her from the troubled circumstance he found himself in and place her in a boarding school in Beirut until such time as his life was more settled. His brothers tried to persuade him to go to the Holy Land on his way to Lebanon in the hope that meeting Shoghi Effendi would have a positive effect on their wayward brother, but Raḥmat was preoccupied with his own turmoil and not interested in any spiritual matters. By way of encouraging him to carry out their wish they gave him a portrait of 'Abdu'l-Bahá painted by a well-known Persian artist and asked him to take it to Shoghi Effendi. The account of how Raḥmat met Shoghi Effendi and became a changed man is another story. Suffice it to say that Shoghi Effendi told Raḥmat he had written to the Bahá'ís in Iran advising them not to send their young children to Beirut before they had completed their secondary education. However, in his daughter's case, and given his personal circumstances, it would be all right to leave her in Beirut.

As Gloria was the only Persian child in her school the undergraduates and student nurses from Iran decided to take her under their wings. They included her on many of their outings and the Bahá'ís amongst them sometimes took her with them when they went on pilgrimage to the Holy Land. Gloria's guardian was anxious that she should learn to read and write Persian so he asked Faizi to give her lessons whenever he could spare the time and Faizi would sometimes go to her school in the evenings to tutor her. His student, however, was not always inclined to concentrate on any more lessons after a full day in class and seeing her friends playing in the garden. Understanding her lack of enthusiasm, Faizi never forced her to study but would instead engage her by giving her interesting clippings from magazines or teach her through playing games. He would sometimes take her for a walk by the seashore and once took her to see a film but she fell asleep halfway through and he had great difficulty getting her back to school.

'Who could have known', my mother wrote before her death, 'that this young man was destined to change the normal course of my life and take me with him on the journey of a life of unusual experiences so that I could be a witness to the amount of work he accomplished, the services he rendered and the sacrifices he made for the Cause which was so dear to his heart?'

A few years later when Gloria returned to Tehran Faizi wrote in one of his letters to his brother, 'If you see Gloria 'Alá'í give her my greetings. I will not forget my dear Gol' (Gol, meaning flower in Persian, was Gloria's nickname).

Bahá'í Activities

With the increase in the number of Bahá'í students at the university, Hasan Balyuzi decided one day to call everyone to a meeting in one of the university halls. After giving an encouraging talk he suggested that they should have classes to practise giving talks, in both Persian and English, on various Bahá'í subjects. His fellow Bahá'í students were all in favour of this suggestion and began holding their meetings every Sunday afternoon in the home of the Iqbal family, one of the long-established Bahá'í families in Lebanon.[1] They started by drawing up on a large sheet of paper a programme for one academic year and then recorded the names of the speakers and the subjects they were going to tackle. Hasan Balyuzi helped them with the references they needed from the writings and on his suggestion they sent a copy of the programme to Shoghi Effendi. Shoghi Effendi's response was to encourage the students to continue with their Bahá'í studies, which gave them added incentive to persevere with their plan.

Having sent their programme of classes to Shoghi Effendi the Bahá'í students, again on a suggestion from Hasan Balyuzi, wrote to him asking for permission to go on pilgrimage during their Christmas, mid-year and Easter holidays. Shoghi Effendi gave his permission and instructed them to go in groups rather than all together. As each group's turn came they would hire a taxi to take them to the door of the Master's house, now Shoghi Effendi's home. Of those days Faizi has written, 'All doors of gracious bounties and spiritual upliftment were flung wide open for us. Those days were indeed like unto the flood of the sun's rays penetrating through an opening in the ceiling to a dark room. We were impatient for such spiritual upliftment . . .'

First Meeting with Shoghi Effendi

Faizi's turn to go on pilgrimage soon arrived (his notes about his first meeting with the Guardian make no mention of anyone else being there). He was 20 years old, felt inadequate and was in trepidation because he felt his knowledge of the writings was limited. At the same time he was eager and impatient to meet the Guardian of the Faith he had come to accept. Hasan Balyuzi, who had already been to the Holy Land on several occasions, had given all the students some guidance on how to behave but Faizi wondered how he would react in the Shrines of Bahá'u'lláh and the Báb. What would his feelings be for this man his friend had spoken about with such love and respect? He was mulling over innumerable questions and had so much on his mind that he paid no attention to anything during the drive from Beirut and before he knew it the taxi had stopped in front of the gate to the Master's house and the driver was asking him for his fare.

Getting out of the taxi, Faizi stood for a moment and looked through the high iron gates at the large stone house sitting at the end of a wide gravel path. He hesitatingly opened the gate and walked up the path. A member of staff asked him to wait in the garden. He roamed around the small garden, 'pacing aimlessly . . . waiting to hear the voice of the Guardian'. After some time someone called him and invited him to enter the house. Keyed up and trying to control his excitement, he walked up the wide steps leading to the front door, entered the house and was guided across the large hall to the room opposite where he was, once again, asked to wait. He took a seat near the door. He did not know that the seat he had chosen to sit on was the one the Guardian always took when meeting with the pilgrims.

Time stood still for Faizi as he sat in the hushed setting in silence. Suddenly the Guardian came out of one of the rooms leading off the hall and walked straight to where Faizi was waiting. Faizi's eyes fell on the one who was to become the inspiration that shaped his life; it was the pivotal moment in which the direction of his life changed forever. Of that first meeting Faizi wrote:

> We Persians have been taught from childhood to stand up when someone older enters the room and to show respect. I, however, forgot all I had been taught and remained seated as if nailed to the chair. The Guardian, who was in the flower of youth and full of spiritual strength with heavenly majesty, came forward and said, 'Come, let us meet each other as two brothers' and with great calm lifted me from my seat. Filled with shame and my eyes streaming with tears I found my head resting on his shoulder.

The Guardian then bade Faizi be seated where he had been. He asked him about his future plans. He encouraged Faizi to study English, Arabic and Persian and then said, 'Let us go to the Shrine of the Báb.'

In later years, when recalling this period of his life, Faizi felt that being young at the time he had 'not understood or appreciated the value of those days'.

Studies, Plays and Relaxation

Faizi returned to Beirut with his heart singing. The Guardian had advised him to study English, Arabic and Persian, so he threw himself into his studies. Judging from his notes and diary of the time, his thirst for knowledge was unquenchable as he attended lectures on history, psychology, literature, education, etc. But he was a balanced man and did not spend all day and every day poring over his books. He loved acting and together with Hasan Balyuzi wrote plays and participated in the theatrical performances the students put on throughout the year. One of the plays they mounted, on Saturday 3 May 1930, was a five act play written by Faizi entitled *Sháh Abbás the Great*. Hasan Balyuzi was not only in the play but was also the director and Faizi played the lead romantic role. Of his friend's writing Faizi has recorded that 'his prose in Persian was very firm and poetic' and of his acting that 'he recited from memory more than 50 lines of the long poem of one of the Persian poets on the ruins of the Persian capital of old Persepolis with great enthusiasm and lamentation'. The two friends also started a Persian journal for the Iranian students in Beirut for which they wrote articles, anecdotes and short stories.

Another activity of Faizi and Hasan Balyuzi was to visit the few elderly Bahá'ís in Beirut who had lived in the Holy Land for some years before moving to Lebanon. They loved listening to the stories these believers had to tell of the time of 'Abdu'l-Bahá and sometimes invited them to talk about their experiences to the other Bahá'í students.

Faizi also enjoyed going into town and to the cinema. I remember him telling me that he and some of his fellow undergraduates could not always afford starched collars, so when they wanted to look very smart they cut out white cardboard collars for themselves. They were such dab hands at it that the collars looked real. One entry in Faizi's diary reads:

> Being penniless is bad, especially for those who don't want to show it. I have one set of clothes; it is winter and the weather cold and rainy and I have no money. When I got my money yesterday it all went towards paying my debts – 22 liras for my teeth – I still owe money but have nothing left. I need a lot of things but I'm not worried. God is great. I am writing this down so that I don't forget these days.

It seems that Faizi, and a number of other Bahá'í undergraduates, did not regularly return to Iran for their summer holidays, but the few times he did Faizi involved himself in all the activities of the Persian Bahá'í community. During the holidays that he and some other students remained in Beirut they continued with their classes on public speaking and Hasan Balyuzi suggested to them that they should concentrate on first writing down and then giving their talks in English. This proved to be beneficial for the new undergraduates, as it helped them learn English very quickly.

Visits to the Holy Land

Faizi and Hasan Balyuzi went on pilgrimage together as often as they could. On one occasion a gardener came to the Pilgrim House looking for them. He gave them a packet wrapped in a silk handkerchief and told them, 'Shoghi Effendi has sent this to be given to you two and he said that you would translate it and send it back to him.'

The young men opened the packet with reverence and great excitement to find a document written by Queen Marie of Romania in praise of the teachings of Bahá'u'lláh. They immediately set to work and took two days to translate the manuscript from English into Persian. As soon as they were satisfied with their work they sent it back to Shoghi Effendi and hastened to the Master's house the same day to accompany Shoghi Effendi to the Shrine of the Báb. When Shoghi Effendi came out of the house and they started walking up the mountain, the two fully expected to hear him comment on the translation. Shoghi Effendi, however, as was his custom during their walk towards the Shrines, shared with them the news he had received from the Bahá'í world. As they reached their destination he turned to the young men and said, 'I received the translation. It is correct but not eloquent. I changed some phrases.' The two were so happy that their Guardian had accepted the little work they had done for him and begged Bahá'u'lláh to confirm them 'to be forever at his service'. They were by now aware of what a heavy burden the Guardian was carrying.

On the few occasions the students took Gloria with them to the Holy Land she found herself alone much of the time and spent her days roaming around the gardens on Mount Carmel or sitting inside the Shrine of the Báb. At times she would go to the house of 'Abdu'l-Bahá but was not interested in seeing any of the members of the Guardian's family, many of whom lived together in that house at the time. The only person she was eager to be with was Bahíyyih Khánum,[2] so when she saw her sitting alone she would go quietly into the room and sit beside her. Gloria knew nothing about the Faith at the time and was not aware of Bahíyyih Khánum's station and her services to the Cause of her father; she 'just loved her and wanted to be near her'.

One day when Gloria was with the Persian students in a meeting they had with the Guardian, Shoghi Effendi asked her to say a prayer. She was too embarrassed to tell him that she did not know how to pray in Persian.

Faizi came to her rescue and said, 'She knows a prayer in English; would you permit her to say it?'

The Guardian gave permission and she stood up and said a prayer given to her by a European lady who had been on pilgrimage and which she had memorized. After she finished the prayer the Guardian remarked, 'What a sweet pronunciation she has.' He then turned to Faizi and said, 'Teach her to pray in Persian.'

At the same meeting the Guardian asked Faizi to chant and Faizi chanted part of a long Tablet of Bahá'u'lláh, at the end of which the Guardian again remarked to one of the older Bahá'ís in the gathering that he was sure the believer had not heard such beautiful chanting for a very long time.

The following morning when the pilgrims were on the slopes of Mount Carmel with him, Shoghi Effendi said to Faizi, 'Bahíyyih Khánum heard your voice when you chanted the Tablet of Bahá'u'lláh last night. Would you go and chant for her?' The request was 'so sudden' that Faizi 'could not properly fathom the greatness of this bounty'. He assumed his friend would go with him but Hasan Balyuzi told him he had to go on his own.

Following Balyuzi's advice, the anxious Faizi was at the Master's house at nine o'clock the next morning. He was admitted to the same room where he had first met the Guardian and sat by the door. Bahíyyih K̲h̲ánum was sitting in her chair, 'Abdu'l-Bahá's wife was standing by her side and the Guardian's mother had her arm on her shoulder. There were a few other women present as well. At a bidding from Bahíyyih K̲h̲ánum, the Master's wife turned to Faizi and said, 'Please chant for K̲h̲ánum.' One can only speculate how the young student felt as he cleared his throat to chant for these three distinguished women. He chanted a Tablet of 'Abdu'l-Bahá addressed to a man who had suffered one whole night at the hands of a group of fanatics in the vicinity of Yazd and each sentence had a refrain 'No more sufferings, why sorrows?' which greatly moved Bahíyyih K̲h̲ánum and all those present.

ೞ

On another occasion the Guardian asked the Bahá'í students to prepare a programme to entertain Bahíyyih K̲h̲ánum. They prepared one with music, chants and songs and went to the House of the Master full of excitement. Bahíyyih K̲h̲ánum was seated on a chair beside the Master's wife with the younger ladies of the family standing behind them. At the end of the programme one of the ladies, speaking on behalf of Bahíyyih K̲h̲ánum, asked if any of the students could sing the tune of *Kúchih-Bág̲h̲í* (a rather sad, haunting tune sometimes sung in Tehran by a lone labourer returning home in the evenings). One of the students who was familiar with these particular songs began singing, his heartfelt rendition probably bringing to Bahíyyih K̲h̲ánum's mind memories of her childhood days in Tehran with her beloved father.

ೞ

One evening Faizi and some other students who were staying at what was then the Eastern Pilgrim House went out onto the balcony from where they could see the light in the Guardian's room lower down the mountain. They decided to stay up and see when the light went out. They waited till two in the morning but the light was still on. The following evening they went as usual to the Master's house and as soon as they greeted the Guardian he told them that he was obliged to stay up late at night because he had a lot of work but that they should go to bed early.

※

Shoghi Effendi was always very kind to Hasan Balyuzi and Faizi. On one occasion when they were in the Holy Land on their own he told them he wanted to send them to the Mansion of Bahá'u'lláh in Bahjí but that they were not to enter into any discussions with the Covenant-breakers[3] who lived there at the time. Faizi and Balyuzi found the Mansion in a terrible condition: not only was it badly in need of repairs but it was unclean and coal was stacked in the room which had belonged to Bahá'u'lláh. Hasan Balyuzi could not control himself and asked the person who was showing them around why the place was in such a bad state. The man answered it was because Shoghi Effendi had not given them any money, to which Balyuzi responded that one needed a broom to clean a house, not money. As the Guardian had told them not to enter into any discussion with these people, that was all that was said. They held their tongues and left.

Hasan Balyuzi and Faizi were again in the Holy Land in February 1932. The Guardian had by this time taken possession of the Mansion and the two were among the first group of pilgrims who were allowed to visit the renovated and furnished building and sleep there for two nights. On 4 February 1932 Faizi wrote to his brother from the Mansion:

> However much I describe things or express my feelings to you it is not enough. My hands shake and my heart beats with the extent of my joy . . . I arrived in Haifa with Jináb-i Balyuzi

two days ago and met the Guardian the same afternoon in the gardens of the Shrine of the Báb . . . The Guardian asked about our studies . . . We then went walking on Mount Carmel and all during our walk the Guardian spoke about the importance of not interfering in political matters . . . We were in the presence of the Guardian at night as well; he asked me to chant a prayer. He sent us to Bahjí the following day and told us to spend two nights there. Do you know what a great honour this is for us, to spend two nights in such a historic place?

I cannot describe to you the beauty of this building . . . I have taken a lot of photographs and will send copies to you from Beirut.

We must return to Beirut in two days. Perhaps I'll be able to come again this year, which of course depends on the Guardian's permission; but he is so kind to us students that he may give us permission . . . I cannot tear myself away from here.

Last Year in Beirut

Hasan Balyuzi graduated with a Master's degree in history and left Beirut for London. The students were so sad to be losing such a dear and close friend and none more so than Faizi. Together they had raised the spirits of their fellow students to greater heights; together they had written plays, acted, laughed and joked and, more importantly, been fellow pilgrims to the Holy Land and the recipients of so much kindness, love and bounty from the Guardian. But Hasan Balyuzi never forgot his friends. He continued helping the young Bahá'ís in Beirut and energizing them through his encouraging and inspiring letters.

☙

For Faizi, his years in Beirut were unforgettable. Although the university 'became a cage' after he met the Guardian and he wanted 'to be left free to soar in the firmament of love and servitude', he nevertheless made the most of what university life had to offer him and was also fully involved in the activities of the Bahá'í community in Beirut. He was a young man and he and his friends were typical undergraduates: they studied hard when they needed to, they went to the cinema and kept up with the latest Hollywood films, they wrote and acted in plays, they composed amusing rhymes and generally had a good time when they got tired of hard work. These few extracts from Faizi's diary (1932/1933) give some insight into his life as a student.

6 January
This afternoon was completely wasted – I didn't go to class – went into town then visited Dihqán – two young men from Ethiopia came to say goodbye – they have been very good and kind friends and their sudden departure has upset me. We ate at half past eight this evening and had a good discussion around the meal table about the great scientists and how much they worked for the good of humanity, also about some of the psychologists.

12 January
We studied Byron's life today. Our conversation at lunch was about the disappearance of the old Persian children's games. I stayed in in the afternoon and worked until Dihqán came and we spent some time together talking nonsense; then 'Alá'í came and we went with him to take a photograph after which I went to a bookshop and bought a book of Byron's poetry and one on philosophy.

13 January
I didn't go to the lecture on psychology today because my two Ethiopian friends were leaving at about half past nine in the morning and I had to see them off. I returned to College Hall and had a breakfast of milk, bread, butter and jam then started studying. Varji came around lunchtime and we had a

very interesting discussion about Byron, Keats and Shelley. We had another discussion about philosophy round the dinner table. Varji said that science must control art, which was a hollow statement to make; and then during the discussion he said that he could not differentiate between science and art . . . Our intense discussions came to an end at eight and we spent the rest of the evening reading some of Byron's poems.

14 January
We spoke about the new game of yoyo at lunch. There has been no rain in one of the areas of Lebanon and the people think it's because so many people are playing this game. Their belief is so strong that the government has said everyone should stop playing it. Coincidentally, the day after this edict it rained for three days. I stayed in my room in the afternoon. Fu'ád came and we started by joking with one another and then entered into a conversation about Persian and Arabic poetry. Fu'ád does not know any Persian but was of the opinion that Persian poetry is not better than Arabic poetry. I asked him, 'What about Russian poetry?' He replied that he did not know any Russian so I told him that he expresses a lot of opinion for someone who does not know. My life this year has been full of happiness. When I get up in the mornings I see my friends and become happy. Their company has such an effect on me that I become upset if I sometimes don't see them; my friends are all precious to me, God increase them.

☙

I came home after church and finished off an assignment on education and took it to my tutor. I then continued reading my book. After lunch I read some French poetry then finished the novel I was reading.

☙

Today I'm writing a play about Alexander and hope it will be good. Two of my house mates are in their rooms studying; Varji is at his desk trying to study but I keep teasing him that all the medical students do is memorize their lessons.

15 January
Sundays are for sleeping. I stayed in bed until nine o'clock and at eleven went to a Bahá'í meeting. After lunch I read and at five o'clock went out. Varji joined me and we had a long walk along the seashore.

20 January
We studied Shakespeare's *Romeo and Juliet* in class today. Shakespeare is such a skilled playwright, and unless one pays deep attention to and studies his works in depth, his masterpieces will not be understood or appreciated.

27 January
It is the first day of the mid-year holidays. I wasted the day doing nothing. In the evening 'Alá'í and I went to the cinema to see *Shanghai Express* with Marlene Dietrich.

16 March
We went to a drawing class at half past four – I showed the tutor some of the drawings I had done and he liked them very much and encouraged me to continue.

19 April
I woke up at nine o'clock this morning – Dihqán came at half past and suggested we go to the cinema but when we got there, there was nothing on so we went to Aḥmad and spent some time talking . . . My brother was with me on my way back to my room and we discussed many subjects, especially about love, and that people, especially men, must not pursue the one they love but must behave in such a way that both parties move

towards each other rather than have one chasing the other. I told him the time will come when he will say to himself 'Faizi spoke the truth'.

Saturday 14 May
Our psychology class went to the mental asylum with Professor Seely. It is a beautiful place on top of a hill . . . Seeing the people suffering from insanity had a deep effect on me and I could not write anything for three days. Each one of their facial expressions touched my heart.

Last Visit to Shoghi Effendi

Faizi returned to the Holy Land a few more times on his own. One day when he was in the Pilgrim House the caretaker came to him and said that the Guardian was on the site of the Shrine of the Báb and wanted him there. Faizi immediately set off and started running in his haste to reach the Guardian as quickly as possible when he heard the Guardian calling out to him, 'Don't run, you will get tired.' Faizi said that from that time on he never ran after anything and left situations to eventually sort themselves out.

Khán did not live long enough to enjoy his son's success at university and died sometime before Faizi graduated in June 1933 with a BA in education. It is not clear why it took him so long to get his degree but it could be that, like many of the undergraduates, he had to spend a good part of the time becoming proficient in the English language before he could tackle the course work.

Before returning to Iran Faizi sought permission to go to the Holy Land. So deep was his devotion that bidding farewell to the Guardian without knowing when he would be able to see him again was very difficult for him. The scene as he walked on Mount Carmel on his last night in the company of the Guardian after they had been to the Shrine of the Báb was breathtaking, with moonlight shimmering on the Bay of Haifa. As Faizi walked behind him the Guardian turned and bade him come forward and walk in step with him 'in a brotherly manner'. He patted Faizi on the shoulder and said, 'Jináb-i Faizi, you will be going to Tehran tomorrow,' which Faizi affirmed. He told Faizi to be different from others and warned him to beware lest materialism take possession of him. Faizi immediately understood that as far as making any money was concerned he was not destined to become rich.

Faizi left the Holy Land the following day with a heavy heart but his deep sadness was assuaged by the fact that he had on his lap a small bouquet of flowers the Guardian had given him that morning to lay, on his behalf, on the grave in Isfahan of Mrs Keith Ransom Kehler.[4] He did not know it then, but he was never to see the Guardian again.

4

Return Home

On his return to Iran Faizi immediately made his way to Isfahan but, owing to circumstances beyond his control, he was not able to reach his destination at the time arranged by the Guardian. The Guardian was advised of this and the date was changed to one or two days later, the day of the commemoration of the martyrdom of the Báb. Faizi and many of the Bahá'ís of Isfahan went to Mrs Ransom Kehler's graveside that afternoon and at exactly four o'clock, the time set by the Guardian, Faizi placed the special bouquet on Mrs Ransom Kehler's grave. He then spent a few moments by the graves of the King of Martyrs and the Beloved of Martyrs[1] before leaving the cemetery.

Having fulfilled his duty Faizi proceeded to Tehran and was reunited with his now widowed mother. Although he was anxious to start teaching at Tarbíyat School as soon as possible, there was no escape from doing his one year of national military service. He was, however, spared the rigours of military training because of his academic qualifications and was given the rank of an officer.

The military officers in those days cut fine figures and tended to make a show of their rank by parading themselves around in their fitted uniforms, polished high boots and shining swords hanging by their side. Faizi, who liked dressing well but never liked drawing too much attention to himself, had a habit of covering his uniform with a cape, which, according to those who knew him at the time, actually had the effect of adding to his dignified stature and made him even more attractive to everyone.

During his year of military service Faizi attended Bahá'í meetings and conducted Bahá'í classes whenever he was off duty. He also tutored a group of young women who had asked him to teach them English. He invited Gloria (who had returned to Tehran before him), to join this class but she went once or twice and then stopped attending because she felt embarrassed being in a group of women who were not only much older than she was but also knew less English. Faizi had first seen Gloria again when her parents invited him to a garden party in celebration of her twelfth birthday. He took her a small gift but did not stay long.

One of Faizi's Bahá'í class students remembered that among her fellow students were Fayḍu'lláh Miṣbáḥ, Mihdí Samímí, Behjat 'Alá'í, Abdu'lláh Fáḍil and Ḥusayn 'Alí Vaḥdat, all to become well known in the Bahá'í community for their services to the Faith. She recalled that one day when Faizi was talking to the class about the Hands of the Cause of God she had, without thinking, piped up, 'You are one of them.' Faizi's reaction to this remark was to bite his lip in shock; he was mortified.

In 1934 Faizi was appointed to the National Education Committee where he served with 'Alí-Akbar Furútan.[2] Mr Furútan's recollection was that there were a number of specialists in the field of education on this committee, such as Dr Húshyár and Dr Rawshan (and, of course, himself) but that they were all 'in awe of Faizi's intelligence and level of knowledge, especially as he was fluent in Persian, Arabic and French', and that, more importantly, Faizi's knowledge of the writings on this subject was a great help in their consultation.

The Bahá'í community in Tehran now looked upon Faizi as a respected, educated man with knowledge of child education, but it was not Faizi's way to point out or talk about practices he believed should be done away with. There are two examples of how he introduced change and how he conducted himself as a teacher. They are not so much examples of the result of academic study but rather of the teachings of Bahá'u'lláh honing his own innate qualities.

All the Bahá'í classes in Tehran ended their year with an examination in the Bahá'í Centre. The large hall in the Centre was divided into ten sections and a table and two chairs placed in each division, one chair for the class teacher and one for the examiner. The students of each class stood in groups in their own section and as each student's turn came he or she would walk up to the table and stand in front of their class teacher and examiner to be questioned about their year's work. Faizi made a small but significant change the one year he was involved in this examination process. As soon as he entered the hall and saw the arrangement he walked to his section, placed a third chair for the student being examined and a bench for the rest of his class to sit on while waiting. He believed children had the same right as adults and should always be shown respect and consideration. The other teachers immediately understood what he was doing and followed suit and the new arrangement was adhered to in subsequent years.

One day the teachers of several of the Bahá'í classes decided to take their students on a picnic together. When they arrived at the picnic site the teachers, as was the way in those days, settled down together and left the children to amuse themselves. It would have been considered 'undignified' for the teachers to bring themselves down to the level of the students and it would never have occurred to the students to ask their teachers to join them in any of their games and activities. Faizi did the 'undignified' thing: he gathered the students around him and started playing the popular game of five stones with them. The other teachers looked on in amazement and called out to him, 'Jináb-i Faizi! You are playing!' to which Faizi replied, 'Don't be jealous. We will include you in our games!' But this was too dramatic and quick a change of behaviour for the teachers who were not yet ready to become playmates with the children!

༄༅

Throughout his years in Beirut Faizi never lost sight of his greatest wish: to return to Bahá'u'lláh's native land and spend the rest of his days teaching at Tarbíyat School. Not only did the fire of this hope never extinguish but it was set ablaze by the continual encouragement he received from the Guardian every time he went on pilgrimage.

Towards the end of his military service Faizi spoke with such excitement and impatience about being so close to reaching his goal that even his commander knew what his plans were. Impressed with his officer's character and conduct, he told Faizi one day, 'I have heard you are going to serve in Tarbíyat School. I'm going to send my children there and you can train them however you like.'

It was during Faizi's year of military service, 1933–4, that, because of his deteriorating health, Jináb-i Miṣbáḥ retired as principal of Tarbíyat School and, with the Guardian's approval, 'Alí-Akbar Furútan was appointed in his place. It was also in this year that the first National Spiritual Assembly of the Bahá'ís of Iran was elected and with it came an escalation of the movement to close down Tarbíyat School. Although Reza Shah[3] initially showed little hostility towards the Bahá'ís, he now rose in opposition with those around him feeding him with information that Tarbíyat School was causing problems for the country. Their argument was that the children who attended this school were being influenced by the spirit of the Bahá'í Faith and that most of them looked favourably on the Bahá'ís once they finished their education. They put it to the Shah that the school should be closed before its influence spread too much. The Shah agreed but he needed an excuse to issue such an order. Mr Furútan, together with the support of the newly-formed National Assembly, dealt with the ever-increasing accusations made against the school with complete honesty and openness and showed that the school was a law-abiding institution which concentrated on the welfare of its children. The excuse the authorities wanted came when the Guardian sent a telegram to the National Assembly with a message that all independent Bahá'í institutions should close on Bahá'í holy days, including all Bahá'í schools.[4]

As fate would have it, 20 days before Faizi's discharge from the army news came that the government had ordered all the Bahá'í schools to be closed.[5] This turn of events devastated Faizi. His plans, his hopes and his dreams were dashed to the ground and he had no control over his disappointment. He became sad and melancholic and spent some time after his discharge wandering around without a job in the hope that the school would be allowed to reopen.

There were not many in Iran at the time with a good standard of English and the administrators of the oil company in Tehran, having heard of Faizi, were very keen to employ him. He eventually, and reluctantly, accepted a post in the company. The salary was excellent and he had prospects of climbing to the top of an important career but his heart was not in riches and high positions and the Guardian's counsel to him that he should stay clear of materialism was constantly in the forefront of his mind. Of interest is that Faizi had not until now formalized his membership of the Bahá'í community but on 14 February 1935 he made his way to the office of the Local Spiritual Assembly of Tehran and registered his name.

Faizi's character belonged to an age of heroes riding out in battle to conquer the despots of this world and to champion the cause of the downtrodden. He loved Greek mythology, he revelled in stories about great feats of bravery carried out by noble men and his heroes were the early believers who had laid down their lives for the Cause he was so passionate about. He wanted to throw himself into the arena of service, dedicate himself to helping his fellow man and put his shoulder to carrying the Faith forward. Instead he found himself sitting in the lap of luxury behind a desk dealing with the high finances of an oil company. The contrast between his aspirations and what he was actually engaged in was too much for him to bear and he 'spent every day swearing' at himself until he eventually became ill and bedridden.

At this lowest point in his life a friend of Faizi's who had come to visit him mentioned that the Bahá'ís in Najafábád (a large village north of Isfahan), whose school had been closed along with all the other Bahá'í schools in the country, were looking for a teacher for their children. This news was 'like a light of hope' shining on Faizi's heart and his 'whole being took life'. He immediately volunteered to go. Many of the Bahá'ís, however, discouraged him, saying that he could do much more for the Faith if he stayed in Tehran. His colleagues in the oil company and other friends thought he was out of his mind giving up such a lucrative job to go and teach village children. My father was all heart but he also had wisdom and faith and one of his strongest characteristics was that he stood like a rock in the face of any opposition if he was convinced he was doing the right thing. He knew this was his lifeline and he was determined to go despite discouragement from many of his friends and the unkind and sarcastic remarks he received from some of them. Although saddened by the negative comments, his 'path of life was already illumined' and he resolutely kept to his plan. One of the few people who encouraged him in his decision was my maternal grandfather, Raḥmat 'Alá'í.

Faizi wrote in his diary, 'God knows with what joy and enthusiasm I wrote to the National Assembly and requested that they give me the honour of undertaking this task. A thousand thanks that that esteemed body accepted my offer.' In response to the National Assembly's letter to the Guardian stating that Faizi had offered his services, the Guardian's secretary, writing on Shoghi Effendi's behalf, wrote:

> ... the Guardian states that this decision which has been spontaneously taken by him will attract divine blessings and is a clear proof of the high resolve, the purity of motive, the self-sacrificing spirit of that favoured servant of the Sacred Threshold. The Guardian is infinitely grateful to him and is well pleased with him and is fervently praying for the success of that luminous and active youth.[6]

Notwithstanding his enthusiasm, Faizi felt quite inadequate and saw himself taking up this post 'to learn steadfastness' from the old Bahá'ís still living in Najafábád. Although others regarded him as a very knowledgeable Bahá'í, Faizi himself felt he had 'brazenly entered this sacred field' which he saw as 'not an arena for anyone to enter' but one in which revered people 'go to guide the weak and poor' such as he himself. He was not being falsely modest; he genuinely believed this and throughout his life sought to sit at the feet of the early believers, to hear their stories and to learn from them. What had given him the courage to rise up to the challenge were the words of 'Abdu'l-Bahá that even if one did not know the alphabet one should rise and serve.

Having received the Guardian's sanction, the National Assembly wrote to the Local Assembly of Najafábád to tell them they had a volunteer. They also had to send a photograph to the Assembly of Najafábád so that they could see what their new teacher looked like. One look at Faizi's clean-shaven face made them decide that he looked too young and it was therefore possible that the Local Assembly of Najafábád would think he was too inexperienced. In addressing this problem Faizi was told to grow a beard to add more weight to his manly features before his photograph was taken!

Mádar-jún was not going to be separated from her son again and resolved to accompany him. Together they packed up house and home and moved to Najafábád, taking with them their old servant and Hooshang, a young lad Mádar-jún had taken under her wing and who was to become my parents' adopted son.

As for Faizi's relationship with Gloria, although her father met Faizi at Bahá'í gatherings and they became good friends, she saw little of him in those days. Contemplating the news that he had decided to go to Najafábád to teach the Bahá'í children there, she decided that this was one person she did not want to lose touch with.

5
Najafábád

Faizi referred to his five years in Najafábád as 'five delightful years. Five years full of spiritual upliftment, discipline and benefit. Five years which always stand as a shining spot in the dark hours of my whole life. It seems that from an unseen source threads of light and happiness had been focused on these years.'

Brief History of Najafábád

One of Bahá'u'lláh's much loved apostles, the famous and respected *mujtahid* Zaynu'l-Muqarrabín came from Najafábád. When he became a Bábí in 1851 a large number of his followers in Najafábád accepted the new Faith and distinguished early believers such as Jináb-i Varqá, Ḥájí Mírzá Ḥaydar 'Alí and Abu'l-Faḍl visited the area to help in guiding more seekers to the new Cause. These early believers became the target of the animosity of the Muslims but, despite the severe hardships they had to endure, they remained firm in their faith.

In the early days of the Faith many believers from Najafábád walked all the way to the Holy Land, sought the presence of Bahá'u'lláh and brought back His messages and Tablets to His followers in Iran. Others took cuttings of plants from Najafábád which they planted in the gardens surrounding the holy places and nurtured them until they were established. Many remained in the Holy Land as gardeners in the Bahá'í gardens.

The First Bahá'í School in Najafábád

With all the opposition and difficulties these early believers had to face, who would have thought that they had time to think of their children's education? Nevertheless, with 'Abdu'l-Bahá's encouragement and under His instructions they started to build a schoolroom in 1910. As soon as the local fanatics heard what the Bahá'ís were doing, they gathered in a mob and, with beating drums, set out to raze the half-built schoolroom to the ground. Realizing what was about to happen, the Bahá'ís decided to defend the building as best they could.

A year later when the schoolroom had been completed and a teacher brought to tutor the children, the fanatics rose again, intent on destroying the school. It was the anniversary of the martyrdom of Imám Ḥusayn and the mourners set off towards the Bahá'í area of Najafábád beating their drums loudly and making a lot of commotion. Once again the Local Assembly of the time decided that it had to defend the school. The youth of the community positioned themselves on the roofs of the houses and the Assembly sent the mob the same message they had a year before. When the mourners saw that their road was blocked they were in a quandary about what to do and stood at the edge of the Bahá'í neighbourhood for about half an hour beating their drums. Seeing that their persecutors were neither moving forward nor retreating, the Bahá'ís sent them another message saying that as they, too, respected the day of Imám Ḥusayn's martyrdom perhaps the mourners would like to bless their quarter by circumambulating it, but that if they were still determined to attack then the Bahá'ís would defend themselves. The leader of the procession agreed to a peaceful solution and he and his mourners were served with refreshments by the Bahá'í community before they left the quarter.

Rooms were gradually added to the same schoolroom and eventually the boys' school was formally established and recognized by the government.

In 1928 the Bahá'ís of Najafábád succeeded in establishing a girls' school as well. Two teachers from Tehran came to run the girls' school. These two self-sacrificing sisters endured many hardships and there was a time when the enemies of the Faith were so threatening that the Local Assembly had to arrange to have them guarded. In time, however, they raised the standard of the school to such a level that it became known as the best girls' school in the whole area.

Both the girls' and boys' schools consisted of the first six primary classes and together they had about 360 pupils. The teachers were all Bahá'ís and the pupils went to Isfahan for the final examinations and to receive their national certificates. When in 1934 all the Bahá'í schools were closed by Reza Shah, the Bahá'í parents and Local Assembly of Najafábád were in a dilemma trying to decide whether they should send their children to government schools or not. Shoghi Effendi advised the Local Assembly that if the two schools were not permitted to re-open then the children could attend the government schools, but the parents were not duty bound to send them. On receipt of this letter the parents unitedly decided not to send their children to the government-run schools. In any case, the school authorities would not admit the Bahá'í children as the clergy had told them to shun Bahá'ís. One lady in the community came forward to take on the responsibility of teaching the fifth and sixth primary classes in her own home without a salary and she did this for nearly two years. However, the education of the rest of the children was being neglected and it was under these circumstances that the Local Assembly of the village wrote to the National Assembly in Tehran asking for someone to be sent to them to tutor their children.

The New Teacher Arrives

When Faizi and his mother went to Najafábád in the autumn of 1936 they left behind a comfortable city life. Faizi's monthly salary of a thousand *túmáns*[1] dropped to 30 *túmáns* which he was to receive from the Local Assembly of Najafábád, but this did not bother either one of them in the least. The Najafábád they were going to was a typical large Persian village of the time. Its population was about thirty thousand and 90 per cent of the inhabitants were farmers. The streets, wattle and daub dwellings and bazaars were dusty, flies were rampant and levels of hygiene were, in general, very low. Most of the homes had a small, putrid-smelling enclosure by the entrance with a hole which was used as a toilet. The hole was covered with earth and when the contents had dried they would be taken to the fields to be used as fertilizer. Those who did not have fields sold the dried content of their toilets to the farmers. Sometimes the price would be argued and occasionally there were quarrels and fights which escalated to such a point that the head of the village had to intervene. The sheep, cows and donkeys lived in the same dwelling as their owners and their dung was piled by the front door to dry, also be sold or taken to the fields.

Of the population of Najafábád about two thousand were Bahá'ís, most of whom lived in a separate quarter of the village. The community was united and loving, and although the knowledge of the Faith among the believers was limited, they were devoted believers and from early days had developed a strong tradition of paying their Ḥuqúqu'lláh[2] every year. Some of the Bahá'ís were shepherds but the majority owned orchards outside the village where they grew almond trees and a few other crops. The farmers with orchards had devised an interesting method of calculating 19 per cent of their profits: every nineteenth tree was marked and when the nuts of these trees were harvested the proceeds were given for Ḥuqúqu'lláh.

First Night in Najafábád

On arrival in Najafábád Faizi's small family stayed in the home of one of the Bahá'ís and on the evening of the same day Faizi was guided to the meeting organized to welcome him. He was greeted by the host who was standing by the entrance to his house welcoming every arrival individually with great courtesy and love. Two large stone steps led from the courtyard to adjoining carpeted rooms. As the friends arrived they took off their *givihs*,[3] entered the rooms, sat where they found space on the carpet and leaned on cushions against the wall. The oil lamps placed around the rooms together with the fires burning in the fireplaces bathed the gathered friends in a warm glow while members of the organizing committee served tea and then collected the empty glasses. The ambiance of the gathering stirred Faizi, as is evident from this entry in his diary:

> The friends, children and adults sat quietly but it was clear that their hearts were connected. The atmosphere was wonderfully spiritual. The women, with loose hair and calm dignified faces, full of patience and forbearance, sat with their children in a separate room, many of them sisters and daughters of martyrs. The men sat noble, their faces weather-beaten, their eyes bright with the spiritual sun and the lines on their foreheads tracing their suffering in the path of the Faith. Among those present were some who had travelled on foot to see Bahá'u'lláh in the Holy Land and brought back His Tablets to their native land and those who had gathered the scattered remains of the martyrs in their area and now protected and kept their families under their wings. The presence of these reminders of the heroic age of the Faith had a profound effect on me who had only tasted the blessings of the teachings and had up to now lived in comfort and never suffered in any way for my belief. I felt so ashamed. Who was I compared to these mountains of steadfastness, these waves of love and kindness, these shining stars of the firmament of true knowledge?

So many friends attended the meeting that night that all the rooms, porch and steps of the house were overflowing. Faizi's already highly pitched emotions soared when an elderly believer opened the meeting with a beautifully chanted prayer. Then the spellbinding voice of a woman in one of the adjoining rooms rose in a chant of one of Bahá'u'lláh's poems. A hushed silence followed as the assembled friends turned to the man sent by their National Assembly to educate their children and they waited patiently for him to address them.

With difficulty Faizi forced himself to take some control over himself as he slowly stood up to thank the friends for giving him such a warm welcome. He asked them to pray for him so that he would, by associating with them, become worthy of serving them. He explained that his wish was to serve the Faith by training their children according to the teachings and then, with great tenderness, he asked the parents to send their children and youth to him so that he could organize school lessons and Bahá'í classes for them according to their ages and abilities. As he swept his gaze over the faces of the men, women and children with whom he felt he had already established a bond, he lost control and tears welled up in his eyes. He sat down, unable to say more.

The Family Settle In

The Assembly decided that Faizi and his family should live in the now empty girls' school. They lived very simply, carpeting their rooms with straw mats and tying benches together to make beds for visitors. Faizi packed his city clothes and started wearing simple shirts, jackets and trousers made out of the cotton denim-like cloth woven in Najafábád and friends remember that he wore a particular eau de cologne that 'lingered wherever he went'.

Added to all the duties which were placed on his shoulders Faizi was also responsible for the members of his household. Apart from Mádar-jún and Hooshang, there was an old, bent-over man by the name of Muḥammad Háshim who from his youth had served in Faizi's household in Qum. This man had reached the twilight of his years and was no longer able to work. Faizi took him under his wing and ensured he was well cared for to the end of his days. When Muḥammad Háshim died he was buried in the Bahá'í cemetery in Najafábád. The family was later joined by two relatives from Qum, a youth and his mother, who had come to visit and never left.

Mádar-jún

It was Mádar-jún who supported all their dependents on the small pension she received from the government and it was she who ran the household and did all the domestic chores while Faizi was engaged with the education of the children and other Bahá'í activities. Although she had been born and bred in a very strict way in an Islamic tradition and was still a Muslim, she was broad-minded compared to many of her compatriots and mixed very freely with the Bahá'ís. When she was still living in Qum she would become upset every time her brother, the most important mujtahid of Qum, attacked the Faith from his pulpit, even though she knew nothing about the message of Bahá'u'lláh. She could not understand why she felt as she did and was at times so afraid of her feelings that she would, after her obligatory prayers, commune with God, asking Him to forgive her if she was being sinful, and to help her accept and be happy with what her brother was preaching about the Bahá'ís. Years later, after he had graduated from university, Faizi gave Mádar-jún a number of different photographs to look at and deliberately put a photograph of the Guardian as a child among them. Mádar-jún looked at the pictures one by one but when she came to the one of the Guardian she stared at it for a while and then asked Faizi, 'Whose photograph is this? He is different from the other children.' It was in Najafábád that she dreamt of the Báb and became a believer. Faizi used to joke and say that even though his mother considered herself a Bahá'í she was really a Bábí at heart!

Setting to Work

When Faizi arrived in Najafábád there were about seven hundred youth and children. He was faced with four hundred boys and girls who were now without any education, and the government representatives, in particular the head of education of the area who knew why Faizi was there, waited in readiness to scatter the smallest gathering of children. Although he had a degree in education,

Faizi was 'completely inexperienced' in organizing such a large number of children and 'felt helpless'. Nevertheless, he immediately set to drawing up a timetable, from kindergarten children to classes for adults. He did not really know how he did it but within the space of two weeks 20 educational classes and Bahá'í classes were established in the homes of the Bahá'ís and 'began running like a well-organized factory; an unseen hand had tightened every screw and set the wheels in motion'. Faizi went from house to house from morning till afternoon. Most of the homes belonged to farmers and were full of sheep pellets and the dung of donkeys and cows but he never showed any distaste or discomfort because he genuinely never paid much attention to such things. Rather, he focused his attention on the immediate needs of the children. He would enter the house 'with a radiant face and smiling lips' and go to the room where the children were gathered sitting on a carpet and eagerly awaiting his arrival and the start of their lesson.

With the salary Faizi received from the Assembly he bought his pupils paper, pens and books. The children loved drawing on outside walls with charcoal pencils, so on one of his trips to Isfahan Faizi bought coloured pencils for them. One day he told them to draw on the wall of a room in their homes so that they could keep their drawing. The parents immediately complained to the Local Assembly about this so he decided that perhaps it was not such a good idea! When he could not get what he needed to encourage the children in their endeavours he would give them interesting pictures cut from foreign magazines, which for the children in those days were very exciting and entertaining.

Faizi was always methodical in the way he planned classes and lessons. Apart from the lessons the pupils had to study in accordance with government regulations, they also had well-organized Bahá'í classes, from which they graduated as youth to systematically study the Kitáb-i-Aqdas,[4] the Kitáb-i-Íqán, *Bahá'u'lláh and the New Era* and the writings in general. With the limited resources available to him he tried to make his Bahá'í classes as interesting as possible. One of the things he did was to buy booklets for every single one of the younger children and write a prayer in each in beautiful calligraphy as a keepsake. He then asked each child to write a prayer they knew, not in their own book but in that of one of their fellow pupils. In this way they learned new prayers from one another and also practised their best writing when writing their prayer in their friend's book. He also took photographs of the different Bahá'í classes and gave copies to the children to frame and keep. This simple act added to the children's feeling of worth.

Work would be set for the children on a weekly basis and every now and again a meeting would be held where they would read poetry, chant prayers and give talks to their gathered parents. Each Bahá'í class was like a little community: they contributed to the Bahá'í funds and involved themselves in the wider community. Some of the younger children, who knew that any money given to the Bahá'í funds had to be given anonymously, devised an amusing way of making their little contributions. They would run up behind Faizi when they saw him walking down the street, and whispering 'for the funds', slip a few coins into his trouser pockets. Faizi would not stop walking, nor would he turn round to see who the children were.

Every effort was made to encourage the children and youth to put into practice the principles they learned in these classes, such as having good manners, being clean and reading from the writings every day. This advice was repeated by the Assembly at the 19 Day Feasts but Faizi himself never told the parents that keeping their children clean and tidy was as important as wanting them to know how to read and write. In these matters he taught by example: with the remainder of his salary he bought the children toothbrushes, combs, socks and small pocket handkerchiefs and was seen on many occasions to be combing their unkempt hair, dabbing attar of roses on their faces and rubbing cream on their chapped and cracked hands in winter.

As months went by not only did the standard of education in the community as whole rise but so too did the standards of hygiene and cleanliness, to such an extent that it surprised visitors. One day one of the Bahá'ís from another community came to a gathering in Najafábád with an Armenian friend. The friend was quite taken aback to see peasant women reading prayers and giving talks and that both they and their men folk were in clean clothes and sat at the meeting with such a high degree of politeness and love. He found it difficult to believe what he was experiencing because, as he told his friend, he was used to different conduct from Persians.

The older age groups were mostly youth who had finished their primary education. They either worked in the fields or in the market so Faizi organized special classes for them which he conducted very early in the mornings before they went to work and late at night. They were encouraged to take down notes of what they had learned and use their notes to give talks in meetings. Also, as Bahá'ís were not free to publish Bahá'í books, the students had to copy the books they were studying. Without their efforts the classes would never have succeeded. Working by the light of an oil lamp after a hard day's work, some of the students succeeded in copying several books.

Faizi motivated the youth with his lively classes so that they all attended enthusiastically. He never reproached any student for not delivering an assignment. One of his students remembers that at the end of one class Faizi gave him a subject to prepare and give a talk on the following week. During the week this student heard that Faizi had gone to Isfahan and that it was unlikely he would be back in time for the class, so he decided to postpone preparing his talk until the following week. On the day of the class the students gathered together as usual, even though they thought Faizi would not be there. However, it was not long before Faizi, together with another Bahá'í, entered the room and started the session. When it came to this student's turn, the young man apologized profusely for not having prepared his talk. He recalls that, 'all Faizi did was to give me such a look of love that it will never be wiped from my memory'.

The students were not given grades in their Bahá'í classes but were rather trained to progress in a spirit of love, friendship and cooperation. Faizi believed that in this way, when they grew up and became involved in activities in the community, their attitude and behaviour would be the same. He was of the view that if a child works and expects to be given a grade for every question he answers, he will as an adult expect to be rewarded for every deed he does. His philosophy was that the teacher must be aware of every individual child's circumstances and if a child has a difficulty then the teacher must find the reason behind it and help the child; that the teacher must not be unenthusiastic and simply ask the children questions like a machine but rather approach them with warmth and feel that he is being of some service to them. This was completely different from the methods of education prevalent at the time. Faizi's opinions were not so much the result of his studies but rooted in what he remembered of his own education at Tarbíyat School and in the teachings of Bahá'u'lláh.

Another improvement in Faizi's conduct of his lessons was to do away with registration at the beginning of every Bahá'í class because the children and youth attended them willingly, unless they had good reason to be absent. The older ones would be tested every few weeks on the book they were studying. The test would consist of 15 to 20 questions on, for example, the meanings of words and their use. The students would all be given the questions beforehand and told how many marks each question carried so that they could prepare themselves. The 'purpose of the tests was not to pass or fail anyone; they were aimed at helping the students themselves identify the areas they were weakest in and improve their knowledge'. The Local Assembly made arrangements for the final examinations for the students who had completed all the Bahá'í classes and it was up to the students themselves to put their names down for the examination. There were no invigilators present during the examinations because the students were trusted. No one ever cheated.

The following is an example of an answer given to a question put to students in a final examination:

Question: In the Book of Aqdas Bahá'u'lláh says that difficulties and tribulations are the cause of strengthening the tree of the Cause of God. Discuss.

Answer: This answer will be from the point of view of agriculture. Sometimes it happens that when a tree is planted water does not reach its roots easily because of the hardness of the soil. To solve this problem an ants' nest is brought near the tree and the ants start attacking its roots. The ants' activity not only does not harm the roots but the fact that they make hundreds of holes in their attack enables the water to reach the roots with greater ease and ensures the survival of the tree. In the same way attacks on the Cause makes it stronger.

The Local Assembly took the teachings of the Faith on the education of children so seriously that it established a fund in 1939 to subsidize the education of a group of youngsters who had to work in shops to help provide for their families and were therefore not able to attend any classes to complete their primary education. The whole community responded immediately and the money for this fund grew annually, enabling the number of children who sat for the national examinations to increase each year.

After two years of twice weekly Bahá'í classes Faizi, with encouragement and financial support from the Local Assembly, sent five of the youth who had completed their primary education to Shiraz and five to Tehran to visit the holy places, to meet the Bahá'í communities in those cities and to see how they organized their activities. Their visits were very successful and on their return a feast was arranged at which they reported back to their community what they had seen and learned. They were then given the responsibility of conducting the Bahá'í classes for the younger children under Faizi's supervision. The new teachers made sure the children in their respective classes came to class clean and tidy and the children responded to this standard to such a degree that they stood out among the other children of Najafábád. One day a government official who took every opportunity to oppose the Faith saw a group of Bahá'í children on their way to the Bahá'í class and noted that they were all wearing clean clothes, their hair was combed, their hands and faces clean and their eyes healthy. He was amazed and remarked, 'I wish all the other children would become like this.'

Years later as he travelled the globe, Faizi met dozens of these same children scattered around the world, many with high academic qualifications and holding important positions but still looking up to him as their teacher and example in life.

Beyond the Children

There were several communities in the vicinity of Najafábád that were deprived of any schooling or Bahá'í education for their children, nor did they have the means to put into practice the teaching that all children should receive an education. As soon as there were enough youth to help him with his work, Faizi encouraged and guided several of them to undertake visits to these communities and help establish classes for the children. In one village where all the inhabitants were Bahá'ís they eventually succeeded in employing a full-time teacher. In another village which was closer to Najafábád one of the youth volunteered to teach the children of the three Bahá'í families living there and would cycle to the village early in the morning to tutor the children until noon. After a few months the progress of the children was such that when they sat for an exam no one could believe the level of their progress in so short a time. Eventually, with the help of the youth of Najafábád and under Faizi's guidance, many of the surrounding villages were able to educate their children.

Faizi was instrumental in the appointment of a youth committee in the community. His great love for sports and exercise led him to help the committee arrange activities such as hiking, climbing and a football team in which he himself played. Apart from these activities the youth also undertook to walk or, if they had bicycles, cycle to surrounding villages on well-organized travel teaching trips.

Once the classes and activities for the children and youth began to run smoothly Faizi turned his attention to another principle of the Faith he was always very enthusiastic about and continually promoted: the equality of women and men. Organizing classes for the Bahá'í women in the village was no easy task owing to the women's heavy daily routine. They rose before sunrise every day and worked till late at night helping their husbands in the fields or orchards. They also cooked, washed clothes and generally took care of their families so they had very little time for themselves. Nevertheless, many were keen to learn and attended Faizi's twice weekly special classes for women in which they studied *Nabíl's Narrative* and other books. The literate women would copy the passages Faizi read out to them and then rewrite these pages in good writing in another book when they returned home so that they eventually had a copy of the book they were studying. Faizi would give prizes to those who made a special effort to produce beautiful pieces of work.

Faizi's free evenings were usually spent with the rest of the community in the homes of the friends but what a number of them enjoyed most was to gather in his room. A group of youth undertook to prepare the samovar for tea and they would start the evening. Those with good voices would chant or sing poems. If someone had come across a beautiful Tablet or interesting part of a prayer he would read it out to the rest. They would sit together till late at night telling stories and reminiscing about the older generation of believers and their deeds and activities in promoting the Faith of Bahá'u'lláh. One of the friends, an old man of about 80, would chant a long prayer he had started to memorize but then stop at a certain point, explaining that that was as far as he had memorized.

The 19 Day Feasts were held in clusters of about 60 people from the age of 15 upwards. The meetings were held in the homes of the Bahá'ís where they would sit in rows, sometimes one behind the other when the room was small, on the carpeted floor. When Faizi joined the community many of the friends would gather together on Friday nights (in summertime in the grounds of the girls' school where Faizi lived and in winter in the large room of the boys' school) and Faizi would give a talk and deepen them in the teachings. Added to this, two or three of Faizi's friends from Tehran and other cities would come to visit him every week. They were welcomed with warmth by Faizi, his mother and the community and had such a good time that they always left reluctantly. On return to their respective communities they spoke with such enthusiasm about the Bahá'í community in Najafábád and the fantastic time they had had that the number of Faizi's guests increased week by week.

The Cemetery

One afternoon, not long after Faizi's arrival in Najafábád, the children invited him to go with them to the Bahá'í cemetery to pay their respects to the martyrs buried there. They and the few adults with them first gathered in a room in the cemetery to hear one of the older believers speak to them about the martyrs. The sun was beginning to set when the narrator began to relate to the silent, pensive gathering the story of the grave where three men were buried together.

It was during one of the periods of persecution when news reached the Bahá'ís of Najafábád that three Bahá'í men had been killed in Isfahan and their bodies flung unceremoniously outside the city. The Bahá'ís of Najafábád were themselves facing intense opposition from the Muslims and knew that it would be very dangerous for anyone to try to find and collect the bodies. One Bahá'í woman, however, thought to herself that the bodies of her fellow believers could not be left where they had been flung and, without telling anyone, decided to go to Isfahan to retrieve them. She waited for the sun to set before quietly setting off on her own with her donkey. Reaching the city in the dead of night, she searched for and found the bodies, put them onto her donkey and returned to Najafábád, reaching her home before the break of day. Hiding the bodies, she waited for darkness before taking her secret load to the village cemetery and, as silently as she could manage, dug a shallow grave. She placed all three bodies in it, covered them with earth and made the site as unobtrusive as possible so that no one's attention would be drawn to it. To remember where she had buried her fellow believers she marked their grave with three stones. When the Bahá'ís of Najafábád acquired their own cemetery they transferred the three bodies from the Muslim cemetery and, once again, buried them together in one grave, placing the same three stones on their new resting place in memory of the brave woman.

Summer Schools and Travel Teaching

Faizi helped organize the first summer school ever held in the area of Najafábád. A group of youth from Isfahan and Tehran attended. Faizi also initiated teaching trips at the end of the summer schools, when the youth went to the surrounding villages to meet their fellow Bahá'í youth there. This was the beginning of many such trips which generated much warmth, enthusiasm and friendship among all the youth of the area.

Faizi's energy during this period of his life seems to have been boundless. His work extended to the neighbouring city of Isfahan where he held a regular deepening class for about 20 youth on Thursday afternoons. Here they studied such books as the Kitáb-i-Íqán and learned how to give talks. Faizi would stay the night in the city and spend Friday mornings visiting the 20 different Bahá'í children's classes to guide and advise the teachers. An advice he repeatedly gave to the tutors was that they should not let the children develop a habit of studying for the sake of getting high marks, or coming first in class, but because it was beneficial to them. On Friday evenings there were general meetings where 60 to 70 gathered to study various Bahá'í books under scholars such as Mr Ishráq-Khávari, Mr Fáḍil Mázandárání and Mr Núshábádí, who were at the time living in Isfahan. If Faizi did not have a meeting to attend in Najafábád, he would join these study classes. During one of these meetings a person declared that every Bahá'í should have a copy of the Aqdas[4] in his home but he did not have one. The next day Faizi sent him a copy. Opening the book the man saw an inscription indicating that Núru'd-Dín Fatḥi-A'ẓam (Faizi's first Bahá'í class teacher) had given the book to Faizi as a gift, so the man felt he should return it. But having given the book as a gift, Faizi would not take it back.

There were three young men who would not leave Faizi's side during the two days he was in Isfahan. They shared the same sense of humour, had the capacity to see the funny side of life in many situations and passed many happy hours together when not in class, not only exchanging their fund of jokes but also discussing serious subjects. One day one of these friends told Faizi that he had been sent a container of molasses to give to him, but having had a taste of the molasses he thought it would be better if he had it himself and in return say some prayers for Faizi. Instead of telling his friend, as would have been the Persian way, that he was welcome to the molasses, Faizi responded, 'Ṭáhirí, you bring me the molasses and pray to God to send you molasses from somewhere else!'

Apart from encouraging the youth to visit Bahá'ís in other villages, Faizi himself would regularly take two or three of the friends with him to visit believers, who were mostly farmers, in nearby communities. They would walk to the closer villages and, if a car could be found, drive to the ones which were further away. None of Faizi's meetings were solemn: there was serious discussion about the Faith as well as amusement and laughter. The atmosphere of meetings with him was inspiring and enjoyable. Faizi himself would relate interesting stories and anecdotes and he encouraged other Bahá'ís to recount what they knew about the early believers.

It was on one of these teaching trips that the host spanked

his little boy for some misdemeanour and ordered him to sit in the corner of the room and not move. The meeting went on for so long that Faizi, after a long, tiring day, started to yawn. He yawned so much that tears rolled down his face. The little boy, who had obeyed his father up to that point, immediately called out to Faizi from across the room in a voice full of understanding, 'Mister, are you crying for my sake?' Everyone burst out laughing and the child's father was persuaded to excuse his son.

Travelling in Style

When one of the Bahá'ís in Najafábád bought a car, a Ford which had to be started with a handle, Faizi and his companions would sometimes hire it and its owner-driver to travel to the far-flung villages. The first time they hired the car was to visit a fortress where ten Bahá'í families lived, each family with only one room. The group consisted of the driver, Faizi and three others. The road they had to take, however, which was meant for pedestrians and donkeys only, was full of potholes and twists and turns. Nevertheless the enthusiastic band of travel teachers started their 40 kilometre journey at three in the afternoon on a Thursday in November in full confidence that their driver and his vehicle of the modern age would get them there in record time. It took them four hours to reach their destination. Most of the journey was taken up with the passengers getting out of the car every few kilometres to push it out of the potholes and ruts in which it repeatedly got stuck, or jumping out to turn the handle every time the engine stalled. Instead of feeling agitated and disgruntled, they spent the entire journey laughing at what they considered to be a hilarious situation. They joked about 'the iron carriage' and marvelled that the owner did not take offence at the way they spoke about his pride and joy which had taken them to the middle of a deserted place where there was no one to be seen. Faizi observed that the degree of their contentment with life must have been such that they were happy with a vehicle whose wheels had to be turned with the strength of the passengers' muscles! One of the companions calculated that from Najafábád to where they had reached the car had actually given them a ride less than the distance they had pushed it and that it would have been better if they had decided to walk to the fortress because they would at least have been saved from having to use so much of their own energy pushing it. And so they spent the journey in happy camaraderie until, at last, they arrived at their destination at seven in the evening, being greeted with great excitement and love by the Bahá'ís of the fortress.

One of the villagers gave over his room for the meeting and they all gathered there, first to read prayers. Then Faizi spoke to the gathering about the steadfastness of their fellow believers in faraway countries after which a large cloth was spread in the middle of the room over the carpet and the community provided a simple supper of bread, butter, cheese, milk, yogurt, eggs, rice pudding, grape syrup and jam, which was enjoyed by all. At eleven o'clock the travellers prepared to leave and the whole village – men, women and children – accompanied them to the car. Bidding farewell to everyone, the passengers piled into the car, the driver slid into the driver's seat, the car doors were closed and a ready volunteer was asked to turn the handle. Nothing happened. Again the handle was turned with great vigour but no matter how many times it was turned the engine refused to start. Resigning themselves to having to stay the night at the fortress and return to Najafábád the following day on donkeys, the visitors, much to the delight of their hosts, wended their way back to the fortress. The friends, who were far from tired, wanted to resume their meeting and started asking Faizi questions about the teachings. After some time a young villager who had been listening intently to their visitor's answers and explanations, hesitantly took out a notebook from his pocket and holding it diffidently in his lap asked Faizi if, with permission, he could ask him some questions, explaining that he had for a long time been writing his questions down but had kept them to ask of someone who could give him convincing answers.

Faizi warmly encouraged him and said, 'My dear, ask whatever is in your heart!' and the man, overcome with emotion at this response, opened his small booklet to start.

But before he could open his mouth someone said, 'It is two and a half hours after midnight; Faizi is tired and needs rest. You ask your questions of him in the morning.'

Faizi, however, smilingly responded, 'Anyone who himself wants to sleep should but, please, do not express an opinion on my behalf. Whoever wants to go to sleep do so; everyone is free to either sleep or stay awake. I may not have the opportunity again to spend such enjoyable, sweet hours.' He then turned to the questioner and asked him to start asking his questions.

One of the questions the man asked Faizi that night was this:

> As Bahá'ís we are told to guide the people to the message of Bahá'u'lláh, but however much we associate with the Muslims, show them kindness and help them in their problems, the moment we start saying anything about the Faith they stop listening. What are we to do?

Faizi's reply was that we have been told to show kindness to all the peoples of the world and this we must obey but it is not so that they become Bahá'ís or that they praise us. Not everyone is the same. Kindness will have its own effect. Quoting 'Abdu'l-Bahá, he said we must not be silent, nor troubled and sad because of the responses we receive but with strength and bravery and a confident heart proclaim the message in whatever way we can. If it is the Will of God He will guide them.

The gathered friends were so engrossed in the session of questions and answers that before they knew it, it was five in the morning and dawn had broken. They rose and went outside to stretch their legs, do their ablutions and say their prayers while the host once again spread a cloth on the carpet of his room and served a breakfast of bread, cheese, tea and fresh milk.

The Bahá'í community in the fortress felt that they had had a precious time and had learned much, and Faizi felt that had the car not broken down they would not have been given this fortuitous opportunity to spend such an enjoyable and fruitful time with this special community.

The donkeys were ready for the travellers but the owner of the car was dejected about leaving his vehicle behind and wondered how he could get it back to Najafábád. Turning to him, Faizi said, with an air of complete confidence, 'Don't be despondent. We will go right now, put the handle in the engine and it will start.'

With the villagers following them they rode on their donkeys to the car. The driver, to humour Faizi, sat in the driver's seat and another person turned the handle. To the amazement of all, the car burst into life. Everyone was overjoyed and the travel teachers returned home in the car, stopping only a few times to push.

Public Showers

Few of the homes in Najafábád had a bathroom. As the public baths were dirty with stagnant water, the Bahá'ís had built a small bathing hut next to the girls' Bahá'í school where there was a 40 metre deep well, but washing in this hut was difficult. Water had to be drawn up and poured into a large cauldron. A wood fire was lit underneath to heat the water. Only one person at a time could stand in the small room to wash. All this was such a palaver, especially in the cold of winter, that those who had no bath in their house made do with very basic washing in their own homes.

Less than a year after arriving in Najafábád Faizi was elected onto the Local Assembly. According to a member of the Assembly of the time, one of his first suggestions was that public showers should be built for the Bahá'í community. This was agreed and a committee for the building was appointed, with Faizi as one of the members. This committee had first to decide how much money was needed, where there was land with water for sale, and so on, and once all these decisions were made the friends were invited to give donations towards the funds needed.

Two hundred men of the community were invited to the first meeting in the home of one of the Bahá'ís. The assembled men sat round the room, two or three rows deep. They were given details of how much the building of the public showers would cost. The plan was to build two public showers next to each other, one for men and another for women. The first donations to the shower fund were made. In the end, however, there were not enough funds for two shower buildings so the Assembly decided on one building for everyone.

After this initial meeting a member of the Local Assembly was asked to attend the meetings arranged for the rest of the community to encourage the friends to make donations to the building fund. One night about 20 friends were invited to such a meeting and in the course of his encouraging words the Local Assembly member mentioned that Faizi, who was not from Najafábád, had donated the only carpet he had in his room towards the fund. One of the attendants, whose own monthly income was about 15 *túmáns*, retorted that Faizi could afford it as he received 30 *túmáns* from the Assembly every month. All the others present immediately raised their voice in protest and asked the man why he had ruined the spirit of the meeting. They reminded him that Faizi had left a comfortable life in Tehran and a thousand *túmáns* a month post to come to Najafábád and spend his life serving the Faith and teaching their children; and that he spent the 30 *túmáns* the Assembly gave him not on himself but on buying what the children needed. The man apologized and the meeting ended. Unfortunately, this incident somehow reached Faizi's ears. As he matured Faizi learned to deal with his exceptional sensitivity and not allow hurtful remarks to affect him too much. But at this stage of his young life the remark devastated him, so much so that he withdrew into himself with deep sadness, feeling that his fellow believers had misunderstood his motives.

One day the same Local Assembly member, who was a close neighbour and in the habit of visiting Faizi almost every morning, went to see his friend. Faizi was nowhere to be seen. He asked

Mádar-jún where he was. In a worried tone she told him that he had locked himself in his room and told her that if anyone asked for him he was not available, or if the children came for him she should tell them that their class was cancelled because he was tired. The man was perplexed and thought to himself that this was very unlike the person he knew. He remembered that once when Faizi had had a sore throat and was running a high temperature, he himself had gone to all his classes to tell the children he could not teach that day. So the friend suspected that something was afoot and that tiredness was not the reason for Faizi's behaviour. He went to the chairman of the Local Assembly, called the rest of the members and together they went to Faizi's house.

Mádar-jún told them she thought Faizi was praying in his room because she could occasionally hear his voice, so they went and stood outside his door. They knocked, told him who they all were and asked him to please allow them in. When Faizi opened his door they noticed that his eyes were red, his face pale and it was obvious that he was extremely sad. But he greeted and embraced each of them with kindness and invited them into his room. They all sat down and his friend asked Faizi if they were permitted to ask what the reason was behind his sadness. After a moment's silence Faizi said, 'My sadness is that I am guilty of not being detached.' They asked what had happened to make him think so and he replied that he should not have taken even one dinar[5] from the Assembly. His friend immediately guessed what the cause of his despondence was. He told Faizi what the response of all those present had been to the one man's comment and then in jest added that if people did not say such things about him he would not go to heaven. This made Faizi laugh and he began to gain some emotional equilibrium.

The community rose as one in their eagerness to support the new building project and everyone gave according to their means. Some of the friends who could not contribute money set aside one month, some two months, to work for free as labourers under the supervision of the builder who was a Muslim. When the required amount was raised it was decided to buy an old building between the boys' and girls' schools. Work started on the first day of the Intercalary Days. Field workers, shepherds, drivers, merchants and labourers all came together, each with a particular responsibility. Some started pulling down the old building to prepare the ground; some climbed up the mountain to roll down stones for the new building; others took their donkeys to the foot of the mountain to collect the stones. Mádar-jún cooked the meals for the stone collectors during these special days, which Faizi arranged to be taken to them.

The daily programme thereafter was that the workers gathered at the foot of the mountain near the village before the break of day and said prayers. They then had the breakfast prepared by their fellow villagers. As the sun rose they climbed the mountain and cut stones, rolling them down the slope, and chanting and singing in a great spirit of fellowship.

It took six months for the public showers to be built. The day they were opened the Muslim dignitaries of Najafábád were invited to come and see the building and were served with sweets and sherbet by the Bahá'í community. This was not only the first public shower (as opposed to bath) in the area but one which had clean water pumped directly from a well into its tanks. It soon became famous and the envy of all. The non-Bahá'ís who knew that Faizi was behind the project regarded him as a special man.

The Learned Baker

An example of the high regard many of the Muslim inhabitants of Najafábád had for Faizi was a learned man who owned a bakery in the village square and had a number of people working for him. He was tall and handsome, enlightened in his thinking, a good man and a good conversationalist who knew many poems by heart. One day he asked one of the Bahá'ís to arrange a meeting between himself and Faizi. It was summertime and on the appointed day at three in the afternoon he arrived with two of his friends. After the preliminary greetings and expressions of politeness the man asked Faizi where and what he had studied. Faizi gave him the information he wanted. The baker then spoke about life after death and asked for Faizi's views about the consequences of one's behaviour and actions in this life. With gentleness and dignity Faizi answered all his questions in a full and clear way while his guest and his companions listened intently. Fruit was then served and their conversation turned to various other interesting subjects. After three hours Faizi's guests left with great courtesy, respect and happiness.

A few days later when the Bahá'í who had arranged the meeting went to buy bread, the owner took him inside his bakery to a private corner.

'You know me as a man who does not stand on ceremony and speaks frankly,' he said. 'I am now 55 years old and it is 40 years that I have been studying literature and poetry. I have met many learned and good-hearted people but I have never met anyone like Faizi . . . He is an amazing, unique man . . . Let me tell you that you don't appreciate or value this beloved person and he will eventually leave you. I am amazed that a man such as he has come to live in Najafábád to waste his life. The world must benefit from him and hear what he has to say. When I met him in your house I wanted to kiss his feet but realized that he is weary of such things. I want so much to meet this man again and continue our conversations but you know that if I continue meeting him no one will buy bread from me. My two friends feel the same way about Faizi as I do.'

Encouragement

After the euphoria of their united effort to build the public shower, the Bahá'ís of Najafábád became a little slack in making use of it on a regular basis. Many of them, despite their children's success, also questioned Faizi's unorthodox methods of education. They became somewhat indifferent about the education of their children and started to lose sight of the fact that they had in their midst someone whose talents and abilities they could continue to use to help with the progress of their whole community. After consultation on the state of affairs the Local Assembly decided to organize a meeting of some 150 male members of the community and to ask Faizi to speak to them.

The gathering took place on a Friday in the grounds of the boys' school. Faizi began by telling the assembled men that what he was about to say was in no way to put himself forward or to claim to be someone special but there were truths he wanted to voice in all love and sincerity. He then related an event that had happened to him several years before.

Once during his student days in Beirut he received a telegram from Shoghi Effendi inviting him to the Holy Land. He went immediately. Shoghi Effendi gave him a bouquet of flowers and asked him to go to Tehran without delay. He was to give the flowers to the National Assembly of Iran. They were to take the bouquet to Isfahan and place it on the resting place of Keith Ransom Kehler.

Faizi set off straight away. He travelled by bus to Baghdad and from there by car to Kirmánsháh (525 kilometres from Tehran) but he could not find any transport from Kirmánsháh to Tehran. He tried to find a private car with the intention of paying the driver whatever he wanted if he could get him to Tehran as soon as possible. He was in a very agitated and anxious state when a man sitting on a chair outside a nearby shop asked him what he was looking for and why he appeared to be so impatient. Faizi told him he was looking for a car to hire to take him to Tehran. The man asked Faizi what his name was, to which Faizi replied Abu'l-Qásim. The man asked what his family name was and Faizi gave it to him. The man then asked if he knew Áyatu'lláh Fayḍ who lived in Qum and Faizi told him that the Áyatu'lláh was his maternal uncle. In that case, the man said, he would take Faizi himself because he was one of Áyatu'lláh Fayḍ's ardent followers and it would be an honour for him to take his nephew to Tehran. Faizi was extremely grateful to the man and offered to pay for the hire of the car but the man said that they would discuss payment on the way. Faizi then waited the one hour it took for the man to return to his home to make arrangements before they set off on their journey.

On the way the driver told Faizi, 'My friend, money and possessions have no value in this ephemeral world. True friendship is rare. When we find it we must sacrifice for it and spend whatever we have in its path. We lose nothing by doing this but rather profit from it to all eternity and benefit from God's blessings. I am honoured to be taking a nephew of Áyatu'lláh Fayḍ to Tehran. For years I have sought his presence several times a year. Whatever I have is the result of listening to his advice. His prayers for me have had an effect on my life.'

When they stopped for meals the man would not allow Faizi to pay for anything and at the end of their journey he took Faizi right up to the door of Mádar-jún's house in Tehran. However much Faizi insisted that he accept at least a token sum, the man refused. He shook Faizi's hand and left.

Allowing a moment or two to pass in silence Faizi then told those assembled that he related this story to them to demonstrate what attachment some have to their priests. The driver did him such a great favour out of his devotion to Faizi's uncle (who was still living in Qum with many followers). Had Faizi's uncle not been so knowledgeable and able to give good advice, the man would not have held him in such high regard.

The gathered men sat in thoughtful silence. After another pause Faizi put it to them considerately if they had ever asked themselves why he had come to Najafábád? He knew how to teach. Why did they not make use of his knowledge and encourage their children to come to him to learn? Why did they not recognize the value of these days? Why did they not pay more attention to their institutions? Why had their public shower, which had been built with such effort and was the reason why the Faith had come to the attention of all the people of Najafábád, fallen into disuse?

'It is ours!' he pleaded. 'Why are you indifferent to it? You should take care of it and guard it. You are well-informed men of the community, you have knowledge of the writings. From this day onwards you must bend your efforts in serving the Faith. I have as dust fallen under your feet and prepared myself to serve you. Come, let us hand in hand, put the past behind us. We must not waste our lives. We must try to serve the world of humanity.'

Faizi's talk lasted about 30 minutes during which 'his manner of speaking was full of humility and love which radiated from his luminous face – he seemed to be on a different plane'. Faizi never put himself forward, never talked about his scholastic abilities or how knowledgeable he was in the teachings but rather used his skills and knowledge to serve the Faith. He told his fellow believers that night that here he was at their service and he wanted them to use him and what he had to offer for the betterment of their community and the progress of the Cause. Drained by his passionate entreaty he sat down but his words ignited the fire of enthusiasm in the hearts of most of the assembled men.

Marriage

Faizi and Gloria had started corresponding some time after Faizi settled in Najafábád. This letter from Gloria to Faizi shows that their pupil–teacher relationship had changed into an informal friendship.

> My dear brother
> I think I can call you 'brother' once more (if there's no objection) because I can't find any other suitable name for you. 'Old Persian teacher' is the proper name but I think it too odd (not in meaning, of course), don't you? I hope you will write and tell me which you think best.
> Last night father gave me your kind letter, which made me very happy. I am glad to know that you are well and serving the Cause as best you can and hope you will always have good results.

In your letter you said you would like to hear about my activities but I have not much to tell you for I don't do anything important that's worth telling. I only go to my Persian lessons in the mornings and spend my afternoons mostly in translating the book father wrote about Mrs Keith.[6] I have also begun to read a few pages from *The Dawn-Breakers* every night and translate it for father and that's all.

Mama sends her *saláms* to you. Please give my love to your dear mother, and don't forget to write to me.

In 1938, two years after Faizi had settled in Najafábád, Gloria's parents and Mr and Mrs Banání[7] decided to go on pilgrimage to the Báb's house in Shiraz taking Gloria, her brother Manúchihr and one of the Banání children with them. They passed Isfahan on the way and decided to visit Faizi in nearby Najafábád, where they stayed for one night. Faizi greeted his guests warmly and Gloria remembered him turning to her and exclaiming, 'You are a young lady now!'

That evening there was a gathering during which Faizi distributed little prizes to the children. Compared to the formal meetings she had attended in Tehran Gloria found this simple, joyful occasion so different and 'very refreshing'.

The next morning Gloria asked Faizi if she could have a look at his books. He took her to his room, showed her the wall cupboard in which he kept his books and then left her to attend to his own work. She looked around his room and took in its simplicity: the floor was covered with cheap, coarse straw mats woven by the villagers; the only furniture was a chair and a plain writing table on which were scattered text books, manuscripts, writing paper, pens and pencils. Being meticulously tidy herself, Gloria thought 'only Faizi could find anything from among that lot'. She then opened his cupboard to find it packed with books, notebooks and papers 'all pushed together on the shelves in a most disorderly fashion so that if you pulled out a book, one or two others would tumble to the ground'. A few books of English prose and poetry caught her eye and then she came across a little booklet, written in Faizi's own exquisite Persian handwriting. On the cover was a lovely hand drawing of a rose and underneath it was written one word, *Gol* (Rose), Gloria's nickname. To her surprise, she found that it was about her childhood in Beirut and she was engrossed reading it when Faizi returned.

He smiled and said, 'Do you remember the time when you fell asleep in the cinema?'

'No,' Gloria answered honestly.

'Well,' he said, 'it's all written in there.' Then he asked, 'How do you like my life in the village?' After the sophisticated atmosphere of Tehran which Gloria had always found very uninteresting, Najafábád seemed like paradise. She told Faizi that she thought his life in the village was wonderful. At this point Faizi was called and the two families were soon on their way to Shiraz.

Gloria had grown into a beautiful young woman whose hand in marriage had already been sought several times but she had shown no interest in getting married so early in her life. Now, however, she found herself thinking more and more about Faizi and the life he was leading. By the time she returned to Tehran she knew that her feelings for him were much deeper than that of friendship. Faizi himself had already made up his mind that Gloria was the woman he loved and wanted to marry.

On their return to Tehran my grandfather found a letter from Faizi waiting for him. Enclosed in the envelope Faizi had sent Gloria a few famous love poems written in his own hand on beautiful stationery. My grandfather first gave Gloria the love poems and then, after he had read it himself, the letter. Faizi had asked for her hand and said that if she refused to be his wife he would never get married.

Gloria found Faizi's proposal of marriage 'so unexpected' that it left her 'quite bewildered'. It had never occurred to her that he would ask her to marry him one day.

A few days after receiving Faizi's letter my grandfather asked Gloria what answer she would give to Faizi. She found herself in a state of turmoil: on the one hand she had come to realize that she loved him; on the other she wanted to continue with her studies. The next time her father asked her what answer he should give Faizi, she said, 'What do you say, Father?'

He replied, 'I'm not supposed to say anything now. The two who are to be married should be the first to give their consent, then their parents are allowed to give theirs.'

What finally outweighed every other consideration for Gloria was not only the love she felt for Faizi but his 'outstanding qualities and the wonderful work he was doing', something in which she was 'eager to have a share'. She accepted Faizi's proposal.

My grandfather asked Faizi to come to Tehran. When Faizi arrived, my grandfather told him he had written to the Guardian about his wish to marry Gloria and was now waiting for his reply. In the meantime a distinguished Bahá'í had arrived from Baghdad as a guest of my grandfather to meet the Bahá'ís and to visit the Bahá'í holy places in Iran. As he did not speak any Persian, my grandfather invited Faizi to go with them on their trip to translate. This was the beginning of a lifelong friendship between Faizi and this man.

A short explanation about why my grandfather felt he needed to seek Shoghi Effendi's approval for his daughter's marriage is called for. Raḥmat's life was transformed upon meeting Shoghi Effendi in 1926. The Guardian had given him specific instructions to carry out when he returned to Iran. Among other things he was told to resign his post in the army and henceforth consult the Guardian about his personal affairs. Although Raḥmat was embarrassed to take up the Guardian's time with personal matters, he felt obliged to obey the instructions he was given.

The Guardian's response to my grandfather was, 'Regarding the marriage of Gloria K͟hánum and Mr Faizi, the Guardian says that this wedding is the object of God's favours and blessings and will in the future produce praiseworthy results for the Cause.'[8]

Having had an insight into the life Faizi had chosen, my grandfather is said to have told his daughter, 'If you marry this man this will be your life but if you ever try to change him, or his life, I will never forgive you.'

The Wedding

Abu'l-Qásim Faizi and Gloria 'Alá'í married on 26 September 1939. My grandmother, Najmiyyih Lámi' 'Alá'í, who had accepted and treated Gloria as her own child when she married my grandfather a few years after his first wife had left him and Gloria, worked hard to arrange a beautiful wedding.

The wedding celebrations lasted two days, one evening with relatives and one with friends and acquaintances. When he came to take the wedding photograph, the photographer took one look at the petite, less than five foot tall bride and realized he had to reduce the difference in height between the couple so he brought a low stool for Gloria to stand on next to her six foot tall, handsome groom!

My grandfather, who was by this time in great pain with terminal cancer and had only one more year to live, celebrated with immense joy and happiness the union of his beloved daughter with the man for whom he had great affection and respect. A number of Gloria's relatives remembered what a striking couple Faizi and Gloria made and how happy they were on their wedding day. One of them recalled hearing some of the guests whispering to one another about Faizi and wondering why someone with his education was living in Najafábád when he could live a successful life and make good money in Tehran. They simply could not understand that making good money was meaningless to Faizi.

Return to Najafábád: Married Life

On their return to Najafábád as a married couple Gloria soon became involved in the life of the community and helped Faizi in his work. Faizi asked her to give English lessons to a number of keen students and she also taught embroidery to many of the women.

Gloria had a particular ability to create an attractive, comfortable home with very little but with much imagination. She quickly not only transformed Faizi's home but also the school and set about redecorating their living quarters, planting flowers in the school compound and cleaning out the pond. By this time more and more friends, including family members, were visiting Najafábád so that, together with the friends in the village, 'everyone, like unto butterflies, fluttered around Faizi's residence from morning to late at night'.

Gloria's relationship with Mádar-jún was not the usual one between mother-in-law and daughter-in-law. Although Gloria's background was almost diametrically opposite that of her mother-in-law and some of her ways and habits were strange to Mádar-jún in the early days of her marriage to Faizi, Mádar-jún was never impatient with her. She took her young bride under her wing and she and Gloria soon developed a very close bond. The only time Mádar-jún openly showed Gloria displeasure was when Gloria decided to take the puppy her brother had given her for a walk outside the boundaries of the school. When she returned home she saw that Mádar-jún was quite upset with her.

'Decent women', Mádar-jún told her, 'do not go out on the street with a dog.'

Those were the only harsh words Gloria ever heard from her. She only hoped that Mádar-jún would never find out that she rode a bicycle on the streets of Tehran, played the piano and had been taught how to dance!

Knowing that Gloria was a very inexperienced young woman who had spent all her life in comfort and relative luxury, Mádar-jún was reluctant to expose her to the rigours and difficulties of their daily life in Najafábád. She remained in charge of the kitchen and would seldom allow Gloria to help her, saying that it was not the place for her and that she should entertain their constant stream of guests and visitors. But Gloria observed her mother-in-law and tried to learn from her: the way she conducted herself and took care of the family with so much love and without any fuss, never complaining about the hardships she had to endure. It was a common occurrence for Bahá'ís to drop in to visit Faizi on their way to the House of the Báb in Shiraz and Faizi loved their company – he would spend a few hours with them and send them away inspired by the simple life he and the villagers led and by the work he was doing.

Mádar-jún prepared the family's meals in the small mud hut designated as the kitchen and she cooked over a wood fire made up on the floor. The walls of this hut were blackened by the open fire and Mádar-jún's eyes would stream constantly from the smoke when she was cooking. There was no electricity in Najafábád in those days and kerosene lamps had to be lit at night, which made cooking after sunset even more difficult, but Mádar-jún's meals were always delicious. When all had finished eating she would clear away the dishes to wash. As there was no running water at the time she would first clean the dishes, one by one, with a cloth and fine sand to take away the grease and then rinse them by pouring water over them, again one by one, from a watering can so that washing the dishes was no less a job than cooking the meals. A close neighbour at the time recalled that every time he went to visit Faizi – which was daily – he would see Mádar-jún washing clothes or washing dishes, sweeping the floors or cooking in that black kitchen, taking food for the 80 year old family servant and tidying his room or cleaning herbs and vegetables. She did not have a moment's rest. Once when the neighbour saw her washing dishes by the light of a lamp he suggested to her that she should leave them for the next morning when there was more light but she replied, 'My dear, there is work tomorrow as well, a day is not only once. I, by the grace of God, have a family to care for.'

One day, soon after her move to Najafábád, Gloria noticed huge jars of sour cherry jam in the kitchen cupboard. She wondered how their small family could eat so much jam, especially as none of it had been served since her arrival. When she questioned Mádar-jún about the jam, she was perplexed to be told that it would soon be finished and that she would have to make some more. Not many days passed before a youth ran to their house one morning and announced that a busload of Bahá'ís had just arrived in the village and were on their way to their home. Mádar-jún was quite unperturbed and prepared to receive them. Faizi left his work and hurried home to welcome the guests. Gloria was touched to see how mother and son warmly received the unexpected guests and were genuinely glad to see them. There was a lot of laughter and excitement and everyone seemed very happy. But the thought raced through Gloria's mind as to why they had not been informed of their coming and what on earth were they going to give them for lunch only a couple of hours away? Two of the men went to the market to buy lamb to make kebab and Mádar-jún and a few of the Bahá'í women living nearby disappeared into the kitchen. A huge pot of rice was put over the fire and out came the sour cherry jam jars for Mádar-jún to cook the famous Persian dish *álbálú polo*, rice mixed with sour cherry jam and saffron.

Faizi took no interest in household affairs. He never knew how much his mother spent, who did the cleaning and shopping and what was being cooked. He was fond of good food but would eat anything that was served without a fuss. When lunchtime came Mádar-jún would wave her magic wand and, lo and behold, a large white cloth was spread on the floor on which were placed dishes and platters of her mouth-watering cooking and all the little delicacies that Persians serve with meals: pickles, fresh herbs with cheese and yogurt, for which Najafábád was famous. Not only did Faizi not help with any household chores but there was no way he would have been allowed to do so even if he had wanted to as in those days the roles of men and women were very clearly defined and the boundaries never crossed. Gloria, however, worked on him to be tidier with his books and papers. She never succeeded.

The Library

Another of Faizi's achievements in Najafábád was to initiate the establishment of a Bahá'í library. There was history behind the building where the library was to be housed. When Mírzá Asadu'lláh Iṣfahání had the duty of transferring, in great secrecy, the remains of the Báb to the Holy Land, one of the places he stopped en route was Najafábád. Arriving at Ḥáj Báqir's house, he placed the trunk containing the sacred remains, which had been tied on his back, in one of the rooms, telling everyone that it contained writings and Tablets. The friends in Najafábád came to visit Mírzá Asadu'lláh during the one day and night he was a guest in Ḥáj Báqir's house but none of them, not even the owner of the house, knew what the trunk really held. Only after he had delivered his precious load to 'Abdu'l-Bahá in the Holy Land did he write to Ḥáj Báqir to tell him what the trunk had contained. The chosen room for the library was opposite this room.

The youth responded with enthusiasm when the Assembly made the decision to establish a library and it was set up with astonishing speed. Once again the community was called upon to assist. They were encouraged to contribute towards the cost of shelving and the other furnishings as well as to donate some of the books they had in their possession.

Naw-Rúz was approaching. It was Faizi's second Naw-Rúz in Najafábád, and as was the Persian custom, he had bought a thousand silver quarter-rial coins from the bank to give as gifts to the friends. However, he was not just going to give them the coins. A story explains the background to the imaginative and gracious way he presented his gifts to his fellow Bahá'ís and encouraged them to donate towards the library.

One of the many incidents related to Faizi when he arrived in Najafábád was that of 'Alí Asghar, one of the local Bahá'ís. 'Alí Asghar had permission from Bahá'u'lláh to go on pilgrimage. He went with Ḥáj Ibráhím but on arrival he became very ill and died before he could gain the presence of Bahá'u'lláh. Bahá'u'lláh gave one of His own cloaks and a Tablet written in honour of 'Alí Asghar for Ḥáj Ibráhím to take to 'Alí Asghar's wife and three year old son. When Ḥáj Ibráhím arrived back in Najafábád he invited a few of the friends to 'Alí Asghar's house and related the circumstances of his death and then, in their presence, handed over Bahá'u'lláh's cloak and Tablet to 'Alí Asghar's wife and son. The gathered friends respectfully kissed the cloak and the Tablet was read out.

A few days before Naw-Rúz Faizi went to 'Alí Asghar's widow, who was now old and frail, and asked her permission to borrow Bahá'u'lláh's cloak for five days. He decorated one of the rooms of the girls' school with beautiful curtains, a photograph of 'Abdu'l-Bahá and white almond blossoms. He then spread the cloak on a table placed at the top of the room and scattered the thousand silver coins on it. On the edge of the cloak he placed a card and in beautiful calligraphy wrote, 'Take a Naw-Rúz gift from the sacred hem of Bahá'u'lláh and help the Bahá'í library.' When the friends came on Naw-Rúz eve for the three days of the holiday to wish Faizi and his family a happy new year, he would first offer them sweets and then direct them to the room he had prepared. The effect of his arrangement and the revered atmosphere in the room was such that it moved everyone who entered. The friends took a coin each and then contributed in kind, or with books, to the library.

Preparations for the library started in 1939. Bahá'í books kept for years in the homes of the friends were donated, many of them original copies in the handwriting of Zaynu'l-Muqarrabín. At the same time the children were encouraged to start their own small libraries at home. The donations included not only handwritten Tablets and books, for example the Hidden Words and the Íqán, but also the Qur'án and scriptures from other religions, the works of famous Persian poets such as Sa'dí, Mawlaví and Ḥáfiẓ, and many other books – together about six hundred volumes. Tables and chairs were bought and opening times fixed. The completed library was a single room but it had a wonderful atmosphere. When news of its establishment reached Shoghi Effendi it pleased him and he said he, too, would send books for it.

As for the name of the library, one night, before the books were transferred to their permanent place, Faizi asked one of his friends to go with him to the meeting of the library committee. He was disturbed by rumours about the name some of the friends wanted to give the library. On the way to the meeting he told his friend that they were going to choose a name for the library that night and that in his opinion it should be named after the first believer from Najafábád, Zaynu'l-Muqarrabín.

All the members of the committee were present when they arrived and were seated around the room. Faizi was both the chairman of the meeting and the representative from the Local Assembly. When the meeting opened he put forward to the committee his suggestion for the name of the library but some of the members disagreed and wanted to name it after Faizi. The friend who had accompanied Faizi noticed that the 'colour drained from Faizi's face and he became visibly dejected'. The committee was silent for about a minute and no one spoke. The friend asked permission to speak. He argued that if the library was named after Faizi it would be a great insult to the man. He asked them if they had forgotten everything Faizi had repeatedly mentioned in all his talks, that everything they did in serving the Cause should be done namelessly and not for the sake of recognition and fame. He reminded them of a story Faizi had related to demonstrate this point.

Someone built a mosque and on the day it was completed he asked a calligrapher to come and inscribe in large writing on top of the entrance that he was the builder. As the calligrapher was about to climb the ladder to begin his work a passer-by paused and asked whose house the building was. The builder replied that it was the house of God. The passer-by asked why he had built it, to which the builder replied he had built it for God.

'And now,' questioned the passer-by, 'you want to put your own name on the entrance?'

The builder said he wanted to do that so that everyone would know he had built the mosque.

The passer-by observed, 'Then you have not built it for God, you have built it for yourself. If you have really built it for God, inscribe my name instead to prove that your motive is sincere.'

The committee resumed its consultation, which went on for a long time, but Faizi remained silent. In the end it was decided that as they could not agree the Local Assembly should make the decision.

The Local Assembly decided to name the library after Zaynu'l-Muqarrabín and a photograph of him was enlarged and hung in the room together with photographs of other great teachers of the Faith. The only picture they could not find was that of the scholar Abu'l-Faḍl.

Faizi's friend thought that there must be a picture of Abu'l-Faḍl in one of the Bahá'í journals and it was decided that he and Faizi would try to find it. When they began their search they were faced with about five hundred editions of the journal, which had not yet been put in any particular order, so looking through every single copy to find the photograph was not going to be an easy task. They stood staring at the piles for about half a minute, wondering how they should start and how long it would take when Faizi pointed to a particular pile and said, 'You pull out one copy and I will pull out another from this pile and Abu'l-Faḍl's picture will be in one of the two copies.'

The copy pulled out by Faizi's friend had the photograph they wanted. In total amazement the friend asked Faizi what it was that caused him to make his suggestion with such confidence. Faizi replied that he did not know himself but added that it could have been Abu'l-Faḍl's pure soul which had inspired him.

Hooshang

Hooshang was the lad Mádar-jún had taken under her wing long before Faizi married. Hooshang remembers Faizi as 'everything a little boy could want in a father'. He remembers that Faizi never thought of himself but rather 'what the Plan is and what has to be done'. He 'never saw Faizi worry or be sad and he never sowed the seeds of fear or worry for the future; he wanted everything to improve and do better, not so much for himself, but for the Bahá'ís'.

He recollects that Faizi was a strong man and that one of his favourite games was to swing on Faizi's arm as he held it at a right angle to his body. Hooshang also remembers that Faizi was very firm with him, and he was a stubborn lad. However, Faizi knew how to get him to behave for, as Hooshang says, 'He knew that if he asked in a particular way I would want to do it for him anyway.'

In later life Faizi would remember with amusement the night that he had painted black the faces of Hooshang and two of his friends while they were fast asleep. When the lads woke up the following morning each laughed uncontrollably at the other two, not realizing that his own face was also painted black!

Hooshang was initially quite resentful of Gloria's arrival but in a matter of months he realized that for the first time ever somebody was interested in him. Mádar-jún was always like a grandmother to him, someone who cooked his meals and was his provider. Faizi was somebody he looked up to. But here was someone who was interested to know what he was wearing, what he was eating, how he talked and how he walked. He soon became very fond of Gloria and started helping her with her gardening and little tasks around the house.

Gloria had two younger brothers, Manúchihr and Manúshán, whom Faizi loved very much. Manúshán was a small child at the time but Manúchihr was only eight years younger than Gloria and would come to Najafábád as often as he could with family members. He and Hooshang soon became lifelong friends.

An Idyllic Life

Faizi's sincerity and love was for everyone so all felt close to him. In time he came to be regarded as so much part of every Bahá'í family in Najafábád that if they had any problem they would share it with him. When differences arose the parties involved would want advice from him. In every matter, whether it be work or their children's marriage, the well-worn road to Faizi's house would be taken.

Faizi's daily routine was not confined to classes and formal meetings. If there was no meeting to attend he visited the friends in their homes, inspiring them with stories from Bahá'í history or sharing with them some of the rare Tablets of Bahá'u'lláh which he had come across and transcribed in beautiful calligraphy. He loved to sit with the older generation and hear from them about the first courageous Bahá'ís of Najafábád in the days of Bahá'u'lláh. All his life he gathered stories about the early believers and recounted them to other Bahá'ís, touching their hearts and giving them an insight into the sacrifices that had laid the foundations of the Faith. Often he would encourage a youth to serve the Cause by telling him of the great deeds of one of his own ancestors about whom he himself had known nothing. His habit and love of recording stories about the history of the Faith continued throughout his life.

What little free time he had Faizi spent on drawing and calligraphy. He would transcribe prayers in the children's books in his beautiful writing and always had pieces of work to send to friends when he wrote them letters. Any drawings he made of scenes and other subjects he gave to the children as presents.

Faizi stayed in Najafábád for four and a half years until he had trained enough teachers to carry on his work. During this time he had, at the request of the National Assembly, travelled to other parts of Iran as well, met with Bahá'í communities and translated for visitors from abroad. He had also translated into Persian some of the Guardian's letters to the West and prepared a condensed version of *The Dawn-Breakers*. He based his notes on these when teaching Bahá'í administration and history at the newly-established summer school on the outskirts of Tehran.

Leaving Najafábád

Faizi himself wrote that the real reason he left 'this corner of heaven' was because he 'could no longer bear the weight of all the love' showered on him.

'I will never forget the dear children,' he wrote, 'the little ones coming out of their classroom and bringing their shoes to me asking, "Master Faizi, is this shoe for my left or right foot?"; little, tender fingers dropping coins in my pocket and whispering, "For the library", "For the bath", "For the poor"; parents coming to me and asking for Bahá'í names to choose for their newborn.' He also felt that enough young Bahá'ís had been trained to continue the children's education and classes for the youth and that his services could now best be used elsewhere.

Knowing that he was going to leave, Faizi sent a report of all the activities in Najafábád to the Guardian ,who responded via his secretary saying, 'This account was safely received and was read by the Guardian with the utmost care. It is indeed in every way comprehensive, correct, sound and exact.'

News that the Faizis were going to leave Najafábád soon spread through the community. The Local Assembly, being sensitive to the fact that Faizi did not have the emotional strength to bid farewell to two thousand of his dear ones, did not set a time for their departure. It was a late autumn midnight in 1940 when, having said goodbye to members of the Assembly, Faizi and his family found themselves in a car driving slowly through the same streets in which he had, four and a half years earlier, arrived full of hope and enthusiasm. The quiet of the night and the thought that his beloved children and friends were sleeping in their homes while he slipped away filled him with deep sorrow. Gloria, Mádar-jún and Hooshang were in their own world of sadness and none of them spoke during the entire drive to Isfahan.

What Faizi had hoped to avoid came about the next day. One of the Bahá'ís of Najafábád was in Isfahan on a visit and was to return home that day. He and Faizi had lunch together in the home of one of the friends and then the driver called out that he was ready to leave. With tearful eyes Faizi embraced his friend. This final separation from Najafábád was such a wrench for him that he went out and 'wept for several hours under the tall trees'. Nothing consoled him.

6

Qazvín

From Isfahan Faizi and Gloria returned to Tehran, where they were invited to meet with the National Assembly on 2 October 1940. Faizi put it to the Assembly that he felt his assignment in Najafábád had come to an end and that his presence there would be of no further benefit to the community. He also referred to a letter he had received from Shoghi Effendi, written on his behalf by his secretary, in which Shoghi Effendi had wished that he would travel around Iran to deepen the friends and to further develop his lessons and translation work. After consultation the National Assembly recommended that Faizi and Gloria go to Qazvín for one year to help the community establish efficiently-run children's classes and study classes. To support himself financially Faizi was to spend some hours in the day either teaching in schools or translating.

When the train from Tehran carrying Faizi, Gloria, Mádar-jún and Hooshang pulled into Qazvín's railway station around lunchtime on a cold October day, the family was greeted warmly by one of the Bahá'ís, who took them to his house. They stayed with this man and his family for the first month while two rooms next door were prepared for them. Faizi and Gloria never forgot the kindness this loving family showered upon them during their entire stay in Qazvín.

Qazvín is a city about 165 kilometres northwest of Tehran, south of the Alborz mountains and about 1,800 metres above sea level. Faizi's arrival started a new period of activity for the large Bahá'í community of the city and the keenness of the friends to take advantage of what he had to offer was 'without precedence'.

Having experienced some degree of scepticism in Najafábád because of his unconventional teaching methods, Faizi approached the youth 'in a deferential and imploring manner' and begged them to attend the classes so that together they could achieve something. However, one of the youth approached him and told him he had no need to plead with them to attend classes because they had been waiting a long time for someone to come and help them in their Bahá'í studies, so Faizi quickly realized that his presence in the community had been eagerly anticipated. He immediately set about establishing three different classes: one for young children, which took place once a week; a second for older children up to the age of 15 and a third for the youth and adults. Between 30 and 40 people attended this last group but their level of knowledge, both Bahá'í and general, varied. Faizi, however, 'taught with such skill that he met the needs of all and satisfied everyone'. They were all ready for tuition and, as one of the students recalled in later years, 'like burning coal covered in ash', waiting for someone to fan them into flame. In the course of his year in Qazvín Faizi 'brushed away the ash' and generated a great sense of unity between all of them.

Previously, study classes for youth and adults had started with 50 participants in the first session, 40 in the second and so on until they were eventually cancelled. Not so with Faizi's classes. The students found themselves drawn by that natural love he had for everyone, by the way he kept their attention during class, by the absorbing manner in which he conducted the lessons and by the way he related an apposite story at particular junctures. As always, all of his sessions started on time and finished on time and no one missed a class. None of the students ever heard a negative comment from Faizi and they all 'felt nothing but kindness from him'.

Faizi had a daily programme during the year he was in Qazvín. He attended dawn prayers with the community and then returned home for breakfast. After this he conducted a class on the Kitáb-i-Aqdas with a group of older youth and adults until half past seven when the youth had to go to school and the adults to work. The rest of the youth were divided into two groups and were allocated three days a week each (Saturdays, Mondays and Wednesdays; and Sundays, Tuesdays and Thursdays) for Bahá'í classes after school, when they would gather at half past four 'without the least sign of tiredness', despite having spent nearly all day in lessons. Fridays were devoted to Bahá'í classes for the children in the mornings and younger youth in the afternoons.

Faizi also conducted a class on *Bahá'u'lláh and the New Era* three evenings a week for those youth and adults who were not able to attend the afternoon sessions. But such was everyone's keenness to attend all Faizi's sessions that many of the afternoon students joined this class as well, swelling the numbers to 40 or 50, with the students' enthusiasm increasing by the day, along with their love for their teacher.

One of Faizi's students, who was 17 years old at the time, wrote in his recollections, 'I don't know what secret he had in being able to give so much love to all, to encourage when it was needed, to be appropriately humorous, to move one when needed. It never happened that Faizi raised his voice in a class or told anyone off; he never talked down to a student.' A child whose behaviour was contrary to what he had been taught was dealt with by Faizi in such a benevolent way that the child himself would become aware of his misdemeanour and change.

In brief, every day and every hour of Faizi's classes were fresh and new for his students and he would never allow them to become tedious. His method of teaching and the quality of his relationship with the students were such that they would gather earlier than the appointed time for their classes. When they finished studying their chosen book Faizi would set them an exam. One of his students remembered Faizi telling his group that as Bahá'ís they were all expected to be honest so there was no need for an invigilator and that he would return after one hour to collect the answers to his questions. This Bahá'í remembers that they all sat for the exam in an orderly manner and remained silent while writing their answers.

Troublemakers

A group of other youth would invariably be standing in the street jeering at the Bahá'í boys and girls as they came out of their classes but neither the young children nor the youth paid any attention to the abuse. Rather, their relationship with one another in the face of such behaviour strengthened so that they were able to support each other in school. With their unity and exemplary behaviour, they soon stood out from the other students.

The troublemakers' machinations were not only aimed at the children and youth of the Bahá'í community but also at the adults. The son of one of the Bahá'ís in Qazvín was mixed up with a gang of ruffians in the city. Faizi censured this young man, telling him that his conduct was not that of a Bahá'í and that he should set a better example for his peers. Instead of taking heed the lad relayed Faizi's reprimand to the gang and some of the tough ones in the group decided to beat Faizi up. They found out what time he finished his afternoon classes, chose the strongest to do the job and waited in the street. As soon as Faizi was seen in the distance the chosen youth started walking slowly towards him with the intention of picking a fight. However, the closer he got, the bigger Faizi appeared to him and when he was about four or five metres away he realized that the man he was about to attack was big and strong and could 'squash him like a ripe tomato'. By the time the thug reached Faizi he had completely lost his nerve and instead greeted his intended victim respectfully. Faizi, who had guessed why the ruffian had been making a beeline towards him, responded politely and told the lad, now skulking away, to return to the one who had sent him. As soon as this ruffian sought out the Bahá'í youth he shouted, 'What are you trying to do to me? Are you trying to get me killed? This man is a giant!' The Bahá'í youth later apologized to Faizi and became more involved in Bahá'í activities.

A Distinguished Visitor, Making New Friends and an Amusing Incident

Faizi threw himself into developing and strengthening community life by organizing lunches, dinners and picnics for everyone, encouraging the youth in sports activities and joining their volleyball team himself. As an extension to his study classes he trained the youth to give talks and to recite Bahá'í poetry, prayers and Tablets. He also linked the Qazvín youth to the Bahá'í youth in nearby communities and visits to neighbouring Bahá'ís developed into a regular activity. The month of fasting took on a different fervour the year Faizi was in Qazvín. Faizi's students and some of the other friends gathered to break the Fast together and then spent the rest of the evening reading *Nabíl's Narrative*.

It was a few days into the Fast that year that Jalál Kházeh[1] visited Qazvín. Faizi had heard a lot about Mr Kházeh and wanted very much to meet him. His first impression of this 'radiant young man' was that he was 'like a flame of fire warming and shedding light wherever he went'. Mr Kházeh spent every day of his visit, from morning to evening, with the friends, enthusing them with his knowledge and fervour and amusing them with his sense of humour.

One freezing day when the youth had gathered in a meeting with him they felt the cold so much that they started complaining. Mr Kházeh asked them to pray for a few more people to turn up to warm the room and then related to them the story of a travel teacher who got stuck on his way to Tabríz and was forced to spend the night in a coffee shop. As it was very cold he asked the owner to make a fire. The owner called out in a loud voice, 'Bring in the cows!' whereupon three or four large cows ambled into the coffee shop and with their breath warmed the room!

Towards the end of the Fast Jalál Kházeh left for Hamadán, approximately 550 kilometres southwest of Qazvín. Before leaving he encouraged the friends to visit Bahá'ís further afield. After some discussion a number of youth decided to take up his suggestion and to visit different communities for Naw-Rúz. On the last day of the Fast ten of them set off for Hamadán, eight went to Ra<u>sh</u>t and Pahlaví and five went to Shiraz. Faizi accompanied the group going to Hamadán, while Gloria went with the youth going to Ra<u>sh</u>t and Hooshang went with the group going to Shiraz.

Faizi's group set off at eight in the morning. They spent their journey reciting poetry and singing songs until, a few kilometres from Hamadán, they saw a number of people cycling towards them and calling out enthusiastically their welcome and joyous greetings. As they got closer the figure of Mr <u>Kh</u>ázeh appeared in the middle of the road, his arm up to stop the bus. The Bahá'ís disembarked and greeted their fellow Bahá'ís with great joy and excitement. By the time they returned to the bus to continue their journey the sun had started to set and they broke their fast with the sweet bread Mr <u>Kh</u>ázeh had thoughtfully brought for them.

It was during this trip, while the youth were walking in the street with Mr <u>Kh</u>ázeh, that his secretary came up to him with a telegram from the ministry of war in Tehran elevating Mr <u>Kh</u>ázeh, who was in the army, to the rank of colonel. But he paid no attention to his rise in rank and asked those present not to mention it in any of the gatherings. Most in the group respected his wish but one of them could not contain himself and wanted to, in one way or another, tell everyone. When they arrived at the home of one of the friends where a large number of believers were gathered, Mr <u>Kh</u>ázeh asked this friend to open the meeting with a prayer whereupon the man said, 'If you were below the rank of a colonel I would not obey you but what can I do? You have just received a telegram saying you have been made a colonel!' Soon after one of the Bahá'ís told Mr <u>Kh</u>ázeh that it did not become his rank and station to be seen walking in the streets with the Bahá'í youth. Mr <u>Kh</u>ázeh's response was that he was weary of his rank and wished that God would help him succeed in spending all his days and nights in the service of his Faith.

During their time in Hamadán the visiting youth attended deepening classes with their fellow youth, children's classes and other meetings and generally took part in the community's weekly activities. One day they hired a bus to visit another Bahá'í community not far away. On their way a hatless and barefooted soldier brandishing a gun stopped their bus and started to give orders. He commanded the driver to take him to a place 60 kilometres out of their way without any payment. When the driver refused the soldier threatened him with his gun and insisted that he take him to where he wanted to go. Mr Kházeh (who was not in uniform), was sitting quietly throughout this altercation but eventually he stood up and commanded the soldier to get off the bus. The soldier did not move. He looked disdainfully at Mr Kházeh and continued with his demands. No matter how many times Mr Kházeh told him that he was a colonel and was commanding him to leave the bus or face arrest, the soldier paid no heed.

Sitting at the back of the bus with his black hat pulled down over his heavy eyebrows was a rotund Bahá'í known for his very deep voice. Suddenly this man bellowed out, 'Man! I'm telling you to get off the bus!' Jumping to, the soldier obeyed immediately and scurried away. The bus continued on its way and Mr Kházeh laughed that his high authority had had no effect whereas his fellow Bahá'í's voice had put the fear of God into the soldier!

After eleven days the time came for the Bahá'ís from Qazvín to return home and many of the friends gathered at the garage where the bus was preparing to leave to bid their visitors farewell. A prayer was chanted, eyes were tearful at the thought of separation from one another and some sobbed openly, such was the bond that had been forged between them. It was dawn the following day when the travellers arrived back in Qazvín but despite their weariness they went straight to the house where the rest of their companions who had gone to Rasht had already gathered (the group from Shiraz returned a few days later). Afterwards, at a meeting specially arranged for the youth who had gone away, the groups gave accounts of their adventures to the rest of the community, uplifting their spirits and encouraging them to undertake similar travel teaching trips in the future.

Another Library

When Faizi stopped over in Isfahan on his way to Qazvín, the great Bahá'í scholar 'Abdu'l-Hamíd I<u>sh</u>ráq-<u>Kh</u>ávarí, told him that a large number of Hakím's² books and precious papers were held by some of the Bahá'ís of Qazvín and that it would be good if they were all brought together. Within two months of Faizi's arrival in Qazvín the Local Assembly decided to establish a Bahá'í library dedicated to Hakím. Hakím's house, which was in Shoghi Effendi's name, was where the friends gathered and had their meetings, as they had during the time of Hakím himself, and the Bahá'í school which the government had closed had been in this same building. As soon as the decision was made work began on converting the southern wing into a library and guesthouse.

Faizi had a talent for getting people involved and undertaking tasks, and under his guidance and encouragement the younger Bahá'ís in the community soon set to work. They first collected the many Bahá'í and other books that had been donated, which eventually numbered over three thousand, repairing those that needed repair. They encouraged the friends in meetings to support them in their work, either financially or by donating more books. Some of the youth were appointed to undertake special tasks. One was responsible for collating the books and magazines, another for the handwritten documents and the rest took on other responsibilities. One of the Bahá'ís who was an ironmonger and also a very good painter and decorator offered to decorate the library free of charge. The paint he chose was a beautiful shade of green which, with the black framed pictures on the walls, 'created a truly wonderful sight'.

The twelfth day of Ridván 1941 was set for the opening of the library and the Library Committee sent invitations to the National Assembly and other institutions. A programme was arranged and on the afternoon of the eleventh of Ridván the friends from Tehran arrived at the railway station. Everyone gathered in one of the homes for an evening of celebration with poetry, sweets and pastries while a few of the youth worked until two hours after midnight putting the finishing touches to the library.

The following day the Bahá'ís of Qazvín and their visitors gathered at the library. The dedication started with a prayer, after which a representative from the Youth Committee read a prepared speech welcoming the visitors in the spirit of Ḥakím. Everyone then viewed the pictures and books and were served with refreshments. Some made gifts of precious books to the library but the most precious gift was from Shoghi Effendi, who transferred the ownership of Ḥakím's house to the Local Assembly. The library was used by all the friends and many eminent scholars. Among them was Mr Ishráq-Khávarí, who came to Qazvín a number of times to use it for his research. He used to say that the Bahá'ís in Qazvín should appreciate the worth of their library because in his view, after the Bahá'í library in Tehran, it had the most prized books in the country.

Preparing for Service

Eight of the Bahá'í youth in Qazvín decided to take advantage of Faizi and devote all their time studying the writings with him, as they felt this would enable them to more fully serve the Faith. Under Faizi's tutelage they gathered very early in the mornings in one of the rooms of the library to study the Torah, the New Testament and the Qur'án. At noon they went home for lunch and returned at two to continue studying the Guardian's writings until four in the afternoon. From four o'clock they took part in the community classes studying *Nabíl's Narrative* and other books. Any spare time they had was spent running the library.

The Local Assembly of Qazvín decided to help these students by buying a typewriter. One of the Bahá'ís was sent to Tehran to purchase it. On his return two of the students who knew how to type started copying selected documents.

The eight students progressed steadily and reached a point where they were ready to go out into the field of service. When

Faizi was asked by the National Assembly to attend a summer school in Tehran to conduct a course on *Nabíl's Narrative*, it was arranged for a few of the youth from this special study class to go with him.

Summer School

Faizi had prepared a summary of *Nabíl's Narrative* in Persian and, using a number of other translations and documents, he started his classes from the first day of the summer school. Initially only seven attended his course but these seven enthused so much about his gripping sessions that his second course of study began with a full room.

Azíz Miṣbáḥ, Faizi's headmaster at the Tarbíyat School also conducted sessions at the same summer school, although he had by this time lost his sight. Jináb-i Miṣbáḥ had a reputation for always arriving on time for his sessions and it is probably because of the good example he set that Faizi's classes, also, always started and ended on time. (In fact, Faizi did not like to keep people waiting, always liked to be on time for everything and would get quite agitated if he were ever delayed in any way). Faizi recalled that the organizers had placed an easy chair in Jináb-i Miṣbáḥ's class for his use and provided benches for the students to sit on. When Jináb-i Miṣbáḥ arrived for his first session he asked if all the others also had easy chairs and was told that he was the only one. He refused to accept this special treatment and asked for a bench to be brought for himself as well.

Leaving Qazvín

On returning to Qazvín from the summer school both Faizi and the students were eager to go further afield into the arena of service. Although Faizi and Gloria had decided to move abroad, the National Assembly felt that Faizi's services were needed in Iran. However, Faizi asked the National Assembly to reconsider its guidance and to release him from his post. As soon as permission was granted he and Gloria started to gather their belongings and make ready to go to Iraq, the stepping stone to the Gulf states, where they hoped Faizi would find employment.

Faizi formed attachments very quickly and had established a deep and warm relationship with the Bahá'ís in Qazvín during the one year he was there, so cutting this bond of affection was difficult. Not only did Faizi have a loving relationship with his students but also with the rest of the community, as young and old alike were captivated by his noble character and behaviour. No wonder that the day of his departure was a mournful one for all. Everyone was sad, especially the youth who had sought his company day and night. One of the Bahá'í students who had spent nearly all his waking hours with Faizi during that year wrote the following in his recollections:

> During all this time I never once heard him speak ill of anyone or put anyone down. He had a remarkable capacity to associate with everyone. Although he was a highly educated man, when he met someone who was on the face of it uneducated he conversed with the person with such love and drew him in in such a way that after a while it seemed as if they had been friends for years . . .

Faizi and Gloria were hoping to leave Qazvín quietly but when the friends became aware of the time of their departure a large group went to the railway station to seek them out, searching in every carriage until they found them. They surged closer, calling out expressions of love, and Faizi found himself trying to hold back his tears with great difficulty. The train started to move and within seconds was out of sight.

'Faizi had gone but the perfume of his presence lingered in every home,' remembered one of the youth of the time.

Having bid farewell to their mentor, the youth of Qazvín did not sit still. Each one of them rose to serve the Faith. In the short period Faizi had been with them he had nurtured them to such a degree that with the flame of faith and love for the Cause burning in their hearts they forsook everything and everyone and set off on the road of teaching. A number of them left their work and studies to teach the children in the villages. Many of them scattered far and wide around the world and are to this day, together with their children, being of service to the people of their adopted countries. Those who stayed behind have remained firm in their faith and they and their families are currently enduring the difficulties showered upon them in their homeland with patience and fortitude. Some have even given their lives for their Faith.

Faizi and Gloria never forgot their time in Qazvín. In his account of the events of that period of his life Faizi wrote, '. . . many a day in times of loneliness Gloria and I gave strength to our hearts by recalling such moments.'

7

Preparing to Leave Iran

On their arrival in Tehran Faizi and Gloria sold most of their belongings to lighten their load. Amidst the confusion of the Second World War, Faizi was lucky to get a one-year passport including Gloria on it as his dependent.

Before leaving Tehran Faizi sent a telegram to his beloved mother asking her to come to Tehran if possible so that he could see her before leaving the country. She agreed, even though it was difficult for her to travel in winter. Her emotions were in a turmoil. She had been separated from her son before but afterwards they had resumed living under one roof. This forthcoming separation, however, being in the path of service in a distant land, had no hope of reunion in the future. She remained calm and quiet throughout their last few days together, which added to the depth of Faizi's own sorrow. Pouring his feelings onto paper Faizi wrote,

> It is not only now that she is quiet. She bore all the hardships and difficulties throughout her life with calm and without saying anything. I cannot put into words the love and devotion I feel towards her sacred being. I have failed to reciprocate all my mother's kindness and self-sacrifice.

Mádar-jún joined Faizi and Gloria, Gloria's two younger brothers and mother (now widowed) in the home of Gloria's mother for their last few days in Tehran. Mádar-jún did not eat much, nor did she talk and was always deep in thought. Faizi recalled how he 'burned with the fire of separation' from his mother during the years he was away studying and how he longed for the day he could make up for all her suffering. He wrote on the eve of leaving his homeland, 'Until now I have not succeeded but rather added to her sorrows. O God, forgive me and make her happy with me.'

The night of departure arrived – 7 January 1942. Clouds covered the skies of Tehran and it was raining. Faizi and Gloria were a very popular couple in the Bahá'í community and when they and their four travelling companions arrived at the railway station they found about five hundred of their family, friends and Bahá'ís gathered to see them off. Faizi's dear brother was the first to come forward and help them with their luggage. He had sacrificed so much to enable Faizi to continue his studies in Beirut and he now placed a wad of money in his brother's pocket, saying, 'You will need this.' The respect and love Faizi had for his brother from his childhood 'increased a hundredfold', as did his 'sense of shame', feeling that 'in the face of all his love, kindness, support and self-sacrifice' he had not been able to do anything for his brother.

Once their suitcases were placed in the luggage compartment Faizi and Gloria bade farewell to the gathered well-wishers whose love 'reached the sky'. As the moment of departure drew near, everyone expressed their affection for this special couple in their own way: some had brought fruit, some sweets and pastries, some told jokes, some embraced them and a tearful group watched from a distance. Faizi and Gloria, charged with high emotion, wondered to themselves how they were able to leave these friends and go to a different country where they would be deprived of all the love and companionship of these wonderful people. The time of departure was minutes away. They boarded the train.

At the last moment Gloria's mother lifted Gloria's little brother Manúshán to once again hug and kiss his adored sister. As the train blew its whistle and started slowly to move away, Faizi gazed on the faces of his friends, whose cries of 'Alláh-u-Abhá!' rose in farewell. He suddenly saw the guard roughly thrust away an arm. Mádar-jún had stretched out her hand to touch his for the last time but the train had by now gathered speed. Every time Faizi recalled 'the harsh treatment of such innocence' his heart melted. For some distance from the station the travellers saw groups of

Bahá'í youth standing on the verges, waving and calling out their goodbyes as the train passed by.

'Farewell my faithful friends,' Faizi whispered to himself as he waved back.

Gloria was by now sobbing her heart out, and as much as he tried, Faizi could not console her. He thought to himself that although they were enduring this separation for the love of God, it was the very same love that God had generated in their hearts that caused such heart-wrenching sadness at this moment of separation.

After Faizi and Gloria left Iran, Mádar-jún lived alone in her house in Tehran, recalling the memories of the few years she had spent with her son and daughter-in-law in Najafábád and Qazvín and wistfully telling her visitors that she wished she could see them more often. Some years later, a friend visiting Faizi in Bahrain told him of Mádar-jún's wish and asked him if he had a message he could take back to her. While Faizi longed to see his mother and agonized over her sorrow at their separation, his message to her was that this life is so short and ephemeral that one must set aside one's personal wishes and longings in the path of service, that they would soon see each other in the next world and that their reunion would be forever.

The Beginning

As the small group gathered together in their third class compartment, deep in their own thoughts, they were unaware that two members of Gloria's family had secretly boarded the train to travel with them as far as Ahváz. As soon as the train was on its way Gloria's uncle, Ni'mat 'Alá'í, and his wife lifted their spirits by surprising them and taking them to their second class carriage where they had reserved seats for them.

The travellers arrived in Ahváz on the evening of the second day of their travels to find Colonel K͟házeh and a number of other friends on the platform to greet them. They were all taken to Mr

Kházeh's house where they met some of the Bahá'ís of Ahváz. The next night a large meeting was organized and the following day the travellers prepared to go to Khurramshahr and from there to Ábádán, the port from which they were to sail to Iraq.

The time came to say goodbye to Gloria's uncle and aunt. Separation from them was especially difficult for Gloria and Faizi's heart ached when he saw Ni'mat 'Alá'í hold Gloria in his embrace as she sobbed 'like an April shower'. It was as if Ni'mat was embracing his niece on behalf of her father. This time Faizi did not try to stop Gloria's tears as he felt her sobbing might lighten her heart.

By evening they had gone through customs and boarded the boat which was to take them to the Iraqi port of Basra. There was a good wind and the boat sailed with some speed out of Iranian waters.

8

Baghdad

As the vessel carrying the hopeful travellers approached Iraq it was met by a launch of the Iraqi port authorities and told that it did not have permission to enter Basra. The passengers were forced to return to Khurramshahr.

This minor setback did not daunt the small group. They enjoyed the unexpected extra time with the Bahá'ís in Khurramshahr in a wonderful meeting that evening then spent the following day making arrangements to travel to Iraq by car, made possible with the help of the friends in the city.

Once again they set off for their destination. They began their journey just before noon and arrived at the customs in Basra at about four in the afternoon. Exhausted, they sat with other travellers in the custom house waiting for their turn. A customs official gave each of them a piece of paper on which they had to list their possessions, especially carpets, and charged each a sum of money.

Having successfully completed the paper work they were told that they were free to go, so they took a taxi to the railway station from where they intended to travel to Baghdad. Basra's railway station was 'extremely dirty and the ground and walls wet with humidity', even though it was supposed to be the cool season. The pilgrims for Najaf and Karbilá[1] had lit braziers in every corner and were busy drinking tea and smoking their hubble-bubbles. Faizi, who had left the group to buy tickets for everyone, was told that apart from third class tickets there were none available. Thinking of his elderly companions and wondering how they could endure travelling in the grimy third class carriages, Faizi went to see the stationmaster. For reasons he could not fathom, the stationmaster said he would arrange for Faizi's group to have a compartment to themselves and he himself came to the platform to make sure their luggage was boarded. The group were so grateful to this man that they all prayed for God to keep him safe and then spent an enjoyable night relating stories to each other before falling asleep in total exhaustion. They woke up early the next morning, had tea and milk and were happy to have got thus far without much difficulty.

The weather improved somewhat as they travelled north. It was nearly noon when the train pulled into Baghdad railway station. The crowd of passengers descending from the train was greeted by almost an equal number of guesthouse proprietors trying to persuade passengers to go to their particular boarding house.

Faizi left Gloria and his travelling companions in the station to find accommodation. He managed eventually to extricate himself from a persistent landlord and walked into Baghdad in search of the three houses where he knew about 40 Bahá'í men and women from Iran were staying before proceeding to their destinations. In the meantime his fellow travellers had been found by some Iraqi believers who had been notified of their imminent arrival by the friends in Iran. By the time Faizi found the houses, everyone was already all gathered there to enjoy the delicious lunch prepared for them.

One of the Bahá'ís of Baghdad wanted the Faizis to stay with him but they did not accept because they did not want to be a burden to anyone, nor did they want to be separated from their travelling companions. However, this man's long friendship with Faizi, which had begun when he had visited Iran and Faizi had been his translator, and his deep love for and friendship with Gloria's father, won the day and he took the couple to his home where they stayed for the year they were in Baghdad.

The morning after their arrival Faizi, who always had a great sense of history, took Gloria with him to be photographed as a mark of the next phase of their life together.

In the year that Faizi was in Baghdad he started Bahá'í classes for the youth and 'generated a new spirit amongst the friends'. Together with Gloria he spent the whole of every Tuesday with the Persian Bahá'í families. The families' furniture was very basic – in fact, they did not really have any furniture – so on the days they met they placed suitcases and boxes around a room for everyone to sit on and together chanted prayers, read from the writings and told each other stories until nearly midnight.

Faizi must have also sought permission to travel teach during this year, as indicated by this extract from a letter written on behalf of Shoghi Effendi:

> Regarding Mr Abu'l-Qásim Faizi's travels in the provinces of Iran to diffuse the divine fragrances, this suggestion has the approval of the beloved Guardian who states that this distinguished youth should be continually encouraged . . . His services are very important and his travels to Bahá'í centres will produce excellent results. The Guardian does not forget the countless services that active servant of God rendered in Najafábád, and it is the Guardian's high hope that Mr Faizi may be enabled to render greater service, engage in more important undertakings and win more signal victories in the days to come. This is the Guardian's wish for him under all conditions and circumstances.[2]

The Search

Faizi had set his heart on going to Ahsá, as he believed it was where Shaykh Aḥmad-i-Ahsá'í[3] was from, but he was happy to go to any of the Arab countries. He and Gloria began a daily routine of going through all the newspapers in search of employment in any of the Arab states. Optimistic though he was, Faizi reached such desperation at one point that he wrote to a friend, 'There is no hope yet of my going to Ahsá or Bahrain but the thread of hope has not been severed . . .' In a letter to Naysán when he, too, was experiencing some difficulty settling in another country, Faizi recalled his own one year in Baghdad and wrote, 'I never lose hope. Nor do I get disturbed. Such events teach us patience.

A good lesson to be learned.' He then reminded him of the song in *West Side Story* and advised him to 'keep cool'!

Faizi decided to apply for teaching posts and was overjoyed when on 5 April 1942 a letter arrived from the principal of Manama College, a boys' secondary school, offering him a position, pending a formal application and a note of his qualifications. With a heart full of hope Faizi completed his application immediately and posted the document. He and Gloria then waited anxiously for a reply.

On 18 July 1942 the Faizis received a telegram from Shoghi Effendi:

PROFOUNDLY APPRECIATE COURAGE SELF SACRIFICE CONSECRATION SERVICE PRAYING SPEEDY REALIZATION HIGHEST HOPES

At last the long-awaited letter from the Education Department of Bahrain arrived for Faizi, offering him a position and setting out the terms of his employment. Faizi and Gloria were thrilled! By this time they had just enough money to buy two one-way tickets on a ship going to Bahrain. They packed up the little they had and made their way to Basra where they stayed for 15 days to await a ship that would drop anchor at Bahrain on its way to India.

They set sail nearly one year after they had arrived in Baghdad.

9

Bahrain
The Lonely Years

A Brief History of Bahrain

Bahrain consists of several small islands close together in the Persian Gulf off the coast of Saudi Arabia. It has a history going back more than five thousand years. Its inhabitants were amongst the first to embrace Islam and its significance for Bahá'ís is that it is from this clutch of islands that Shaykh Aḥmad Aḥsá'í, a Muslim scholar and the first man to actively prepare his students for the coming of the Báb, came. In more recent times, and before the discovery of oil on the island, Bahrain was known as a pearling centre. With its extremely hot and humid climate, it produced little apart from dates, fish and a few greens and relied on the import of rice, potatoes, live animals and fowl and other produce from Iran and India. These came on *dhows*[1] sailing up and down the Persian Gulf, and as there was no refrigeration the livestock and chickens had to be slaughtered on the day they were to be sold. Although Bahrain was the first place in the Persian Gulf to sink wells after the discovery of oil in 1932, in the 1940s its wealth had yet to benefit the majority of the inhabitants, who were still living under primitive conditions. There was no mains water and when water was eventually piped into dwellings it was brackish and unsafe to drink unless boiled.

The population of Bahrain at the time was composed of three main groups. The original inhabitants, the Bahárnas, were Arabs who belonged to the Shí'í sect of Islam, the rulers were Sunní Arabs and the third group, the Bandarí, were Persian Sunnís who originated from the coast of Iran. Besides these three main groups there was a small community of Persian Shí'ís who were mostly from the south of Iran.

The First Bahá'ís in Bahrain

Very few ships sailed the Persian Gulf in the winter of 1942 as it was during the Second World War and the passage unsafe. The few that did sailed with vigilance from India and Pakistan to Iraq and back once every two or three months and blacked out at night. The ship on which Faizi and Gloria travelled from Basra took eleven days to reach the island of Bahrain and arrived there on 25 December 1942. In those days ships dropped anchor far off shore and passengers had to disembark into the launches sent to transport them to the port by descending on ladders let down the side of the ship. This was tricky for the uninitiated even when the sea was calm and very precarious in winter when the waters were rough. The small launches would not only ride up and down with the waves but also sway away from the ship with every swell so that passengers had to be precise in timing when to step off the ladder into the launch, otherwise they were in danger of falling into the heaving water between the ladder and the launch and drowning. Faizi, in full Arab dress, disembarked first and got himself and their luggage into a launch then looked on anxiously as Gloria, also appropriately dressed and covered from head to foot, struggled while trying to stop her veil from slipping off her head and her shoes from slipping off the rungs of the ladder.

Before disembarking the Faizis were surprised at the unexpected arrival from the shore of an Englishman who had come on board specifically to see them. After introducing himself as Mr Waklin (the Head of Education in Bahrain with whom Faizi had been in correspondence), he told Faizi that he had seen his application and knew he was a Bahá'í. Mr Waklin and his wife were to become friends with the Faizis and he was to prove himself to be just, fair-minded and a faithful friend.

Although Faizi had set his heart on going to Aḥsá he was

happy to have succeeded in getting permission to enter Bahrain and his feeling of exultation was beyond measure when he and Gloria arrived in Manama, the largest island of Bahrain. Little did he know at the time that his wish had come true. In a letter dated 15 July 1944, written on behalf of Shoghi Effendi to an individual believer in one of the other Arabian countries, Shoghi Effendi referred to Bahrain as 'the birthplace of <u>Sh</u>ay<u>kh</u> Aḥmad-i-Aḥsá'í'.[2]

First Few Months

Faizi had accepted the accommodation offered in his contract for the first month so that he and Gloria would have somewhere to live when they arrived. This place had one very large room with a small room attached. As it was the winter season and they did not have many possessions or proper bedding, they decided that the large room would be too cold to live in, so they settled in the small one. The only problem was that this room was so small that when they slept on the floor at night they had to leave the door open so that Faizi could stretch his legs.

The school in which Faizi was to teach was, at the time, the only secondary school in the whole of Arabia. It had been newly established by the <u>Sh</u>ay<u>kh</u> of Bahrain; the teachers were from Lebanon, Syria and Egypt and the students from the well-connected and rich of Bahrain. Faizi's daily routine was to leave Gloria every morning and go to the school to teach. He would return home for lunch and in the afternoons did what the other teachers were in the habit of doing: going to the bazaar and visiting the shops and merchants as part of their social life, becoming better acquainted with some people and making friends. One of the most important assets both he and Gloria had was that of the four languages they both spoke one of them was Arabic.

Finding a house to rent was not easy. Except for the rich merchants and a few foreigners in Bahrain, the rest of the inhabitants lived in small, usually one-room *barastís*.[3] The *barastís* were so close together that a whole district would go up in flames within minutes if a woman was not careful with her cooking fire. There were very few houses for rent and most of these had no sanitary facilities, for at the time many of the inhabitants said that no angel would enter a house that had a toilet, so most of them used the waterfront in the evenings. The women, who could not be recognized because their faces were hidden under veils, would spread the skirt of their long, black veils around them for privacy.

After one month Faizi managed to find a small house in a narrow street near the bazaar. It had a small courtyard and a single room but no electricity or water. It did, however, have a hole in the ground for a toilet and he and Gloria resigned themselves to no angel ever coming near them. A syphilitic water carrier would deliver two skins of water once a day. The water, which would wash over the sores on the carrier's hands as he emptied the skins into the containers provided, had to suffice for drinking, washing, cooking and everything else. Gloria used to boil their drinking water on a small kerosene stove she had brought with her from Baghdad. After the water boiled, she let it stand until it was lukewarm then poured it into an earthenware jug to cool down. As she and Faizi were respectful of the island's customs and very careful not to behave or act in any way that would cause offence, Gloria seldom left the house and certainly did not go to the market to buy food. Faizi, as was the custom among the Arabs, bought what he could find in the market on a daily basis and Gloria prepared their meals.

Although Gloria did not leave the house – and in fact had nowhere to go at this time – she was not left alone. As soon as Faizi left for work in the mornings the women in the neighbourhood, who had very quickly realized that a foreign woman was living in their midst, went to the house to keep her company. They were simple, unsophisticated local women and the few foreign women in Bahrain at the time never socialized with them, let alone allowed them into their houses. Almost daily the women would arrive with their children and look over everything in the house. They would open Gloria's suitcase, take out her clothes and show them to one another. They cracked and ate the *banak* (nuts) they had brought with them then threw the shells on the floor. They would ask Gloria if she had gold and when she told them she had only her watch and wedding ring they would turn to each other and whisper that her husband did not love her. Gloria accepted that this was the normal conduct of these women and did her utmost to be welcoming and treat her visitors with love and kindness. However, what she found most difficult to cope with was her visitors' use of the drinking water. She had placed a ladle on the water jug to pour the water into the glasses she provided but the women and their children drank the water from the ladle and poured the remainder back into the jug so as not to waste a drop. Her guests and their children generally stayed until the noonday call for prayer when they would leave because they knew the men would soon be returning home.

Perhaps the most testing of the women's customs for Gloria was spitting on the face of a newborn to ward off the evil eye, a practice in many cultures, and then rubbing the spit all over the child's face. One can only imagine what Gloria went through at my birth when one by one the women solemnly spat on my face and rubbed it in! My brother, Naysán, was spared the ritual as by then our family had moved into a different neighbourhood and Gloria had learned to be a little more assertive.

One day one of the Christian missionaries, Dr Harrison, who was well known on the island, paid them a visit. In the course of their conversation Gloria told him that she had not yet seen a healthy eye in Bahrain and that many people were either blind or had trachoma. Dr Harrison informed her that trachoma was the least of their problems because many of the Bahrainis had tuberculosis and venereal diseases, all of which were infectious. When Gloria asked what she and Faizi should do to protect themselves he said they should not let anyone into their home. He told her that the Christian missionaries seldom let any of the natives pass the threshold of their houses – their association with them was in their missionary school, the hospital or in the streets and bazaar. Of course that advice was not acceptable to Gloria, who was beginning to regard her daily visitors as her friends. She once again asked Dr Harrison what to do if someone came to her house and asked for water. Dr Harrison replied that the glass from which this person drank should either be thrown away or boiled. Throwing the glasses away was not an option. For several days Gloria boiled the used glasses but in the end she decided that with the lack of water this was not practical, so she relied on God's protection and just washed them with soap and put them in the sun.

A New Neighbourhood

After some time Gloria was asked to teach English in the American school for girls in the mornings, which she accepted. Soon after Faizi found a two-room house above shops in another neighbourhood in <u>Sh</u>ay<u>kh</u> 'Abdu'lláh Road. This was where our family lived until 1957.

More of the inhabitants had by now moved into concrete dwellings which were generally two storeys high. These houses consisted of rooms built around a courtyard; the windows facing the street were shuttered and always kept closed for privacy. Some of the Faizis' new neighbours, however, were quite poor and still lived in *barastís*. The neighbours kept hens and a cow or two or goats in the yard and usually had two baskets hanging from the ceiling of their lodging, one containing dates and the other coarse salt. Their breakfast consisted of dates and bitter coffee and the women's lunch was the same. Guests would not be served anything until they were about to leave at which time the date basket would be brought down, the ever-present flies would be brushed away and the dates offered with black, unsweetened coffee. The men returning from work in the evenings would bring home a few fish hanging from a string which their wives would cover with coarse salt and leave for a short time. They would then wipe away the salt and set the fish to cook on a tin over a fire made from palm wood. When the fish was cooked they would gut it and give the innards to the chickens before eating it with boiled rice.

The first person who showed Faizi any friendship was a man named Kavash (he may originally have been from Iran) who would sometimes buy fish for Faizi and Gloria from the market. He showed them much kindness. In time the Faizis became friends with their new neighbours, all of whom were Bahrainis with the exception of one family, who were Persians. This family was generous, kind-hearted and fair-minded and its members were to become some of the Faizis' most faithful and supportive friends throughout the years they lived in Bahrain.

Laying Foundations

Faizi had a great sense of history and liked to begin projects on special days of the Bahá'í calendar. The night he and Gloria left Tehran for Baghdad one of the friends who had come to bid them farewell at the railway station had given Faizi a sealed envelope. On the ninth day of their first Riḍván in Bahrain Faizi wrote a letter to this friend in which he said:

> I opened the sealed envelope you gave me at the railway station when we left Tehran to find the sum of money you had given with so much love . . . I'm sorry to have taken so long to send you a receipt but I wanted to wait until the money reached its rightful place before doing so. Gloria and I have today, the ninth day of Riḍván, established the first Bahá'í fund box . . . The first donation placed in the box was the 20 *túmáns* (20 rupees) with your card and our minds put to rest that the money reached its rightful place . . . We hope you will accept this first receipt from our fund box.

Faizi and Gloria themselves made their own first contribution with the sum of ten rupees.

From having lived in large Bahá'í communities bubbling with activities and good-humoured camaraderie full of enthusiasm, the Faizis now found themselves living on this small island to which only their eagerness to serve the Faith and their love for Bahá'u'lláh had drawn them. They had succeeded in their quest and were determined to make a life for themselves in Bahrain. Life on a daily basis, however, was not easy. They knew it was going to be very hot for most of the year but as soon as the sun began gathering strength after the cool of the winter months and Bahrain rapidly turned into the hottest of Turkish baths with temperatures soaring into the forties and levels of humidity rising to 96 per cent, they did not know what had hit them. When their friend Mr Waklin asked Faizi if he and Gloria intended to leave Bahrain for the summer, Faizi reminded him that according to his contract he was not permitted to return to Iran. He was told, however, that arrangements would be made for them to go to Iran for the summer and Faizi spent this holiday travelling around the provinces, meeting with and helping encourage the friends and youth in their activities.

Return Home

Arriving back in Bahrain after their holiday, Mr Waklin once again came to the ship before the Faizis disembarked, this time to inform them that his department had made a new ruling for the foreign teachers: neither they nor their wives had to wear traditional Arab clothing. Gloria was reluctant to remove her veil as she had not been seen without one since her arrival and she thought it would be more prudent for her to continue wearing it for the time being. However, Mrs Waklin, who had come to the boat with her husband, insisted that Gloria leave the ship without her veil and hid it from her so that Gloria had no choice but to arrive back unveiled. Gloria continued to show deference by being very careful how she dressed when she went out of the house and seldom ventured out of her neighbourhood. When men visitors, other than close friends, came to the house she would not enter the living room. Some years later when the rulers were discussing the question of women removing their veils, the Faizis heard that a comment had been made in the meeting to the effect that if they could be sure all the women would go out of their houses dressed as Mrs Faizi dressed, they would give consideration to the lifting of the veil.

A New Companion

Two years after their arrival in Bahrain a young man became acquainted with Faizi through one of his friends. These two young men would usually drop in to see Faizi every morning before work. Gradually they began to speak about the teachings of Bahá'u'lláh and in time both expressed their interest.

The first Bahá'í group in Bahrain consisted of Gloria, Faizi and three others. They sent their first telegraphic communication from Bahrain to Shoghi Effendi with greetings for Naw-Rúz:

> CONGRATULATIONS TRIUMPHAL TERMINATION FIRST CENTURY BAHAI ERA GLORIOUS COMMENCEMENT SECOND HUMBLY SUPPLICATE CONFIRMATION GROUP.

In reply Shoghi Effendi sent a telegram to Faizi which he received on 21 March 1944:

> DEEPEST LOVING APPRECIATION REMEMBRANCE GROUP HISTORIC OCCASION PRAYING SIGNAL SUCCESS PERSEVERE.

The group never met again although the young man retained his interest. Faizi understood from Shoghi Effendi's message what he and Gloria had to do: they had to live their life according to the principles they believed in and be patient.

On 25 May 1944 Faizi received another telegram from Shoghi Effendi:

> HEARTFELT CONGRATULATIONS BRILLIANT HISTORIC ACHIEVEMENT LOVING REMEMBRANCE SHRINES PROUD YOUR SERVICES.

On the first day of Riḍván the Faizis sent a telegram to Shoghi Effendi saying simply 'RIDVAN GREETINGS'. Shoghi Effendi's reply came immediately after the one above:

DEEPEST LOVING APPRECIATION GREETINGS PRAYING INCREASING SUCCESS HISTORIC MERITORIOUS LABOURS.[4]

The Family Man

My father's status in life changed two years after landing in Bahrain: he became a father. His joy when my mother told him that she was pregnant was immense and, very unusually for men of his generation, he wanted a girl. He was so sure that they were going to have a daughter that he and my mother gave me my name long before I was born.

When her time came my father took my mother to the hospital and stayed – again, not something husbands did in those days, especially not in Bahrain. He walked up and down the hospital corridors while he waited and at about five in the morning he stretched out on a bed and fell asleep. He dreamt that a dear friend of his in Baghdad was telling him about the Guardian, at which point he woke up and saw a nurse walking towards him to tell him that he had a daughter.

My father was very much a romantic at heart. When he brought my mother home from hospital he quickly went into the house before her to put on a record so that music would be playing as she entered. The friends and acquaintances my father had made by this time did not share his delight at becoming a father. He could not understand their lack of enthusiasm, and at times commiseration, until he realized that it was because his firstborn was a girl and not a boy.

Daily Living

During the war there were not many provisions and Bahrain itself had nothing except dates and fish – and even these were in short supply as most of them were taken to 'Awálí, where the oil refinery was and where the foreign oil company workers lived. In normal times flour, rice and other grains and cereals were brought from India while from the ports of Iran goats, onions and potatoes used to be brought on sailing boats. But during the war normal traffic in the Gulf was hampered and provisions in Bahrain became fewer and fewer by the day. Old, bitter and bad-smelling flour which had been stored at the customs was allocated to be baked into bread for the people.

It was during this period that the friends in Najafábád wrote to the Faizis saying they wanted to send them a gift but needed to know what might be useful. In reply the couple asked for *lavásh*, a thin flat bread made with flour, water and salt which dries very quickly and which they therefore hoped would keep on its way to them. The friends in Najafábád, unaware of the dire situation in Bahrain, thought to themselves that ordinary bread was found everywhere and it must be that Mr and Mrs Faizi craved the special bread made in Najafábád with flour, milk, eggs and oil, so they prepared and posted the special bread to them. The parcel reached the Faizis after four months, riddled with maggots. In any other circumstance Gloria would have thrown the bread away but given their situation she broke the bread into small pieces, placed the pieces in the sun to kill the maggots, picked the maggots out of the bread once they were dead and then she and Faizi ate the bread. It was 'the best food' they had had for a long time.

On another occasion someone sent them a box of grapes. These, too, had become rotten on the way and only one bunch was edible. On yet another occasion one of their American friends working in the oil company came to visit them with an orange in his hand, which he gave to my mother. When he left she juiced the orange for me and she and my father shared the pith. The workers in the oil company did not suffer from the shortage of food but they were not permitted to associate with any of the inhabitants of Manama so this friend was not able to visit my parents again. Once the war ended, however, more ships came to Bahrain bringing provisions and in time there was a reasonable supply of food, including tinned food.

Deportation

About two and a half years after they had settled in Bahrain a very fanatical Sunní Muslim stirred some of the merchants in the bazaar to rise up against Faizi. They signed a paper declaring that Faizi was an infidel who was leading their youth astray and took their petition to the <u>Sh</u>ay<u>kh</u> of Bahrain, who ordered Faizi to leave the country within 24 hours on a boat anchored offshore.

It was Mr Waklin who brought news of the deportation to Faizi. He was so upset that he could not hold back his tears as he told Faizi that he had gone to the <u>Sh</u>ay<u>kh</u>'s English advisor and begged him to do something because Faizi was the best teacher he had. But the advisor had told him that the <u>Sh</u>ay<u>kh</u> was very angry, that there was nothing he could do and that Faizi had to leave Bahrain within the ordered 24 hours. As soon as this friend left, our Persian neighbour who had heard the news came to see them, sobbing as he walked up the steps to the house. While these friends were with them the Faizis concentrated on consoling them but once they were on their own they wondered how it could be possible that they had to leave Bahrain, a place to which they had grown attached, where they had made friends and wanted to remain to the end of their days.

After some thought Gloria told Faizi that the <u>Sh</u>ay<u>kh</u> had ordered *him* to leave but had made no mention of her, so she would stay and somehow or other earn a living. But she had not really thought through her proposal. Faizi knew that a woman living on her own in Bahrain was out of the question. After further consultation it occurred to them that, apart from the <u>Sh</u>ay<u>kh</u>'s

English advisor, there was one other Englishman, the British government's political advisor for the countries in the Persian Gulf, whom they could approach. They decided that Faizi should go to him and explain that as it was war time whichever country he was deported to would believe his expulsion was on the grounds that he was thought to be a spy. He intended to ask the advisor to write a letter saying that he had been asked to leave because he was a Bahá'í.

As Faizi set off to see the British political advisor Gloria started to pray. It did not take long before Faizi returned to tell her that the political advisor had changed and been replaced by a new head for the Persian Gulf. On arriving at the official's residence Faizi found the new head strolling in his yard and Faizi asked if he could speak to him. When he explained that the Shaykh had ordered him to leave Bahrain, the man asked if he was a Bahraini. Faizi replied that he was not and that he had a Persian passport. The response of the new official was that the Shaykh could only expel his own countrymen and that expulsion of foreigners was the responsibility of the British. He told Faizi to return home and that he would talk to the Shaykh. This was the beginning and end of the matter. After that no one said anything about Faizi leaving Bahrain. However, Faizi heard that the Shaykh had cut short his teaching contract, their only source of income as Gloria had stopped teaching six months previously when I was born. They now had no income.

Notwithstanding the bleak financial situation in which they found themselves, the two were jubilant that they had not been forced to leave the island. With renewed zeal they prepared themselves for any further tests which they knew they would have to face.

Survival and Faithful Friends

Faizi and Gloria were now completely isolated. They had become the talk of the town and the atmosphere in the marketplace was extremely tense. People came to different conclusions about their case and the Faizis later learned that not everyone was prepared to condemn them. Although they were not without friends, these friends did not consider it wise to approach them at such a time.

It is understandable that the Faizis' presence in Bahrain must have puzzled many people. It was clear that Faizi could get a good job in another country where living would have been much more comfortable. He was not preaching his religion as the missionaries were. Why then were he and his wife so eager to stay in Bahrain, even when the Shaykh wanted them out?

Of the many friends they had made the water carrier remained faithful and continued to deliver his two skins of water every day. One other who refused to stop coming to our house was Maryam, Gloria's daily help. Maryam was a Bahraini of Persian origin and had a family of her own but she was very attached to our family, as we were to her. As there was no longer any money coming in Gloria told her she could not pay her and that it was better if she sought employment somewhere else. Maryam responded, 'No, madam. I will not go anywhere else. I don't work for the money. I come here for your sake.'

As weeks went by the tenacious couple's financial situation became very difficult. There came a point when they had finished their small store of rice and lentils and had just enough money left to buy water and bread but nothing else. Gloria did not want Maryam to find out that they did not have any food to cook so she told her that as the weather had become very hot she should come early in the morning and return to her home before the heat of midday but Maryam was aware of the couple's situation. One morning she asked permission to go to the bazaar as she had something urgent to do. Gloria was very surprised with this request because Maryam had always said that it was not proper for women to go to the bazaar and never went near the shops herself. She returned after some time and put a plate of _khalaṣ_ dates in front of Gloria, saying, 'I saw they were selling _khalaṣ_ dates in the bazaar and bought some for you because I know you like them.' She then left immediately with tears in her eyes. Maryam remained with us until she decided to stop working but Gloria and Faizi never forgot her kindness to us and Faizi continued to send money to her at regular intervals for as long as she was alive.

One other person remained loyal in his friendship with Faizi: Ibráhím Al Arrayed, a well-known and erudite Arab scholar living in Bahrain whose company Faizi enjoyed very much. At the time when anyone who went to the Faizis' house would be labelled a Bábí and matters would be made difficult for them, this man behaved with great courage and magnanimity in openly showing his loyalty to his friend.

The Prize and the Consulate's Advisor

Faizi could have written to either the National Assembly of Iran or his family for financial help but, apart from not wanting to worry them, he knew that all their letters were censored. As the little money they had dwindled even further he remained calm and confident that a door would be opened to help them out of their difficult situation. Gloria, however, was not prepared to see their child die of starvation and told the Almighty that if He was going to perform a miracle He should do it quickly.

One day, when payment for the next delivery of water meant that their purse would be completely empty, Faizi heard that a boat had anchored offshore. He went to the port to see if any letters had come for him as in those days the post was not delivered to houses. (I remember some years later when the postman delivered our letters my father amusingly showed me an envelope he had just received. It was addressed 'Mr Faizi, Persian Gulf'. It had come directly to our house from the sender in Europe without any apparent delay.) Faizi returned home after a short time with a beaming face. He took Gloria by the hand, sat her down and then gently put a cheque for 80 rupees in her lap saying that the miracle she had been waiting for had happened. Faizi had, the previous year, entered a story-writing competition for a magazine

BAHRAIN: THE LONELY YEARS

published in India and, unbeknown to him, had won first prize. The magazine had mislaid his address and not found it until a year later, which explained the delay in sending him the prize money. The 80 rupees was enough for them to live on for several months.

While Faizi and Gloria were going through this testing period two of Faizi's students had risen in his defence and questioned their fathers, asking how could Faizi be an infidel when he was the only teacher who encouraged them to say their obligatory prayers and to practise human virtues. They persuaded their fathers to meet Faizi and, having done so, the men told Faizi that they were willing to speak on his behalf to the Shaykh. Faizi asked them not to do so.

Eventually those same fathers of the ex-students asked Faizi to give their sons private English lessons. Many years later one of those students, on hearing of Faizi's death, commented, 'Mr Faizi not only taught us English but also how to be human beings.'

To his eternal credit Mr Waklin wrote the following reference for Faizi:

From: Government of Bahrain – Education Department
    4th June 1945

TO WHOM IT MAY CONCERN

Mr Abul Qasem Faizi

Mr Abul Qasem Faizi joined the Education Department of the Government of Bahrain in December 1942 as a teacher of English in the Secondary School in Manama. He worked in this capacity until 23rd February 1945 when he was asked to resign.

During the period that Mr Faizi worked for the Government he proved himself to be not only an excellent teacher but one whose heart and soul is in his work. His influence on the boys and his colleagues was of great value.

The reason for the termination of his services was that certain people strongly disapproved of a non-Muslim, a Bahá'í, teaching in a Government School.

That Mr Faizi is now tutoring members of the Ruling Family is an indication of the value placed on his services.

FJ Waklin
Director of Education

Life Continues

Faizi soon found himself teaching about 90 students from morning till night so that he was exhausted by the time he returned home from his lessons. Most of his students were intelligent young men whom Faizi found a pleasure to teach. Among his students were a few who were not up to learning English but he did not give up on them and was amused by one of them calling out to him from across the street one day, 'Hello Mr Faizi! How is you?'

Faizi was very aware that both his and Gloria's every move and action were being observed by those around them. Even though they had become acquainted and made friends with a number of people there were times when they felt very lonely. It was during one of these periods that they received a letter from Rúḥíyyih Khánum[5] dated 30 December 1945, in which she wrote:

> You must not think that because you are serving so far away you are forgotten! On the contrary all these years I have heard the Guardian speak of your work in terms of the highest praise . . . He [Shoghi Effendi] considers you an example to all your fellow Persian Bahá'ís, and wishes more of them would follow in your footsteps. He will pray for you both . . .'

One can but guess what comfort this letter gave them and what added strength it was to their spirit of steadfastness.

Service to the Community, Family Man, Loss

In wanting to be of some service to the youth of Bahrain a few members of the small Persian community decided to establish a sports club. They named it the Ferdowsi[6] Club and invited people to contribute to its running. Faizi was one of the first members and the club records of 1946 show that he contributed 50 rupees. He also volunteered to teach the youth both sports and English. 'Abdu'l-Karím Khushábi, who was one of the men behind this project, remembers that in the 44 degree heat Faizi would strip to the waist and teach the youth traditional Persian exercises.

Of the two Faizis Gloria was the practical one. Faizi used to deflect any credit from himself by saying that it was Gloria who was the prime mover behind their settlement in Bahrain and recalling that it was she who got all the necessary documents. Faizi had a strong belief that women were the ones who 'ensured the triumph of their family' in the field of service and could, 'more than the men, have hope, endurance and perseverance'. However, he was not passive when it came to seeing to the comfort of his family. For example, when he found out that a man was going to build right next to the house they were living in at the time, he immediately wrote to the municipality, pointing out that as the dwelling was going to overlook his house it would take away his wife's freedom because she would then have to remain indoors to avoid being seen by the neighbour and that this would be very difficult for her in the heat of the summer. On another occasion when we were living in our last house in Bahrain he wrote again to the municipality complaining about the smoke filling our rooms twice a day when the *dhobis*[7] under us made their fire to boil their clothes. He told them that he had complained to the landlord and repeatedly suggested to the *dhobi* men that they build a chimney for their fire but that it had all been in vain.

Two years after my birth my parents were delighted that my mother was expecting again, this time twins. Their identical boys were born in 1946 on the anniversary of the ascension of

'Abdu'l-Bahá while we were on a trip to Iran but they did not live long. One died soon after birth and the other survived for only a day.

My parents returned to Bahrain with heavy hearts. The death of a child, in their case two children, is not easy and a corner of my father's heart always mourned the loss of his two sons.

※

Despite his long hours of daily tuition, Faizi managed to build up a vast correspondence with Bahá'ís in various countries and kept up with news of Bahá'í activities around the world. He took great delight when he was able to participate in any activity from afar. For example, when he read that the Bahá'ís in Beirut were going to establish a Bahá'í cemetery, he wrote the following letter to them:

Dear Bahá'í friends in the city of Beirut,

We have read in the Bahá'í News of the NSA of Iran that the friends in the city of Beirut are planning to establish a Bahá'í cemetery and our beloved Guardian has encouraged the friends to send gifts for this great project. Therefore with our hearts filled with His love and in obedience to His commands we are sending you a small sum of money on behalf of our small community and we hope you will accept this simple gift . . .

We are hoping to receive your joyous news and your prayers for God's protection from tests and difficulties are much needed in these difficult days.

Yours sincerely,
Faizi

※

It was towards the end of this period of isolation that Shoghi Effendi, in one of the letters written on his behalf to Faizi, wrote:

> The letter of that true servant of the Sacred Threshold, that distinguished, active, steadfast and detached soul, was received and brought untold joy and cheer to my heart. The uninterrupted and outstanding services rendered by that luminous youth in recent years have adorned the pages of Bahá'í history and provide an example worthy of emulation by all the friends, especially the believers of Iran.[8]

After six years on their own the lone Bahá'ís on the island were on the brink of exciting changes which were to usher in the birth of one of the strongest Bahá'í communities in the world.

10

Bahrain
Beginnings of a Community

A Surprise Visitor

One day in 1947 there was a knock on the Faizis' front door. Gloria opened the door to see a gaunt man standing there. He said he knew her uncle and that he had a message for her from him. According to the custom of the island, as Faizi was not at home Gloria could not ask the man in, so she told him that he should come back a little later when her husband had returned but the man was not willing to leave. At that moment Faizi arrived and immediately recognized the emaciated man. Embracing him, he cried out, "Ináyat! What are you doing here? Why have you become like this?'

The young man was 'Ináyat A<u>kh</u>aván who had left Iran with the intention of settling in Bahrain. He had taken a sailing boat to cross the Persian Gulf from Iran to Bahrain but a storm had come up on the way and it had taken the boat 22 days to reach port. During that time he had become unconscious through lack of food and water such that when the boat reached Bahrain he had been taken to hospital and nursed for one month until he was able to walk. Although he had been advised not to contact the Faizis, 'Ináyat could not endure his situation any longer. He found out who the Persians living in Bahrain were and through them located the Faizis' house. They met just that once before he was sent back to Iran.

About a year earlier Shoghi Effendi had sent the following message to Mádar-jún:

Faizi and Gloria with some of the students in Qazvín

Faizi's special youth study group in Qazvín. *Standing, left to right*: S. Zahrá'í, H. Hezárí, R. Samandarí; *seated, left to right*: E. Zahrá'í, Faizi, B. Samadání

Bahá'í youth of Qazvín visit the Bahá'í youth of Hamadán

Faizi tutoring at a summer school in Tehran, late 1930s

Faizi and Gloria on the brink of new adventures, Baghdad, January 1942

Faizi and Gloria with pioneers in waiting, Baghdad 1942

Our neighbours, Bahrain

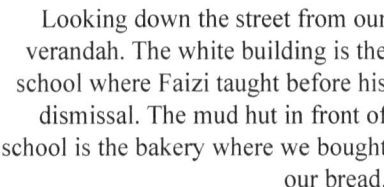

Looking down the street from our verandah. The white building is the school where Faizi taught before his dismissal. The mud hut in front of school is the bakery where we bought our bread.

Faizi and Gloria in indoor
Arab dress, Bahrain

Faizi and Gloria in outdoor
Arab dress

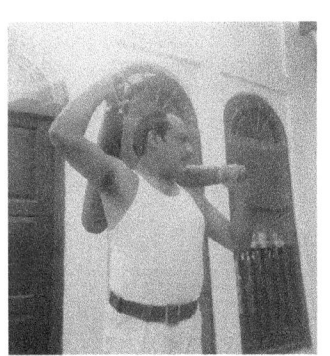

Faizi exercising with his
dumbbells, Bahrain

Faizi in full Arab dress, 1942

Children in the poor neighbourhood of Bahrain which Faizi used to frequent. May is in middle, sitting on the ground.

Left: Faizi distracted from tidying his bookcases, Bahrain

Right: Faizi preparing his lessons, Bahrain

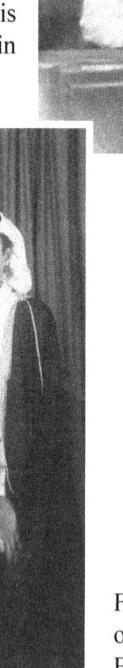

Faizi with three of his students, Bahrain

Faithful neighbours, *left to right:* 'Abdu'l-Karím Khoshábí, Faizi, Ḥusayn Khoshábí

Left: Father, daughter and doll, 1947

Right: Faizi and Gloria in Tehran awaiting the birth of their twin sons, November 1946

Faizi, May and Naysán, Bahrain, 1949

Early pioneers to one of the Gulf states, early 1950s

Pioneers to one of the Gulf states lived in this *barastí* for several weeks at a time, 1950s

Faizi with some early pioneers to Bahrain

Faizi, Gloria, May and Naysán with their family car Bahrain 1951

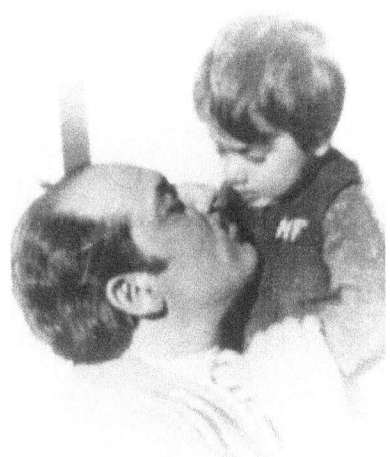

Father and son, Bahrain

Faizi and Naysán exercising together, Bahrain 1954

Faizi relaxing in our main room, Bahrain

The strong man! Naysán and Mansur Rafí'í hanging on Faizi's arms

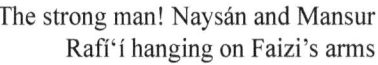

Faizi would always take a launch
out to passenger ships anchored off
shore if Bahá'ís were on board

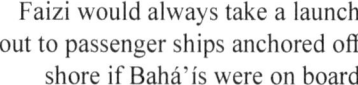

On board the ship from India
to Australia,
25 October 1953

Ustad Ibrahim Urayyed with
Faizi and a visiting friend,
Bahrain, mid-1950s

The worthy efforts exerted by your noble son in Bahrain are indeed an example to be followed by all the Bahá'ís of Iran. The magnificent services of that outstanding servant of the Cause deserve the praise and applause of the concourse on high. Blessed is he and those who like him have forsaken their native land to glorify and exalt God's most great, most sacred and most mighty Cause.[1]

In the summer of 1948 Faizi and Gloria knew they were going to have another child. My mother never spoke to me about the loss of my twin brothers but my father did. Of the many bedtime stories he used to tell me, one was about twin boys. After the death of the twins these boys became my brothers for me, and my father went along with my fantasy until my mother was expecting again and he started preparing me for the arrival of a new sibling. He talked to me about how wonderful it was going to be to have someone to play with, to care for and to grow up with, and he completely enveloped me in his own excitement at the prospect of another addition to our family.

Fellow Believers Begin to Arrive

It was extremely difficult for any foreigner to enter and remain in Bahrain in the 1940s. Trying to think of ways to help the young men from Iran who wanted to come, Gloria came up with a proposal. Knowing that provisions, such as potatoes and onions, were brought in sacks from Iran on sailing boats by tradesmen who were allowed to stay until they had sold their produce, she thought that this may be one way in which new arrivals could make a living. Faizi agreed, but instead of writing the letter himself he asked her to write to Iran and put the suggestion to them because, he said, it was her idea. Faizi's attitude may not seem significant but at a time when society in general was patriarchal and the Bahá'í community was still learning to fully practise the teachings of Bahá'u'lláh on the equality of men and women, it was important.

There were, in general, two types of Bahá'ís who came to settle in Bahrain and nearby states in those days. Some came from the south of Iran close to the Persian Gulf with their wives and children and found it slightly less difficult to adjust to life in these hot countries. The majority, however, were young bachelors who came from sophisticated parts of Iran, many of them having been inspired by Faizi's example. They were not used to the way of life in these countries, nor were they familiar with the Arabic language; they had difficulty getting permits to stay and could not find jobs. The spirit of these early settlers was that of the Heroic Age of the Faith. They were, one and all, truly detached and willing to do anything to achieve their aim. There are numerous fascinating accounts of how they succeeded in reaching and remaining in their chosen area and how a number of them repeatedly returned with their sacks of potatoes and onions until they were able to remain and make a living.

The first person to arrive in this way was a good-looking, resourceful, strongly-built, daring young man. He travelled with an older Bahá'í who did not intend to stay but had come to find out about trading in Bahrain. While his friend was negotiating with the customs men about their merchandise the young man walked out of the customs, mingled with the crowd outside and did not return to the boat. Although he was not sure that it would be wise to contact the Faizis, he decided to find out where they were and to visit them after dark. Delighted as they were to see him, the Faizis were concerned about his safety but he somehow managed to stay on and eventually settled in Bahrain for many years.

૭૦

In February 1949 two Persian youth, Hishmat and Shápur, arrived in Bahrain. They did not travel together but hoped that circumstances would allow them to have contact with one another after their arrival. One day, soon after he had entered Bahrain and before the arrival of his friend, Hishmat was standing outside a government office when he saw a dignified, well-dressed man with a smiling face walking down the street. The figure stood out from the crowd and Hishmat wondered to himself if it could be Faizi. At that moment he saw on the other side of the street a porter in old clothes and with dishevelled hair running towards the bakery. As soon as the porter saw the distinguished man his face lit up. He crossed the road to greet the dignified man and they embraced. As he watched, Hishmat saw the mystery man put his hand into his pocket, take out what looked like a handful of money and put it into the porter's pocket as he was embracing him.

Soon afterwards Shápur arrived and was introduced to Hishmat by a small group of young Persian Muslims with whom they had both made friends in the guesthouse where they were staying. Some days later the young men were in the bazaar looking at various wares when the same dignified man appeared. The two found themselves drawn to him by the 'warm look in his eyes which emanated such love'. As soon as he saw the young men the man's eyes rested on them a moment or two before welling up with tears. Seeing this Hishmat and Shápur quickly left the bazaar. Hishmat told his friend that he had already seen this man and suspected that it might be Faizi.

It was not long before Hishmat and Shápur made friends with another Persian who spoke to them about a fellow countryman with great deference, saying that if eight other people could be found like this knowledgeable man the world would become a better place. The two guessed that it must be Faizi their friend was talking about and eagerly accepted his suggestion that he should arrange for them to visit the man. On the arranged day they 'hastened to the house like parched people' to find their conjecture confirmed. Faizi greeted and embraced them and their friend warmly. His first questions were where they were living, what they did and how they spent their evenings. They told him that they had no employment because they were still waiting for permission to stay and that they spent their evenings in discussion and reciting poetry with the friends they had made. Faizi suggested that they do the same together. Hishmat and Shápur conveyed their 'innermost thoughts and feelings' to their host by reciting the poems of Naím, Varqá and Salmání[2] in praise of Bahá'u'lláh. Having been introduced to him, the two were now able to see Faizi a little more freely. Faizi advised Hishmat not to stay in Bahrain but Shápur stayed on.

Faizi's and Gloria's fourth child, Naysán Raḥmat, was born mid-March 1949, not long after the arrival of Hishmat and Shápur. Although my father would almost certainly have been oblivious of the dust which had gathered in the house in my mother's absence, he wanted to make the place beautiful for the return of his wife and newborn son. There were no flowers for him to buy, so with Shápur's help he carefully cut out pictures of flowers from a calendar and stuck them on the walls of the room to welcome Gloria when he brought her home from hospital. A few days after Naysán's birth, clouds gathered and it rained for two weeks, the first rain in the six years my parents had been in Bahrain.

Family Life

Faizi's income during these early years was still not much and we lived very simply (as one of our friends put it, all our possessions could be fitted into a small van). But Gloria, being an adept seamstress, clever with her hands and with her usual flair for creating something out of nothing, had skilfully made our home attractive and welcoming.

Our home was above a row of shops: a *dhobi*, a café-like shop – from which for nearly a year played, at full volume, the owner's favourite record over and over again from morning till late at night – and one or two other small shops selling sweets, pencils and other similar wares. They all had roofs at varying heights so that we had either to step down or step up to our rooms which were arranged around a small concrete courtyard. It was over the washing line in this courtyard that my father played volleyball with us and our friends; and it was here that once a week he would sit on a low stool with tins of shoe polish while Naysán brought all the shoes in the house to him to clean. He would arrange the shoes in order of size in a semicircle in front of him before starting to clean them. Naysán and I and any of our friends who were there would sit with him and he would tell us a story as he first wiped the shoes clean, then put polish on all of them and moved them one by one into the sun 'for the wax to soak into the leather', then rearranged them again around him and brushed them up to a shine. The stories he told us on these days were always about <u>Khálih Múshih</u> (Aunty Mousie), simple tales which he made up as he went along.

It was also in this courtyard that I have my earliest memory of my father disciplining me. I was about six years old when my parents whitewashed the walls of this outside space. Despite having paper to draw on, this vast, pristine expanse of white was too much of a temptation. To my infant mind, to make what I knew I should not be doing less obvious, I used burnt matchsticks from the kitchen to draw with. It was towards sunset when the black scrawl was spotted. The masterpiece was obviously mine but I was not scolded. Instead my father asked, 'Do you know who did this?'

I glibly replied, 'No.'

He asked me if I was sure I didn't know and once again I denied all knowledge. He knew, and I knew that he knew, I was lying. He told me to stand where I was – which was in front of the drawing – and to come and tell him who I thought had done it when I remembered. I cannot recall how long I stood there before I got tired and decided to come clean. When I told him I had remembered and that it actually *was* me, he hugged me and said that he was so happy I had decided to tell the truth. The only other time I remember him punishing me was when I was about eight or nine years old and shouted out a very bad swear word. He firmly took my hand, stood me in front of the washroom sink and told me to wash my tongue with soap. I refused. He stood close behind me and in a very stern voice said that both he and I were going to stand there until I did as I was told. Eventually I soaped not only my tongue clean but also any memory of what the swear word was. This time he did not hug me but told me off and said he never wanted to hear me use such words again.

My father would very seldom reprimand us. Instead, he had a special look: a slight frown and eyes wide open. When he gave us this look Naysán and I knew that whatever it was we were doing had to stop there and then. Our immediate response was not out of fear but rather because we loved him and understood that he knew best – and that it was so much better than getting the beatings many of the neighbourhood children received for any mischief they got up to.

༄

Our living room was small and simple with two wooden armchairs and wooden benches, which my mother had skilfully covered with cushioning and pretty material, fitted into two alcoves. Most of my father's books and files were kept in bookcases built into another two large alcoves. As mentioned before, my father was not tidy but my mother was meticulous in everything she did and was very tidy. She would occasionally ask my father to sort out his bookcases. He would ensconce himself in the living room to do as she requested but he never got very far. Within minutes he would be engrossed in one of his books, and before he realized it, it would be time for lunch or going out for his afternoon lessons – or we would find him asleep with a book on his lap. My memory is that he never managed to tidy these particular bookcases.

The main room in which we lived and dined and received the daily visits of passing friends was also where my parents had their bed in winter. It was the largest room in the house and the space between this room and the living room was enclosed to create a room for Naysán and me. This main room was the one we would prepare for the festival of Riḍván every year. My parents would bring out the twelve large white cards onto which they had pasted pictures of different flowers and place them in the alcoves for the twelve days of celebration.

During the hot summer months Naysán's and my room would become the storeroom for the winter furniture, as the main room would be emptied of everything except what was absolutely necessary: a rectangular wooden table and several chairs and rush mats which we would spread on the concrete floor to lie on for siestas. There always seemed to be a battle of wills between Naysán and me and our parents over the daily siestas because we never wanted to lie down or to leave my father alone so he could have some rest. In the end he struck a deal with us: we could choose either to have a wrestle with him or to do what he called 'gymnastics', after which we had to let him rest. I regarded myself too grown-up for such games after a few years but Naysán, whose favourite was wrestling, continued until our lives took an unexpected turn.

At night in summer we climbed rickety ladders onto first one roof then the highest roof of our house to sleep on wooden beds, taking with us a white enamel water jug with a matching mug. If my father was home by this time he, too, would come up with my mother, Naysán and me and take over the storytelling, which included stories from the early history of the Faith, after we had said our prayers. The nightly ritual then was for him to point out the different stars in the vast sky above. When the heat and humidity were so great that it was difficult for us to fall asleep, my father would lie down between us and twirl one of his vests fan-like over us to create some movement of air until we fell asleep to the sound of his voice quietly relating tales of heroes from days gone by and from Greek mythology.

To avoid the 40-odd degree heat of the rising sun we climbed down at dawn to the stifling main room below. My mother would go into the tiny kitchen to make morning tea and my father would unbolt the door at one end of the room which opened into a space looking down into the neighbour's yard. He would then turn on the ceiling fan and open the door at the street end of the room.

This door led onto a veranda which ran the length of the house and was shuttered with five openings to the height of an adult. From here my friends and I spent a lot of time standing on boxes and looking down at all the goings on below. Our house was on one of the main crossroads and the comings and goings constantly provided us with interesting scenes of activity. My father was tall and could look out over the veranda enclosure. He would stand there several times a day, with his hands clasped behind his back, gazing across the neighbourhood, whistling quietly or gently chanting under his breath.

The baker was on the opposite corner of the crossroad and it was from him we bought our large, round flat bread every evening (one of my jobs was to pick out the baked weevils before the bread came to table).

Having opened the room in the morning, my father would ensure Naysán and I washed and brushed our teeth while he shaved. I would usually be finished before he had even started and would stand by the bathroom door watching him prepare to shave but at the ready to run away as soon as he stooped down to kiss my cheek when his face was fully lathered. This 'game' continued for years and when Naysán and I had children of our own he continued his teasing with not only us but also with them. With a fresh pair of shorts on, hair brushed and Old Spice slapped on his clean shaven face, my father would then be ready for the day. He would settle at the table after breakfast was cleared away to write, prepare his lessons and attend to his correspondence, all of which he would gather up when it was time to set the table for lunch.

All the early settlers have intriguing stories, stories which will no doubt be collected for future historians to include in their accounts of the early days of the Faith in every country. This is not the place to write about the early Bahá'ís settling in this part of the world but I will relate one or two brief accounts to illustrate the world in which my parents lived and give the reader a flavour of the spirit and resourcefulness of those with whom they shared these years of their life.

BAHRAIN: BEGINNINGS OF A COMMUNITY

The Spectacled Persian

Shápur was a sensitive young man with a love of literature and poetry. He was a rather slightly-built individual with blue eyes and delicate features, always smartly dressed with a spotless shirt and gold-rimmed glasses. Most Bahrainis at the time were not the sophisticated and advanced people they are today and Shápur's appearance began to draw too much attention. He was advised to try and blend in with the locals a little bit more and to remove his glasses in public as they were in danger of causing hostility towards the small community. Shápur's smart clothing very quickly disappeared when he opened a small restaurant to try and earn a living. He even marvelled at how well he could manage without his glasses. After a while he went to Iran, got married and came back to Bahrain with his wife and mother, but as they could not bear the rigours of life on the island, they all returned to Iran. Shápur was arrested after the Islamic Revolution in Iran in 1979 and was tortured savagely for days before being killed, not only for being a Bahá'í but also because he came from a Jewish background.

The Photographer

Another young man was initially one of a small group in Qatar. Qatar is now one of the richest and most highly-developed countries in the world but in the 1940s and early 50s it was, like many of its sister states, as yet undeveloped. In trying to find a job this young man had noticed that there were no photographers in Qatar so he decided to become one himself. He rented a small shop, bought a simple camera, put up a mirror on the wall of the shop and sat down to receive his customers.

Time went by without anyone paying any attention to him or to his shop. After many days an old man walked in and asked, 'What are you doing here? And what is that strange thing you have?'

The photographer explained that he was a photographer and the strange thing was his camera.

'But what is your job?' the man asked.

'I take pictures of people,' he was told.

The man was curious to know what that meant.

It was explained to him. 'When you look into a mirror you can see yourself in it. Well, I can fix that image for you on a piece of paper.'

'Why would you want to do that?'

The photographer responded that when you have your face on a piece of paper you can look at it whenever you like.

'Why would I want to do that? I can look in the mirror when I want to see myself,' replied the man.

'But you keep on changing as you grow older,' persisted the young man, 'and the picture on the paper will show what you look like now.'

'Alláh be praised!' said the old man. 'I will accept His decree and grow old according to His will.'

The now dejected photographer lost all hope of persuading the man to have his photograph taken.

After a long time, when the unsuccessful photographer was ready to give up all hope of interesting anyone in his photographic skills, one of the shaykhs approached him.

'I want you to come to my place, and photograph my wives.'

The photographer could not believe it. How could he photograph the shaykh's wives when, as a man, he was not allowed to see their faces? He told the shaykh he would think about the proposal and give him an answer the next day. That night, he discussed the matter with his Bahá'í friends, who were all puzzled over his predicament. But they finally decided that as the shaykh himself had made the suggestion, he should not be refused.

The shaykh duly returned to the shop the following day and the photographer followed him to his house. When he had chosen a place in the yard where the photograph could be taken, seven ladies came out of the house and stood in a row. They were covered in black veils from top to toe, with not a finger showing. The shaykh, however, was able to identify his wives by the small child each had standing in front of her! That was the end of the young man's hopes of becoming a photographer.

The Communal Money Box

A few young Bahá'í men who had settled in one of the Arab states all lived in one room and went out every morning to hunt for jobs. If they were lucky, one or two of them would be employed as labourers for the day, carrying merchandise on their backs from the ships to different shops. They had a box into which each would put what money he had earned without telling the others who had been lucky with a job that day. At the end of the day the box would be opened. Sometimes it was empty, at other times there might be three or four rupees in it which would buy them a few dates. If it had been a good day there would be enough money to have a decent meal. This arrangement went on for almost a year until one of them found a permanent job and could help support the less lucky ones. The idea of having a communal money box was so practical that it became prevalent among the Bahá'ís who had settled in other parts of the Gulf.

Muḥammad's Search

Muḥammad lived in a village not far from Shiraz in the late 1800s. He was a simple man with a pure heart and he was convinced that a new Messenger had come into the world. He told others about it but people said he had lost his mind.

Muḥammad decided to leave his village and go into the mountains to meditate and pray for guidance. He took some dates for food and retired to the mountain for 40 days. After 40 days he came down and took the road to Shiraz. There he wandered the streets during the day hoping for a clue that might lead him to what he sought. At night he slept in a mosque. One night he noticed that three men came in separately but met together to read some writings by candlelight. The men left the mosque before dawn but came back again the next night. As this went on for a few more nights it aroused Muḥammad's curiosity. He approached the men one night and asked what it was they were reading. They were not prepared to tell him. After pleading with them and telling them how he was longing to find the answer to a mystery he knew had come to pass, the men told him about the coming of two Messengers; but they never returned to the mosque again and he did not know where to find them.

Muḥammad went back to his village, wondering how he could discover more information about the new Messengers. He lost hope of getting anyone interested in what he had to tell them. Then, years later, a Bahá'í teacher came to his village and talked about a new Faith. It was then that his fellow villagers realized that Muḥammad had not been crazy after all.

Muḥammad was an old man and an invalid when the call for Bahá'ís to spread around the world was raised. He told his two sons that they should go. Although his sons were reluctant to leave their old father alone, Muḥammad insisted that they must go in his stead. They obeyed his wish and in time became an integral part of the community in Bahrain.

The Shopkeeper

One of the Bahá'ís in Bahrain found that he could make a modest living by selling tins of tomato paste. He bought the tomato paste from a wholesaler and sold it at a small profit. One day someone suggested to him that he should start importing the paste himself and in that way make more money. The man's response was that if he did that he would put the wholesaler out of business, which he did not want to do. He said that the reason he was there was to become friends with and serve the inhabitants, not to make money.

A Community is Born

Gradually in the course of several years other Bahá'ís arrived from Iran. Some had to go and come several times before they could establish themselves and all had to face countless difficulties and endure much hardship. But their spirit, men and women alike, was strong and in time a small community of adults, youth and children was established. This small group refrained from speaking about the teachings of Bahá'u'lláh to others and drew attention to themselves only by the way they led their lives. Faizi described his new fellow believers as 'wonderful people' who were 'detached from everything' and 'full of the Guardian's love', 'happy and so full of spirit that one would think of them as the owners of all the hidden treasures of the earth'. At the helm of this group was Faizi to whom all turned as to a loving and caring father. They recall that Faizi would look at everyone with such love that they would 'forget all their sorrows' and that whenever the difficulties of daily life swept them off their feet, they would go to him 'to be recharged'.

There was an extraordinary unity amongst the Bahá'í community in Bahrain. The men and women who had in the spirit of service given up their stable lives in Iran were from varying backgrounds: some were not literate, others were highly educated; some came from villages, others from sophisticated lives in cities.

In a letter to a friend, Faizi wrote about a vivid dream he had had during these years which describes well the feelings of these settlers towards each other and everyone else.

'I dreamt', he wrote, 'I was in a meeting.'

> Outside the building was a large peach tree with large, beautiful coloured peaches, but the tree had no leaves. I told those gathered, 'Look how these [meaning pioneers] have sacrificed themselves like the leaves of this tree so that the sun can shine more fully on the peaches to ripen them.' In truth this is the way it is with pioneers all around the world: they should walk

the way of selflessness so that the Sun of Mercy and Kindness shines directly on the people of the land and brings them to maturation.

✧

One of the friends relates that when he first arrived in Bahrain he did not think Faizi was any different from anyone else and that, like the rest of them, he would enjoy a little flattery. He very quickly realized that not only was Faizi tired of such talk but that he would become very uncomfortable if anyone started praising him. Faizi would often compare the human ego to 'a sharp knife' and 'life's journey' to 'climbing a steep cliff with a rope: at any time during this climb the knife could cut the rope, even if one were near to the top of their climb'.

Faizi loved almost everyone who crossed his path. He embraced individuals so warmly that each thought he loved them more than anyone else and many felt that his relationship with them was very special and not the same as with others. The truth is that Faizi had a unique quality: he made everyone feel as if they were special to him because they all were. His fathomless love was completely genuine, totally natural, and the most outstanding quality of his character and personality. (Gloria once said that Faizi was naturally good-natured with noble qualities whereas she had to work at it.) Having said that, the Bahá'ís of Najafábád held a special place in his heart, but it was his friends in Arabia, particularly the ones in Bahrain, who were at the centre of his affections and whom he regarded as his family. To the end of his life Faizi continually wanted news of their well-being, pictures of the children so that he could see how much they had grown and pictures of the babies born after he had left the island. During the summer months he would worry about how they and the rest of his friends on the island were coping in the heat.

The friends in Bahrain remember that 'whatever Faizi had, he wanted the same for others, even cold water'. One day someone gave him a watermelon, a fruit not very easily available in Bahrain at that time. He divided the watermelon into pieces and sent each Bahá'í family a portion. If anyone was heavy-hearted he would not rest until the source of their problem was solved and they were happy again. The members of the community foremost in his mind were the children. At the beginning of each autumn he and Gloria would go to many households where there were children and give the parents vitamins and a bottle of cod liver oil to give to their children in preparation for the winter months.

Community Activities

By way of occupying the young – especially the single men – during the evenings, and no doubt to help establish more common bonds between them, Faizi would ask each one to write down whatever they wanted during the week and then to share it with the rest of the group at a gathering they had every Wednesday night. These were generally quotations from Bahá'í writings, poems or short essays on aspects of their lives. One of this group recalls that despite their varying abilities at reading and writing, Faizi never corrected anyone if they made a mistake or mispronounced a word. His way of making any correction was, at an opportune moment weeks or even months later, to read the same passage or poem out to the group.

Another practical project for the progress of the Bahá'í community was to teach reading and writing to the women who were illiterate. Gloria developed a special course for this purpose and started teaching the women how to read and write in Persian. In time the standard of literacy of a number of them was so high that they were able to enjoy the Bahá'í writings and other books for themselves.

Inevitably, problems and difficulties occasionally arose in such a tightly-knit group of people, but no matter what the concerns were, their fundamental unity was never affected. The adults were all uncles and aunts to us children and my memories of growing up in Bahrain are that we were surrounded and protected by them, that they all cared for all of the children. While we were not spoilt and had to bear many of the difficulties our parents endured, it was never in an unhappy atmosphere but rather one which was warm, loving and full of laughter and fun.

One of my sweetest memories of those times is our small community gathering on the roof of one of the houses at night during the summer months. Here we sat around a cloth spread out on palm leaf woven mats to share a supper, which usually consisted of flat bread, chives or radishes and Kraft tinned cheese. Sometimes those who could would bring boiled eggs and potatoes. All the food would be put in the middle of the cloth and no one knew who had brought what or how much because for some families providing even such a basic meal was difficult. After this simple repast prayers would be quietly chanted by moonlight, or if it was dark, by the light of one or two oil lamps. The adults would relate stories or something amusing that had happened to them since they had last gathered together. Having repeatedly been told not to disturb the neighbours by making too much noise, we children would eventually become drowsy and fall asleep to the murmur of our parents' conversation, either stretching out behind them or curling up with our heads resting on their laps.

Bahrain has nine months of heat and three months of cooler weather. It was generally during the winter months that any Bahá'í visitors from abroad came to our community and, judging by the photographs, it was in these cooler months that most of the photographs of the time were taken. Life during the winter months was much more comfortable. Curtains would be hung, proper beds put up, carpets spread, cushions taken out of storage and plumped up, and for days the smell of mothballs would fill the air while our winter clothes were aired. Naysán and I would often have friends spend the day, and sometimes the night, with us, or we would go to their houses. This constant exchange of children was usually at its height in winter when our parents also seemed to have many more impromptu gatherings. One winter, however, was not so good because all of us children, one after the other, became ill with coughs and colds and a number of us caught chicken pox and measles. My father, who worried so much whenever any of us got ill, held Naysán in his arms when he had whooping cough and walked up and down the room with him trying to comfort him while my mother saw to our other needs. At night he did the same for what seemed like hours to try to put Naysán to sleep. When I came down with chicken pox he sat by my bed every night and moved the palm of his hand very lightly up and down my back to ease the itching until I fell asleep.

'The Fridge'

One of the friends in particular used to be the source of great amusement to the whole community. He was a car mechanic and endured much, particularly during the summer months, when he not only had to contend with the heat while under the cars he was repairing, but also with his asthma. He was given the nickname 'The Fridge' because of the things he said and did. In Persian, meaningless and almost nonsensical remarks and actions are referred to as being 'cold' or 'icy'. 'Naff' is the colloquial word which most closely conveys this dear man's very individual sense of humour. He had, indirectly, made the Guardian laugh when Shoghi Effendi's secretary had read out to the Guardian an amusing anecdote Faizi had written about 'The Fridge'. For example, 'The Fridge' would invite all the friends to his house for lunch during the Fast. Then there was the time he went to the 19 Day Feast with one of his several children fast asleep on his shoulder. When asked why he had not brought his other children he replied that it was because they were all awake.

One day in July Faizi went to his house at nine in the morning when the heat of the day had already reached a high temperature. Faizi asked his wife where 'The Fridge' was and she told him that he was still asleep on the roof. In astonishment Faizi asked why he had not been woken up to come down before he died in the blazing sun and proceeded to climb up to the roof himself to rouse his friend. He pulled back his friend's cover and told him to get up whereupon The Fridge opened one eye, saw who it was, quickly pulled the cover over himself again and with a defiant voice said, 'What? My body is only just warming up!' At this ridiculous remark Faizi burst out laughing, as did his friend, and together they climbed down into the house.

This loveable man's wife was as endearing as he was. In those early days she was not a Bahá'í but had willingly settled in Bahrain with her husband. She was always welcoming and would often invite the friends for a simple meal of bread and yogurt. Despite having to care for her own family of several children under difficult domestic conditions, she would, in her own unobtrusive way, collect and wash the clothes of several of the young single men in the community. I remember her as a smiling, patient and quiet lady who was generous with the little she and her family had at the time.

Visitors

During this period there were one or two western Bahá'ís working in the oil industry who were posted to Dhahran, the main centre of the oil company on mainland Arabia. One was Joseph Peter, an American Bahá'í who was sent to Saudi Arabia in 1949 as a consultant. As he did not speak Arabic, nor did he have any names or addresses, he had no hope of being able to meet up with any of the Bahá'ís.

Joseph was on one of the trips arranged for newcomers to the town of Dhahran when he and the group he was in were taken to a native rug stall. The merchant came out of his shop and bade them enter and be seated. He offered them tea and then showed them his rugs. However, as the foreign group and the merchant did not speak each other's language negotiations, much to the amusement of the growing crowd of onlookers, became difficult and the merchant started to become agitated, fearing that he was not going to be able sell anything. It was at this point that he spotted a young man in the crowd with whom he was acquainted and excitedly gestured to him to come to his aid because he knew the person spoke both Arabic and English. The young man obliged and started to translate for the customers and the merchant.

Joseph reached out to inspect the knotting on a rug. The expression on the young translator's face changed as he caught a glimpse of a Bahá'í insignia on Joseph's ring. Seeing his expression, Joseph realized that the translator understood the significance of the symbol on his ring but neither of them said anything.

Before leaving the shop the translator asked Joseph if he could step aside from the others and then guardedly asked him if he knew the meaning of the ring's symbol. Joseph responded 'Yes'. The young man beamed with joy but quickly regained his composure and confirmed that he, too, was a Bahá'í. The two discreetly established where and when they could meet then Joseph rejoined his group on their walk through the stalls.

Several days later in a meeting at his hut Joseph learned that his fellow Bahá'í was 'Ináyat Akhaván, the same person who had some time before visited the Faizis in Bahrain. He was earning his living as a translator because he spoke Persian, Arabic and English. In the course of their meeting 'Ináyat told Joseph about the Bahá'ís in Bahrain and strongly suggested that he visit them, saying that he would inform them in advance of his visit.

Joseph was excited at the prospect of meeting the friends in Bahrain and made a trip there. 'Ináyat had given him instructions where to go from the pier and as he approached the store he was looking for he saw a handsome young man dressed in a brown business suit standing at the entrance. On seeing Joseph the young man flashed a smile in recognition of who he must be and bid him enter his shop.

Since it was late in the morning and close to the time for the Muslim's noonday prayer, Joseph's guide decided to close his shop and take him to meet some of the friends. While wending their way through dusty streets he told Joseph they were going to see the Faizi family, as they were generally available and spoke English, remarking that their home had become the unofficial Bahá'í centre for Bahrain. This is Joseph's own account of his meeting with Faizi and the small community:

> When we finally reached our destination M knocked on the door and a voice from within bade him open the door and enter, so he stepped in and chanted a Bahá'í greeting which evoked an even more melodious voice from the second floor above . . . inviting us to enter. As we ascended the stairs I could see an imposing young man in western dress beaming a radiant smile, alongside him was his smiling wife who was also in western dress – my immediate impression was that they were Persian . . . I met Abu'l-Qásim Faizi (more affectionately called Faizi at that time), his charming wife Gloria . . . One immediately sensed this young couple were a living example of the Hidden Words 'possess a pure, kindly and radiant heart', for in all their endeavours they reflected warmth and joy, enthusiasm and determination which infectiously affected the small community of Bahá'í friends and others who came in contact with them . . . During the afternoon Bahá'ís from all over the island dropped by to bid me greetings – how they knew I was on the island or where I was proved somewhat of a puzzlement to me for no one had a telephone or car, so I learned never to underestimate the efficiency of the 'Bahá'í grapevine'!
>
> One facet of his life which always impressed me was that every time I visited the Faizis he was constantly occupied either composing, writing or finishing a letter to a friend or acquaintance somewhere in the world – he must have written at least a half dozen or more letters daily . . . When a letter from Shoghi Effendi was imminent he somehow sensed it coming days before and would become especially happy and radiant in anticipation of its arrival. This prescient ability reminded me of another believer whom I had come to know quite well in 1943

while in Honolulu and who eventually would also be named a Hand of Cause. This was Agnes Alexander who likewise would become excited and elated in the expectation of a letter from Shoghi Effendi.

During my stay I was able to attend a number of Feasts in Bahrain, but . . . it was thought best to exercise caution where any meetings of this type were held . . . This meant that it would take a little while for all the friends to get there before a Feast could get started. The community, other than Faizi's wife, Gloria, and their daughter and son, was composed entirely of men and were Persians just recently arrived from Iran. Mostly these newly arrived wore western style dress and represented a spectrum of backgrounds: merchant, labourer, tradesman, gardener, student, etc. The Feasts held were typical of Feasts held all over the world in Bahá'í communities – starting out with prayers and readings which then led into the business portion of the meeting at which point Faizi as chairman would take over. He then issued a call for any reports, following which he reviewed the news, events, old business, etc. Concerning new business he made sure that each member present had a chance to contribute their thoughts and ideas, following which he would recapitulate these inputs, consolidate the choices and the community would then put to a vote the issue at hand and in short order the matter was settled. There was very little oratory, posturing or heat that we in the States may sometimes experience – it was all very calm, quiet and expeditious, so that very quickly all questions of importance had been decided concerning the community and its functioning. With the completion of this phase the Feast was then generally consummated with some simple refreshments like tea and fruit followed by the socializing of those present.

. . . one could sense that here was a person of ability and great spiritual capacity and I certainly was not alone in such an assessment, for the entire Bahraini community of Bahá'ís seemed to concur in that they all turned to him for guidance and direction. My personal observations would capsulate Faizi as an optimistic-realist who, undoubtedly because of his own children, was keenly interested in the youth and their education, had a quickness of wit and a warmth in humour, while conversing would listen attentively and later respond with intelligence and heartfelt sincerity, could in a few words put a person at ease and with the radiance of his smile make them happy.

Faizi was not only a source of strength to the community in Bahrain but also to those settled in the surrounding states. As soon as anyone arrived in a region Faizi would begin corresponding with him, sharing with him news from around the world and encouraging him to remain steadfast under the very difficult conditions in which he was living. His letters contained 'words which sat so deeply in one's heart that everything else would be forgotten'.

Faizi was extremely generous and loved giving gifts no matter how limited his financial situation. He gave according to his means and prepared his gifts with enthusiasm and care. For example, he would send pictures of scenery from Switzerland and other cooler countries which he would carefully cut out of old calendars and magazines. The recipients would hang these pictures on the walls of their *barasti* or mud dwelling as they were the only evidence of green scenery in those hot places without water and electricity, added to which they were reminders and tokens of the sender's love and kindness towards them.

Faizi's letters would be shared among the friends and in their meetings. They were simple letters but 'because they came from the heart they reached the heart of the reader and listeners'.

Another one of his gifts was extracts from the Bahá'í writings copied in his own calligraphy. Calligraphy was Faizi's way of relaxing and he loved creating pieces with words from the writings then sending them to his friends, a practice he continued to the end of his life. To one of his friends who wanted to learn English he sent a few English books with instructions that he should 'start from the small book and go forward' (he had numbered each book). At the end of his note he wrote, 'They cost about 20 rupees. It would have been good if I could have just sent them to you but with an empty pocket one cannot show off and I don't stand on ceremony with you.'

Not only did Faizi correspond with the young settlers but also with many of their parents in Iran to assure them of the young people's well-being. When one of the new brides was very worried because she had not heard from her father for some time, Faizi sent a telegram to the father informing him of his daughter's anxiety and asking him to send her news of himself to put her mind at rest.

The First Local Assembly

Faizi believed that the foundation for the progress of the Faith in any region lay in the way Bahá'ís conducted themselves and practised the principles of the Faith. He gave as an example the importance the Bahá'ís in Najafábád, from the early days of the Faith, gave to supporting the Bahá'í funds such that they set up a system to contribute to them with ease. Another example was of an Assembly that had so many disagreements that it had a negative effect on the community.

The first Local Spiritual Assembly of Bahrain was elected at Riḍván 1950 in a house rented by three Bahá'í families from one of the men who had made every effort to have Faizi deported from Bahrain. Faizi's joy on this occasion was patent. One of the members of that Assembly recalled that what Faizi said on that historic night 'had such an effect on the hearts of those gathered that it became the touchstone of the Bahá'ís of the region'. After observing that the Assemblies around the world were each formed on the foundation of one of the principles of the Faith to which its members tended to pay more attention, Faizi had said, 'Come, let us base the foundation of our Assembly on self-effacement and absolute nothingness. Self should have no place in our midst; we should all be ephemeral and leave no trace of ourselves because our Lord has said "I want no name or sign after you are gone".'

By the time the Local Assembly was formed the community already had an established programme, which now came under its jurisdiction and through which it continued to guide the community from strength to strength. There were several classes for deepening the community in the history and teachings of the Bahá'í Faith and everyone was engaged in some activity. Children were divided into age groups and attended Bahá'í classes every week, 19 Day Feasts were held regularly and arrangements were made for celebrating and commemorating Holy Days. My mother was the teacher for my age group one particular year so our class was held in our home. By this time we had running water (when water pipes were being laid in the streets my father had got permission for a pipe to run to our house at his own expense) and the treat at the end of our Bahá'í class was for everyone, one by one, to go under the 'shower', which was water from a pipe without a showerhead. We all tried to do our best, to learn well what was taught to us and to memorize our prayers. Once a year at Naw-Rúz a ceremony was held to celebrate our achievements and the Local Assembly would present each one of us with a small gift and a beautiful certificate written in my father's calligraphy and decorated by him with stars.

∽

Not a day went by without both Bahá'ís and other friends dropping in to see Faizi, some for a short visit, some for longer. It never ceased to amaze me, from a young age, that no matter how busy he was my father would always welcome every visitor with great affection and enthusiasm, even though he saw many of them every day.

Apart from members of our Bahá'í community, two of our Bahraini visitors stand out in my memory. They were quite different from our neighbours, friends and acquaintances owing to their particular eccentricities.

Mammad

Mammad Ganúkh was a middle-aged man who had neither relatives nor a permanent home. Whenever he visited us my mother would ask him to do a little shopping for her so that she could give him a few rupees. He was an honest man and always brought back the right change but she never knew when she would get what she had asked him to buy for the meal she was going to cook that day, as it often happened that he would return a day or two later. Once when he came in the early morning she asked him to buy her some fresh fish and stressed that he should bring it quickly as the fish would go bad when the heat of the day set in. Mammad promised he would. It was close to sunset when he casually climbed up the steps to our house with two small, limp fish dangling from a piece of string.

'What happened to you?' asked my mother.

'I bought the fish in the early morning, as you wished,' he replied, 'then I sat down to chat with my friends. I could not, of course, bring you the fish until my friends left.'

What could Gloria have said against such reasoning?

If Mammad visited around lunch time we knew that he had had nothing to eat that day so we shared whatever we were having with him; but he never accepted to come into the room to eat with us, preferring to squat down in the courtyard to eat his meal on his own.

Qulúm

Qulúm was a well-known thief on the island. He stood out in a crowd because he had very dark skin, was tall and well-built with a large lump in the middle of his forehead. Qulúm stole when no one was looking and when caught he would be given a short sentence and thrown into prison. Because of his reputation no one would employ him when he was released so he had no other option but to steal again, which landed him back in jail. He was quite used to this routine and spent his whole life in and out of custody.

My father befriended Qulúm. If he saw him in the marketplace he would buy something and pay Qulúm to deliver it to our house. Qulúm responded to this trust. One day when my father returned home he asked my mother if Qulúm had arrived with the shopping. She said he had not and asked my father what it was that Qulúm was supposed to have delivered. When Faizi told her that he had bought some gramophone records and a few other items she said, 'This has been too much of a temptation for Qulúm. I wonder if we will see him again.' My father, however, never doubted that Qulúm would deliver the shopping, which he did a little later.

Towards the end of the Fast one year my father went to the bazaar to buy the Local Assembly's Naw-Rúz presents for the children of the community. He had bought all the presents when he saw Qulúm, so he gave the parcels to him to deliver to our house but Qulúm did not deliver them when expected. My father, however, did nothing and as always remained confident that Qulúm would appear, but in his own time. He did.

Sometimes, when he was very hard up, Qulúm would knock on our door and shyly ask my parents if they would lend him a few rupees. He always paid the money back. Once, however, when he had asked for more than usual, we did not see him for a long time. Several months later he came to pay the debt and informed us that he had been unable to come sooner because he had been in prison.

Fish and Reconciliation

Everyone on the island worked hard during the day – the men to earn a living for themselves if they were single and for their families if they had one, while the women cared for their children and did the daily domestic chores under difficult conditions, shortage of water being the main problem. The money earned was usually just enough to buy the family's basic needs. One of the Bahá'ís was a tailor who only earned enough every day to buy bread and some greens for his family of five children – he did not have the money to buy enough water for them all. Some people had only rice to eat and occasionally some vegetables such as potatoes or okra. They were, nevertheless, thankful and happy and completely confident that things would, in time, improve. In spite of their personal difficulties, one year the Bahá'í community was able to collect three hundred rupees on the day commemorating the martyrdom of the Báb to distribute among the poor and needy inhabitants of Bahrain.

One of the many amusing stories from this period is that of two friends who had a number of children between them. They would go to the market when they had some extra money to buy fish for their families but they would go towards the end of the day when the fish was on the brink of going off and therefore sold cheaply. In time they were able to afford better quality food. The first time they went to the fish stall after their financial situation had improved was at noon one day. The stall holder smiled at them, put up a finger and called out, 'One minute!' He then obligingly dug into the bottom of the pile of fish and pulled out a nearly fetid one, thinking that this was the way these Persians liked their seafood!

The friends in Bahrain remember that Faizi 'always tried to mend broken hearts and console people'. One friend recalled that his wife, who was not a Bahá'í at the time, became annoyed with him one day because of some incident and that her annoyance continued for some time until nearly the month of fasting. The community had decided that each family would invite two families from among themselves to their home during the Intercalary Days. When they drew up the rota in a meeting, this man remained silent because his wife had told him that she would only invite Mr and Mrs Faizi and he had with equal stubbornness said that if this was the case then he would not invite anyone. Suddenly Faizi (who knew nothing of the state of affairs between husband and wife) put an arm around his friend's shoulder and 'in his usual heart-warming voice' said, 'My wife and I will be at your house tomorrow.'

The friend was delighted but at the same time puzzled and told Faizi, 'It seems that you can see into our hearts and knew that my wife had insisted she would only invite you and your wife and refused my request to invite another family also. I obstinately told her that in that case I would not invite anyone.'

On hearing this Gloria told Faizi that one does not invite oneself but Faizi again said, 'We are invited and will definitely be there tomorrow.' Faizi then asked his friend to tell his wife that the Faizis were coming for lunch. The disgruntled wife was so happy at getting what she wanted that she forgot all about what had upset her and the husband and wife were reconciled.

Guarding the Community

Faizi himself wrote that the community in Bahrain was 'so harmonious that in truth we had divine unity'. The one bad habit the entire community did its best to protect itself from, especially us children, was backbiting. If it ever raised its head on very rare occasions, however indirectly, it would really upset everyone.

An example was when the eight year old daughter of one of the families became dejected without any explanation and continued in this mood for a few days. Repeated questioning by her parents to find out what was making her so sad was to no avail until she one day said, 'Uncle X has a lovely face.' After some analysis of her comment her parents guessed the source of her unhappiness. The uncle was a mechanic and of course his work clothes were black and greasy. He had attended a 19 Day Feast without changing into clean clothes because he didn't want to be late for the meeting and one of the immature youth had casually remarked how dirty his clothes were. It was this thoughtless comment that had upset the child, who could not bear to hear anyone say something negative about any of her dear uncles.

Children and Domestic Skills

Faizi was known for the unbounded love he had for children. It was his unaffected and guileless nature that not only drew him to them but also attracted the children to 'flutter like butterflies' around him.

Dr Manouchehr Salmanpour,[3] who was in the 1950s working for the Shaykh of Kuwait and held a responsible position, recalled being chauffeur-driven to our house the first time he visited Faizi in Bahrain. As he stepped out of the car he saw Faizi in his smart working shirt and trousers sitting in the dust across the street playing with a little boy. When he saw Dr Salmanpour arrive he very kindly said goodbye to the little boy, got up and greeted his friend. As they walked up the steps to our house Dr Salmanpour asked him, with some astonishment, what he was doing sitting in the street playing with a street urchin. Faizi's response was that he saw the boy had no one to play with, so he played with him for a little while.

Faizi regarded the children in the community in Bahrain as being like his own. He delighted in all their antics, felt pride in their achievements and worried with their parents when they became ill or suffered in the extreme heat of summer. He once wrote jokingly to a friend that as human beings are never perfect they must spend some time in hell in the world to come but that as those living in these hot countries were practising from now, they would most probably find hell and its fires 'quite a pleasant corner!' Those from colder climes sweated profusely in the heat, which depleted the salt in their bodies; those from the seaside areas of Iran suffered from eye diseases; the children suffered from prickly heat all over their bodies and many had dreadful boils as well. As summer approached Faizi and Gloria would prepare bottles of eyewash for every family and give them to the mothers, showing them how to wash their children's eyes to protect them from the prevalent eye diseases.

A number of friends whose constitutions were not very strong eventually succumbed to the heat and became very ill. One of them was Gloria, who was reduced to 'skin and bones' and who never quite regained good health for the rest of her life. Faizi sent her to Iran for treatment in the summer of 1950 in the hope that she could be helped. He would often speak about her in admiration and in a letter to a friend that year he wrote,

> I hope Gloria can be treated there and return with renewed vigour and joy and resume her services and be prepared for further tests. You have no idea what a strong heart she has. If she had not been here there would have been times when I would have broken and crumbled to the ground; it is she who has constantly held me firm in the face of difficulties and remembers 'Abdu'l-Bahá's trials and tribulations and with the power of her perseverance saved me from the precipice of danger. In all this time she has not wanted a new dress from me, she has been satisfied with the little I have been able to provide and made our life joyful and happy. This is why her absence is so very difficult for me.

༄

Faizi enjoyed giving lessons to the children when he had time and one year arranged for calligraphy classes for the older ones during the summer months. One of his students recalls a particular summer when Faizi was on his own because he had sent Gloria, Naysán and me to Iran for a month or two. She and another two children would go to him in the mornings and stay till the afternoon. He would give them lines written in his own beautiful calligraphy to copy, prepare their reed pens and make up the special ink for them. They would have a simple lunch which he prepared for them: boiled potatoes. She also remembers Faizi taking a look at her efforts in calligraphy one day and laughingly saying, 'If you put this writing in the sun it will start crawling!' He said the same of my Persian handwriting but the strangest thing was that he said this with such affection and in such a peculiarly encouraging tone of voice that we were never discouraged and continued to make efforts in trying to improve our writing.

Added to his daily schedule of writing, studying and being involved in the community's activities, Faizi, in Gloria's absence, now had to also attend to his domestic chores. He wrote to a friend in England,

> Now that I am alone I must do all the work of the house. Early in the morning I say my prayers and pray for my dear ones abroad, including you. Then I read some passages from the writings of the Ancient Beauty and 'Abdu'l-Bahá and then start copying some of the Tablets, the rough copies of which I have. It takes me 20 minutes to write a page like this. Then I boil my milk and make tea. Before going my wife thought I would never be able to do the job, but now I am trying my utmost to demonstrate all my capacities.

One day after putting the milk to boil on the stove (in those days milk was not safe to drink without first being boiled), he hurried back to the room to listen to his newly bought records.

Faizi and Gloria enjoyed the popular songs of the time played on radio, but the music they enjoyed most was classical: Arabic, Persian and European. I do not recall them having any records of Persian music but they did have a collection of Russian and European ones which Faizi would often play. Some of his favourite compositions were Beethoven's 9th Symphony (which he was convinced was inspired by the spirit of the age), Bizet's *Carmen*, Brahms's Violin Concerto in D Major, *Rhapsody on a Theme of Paganini* by Rachmaninoff and Chopin's Polonaise in A Flat Major and Fantasie Impromptu in C Sharp Minor, to name but a few. He would excitedly express his appreciation of any good voice he heard on the radio and thrilled at any musician's mastery of his instrument, particularly Yehudi Menuhin and in later years Bijan Khadem-Missagh, whom he loved and admired.

To return to the milk, Faizi was so engrossed listening to his music that he came to only after smelling the smoke billowing out of the kitchen. The milk had evaporated completely and the pot was black. As he was determined that Gloria should not come back to a ruined cooking pot he spent days scrubbing it with sand before it was again good for use.

On another day one of his friends came to have breakfast with him. Faizi made sure everything was spotless and clean. He laid the table carefully with bread and cheese and when his guest arrived made the tea and brought it to the table with a jug of milk and a bowl of sugar. He then asked his friend if he wanted to drink milk or tea first and the friend said he would first have a glass of tea. Faizi was so happy that he had got everything right for his guest. He carefully lifted the teapot and poured the liquid into a tea glass. Clear water came flowing out. He had forgotten to put any tea leaves in the pot! They both found this hilarious and spent the next two hours over their breakfast laughing at the incident every now and again and later told the rest of their friends about Faizi's domestic skills.

Faizi tried to keep fit by exercising and, in memory of his childhood escapades to watch the *pahlaváns* through their routines, loved to practise his moves when Shírkhudá[4] came on the Persian radio service every day chanting to the rhythm of the beat on his drum.

'Excuse me,' he wrote in the middle of a letter to a friend, 'but Shírkhudá is striking his drum and I can no longer sit still. With your permission I'll get up and exercise and then continue with this letter.'

Although Naysán and I started to go to school during the last years we were in Bahrain, our parents were our tutors for the first years of our education. My mother opened a small primary school for a short period with about 15 or 20 pupils and my father would help her with some of the classes. I remember when the few English children who attended returned to England their parents wrote to mine to thank them and to say that their children had been placed in classes higher than their chronological age because of the high standard of education they had received from them. At home my father taught me how to read and write Persian and I can bear witness to the level of his patience. I was not studious but he patiently kept me interested and did not give up even though it must have been apparent to him that I was not going to develop into a scholar. He always corresponded with me in Persian and expected me to write back in Persian. His persistence has stood me in good stead.

A Wish Come True

19 July 1950 was, as he put it himself, one of the best days of Faizi's life. As he was about to leave the house in the morning he received a note saying that Hooshang was waiting for him in a ship anchored offshore. He immediately went out to the ship in great excitement to meet 'the light of [his] eyes, Hooshang'. When he and Gloria left Iran they could not take Hooshang with them so he remained behind and was taken care of not only by Mádar-jún but also by my maternal grandmother, Najmiyyih, who treated him as one of her own sons. He was now on his way to Bombay and from there to New Zealand to join Manúchihr and Suhayl 'Alá'í (Gloria's brother and cousin) to study agriculture at Massey University in Palmerston North. Of that day Faizi wrote,

> From that day I am so happy that, thank God, my dear Hooshang has entered the road to progress and because he is an intelligent boy I am sure he will progress in his studies. When I returned home I prostrated in prayer that one of my highest wishes has come to fruition.

Community Life

A year after the Local Assembly was formed it decided to divide the friends into different deepening groups, each responsible for studying a particular book. Each group was given the name of the book they were to study: *The Book of Certitude*, *Tablets to the Kings*, *Some Answered Questions*, *The Hidden Words*, etc. They held their deepenings every week and then in the 19 Day Feasts one member from each group would explain to the rest of the community what they had studied during the month. In this way the standard of knowledge about the Bahá'í Faith in the community improved during the year.

1951 saw one of the severest summers in Bahrain. Faizi wrote to a friend, 'Those who were wise fled and those who were in love and without money, such as the Beloved's friends, remained.' That year there was no respite for a few days from the north wind; what wind there was was either from across Arabia, which was hot and full of sand and grit, or from over the sea, bringing with it heavy humidity which, more than anything else, was the cause of further suffering. The effect of such heat on everyone was that all, adults and children, developed severe prickly heat and boils. The situation was so bad that all Bahá'í activities, including the children's classes, were put on hold, except the Assembly meetings and 19 Day Feasts, and in these two meetings nothing much was done because everyone was constantly fanning themselves and drinking water. Every day mothers could be seen with their children under their veils going to the hospital where there was one clinic and three hundred patients with medicine in short supply. They returned home in the heat of the noonday sun with their children no better. Many families mourned the loss of a child or adult that year but the Bahá'í community was spared any fatality.

Despite her own poor health Gloria sometimes took those who needed her assistance to the hospital. One day when she was accompanying one of the ladies she also took Naysán, who had developed boils under his arms. After a few hours Faizi, who was in the house at the time, suddenly 'felt a turmoil' in his heart. He immediately dressed and hurried towards the hospital to see Gloria walking home with tears streaming down her face and Naysán wrapped in bandages lying almost lifeless in her arms.

Faizi would often intuitively feel that someone was ill, in need of help or even about to arrive on our doorstep. He would time and again tell either Naysán or me to go to the front door and be prepared to open it because uncle so and so was about to climb up the steps, and he was invariably right. This was pure magic to me and in reply to my repeated questioning, 'How did you know?! You weren't standing on the veranda, so you couldn't have seen him coming!' he would just smile. He firmly believed that souls who have a deep love for one another can be in spiritual communication.

Gloria had been told the previous summer when she had gone to Iran that the only way she would get better was to have complete rest in Iran, which for her was out of the question. When Faizi wanted her to go to Lebanon for this particular summer she had refused saying that she would not go without him. One of their friends recommended that she should drink borage tea in the mornings, saying that it would help her stomach pains. Faizi would get up very early every morning to make the tea and take it to Gloria so that she could drink it before getting up. In time this seemed to relieve her pain somewhat but then no more borage could be found in Bahrain and she again started feeling unwell.

Such was the heat and humidity that summer that Faizi found it 'impossible to write' as his extreme perspiration simply wet the paper and ruined any writing. He lost much of his strength so that when he returned home at the end of the day from his lessons in 'Awálí he found he could not do anything else, 'just lie around'. However, he was an avid reader and no matter how tired he was he never stopped reading. It was an article in one of the many magazines and periodicals he received which gave him food for thought. The premise of the article was that one does not get tired from work and that it is only extreme worry that can render one incapable. Having read this Faizi felt that the reason behind his fatigue must be his constant worry over his friends and their children and his feeling of inadequacy in being unable to help them.

Friday Picnics

The highlight of the week for the community was going on a picnic every Friday to 'The Garden'. The first 'garden' was a piece of land belonging to the community on the outskirts of town. It had a *barasti*, palm trees, patches of onions and alfalfa and a large well which we children were not allowed to go near. The Local Assembly hired a bus for these Friday outings and Faizi would gather all the children and spend much of the day with us. In later years this land was sold and a better site bought.

    These picnics were not just a day out; there was a programme aimed at educating us while having an enjoyable day. The children would gather at the appointed house early in the morning to wait excitedly for the bus to arrive. Faizi would be there before everyone else and would keep us amused with games, riddles and jokes so that we never became impatient or out of control. When the bus arrived we would all pile in and sit on its wooden benches. Then it would go round collecting the parents who were ready to be picked up. The friends who had cars would pick up the parents who wanted to finish preparing their picnic and leave a little later. A large block of ice would also be brought to the bus to take with us and some of the boys always managed to break off pieces to suck, paying no attention to the protests from some of the parents on the bus who called out that it would ruin their teeth and give them sore throats. Faizi would not say anything and never prevented the mischievous boys from having their fun.

    When we arrived at the garden our parents would relax and enjoy each other's company while we children were grouped according to our age and started classes and activities for two hours with our allocated teacher before it was time to have the picnic lunch. The older children had sporting activities while the younger ones sat on mats under the palm trees either cutting out pictures from magazines and sticking them into their scrapbooks, with a word or two under each picture, or playing with plasticine.

    One of the children from those early days has written about

the significance for her of the activities arranged for our Friday picnic days:

> I who was just rolling the plasticine into a long rope was baffled because I didn't realize that you had to make something. I thought it was enough to feel the lovely softness of the clay under my fingers and roll it about and just glory in the material and its many colours and how they mixed and blended. But Amú-ján (Uncle, which Faizi was called by all the children) showed me the shapes on the back of the packet and made little shapes himself. A little encouragement caused an awakening in me. A new door was opened within, a new consciousness had appeared. This is such a little incident but it has a significance which I cannot communicate clearly; even though I must have been only four or five at the time I remember it to this day. I think it is one of those moments of transformation . . . when our whole consciousness is awakened and pushed to a higher plane.

At noon different coloured cloths would be spread out in a row in the middle of the palm leaf mats the adults had been sitting on and each family would place their food in the centre of their spread. There would be various simple dishes of rice and meat, big pots of stew, platters of bread and cheese and the fare was shared with all.

After lunch the gardener would start the pump and water ran from the well into a reservoir pool from which it flowed into the channels in the garden to water the palm trees. The dishes were washed in this running water and then the adults lay down for a siesta. We children were not interested in resting and wanted to make the most of the freedom we had but were told to keep quiet. Some of us older ones would roam further away to play and sometimes Faizi would stop the younger ones from making a lot of noise by sitting them down around him in a circle and keeping them amused with various sitting games and riddles to solve. After an hour or so our parents would brew tea and we would continue our games in the garden, swinging on the swing with a wooden seat that the young men in the community had strung up for us between two tall palm trees. We were forever having competitions to see how many of us would succeed in swinging high enough to touch the palm fronds with the tip of our toes.

Towards sunset a last pot of tea would be brewed and sometimes cold boiled potatoes and eggs were handed round. Faizi would then gather us children and say, 'Let us start walking to greet the bus' and we would, with a few of the younger men and women, start walking towards town. We raced up and down the sand dunes, we sang songs, we listened to more stories until the bus which had gone to pick up the adults came along to pick us up. By then we were covered in sand and exhausted. The ride back into town was quieter but we would all be glowing with happiness and already looking forward to the following Friday.

Not one Friday outing was missed until the month of fasting arrived in the first year this activity was established. The parents and the rest of the adults in the community did not feel like going to the garden when they were fasting and suggested in a 19 Day Feast that these weekly outings be cancelled until the end of the Fast. When the Local Assembly discussed the suggestion Faizi expressed his deep concern as he did not want to deprive the children of what we enjoyed so much. A member of the Local Assembly at the time remembered that Faizi volunteered to take us on his own, saying, 'Respected gentlemen, don't take away this joy and happiness from me. I cannot bear to see these innocent children who live in small houses be deprived of the one day in their week when they can be free. Please leave me to myself and don't let it matter that I am fasting.'

The Assembly agreed and he and one other adult took on the responsibility of taking us to the garden.

Generous at Heart

Faizi had a certain endearing simplicity. He did not have a shred of pretence about him and his openness and natural manner was almost childlike at times. He was one of the very few people, if not the only one I have known, whose private and public behaviour were the same. He had a generous spirit and took pleasure in giving, usually small gifts, as a gesture of appreciation and love and it did not matter to him whether he knew the person or not. For example, he read an article in the Persian *Bahá'í News* about 'the Italian doctor who was responsible for purchasing the marble for the Shrine of the Báb'. This had such a great effect on him that he sent the Italian gentleman a Persian miniature via a friend, asking this friend to find the doctor's address and post it to him, saying that 'these are the people who will bring all of us honour'. The doctor was Dr Ugo Giachery.[5] He delighted at the thought of Bahá'í youth leaving their homes and families behind to go to different lands. At one time he sent one such group small pieces of his calligraphy, one for each of them. Enclosed in the envelope was a one dollar bill which he asked them to spend – no more than the one dollar – 'on a simple feast of, for instance, just a glass of tea' so that he could share in the pleasure from where he was, 'Because', he wrote to them, 'whenever I think that a group of youth with zeal and enthusiasm are gathered together, talking about their hopes and dreams, drawing up plans of how to serve the Faith, it creates such a world of joy in my heart that I cannot put it into words.'

As the Bahá'í communities in this part of the world multiplied and developed, so did Faizí's workload. Not only had he by now been appointed an Auxiliary Board Member[6] but he was also even more in demand to give lessons, which he did in order to meet his increased expenses as he was reluctant to ask for any financial assistance from Bahá'í funds. When my mother, Naysán and I returned to Bahrain after being away for the summer months, he wrote to a friend,

> May and Naysán go to school and I see less of them because my work is from afternoon till night when I must teach Arabic. A few nights ago Naysán was crying and saying, 'What is the use

of us returning. I don't see you for even half an hour; as soon as you return home you're off to more lessons and meetings.' He speaks the truth. Because it is winter the students want more lessons and I have more work.

New Employment

After spending years working every hour of the day and well into the night giving private tuition, Faizi was approached by the oil company in Bahrain asking him to teach Arabic to their European and American workers so that they could communicate with the Arab workers – an extraordinary request, that in an Arab country its oil company should ask a Persian to teach its employees Arabic. Faizi drew up three month courses and began tutoring the workers three afternoons a week in 'Awálí where the oil company was based and where the foreign workers lived. A company car would arrive at the entrance to our house half an hour before his lessons began and return him home in the early evening. I remember whenever he returned home, especially after these particular days, he would begin whistling his special whistle of three distinct notes as soon as he opened our front door and started walking up the steps, a signal that he was home and for Naysán and me to run up to him for hugs and kisses.

Faizi's work with the oil company arrived at a very fortuitous moment. Working for only three days a week gave him the release he needed to pursue his work for the Faith the rest of the week and to spend more time studying not only the writings but also his other two favourite subjects of history and philosophy. He received an excellent salary and thereafter he and Gloria had no financial problems.

Although Faizi now had a very good income our lives did not change that much. Whatever he earned was also spent in helping many needy people. He could now afford a few luxuries, but despite the heat of the summer, he was not willing to buy a refrigerator as he knew most of his friends could not afford one.

Instead he arranged for blocks of ice to be delivered to our house and whenever any friends dropped in the first thing he would do was give them a glass of water with pieces of ice in it. If anyone became ill it was often Faizi who would go to their help and pay for their treatment without saying anything to anyone, sometimes not even to Gloria. Much of the information about how he helped families came to light only after his death. The following story related by a young man who was a small child when the Faizis left Bahrain is but one such example:

> I was 15 years old when one day there was a knock on the door of our house. I opened the door on an old woman carrying her young grandchild. She was one of my mother's friends so I invited her into our living room as my mother was busy in the kitchen. We had a photograph of Mr Faizi in this room taken during a talk he was giving at a conference in India. As soon as the woman's eyes fell on this photograph she became excited. 'Is this not Faizi?' she asked and I responded that yes, it was. She immediately took the photograph and kissed it and then gave it to her grandchild and told the child to kiss it too. I was taken aback and wondered why the woman showed such devotion to Mr Faizi as I was always under the impression that Mr Faizi was dear only amongst the Bahá'ís. On questioning her I found out the reason.
>
> Many years ago when this woman's husband died and left her with several children to bring up, she tried to earn money by selling peanuts, chewing gum and such things, but never made enough profit to live by. It was Mr Faizi who supplemented her income and gave her a 'salary' every month. As she said herself, 'It was Mr Faizi who raised my children and was like a father to them.'

✂

The only extra possession Faizi bought was a black Wolseley car.

Both he and Gloria started taking driving lessons but, although he was not a bad driver, Faizi did not take to driving. He left it to Gloria to get her driving licence, one of the first women on the island to do so. Once Gloria had her licence she took over driving Faizi to 'Awálí for his lessons, taking Naysán and me with them. Gloria would read and we would amuse ourselves playing outside the hut where Faizi taught until he finished and then we would all return home together. Having a car enabled Gloria to join the other few members of the community with cars to drive those who needed help with transport.

Faizi's ability to give talks and conduct deepening classes began to be recognized further afield and in 1952 he was invited to conduct classes at a summer school in Pakistan. He made new friends there and added them to his correspondence list. One of these friends recalls that when in later years he stopped responding to Faizi's communications as frequently as he used to, thinking that Faizi now had too much work and he should not impose, Faizi wrote to him complaining that 'this was not the way with friends'.

The Green Pen

Visitors to the community from the outside world were always a source of excitement and joy for the Bahá'í community in Bahrain. One such occasion was during one of the Muslim feasts in 1953. Faizi had gone to visit some of his friends to wish them a happy feast and returned home at noon. Soon after his return there was a knock on the door. He called out asking who it was and at the same time invited his visitor to enter. A tall, well-dressed, well-mannered and courteous black man came up the steps and with a heartfelt greeting pressed Faizi into his embrace and kissed him nine times on both cheeks. Faizi was so taken aback that he did not know what to do but to invite the man into the living room. His guest sat down, said his name was Bashír and that he was a Bahá'í from Khartoum who was at the time working in Arabia for a few months with the agriculture department. He had been in search of Bahá'ís but to no avail, until a young man gave him Faizi's address.

That same afternoon the whole community – men, women and children – came in great excitement to meet their visitor. Bashír chanted a prayer, questions were asked, answers given and the whole group were in a world of their own. The following day the men of the community took Bashír to the airport and in front of everyone embraced and kissed him in farewell, while those around them looked on in amazement. In those days there were hardly any black people in Bahrain and the few who were encountered prejudice. Before leaving, Bashír took a green pen out of his pocket and gave it to Faizi, saying, 'I love this pen very much, which is why I am giving it to you.'

Another significant visitor to our small community was Brian Giddings, who at the time was captain of a ship which occasionally dropped anchor off our island. Whenever it did Captain Giddings would come ashore to visit the friends. I remember the first time he walked up our steps and introduced himself as a Bahá'í. My parents were completely overcome with emotion as this tall, gentle Englishman in his white captain's uniform embraced them. It had been a very long time since the small band of believers had had contact with any fellow believers from abroad. News of Captain Giddings's arrival quickly spread as arrangements were made for the community to meet and welcome him and with every subsequent visit the bonds of friendship between him and the friends in Bahrain grew stronger.

Launch of the Ten Year Crusade

When in 1953 Shoghi Effendi launched a ten year plan for the Bahá'í world community, the Ten Year Crusade, with five intercontinental conferences, Faizi and Gloria together with another Bahá'í from Bahrain decided to attend the fourth conference in New Delhi, India, held from 7 to 15 October. Faizi guessed that some of the Bahá'ís from the surrounding countries attending the conference in India would be travelling on the same ship we were to board, the *Dwarka*, so he bought third class tickets, as he knew many of them would travel this way. He and our fellow traveller had a bet: Faizi was sure that there would be other Bahá'ís on board but our friend did not think so and the agreement was that whoever lost the bet would buy the evening meal on the ship for as many Bahá'ís as were on our deck. When we boarded the *Dwarka* the number of Bahá'í passengers rose to 27. True to the agreement, the Indian meal was bought but the curry was so full of chillies that no one was able to finish it.

Some of the Bahá'í passengers had first and second class cabins but as passengers from the lower decks were not allowed on the upper decks, they preferred to leave the comfort of their area to join the friends on the lower deck so that they could all be together during the day.

Among the first class passengers were two Arab millionaires with whom the Bahá'ís on the same deck exchanged greetings every day. One of the millionaires asked one of the Bahá'ís where she was going and why, and she explained that the Bahá'ís were going to New Delhi to attend an international Bahá'í conference. He then asked this lady what the difference was between Islam and the Bahá'í Faith, but as she did not speak Arabic and her English was not good enough, she asked him if he would like to discuss the subject with one of her friends and he willingly accepted. The lady immediately went to Faizi and explained the situation to him. The Arab gentleman invited Faizi to the upper lounge area where he and his friend asked him questions. When Faizi started answering the questions these two men interrupted and spoke to one another, quoting from the Qur'án. Although the lady did not understand Arabic she became agitated when she saw Faizi sitting patiently and 'in silent dignity', listening to what they were saying. She whispered to him that they were taking advantage of his silence but he told her quietly that he had found in his experience that some people need to express all their own views in a discussion without listening to others and that one has

A Friday picnic with some of the friends, Bahrain

Adults and children playing together on a Friday picnic, Bahrain

Faizi in our main room during Riḍván, Bahrain 1950s

Faizi and Hooshang in New Zealand, 1954

Faizi with Bahá'ís in India; Hushmand Fatheazam, *standing far right*, 1955

Faizi and Masih Rowhani, *to his left*, with pioneers to one of the Gulf states, 1950s

Faizi, Gloria and Naysán the day Gloria left for Europe, 1955

Hand of the Cause Mr Samandarí arriving at 'The Garden' for the election of first National Spiritual Assembly of Arabia, April 1957

Left: A very happy Mr Samandarí on the day of the election of the National Spiritual Assembly of Arabia, April 1957

Right: Faizi giving 'The Fridge' a bear hug during the National Convention, April 1957

Delegates in discussion, National Convention, Bahrain, April 1957

The first National Spiritual Assembly of Arabia (one member absent) with Hand of the Cause Mr Samandarí and his companion, General Sohrab, *to his left*

Faizi with Bahá'ís in Basel, Switzerland, before receiving news of his appointment as Hand of the Cause, September or October 1957

Faizi standing by the coffin of Shoghi Effendi, London, November 1957

Faizi helping Hand of the Cause Mr Samandarí down the steps of the Master's House, Haifa, 1957

Hand of the Cause Hasan Balyuzi and Faizi on Mount Carmel, 1961

Hand of the Cause Paul Haney and Faizi, Riḍván, 1961

Faizi with Bolivian Bahá'ís, 1963

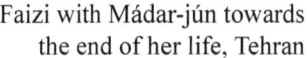

Faizi with Mádar-jún towards the end of her life, Tehran

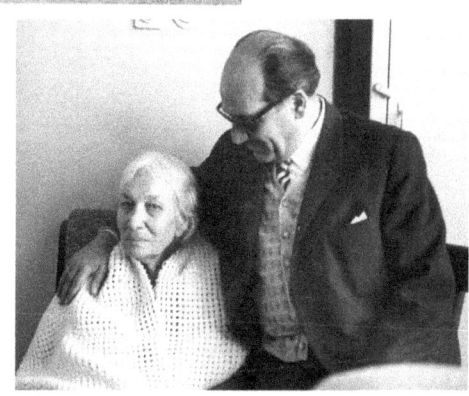

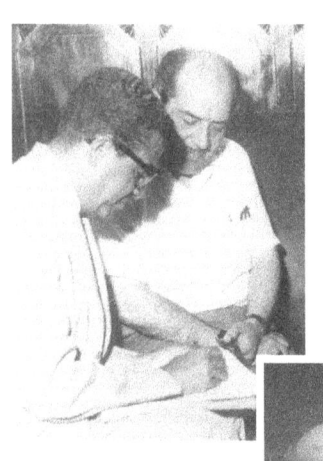

Faizi and Amoz Gibson

Rúḥíyyih Khánum and Faizi

Faizi addressing the Bahá'ís on the last day of the World Congress, Royal Albert Hall, London, 1963

Meeting with the President of India, *left to right*: Shirin Boman, President Dr Zakir Hussain, Shafíqih Fatheazam and Faizi, October 1967

Faizi and Sorab Payman in front of Michelangelo's *David* in Florence, 1968

Faizi and Naysán, late 1960s

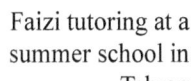

Faizi tutoring at a summer school in Tehran

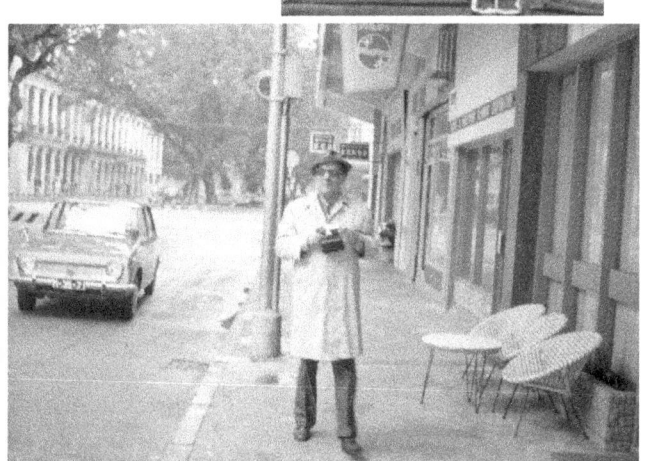

Faizi in Macau, January 1969

Faizi with Bahá'ís of Dahomey (now Benin), 1970

Faizi with Bahá'ís of Brazzaville, May 1970

Faizi visiting Bahá'ís of Najafábád in 1971

Faizi visiting Hand of the Cause Mr Banání and Mrs Banání and their son Hosni, April 1971

to allow them to say all they have to say until they empty themselves and have nothing more to express. And this is exactly what happened. Once they had had their say they gave their full attention to Faizi's explanations.

The journey from Bahrain to Bombay took about ten days. The friends had dawn prayers together every morning and in the evenings gathered to benefit from the learned among them. My memory of that trip is that Faizi was elated and happy throughout the journey and that the Bahá'ís on board never seemed to tire of his company. They spent every day sitting in a large circle, drinking tea, listening to each other's experiences and laughing a lot.

Arriving in India

A number of youth had been given the responsibility of taking care of the needs of some of the overseas visitors who were going to give talks and conduct sessions at the conference. One of them had been told that among the group assigned to her was a believer from Bahrain. She thought to herself that someone from there probably knew little English, so when she met her charge she spoke to him in very simple English and he responded in like manner. Pleased with herself for handling well what could have been a difficult situation, she was later stunned to see the same man on the conference podium skilfully translating the Persian talks into English! It was Faizi. She realized he had responded in simple English on that occasion so as not to cause her embarrassment.

Ten Hands of the Cause attended the conference in New Delhi: Shu'á'u'lláh 'Alá'í, Dorothy Baker, Músá Banání, 'Alí-Akbar Furútan, Ugo Giachery, Horace Holley, Dhikru'lláh Khádim, Tarázu'lláh Samandarí, Valíyu'lláh Varqá and Charles Mason Remey. Faizi was the chief translator at the conference and after the sessions was constantly surrounded by friends wanting to ask him questions. The evening sessions were open to non-Bahá'ís and Faizi would be found there, sometimes until midnight, answering enquirers' queries. He was so exhausted by the last day of the conference that when he was asked to chant a prayer he fainted as he tried to stand up. He was immediately attended to and someone else took his place.

During this period the National Assembly of India had arranged for two groups representing those attending the international conference to meet the president of India and the prime minister, Jawaharlal Nehru. Faizi and Gloria were in the group to meet the president. No one knew that they were really interested in meeting Nehru and they certainly said nothing about their preference. However, for reasons they never understood (it could have been an oversight), their names were placed on both lists so their wish to meet Nehru was granted and he autographed two of his books for them.

A Trip to Australasia

According to the directions given them by Shoghi Effendi, the Hands of the Cause were to travel to different countries after the conference. Mr Furútan, who was assigned to go to Australasia, sought Shoghi Effendi's permission to ask Faizi to accompany him as his translator. They boarded an English ship from Bombay on 25 October 1953 with eight Australian Bahá'ís who were returning home, while Gloria sailed back to Bahrain with my brother and me.

The journey from Bombay to Freemantle took eleven days. On the second day out to sea the Bahá'í contingent gathered together to elect three from among themselves to arrange dawn prayers and teaching activities while they were at sea. They had firesides every three days in the ship's social hall at which more than 50 enquirers attended on each occasion. Faizi was able to have some rest during this trip and recharge his batteries before the ship docked at Freemantle on 5 November 1953. He and Mr Furútan embarked on a tour of 42 cities and localities in Australia and New Zealand where Bahá'ís resided.

An Australian who was not a Bahá'í at the time remembers

that his first impression of Faizi was that he had 'an almost superhuman expression of humility, a total lack of ego' and that it was this quality that attracted him 'so strongly to this remarkable man, and through this to the Faith itself'. 'And yet,' he went on, 'along with this, there was in him an air of nobility; he walked like a prince and when he walked through the market others seemed to step aside as if to pay their respects to a kingly figure.'

During their stay in Australia Mr Furútan and Faizi were guests at the Yerrinbool Summer School (December 1953/January 1954). A few days into the school the committee of youth who had been given the responsibility of supervising and organizing morning and afternoon teas realized that the biscuits kept disappearing during sessions so they decided to keep them in the kitchen where no one was allowed, especially the children who were the chief suspects. However, the biscuits still kept disappearing. Eventually the culprit was found: Faizi. He would go into the forbidden room – no one, of course, thinking of questioning or stopping him – fill his pockets with biscuits, fold his arms and with great dignity walk out and distribute the biscuits among the children.

After having spent so many years in Bahrain, Faizi really enjoyed his tour of Australia and New Zealand and meeting the Bahá'ís from those countries, observing that 'the sun of truth these days shines in multi-coloured shades and each individual glass reflects its own innate and specific colour and beauty'. He particularly enjoyed meeting the friends from Persia who, had it not been for the 'stimulus given to the Bahá'í world by the beloved Guardian' would never have thought of travelling such distances and settling in these far off lands.

Mr Furútan and Faizi visited every centre where Bahá'ís lived, some of them living in very humble circumstances. Many of the friends remember Faizi telling them stories about the believers in Iran and 'peppering his anecdotes with jokes and a degree of warmth and light-heartedness' which held them spellbound. One of the families they visited in New Zealand lived in Dunedin – they were the first believers to settle in South Island and were at the time still the only Bahá'ís there. Faizi, as was his way, embraced the man of the house on meeting him and when leaving, but the man, who was used only to a handshake in greeting and farewell, was a little uncomfortable at this display of affection. This same Bahá'í met Faizi again in Sydney 25 years later but as he approached to embrace Faizi he detected some hesitation on Faizi's part, as if he was waiting for him to make the first move. It crossed the man's mind that Faizi had hesitated because he remembered his unease at being embraced all those years ago, but then dismissed the notion as he thought to himself that Faizi had met thousands since then and there was no way he would remember him. However, his conjecture that this had been the case was confirmed when he read the account of an incident which took place while Faizi was lecturing in Vienna. Years before, when Faizi was involved in organizing and conducting children's Bahá'í classes in Iran, he had asked a boy in one of his classes to say a prayer but the little lad had obstinately refused and in the end said that he could not because he had a bad tooth. This same boy, now a grown-up young man, was in the audience in Vienna and went up to greet Faizi during an interval. To his astonishment, as Faizi warmly embraced him he whispered in his ear, 'How is your tooth?!'

Return Home

It was during Faizi's absence in the winter of 1954 that Mr and Mrs Banání and Mr Samandarí visited Bahrain. Mr and Mrs Banání stayed with us and Mr Samandarí stayed with one of the young Bahá'í couples. Our community had a most wonderful time during their entire stay. It was in January of the same year that the plane Dorothy Baker was travelling on stopped in Bahrain to pick up passengers to London. Among the passengers from Bahrain were the two young daughters of a Jewish family and the teenage daughter of one of the prominent families in Bahrain, all being sent abroad for their education. The plane crashed in the Mediterranean Sea on its way to London and there were no survivors. The grief of the two families was felt by everyone in Bahrain and, of course, the Bahá'í community also grieved the loss of such a shining star of the Bahá'í world.

On his return to Bahrain Faizi immediately started corresponding with the new friends he had made in Australia and New Zealand. His letters to different continents invariably shared news about their fellow believers in another part of the world, giving them information about their lives and indirectly encouraging them to persevere wherever they were. In his first letter to Australasia he wrote,

> These lines come to you full of love and greetings from your brothers and sisters . . . Ever since I returned to Bahrain I am constantly writing to them and telling them tales of love, devotion and sacrifices of our dearly beloved brothers and sisters all over Australasia and still they want me to write to them, and in all their communications they ask me to offer to each and all of you their sincerest love, prayers and greetings.

In another he describes how it took two young men 50 days to reach their destination in a sailing boat. One of the men, who knew there was no medical service where he was going, had taken a bag of medicines with him and set out in the desert, going from village to village and tent to tent treating those he could treat. The other had gone to one of the islands where, apart from the occasional sailing boat, the people had no form of communication with the outside world. They fished and gathered shells and whenever a sailing boat came by they would exchange their shells and dried fish for provisions such as rice, dates and coffee. The friends in Bahrain had tried for weeks to send more medicines and some provisions for the two men but were not able to because there were no boats going in that direction.

'Though apparently in absolute destitution, misery and hardship', wrote Faizi of these young men,

... yet we must see what they write of the ecstasy and joy which is theirs in those far off corners of the world. Words fail me to tell you with what beautiful poems and sentences of love and enthusiasm they fill their letters. They have nothing in mind but to reach their goal town and are ready to bear all hardships and suffer every deprivation because they are sure that the clouds will break away, the clear horizon with full éclat will shine on humanity and their endeavours will not be in vain.

The Avid Reader

Faizi's daily contact with the outside world was through the radio, the books he ordered and the several magazines and periodicals to which he subscribed. Apart from works of literature in Persian and Arabic, he enjoyed the works of many of the European and American writers, such as Shakespeare, Alexander Dumas, O. Henry and John Steinbeck, and revelled in any book on Greek mythology, abridged editions of which he would buy for us to read. He spent any leisure time he had not only enjoying the classics and studying the Bahá'í Faith and the teachings of other beliefs, but also reading on a variety of other subjects. Most of the summer of 1954 was spent 'reading the works of a single author, Stefan Szweig, a German psycho-socialist writer. Of this man's works Faizi wrote,

> ... most of his books and stories show the depth of the human soul in love, hatred, jealousy, etc. I liked them very much. But now I must read lots of books on History, especially History of Civilizations, because I found my little knowledge about this topic very helpful in my general lectures during my tour in India and Pakistan.

I remember how excited he was when he received a number of books he had ordered written by the historians Arnold Toynbee and Will Durant and reading passages out to my mother, who was also interested in similar subjects. Many years later he made this interesting comment in a letter to a friend about something he had come across in a pile of papers he had been given to go through:

> It is about five days that I am here and am drowned in these papers. Some are very interesting. Others are copies of the Tablets and some original letters of the early believers. In one of them I found something which shook me from head to foot and that was an oral statement of the beloved Master quoted in one of these letters. He has said that in the whole of the universe nothing ever dares to stand against God the Creator except 'self or ego'. Now I am more sure of my own statement in the study of history, that the history of man is nothing except the accounts of man's struggle against the Word of God.

In those days Bahrain had nothing to offer by way of theatre, museums or art galleries, although it did have an open-air cinema to which we were taken when a suitable film was being shown, particularly any with Red Skelton or Charlie Chaplin, as my father found Skelton's humour hilarious and regarded Chaplin as a genius. My parents, however, exposed us to the world of art through books and the many publications they had which were filled with copies of well-known paintings and photographs of famous sculptures. My father's pleasure was beyond measure when in later years he was able to stand face to face with many of the works of art he had thrilled over in his books, particularly the works of Michelangelo whose statues of David and Moses were among his favourites.

As children it was the *National Geographic* we looked forward to most and we would spend hours going through every new edition with our friends, marvelling at the photographs. My father also had a habit of cutting out interesting and beautiful pictures from magazines and sticking them in albums for my brother and me and our friends to look through. Going through these albums now I see that they are simple, colourful pictures of garden scenes, flowers, mountains and such like, but they enchanted us at the time and carried us into a world other than the one of heat and barrenness that were our surroundings.

Beginnings of Change

From this time on the pattern of Faizi's future life gradually started to take shape as he would increasingly visit the Bahá'í communities in the Gulf states as well as be invited to summer schools in other countries. Separation from his family was always very difficult for him but he endured it and never allowed it to come between his service and obligations to the Cause. While on board a ship to India in October 1954 he wrote in his diary:

> O God, it is two days now that I am away from Gloria and the children. I cannot endure two days, how am I going to last two months, especially from Gloria who is so weak and unwell? In truth, it was her right to travel to perhaps bring about some change in her health. Please God protect this treasure for me . . . She now has to deal with everything on her own . . . If God grants and keeps her safe for me I will not have any other sorrow. Please God, give me some of her pain so that she can have some relief because she is the one who deserves comfort, she is the one who deserves your blessings, not me. May my life be a sacrifice to you, my Gloria; you have done so much for me . . .

Parenting Alone

By the time Faizi returned to Bahrain Gloria's health had deteriorated even more, so he arranged for her to go to Europe in 1955, not only to seek treatment but also for some respite. Although friends were always there to help and often invited us for meals and a helper came every day to wash our clothes and sweep the floors, Faizi was the one who took care of Naysán and me for the nearly nine months our mother was away. How he managed to do that, teach and remain involved in all the Bahá'í activities I don't know but my memories of those months are that he was always there for us, that we laughed a lot, that we would all sit and write to my mother once a week and that he was not a good cook. His best meal was opening tins of corned beef into a frying pan, mashing it down and cracking eggs on top. He was also good at boiling potatoes and eggs. I remember trying to cook a meal for him during the Fast. I don't remember what I cooked but do recall that, in my ignorance, I put a heaped tablespoonful of turmeric and an equal amount of salt in the boiling water. When it was time to break his fast my father first drank some tea and then I served him the meal. He took a spoonful and immediately ate a large piece of bread before hugging and kissing me for making a meal for him. Although he did not eat any more of the food, he never mentioned the taste or criticized my cooking. It was when I took a mouthful myself that I realized, apart from the turmeric bombarding my mouth, it was saltier than the Dead Sea!

While my mother was in Europe my father had to go to one of the other states to visit the Bahá'í community there. Several families offered to take care of Naysán and me for the one week he was going to be away but he would not accept their offer and took both of us on this trip, even though it would have been much easier for him if he had left us behind.

When my mother returned to Bahrain she told my father the doctors had said that as long as she lived in Bahrain she would continue to suffer with ill health. She, however, was not willing to leave the island she now regarded as her home.

Troubles Brew

It was in this year during the Muslim month of fasting that a Persian Muslim cleric, Falsafí, came on Persian radio every noon to speak against the Bahá'í Faith, which gave rise to yet another period of persecution. Faizi used to listen to Falsafí's tirades, and as much as our parents wanted to protect us, we could sense their anxiety about the state of affairs in Iran. One day when one of our neighbours came to our house at noon while Faizi was listening to Falsafí, he became upset and asked Faizi why he was listening to such prejudice when in their house they turned their radio off every time the man came on, such was the level of this family's friendship and loyalty to my parents.

It was also during this summer that, because of false rumours spread about them by one man, the Bahá'ís in one of the nearby states – men, women and children – were thrown into prison, a number of the men beaten and then all of them deported by boat.

I remember my father becoming very worried one day with some news he had received and then going to an Assembly meeting and not returning home till after we were asleep. That night my mother told Naysán and me that she was going to say a special prayer for some Bahá'ís as they were in trouble. A few nights later my mother took us to the roof but did not stay with us. I lay wide awake with half an understanding of what was happening. The house below was in complete darkness. After some time I heard someone stealthily come up our steps, followed by others at different intervals. It was the dead of night; I could hear nothing except what I imagined was the occasional murmur of quiet conversation in the living room. The men who had gathered in our house were the ones who had been deported. The women had all been taken in by the rest of the community.

Growth and Maturation of a Community

By now the Bahá'ís in Bahrain were a mature, loving, united and well-organized community with smoothly-running activities for adults and children alike. The community had had the excitement of welcoming young and beautiful brides for several of the young men – a few of them coming out to marry without having met their prospective husbands – and organizing the couples' weddings. The foundation of these marriages was the couples' desire to serve the Faith and to my knowledge almost all have been successful and happy unions.

I remember one of the wedding feasts in the Bahá'í Centre. The Local Assembly had bought a huge, round tray and filled it with gifts for the newlyweds, nothing very expensive but practical and useful items for setting up home. One of the Bahá'ís known for his quick wit and repartee placed this tray on his head and swaggered into the room where everyone was gathered, with a group of us children trailing behind him singing and clapping. He placed the tray on the table in front of the simply dressed bride and groom and then began giving them the presents, one by one, with some amusing explanation as to the use of each item. In no time the entire room was helpless with laughter at his hilarious interpretation of what each gift could be used for.

Among other things, the Local Assembly had asked the friends to be prepared for hard times and had itself stored some rice to distribute should it be necessary. An efficiently functioning Child Education Committee, with the help of the young couples, organized the Friday outings, while members of the committee visited the children's homes to teach them how to keep their rooms and books tidy. Of this committee Faizi jokingly commented that, 'Thank God they don't come to inspect my room as even I don't know where my various papers are, let alone anyone else!' The group of young couples themselves studied English with Faizi two nights a week and Faizi would ask them to write the sentences they learned in English, Persian and Arabic so that they would improve their Arabic as well.

In December 1955 Faizi was asked by the Hands of the Cause in Iran to visit Bahá'ís in a neighbouring country. Naysán and I were very upset that our father was, once again, leaving us. As if foreseeing a life of separation Faizi wrote in his diary:

> I am still thinking of my two beloved ones. Naysán said, 'One day Gol-jún [Gloria] leaves us and travels, another day you'; but they must become strong and used to this life of pioneering

and know that being together is not that important; what is important is to be there for the Faith and it is our life's duty. If the Faith requires us to be away from each other forever we must accept it with complete happiness and joy and know that our well-being and blessings lie in that.

In 1956, as the heat of another summer started creeping up, Faizi insisted that Gloria take my brother and me to stay with Gloria's uncle, Núrí 'Alá'í, and his wife who were at the time living in Turkey. He was 'suffering and pining for five months' during our absence which, together with the heat and humidity, put such pressure on him that he felt he could not do much work. While we were away trouble brewed on the island, with the movement associated with the labour unions calling for political reforms and the end of British involvement in the affairs of the island. A curfew was imposed, all the shops and offices were closed and the political situation was unstable for several months. Faizi, who was waiting impatiently for news of our return at the end of the summer season, was afraid that all ports of entry would be closed. On top of his worried state of mind he also became ill. But despite his anxiety and illness he did not lose his sense of humour and wrote to a friend, 'Of course the friends took care of me and Mrs M's soups forced me to remain sick so that I could enjoy her chicken broth for longer.'

A United, Supportive Community

With the summer heat abating and with his family back with him, Faizi threw himself even more diligently into work and his vast correspondence. The Bahá'ís had, of course, remained completely outside the political turmoil during the troubles and by then everyone knew that they never interfered in any political affairs and were only interested in being of service 'to all the people of the world no matter what race, colour or sect they belong to'. What they did do in their weekly meetings was to pray for the whole of mankind to be liberated 'from under the burdens of sheer ignorance and prejudice'. They also shared with one another letters they had received from fellow believers in countries close to them.

One day a letter from a couple was read out at their weekly meeting. Living where they were was very difficult as sailing boats went there at most three times a year so that the inhabitants had to make sure they had enough provisions with them for at least one year and with these provisions they were able to barter for other goods needed for their daily living. With the exception of the letters they received whenever a boat sailed in, the couple were completely cut off from regular news and letters from their friends, Bahá'í administration and the rest of the world. Notwithstanding the very difficult living conditions they wanted to remain where they were, but in this last letter they had written that their provisions had come to an end and that they were going to have to leave by the first available means of transport. This part of their letter made the friends so despondent that they decided there and then that they would do their utmost to help.

News of the couple's predicament spread rapidly to the other Bahá'ís in the area. Some wrote to say that they had collected about two thousand rupees and were sending wheat, rice and any other provisions they could, while others sent money. Faizi was overjoyed and wrote enthusiastically to some of his friends about the demonstration of such support and unity.

Support from the Motherland

Inspiring letters of love and encouragement were continually received from the Hands of the Cause. These letters were immediately sent to the houses of the friends so that everyone had a chance to read them. The Hands of the Cause also had private and individual correspondence with all the centres and friends. Of Mr Samandarí, Faizi wrote at the time,

> Jináb-i Samandarí, though more than 80 years old, weak and

all the time suffering from many ailments, never ceases to go about. His letters are masterpieces of the perfect art of Persian handwriting and full of love, hope and news . . . I myself envy anyone who has a letter from him in the week when I happen to be forgotten by him. He writes to Brazilian friends . . . and to the friends of the Pacific besides writing to so many, many other people in Iran.

Regarding leaving one's homeland to settle in another country, Faizi wrote to a friend:

> As for your statement that pioneering includes difficulties, with all due respect I raise my voice and beg to differ. In my opinion there are no conditions laid for pioneering except obedience and purity of motive. There may be those who remain at home but be counted as pioneers by the Blessed Beauty; and there may be those who have run barefooted across the sands of Arabia but not been accepted . . . pray that even if difficulties are endured they be with acceptance, happiness and purity. In her last talk in Karachi Dorothy Baker related that when she entered the presence of the Guardian the smell of roses made her as if drunk so that she fainted. When she came to she heard the Guardian say to her, 'A thousand welcomes to my martyr pilgrim.' After regaining some strength she asked the Guardian why he referred to her as a martyr and he said it was because she had requested to come on pilgrimage four times and four times he refused and asked her to instead carry out a task which she undertook with joy and resignation. In the same way we don't know who is accepted in the field of pioneering.

It was his love for Shoghi Effendi that gave Faizi the tenacity to endure difficult conditions. Years later in a letter to a friend he wrote,

> When I said goodbye to our dear, dear Guardian and left the

Holy Land for Iran my life became a perpetual yearning for looking at his countenance again. No day passed without me sitting somewhere and closing my eyes and bringing him closer and closer to myself. The way he walked and talked became so vivid in my mind that I thought I am again with him. This strengthened me and kept me and my family alive in the most terrible conditions ever possible for 15 years.

Almost everyone who met Shoghi Effendi fell under his spell but there were those men and women who were charged with such a deep, binding love for him that it completely changed their lives and enabled them to render outstanding services to the Cause of Bahá'u'lláh. Faizi was one of these. He spoke about the Guardian to his fellow believers: about the burden of responsibilities placed on Shoghi Effendi's shoulders, the breadth of his vision for the progress of the Cause, the beauty of his translations of the writings into English and the love he had for all of them. He heightened their devotion and love for the Guardian as well as their enthusiasm to carry out his wishes and plans with complete obedience, confidence and joy. It was this, together with their deep love for Bahá'u'lláh and a firm belief in His teachings, that made these believers tenacious. They did not give up when faced with challenges so severe that it would have broken the resolve of ordinary men and women. They continued to persevere, to return like waves to the shore until they were able to establish themselves and become as one with the inhabitants of their chosen land.

The Gathering

The National Spiritual Assembly of this region was formed in April 1957, 14 years and four months after the Faizis set foot on Bahrain. When the Guardian called for Bahá'ís to settle in this part of the world he advised them to refrain from speaking about the Faith to the inhabitants. Not being able to speak openly about their beliefs focused all their energy on looking within themselves to try to live their lives according to the teachings of Bahá'u'lláh and to developing and strengthening their respective Bahá'í communities. The Bahá'ís of Bahrain were fortunate to have among them a believer of the calibre of Faizi who was instrumental in the maturing process, not only of his fellow believers in Bahrain, but also in influencing the development of the other communities in the Peninsula with his deep knowledge of the Faith, his wisdom, his constant communication with every centre and his countless letters of encouragement to individual believers.

Preparing for the election of the first National Assembly was particularly exciting for the community in Bahrain as Shoghi Effendi had instructed that the delegates should gather for the convention on their island. A representative from the National Assembly of Iran, who was to accompany Mr Samandarí to Bahrain and 17 delegates from eleven surrounding states, were also expected to attend. However, it seemed that all doors from every direction were closed as, once again, the Bahá'ís, for no apparent reason, faced opposition. The head of the visa section had specifically said he would not issue visas to Faizi's friends and threatened to deport the Bahá'ís. The friends in Bahrain made no protest in the face of such opposition; all they could do was be patient and pray for a solution.

With their usual determination all the delegates, except one, eventually got themselves to Bahrain in launches, sailing boats and aeroplanes but with great disappointment Faizi had to go out to the ship carrying Mr Samandarí and his companion to tell them that he had not been able to get them permission to land and asked them to go on to the next port of call. Mr Samandarí's message to the friends in Bahrain was to keep trying as there was 'no lock without a key'.

Two of the young believers who lived in Muharraq (an island linked to Manama at the time by a bridge) but worked in Manama would always be on the lookout every morning as they approached the bridge for anyone who might need a lift across. While Faizi was giving the disappointing news to Mr Samandarí, one of these men was surprised to see his neighbour, the secretary of one of the shaykhs, standing by the bridge. He stopped his car and picked him up. The neighbour explained that his car had broken down that day and was in for repairs. Looking at the young man giving him a lift, the passenger asked him why he was looking so despondent? To avoid the complication of explaining his relationship to Mr Samandarí the Bahá'í said that his uncle was trying to enter Bahrain but could not as he had not been granted a visa. The passenger immediately asked for the uncle's name so that he could put the request to his boss, the shaykh. Our young pioneer made bold and said that as his uncle was an elderly gentleman, he had a companion who would also need a visa. 'Give me his name too,' said his passenger. And thus the head of the visa section was overruled and Mr Samandarí and his companion were granted permission to land in Bahrain just before the cannon sounded the end of Ramadán and the beginning of the Muslim festivities. A moment later and everything would have had to wait for several days, which would have meant that Mr Samandarí would not have been present for the election of the National Assembly.

An amusing story was told by one of the delegates. One must remember that this was many years ago and this part of the world was yet to enjoy the progress and high standards it enjoys today. The delegate related that when three of them went to the hospital for their smallpox vaccinations before travelling to Bahrain they were directed to sit and wait. They waited a while, by which time there was a long queue of people wanting the same vaccination. A man came out and asked them all to stand up, roll up one sleeve and put their arms out. The man then walked down the queue putting a drop of the serum on each arm. He was followed by the doctor with state-of-the-art equipment: a nail hammered through a piece of wood. To the men's horror, the doctor went down the queue scratching one arm after another with the same nail! As soon as they returned home the men washed and squeezed their wounds in the hope of getting rid of any infection they may have contracted. They met up with a friend who had been there longer than they had and told him what had happened, thanking God that at least they had been at the head of the queue and the first to be vaccinated in this manner. Their friend, who was well acquainted with the hospital, laughed and said, 'What? That doctor has been using the same nail for years now!'

Far from the Madding Crowd

On 30 April 1957, in a corner of 'The Garden', 'far from the madding crowd of humanity', in a *barastí*, 27 men gathered in a spirit of love and unity. (Given the strict customs in this part of the world on the association of women with men other than family members, Shoghi Effendi had advised that, for the time being, the women should not be considered for election onto Assemblies. This was for the protection of the Faith at the time. Now both men and women are eligible to be elected.)

'A certain magic power had made them tongue-tied,' Faizi wrote of his fellow delegates.

> They were so weak, frail, unknown and materially poor that no one considered their gathering as anything important. They were given the task of erecting a pillar which could stand all the storms, gales and catastrophes for at least a thousand years. Such a Herculean task for such frail bodies in such cruel circumstances and with so few means was so tremendous that they could not even utter a word.

An unusual quiet gripped the group gathered in the simple, unsophisticated palm leaf hut, each in silent wonder of the power which had brought them together and overcome with feelings of humble servitude. Suddenly the silence of their reverie was broken by Mr Samandarí's voice rising beseechingly in a chant, shaking them from their trance and bringing them into the stupendous reality of the responsibility placed on their shoulders. The distant shore of Arabia could be seen clearly from where the *barastí* stood. Ever sensitive to the world of nature and attuned to the drama of the moment, Faizi recorded, 'As evening descended something unusual happened: the skies darkened, thunder roared like unto the word of God; lightning ensued and with every strike bathed both shorelines in light. Just as suddenly the thunder and lightning passed away, leaving us in silent darkness. And then it started to pour with rain.'

The new National Assembly received the following cable on 5 May 1957:

> GUARDIAN CABLES DELIGHTED ASSURE NEW ASSEMBLY LOVING FERVENT PRAYERS . . . FERRABY

When Mr and Mrs Banání were on pilgrimage just before the election of this National Assembly Shoghi Effendi had told them that its 'firm pillar' will be Faizi.

Destiny

Faizi flew away from Bahrain to another state on 27 June for the second meeting of the newly-formed National Assembly, promising all of us that he would return within ten to 20 days. At the end of the last session of the National Assembly meeting one of the members suddenly suggested that Faizi should go to Tehran on their behalf to discuss a number of their concerns with their sister National Assembly. He was to stay for 20 days before returning to Bahrain. Faizi immediately sent a telegram to Bahrain informing us of his delayed return and headed for Iran.

Making the most of his presence in the country, the National Assembly of Iran asked Faizi to conduct sessions for two weeks at the summer school. Faizi stayed with Mádar-jún during this time but she complained that now that he had returned after ten years she still did not see him because he left the house at seven in the morning and returned at eleven at night. Towards the end of the summer school my uncle received news that his son, who was in

Germany, was going through some difficulties so he asked Faizi (who was close to his nephew and two nieces and who adored him) to go to Germany to help his son. Faizi agreed. At the same time the National Assembly asked him to meet with the Persian Bahá'í youth living there, after which he was asked to participate in the Swiss summer school. Once again, Faizi had to inform Bahrain that his short absence was now going to be two months.

Faizi's original plan had been to travel to India from Iran and on his return visit Bahá'ís in several centres before returning to Bahrain. On hearing that Faizi's return home was delayed one of the friends from Bahrain who happened to be in Iran went to Mr Furútan and asked why, when there were others who could do the same job, Faizi was being sent. He argued, as if he had a premonition, that they only had this one Faizi and they needed him. Mr Furútan explained to him that the decision was not his.

When Faizi left Bahrain it was with a light heart, still rejoicing in the knowledge that a National Assembly had been formed and already looking forward to his return to Bahrain and his life there. Little did he know that he was destined never again to set foot on what had become his homeland, nor did he know that in his first message to that region the Guardian had addressed him as 'the Spiritual Conqueror of Arabia'.

11

The Road of No Return

Faizi was still in Germany on 2 October 1957 when the Guardian's telegram appointing eight new Hands of the Cause of God was sent to the Bahá'í world. They were Hasan Balyuzi, Collis Featherstone, John Ferraby, Raḥmatu'lláh Muhájir, Enoch Olinga, John Robarts, William Sears and Faizi.

Faizi was not aware of this dramatic change to his life until he arrived in the German suburb of Basle. He was astounded when given the news and did not initially accept that it could be true, repeatedly saying, 'I am not worthy of such a rank. God forbid! God forbid!' He broke down weeping when shown the text of the telegram.

Faizi kept to the assignment given him by the National Assembly of Iran and continued to meet the Bahá'í youth around Germany. Towards the end of October the friends in Frankfurt were delighted to be informed that not only Faizi but also Mr Khádim would be meeting with them on 4 November. On the appointed day one of the Bahá'í youth made his way to the Bahá'í Centre in great excitement as he had known Faizi since childhood but not seen him for twelve years. Arriving at the Centre he found Faizi sitting in a corner of an upstairs room sobbing. Faizi rose, embraced the youth and in a voice full of anguish told him that Shoghi Effendi had passed away in London.

Numbed with such devastating news the youth left the Centre to return home and grieve in private. As he stepped out onto the street he saw Mr Khádim, who had just arrived from Paris and was completely unaware of the events of the last few hours, in search of the Centre. As soon as he was given the news Mr Khádim broke down. The young man, seeing that he could not now leave him, guided him to the Centre but outside the front door Mr Khádim

225

asked him to go inside and bring Faizi. The two men embraced in the street and sobbed helplessly on each other's shoulders.

Mr Khádim and Faizi eventually went inside the Centre where the secretary of the National Assembly of Germany was in constant telephone contact with the National Assembly of the British Isles about arrangements for Shoghi Effendi's funeral. Rúḥíyyih Khánum had asked for as many of the Hands of the Cause as possible to be present on the day of Shoghi Effendi's interment. The two men, having with great difficulty reined in their emotions, went to the British Consulate for visas to Britain only to be told that they would have to wait a few days. They returned to the Centre dejected but the youth, who had remained with them, asked Faizi if he had told the British Consulate that the Guardian of the Bahá'í Faith had passed away and that they had to be present at the funeral. Faizi said he had not and immediately returned to the Consulate where he was informed that the Consul had been instructed to issue visas to any Bahá'í who applied. The meeting for that evening was cancelled and the small group remained in the Bahá'í Centre until one in the morning, when Mr Khádim and Faizi went to their hotel to spend a restless night.

In the midst of this shattering news and drowning in the ocean of his own sorrow, Faizi's thoughts flew to the friends on his island home. He wrote them this letter the following day:

> Dear companions, my friends in Bahrain and other centres
>
> Yesterday we received a telegram to pray for the protection of the Faith because the beloved Guardian was very sick. After one hour when we gathered to arrange for a prayer meeting news was received that that holy spirit had winged its flight. In the afternoon a telegram was received from Rúḥíyyih Khánum that we must all be patient and cling to the institutions with one heart and one aim. In the evening a telegram was received that on Saturday 9th the funeral will take place in London and that the Hands of the Cause, members of National Assemblies and

Auxiliary Board Members should attend after which the Hands of the Cause will meet . . . to then announce what they are going to do. This, in brief, is an account of this mighty event which I know you have been waiting to know and which I give you in great haste and in complete sorrow. Memorial meetings should take place throughout the world on the evening of 9th November . . . I will inform my dear ones of whatever happens. Faizi

Faizi kept in constant touch with those he had left behind during this period, advising them firstly to remain firm and secondly to be silent in the face of any possible attacks from the enemies of the Faith and not to enter into any speculation about the Hands of the Cause and where they would be, stressing that all must concentrate on protecting the Faith in complete unity. In another letter he wrote:

> I have no strength or joy to write you a detailed letter. I don't know when I will be saved from this depth of sorrow . . . I still don't know where I will go and what I will do; what is clear is that my visa for Bahrain expires on the 25th of this month and I have to renew it, but how and where I still don't know. I just want to let you know that if you don't hear from me for some time it will be because of the volume of work, but you will always be in my prayers. As God is my witness, I close my eyes and pass through all your homes; I always pray for the children and hope that you don't forget me in your prayers as I am in need of them.

On the day of the Guardian's funeral, as the vast gathering of mourners stood in silence waiting for the coffin to be lowered to its resting place, Rúḥíyyih Khánum 'felt the agony of the hearts around her penetrate into her own great grief. He was their Guardian. He was going forever from their eyes, suddenly snatched from them by the immutable decree of God . . .'[1] She decided that those who wished could pass by the coffin to pay their respects.

For two hours believers who had managed to fly in from around the world filed by the coffin and had their own moment or two with their Guardian. In deep mourning some stood with bowed heads, some knelt, some fell to their knees and placed their forehead on the ground. One of the believers who was a young woman at the time recalled seeing 'a tall, strongly built and gentle man who helped the weak, the old and the feeble to their feet' and that he had bent over, held her hand and helped her to her feet when she was unable to raise herself from her knees. She learned later that the man was Faizi.

Rúḥíyyih Khánum had told Faizi that, if he was able to hold back his tears, she wanted him to chant the 'Prayer for the Dead'. Khánum's request gave Faizi some sense of calm and he chanted the prayer without shedding a single tear. It was his last farewell to his Guardian, which he bade with a burning heart.

12

The Holy Land
A Change of Direction

Faizi had no idea what his future would be, what would happen to his family or whether he would return to Bahrain; nor was he preoccupied with these uncertainties. Many years later, recalling the months after the passing away of the Guardian, he described himself as being 'like a bush thrown on the torrent of the Will of God and carried about', and wrote, 'I had no will of my own in any of these events. They came over me just like waves of the ocean of the mighty Will of God.'

Although Faizi and his fellow Hands were each in their own way struggling with the weight of their grief, their entire focus was on protecting the Cause of Bahá'u'lláh, ensuring the unity of the Faith and fulfilling the plans of the Ten Year Crusade Shoghi Effendi had left behind for the worldwide Bahá'í community to complete.

༚

Twenty-six of the 27 Hands of the Cause gathered at the Mansion of Bahjí on 18 November 1957 for a memorial meeting (Corinne True, because of her advanced age and infirmities, was unable to attend), after which they entered the Shrine of Bahá'u'lláh, and 'in utter humility at the Sacred Threshold'[1] beseeched help and guidance. Details of their deliberations in the following few days are well recorded in Bahá'í history. What was crystal clear in the message they sent out to the Bahá'í world was that the Hands of the Cause were there as a shield 'to preserve the unity, the security and the development of the Bahá'í World Community and all its institutions'.[2] In their first meeting they decided on the formation of the body of the nine Hands of the Cause to reside at the World Centre to 'energetically deal with the protection of the Faith whenever attacks, whether from within or outside the Bahá'í community, are reported by Hands from their areas or by National or Regional Assemblies, or whether they arise within the Holy Land'.[3] They also had the added duty of managing a heavy administrative burden, one that Shoghi Effendi had, with only a few to assist him, managed on his own for 36 years. It was in November 1958 that they took the momentous decision to call on all the National Assemblies to gather in the Holy Land at the end of the Ten Year Crusade in April 1963 to elect the first world governing body of the Bahá'í Faith, the Universal House of Justice.

Faizi, together with the rest of the Hands, was not only now plunged into long hours of consultation but had the added responsibility of simultaneously translating proceedings into Persian for Mr Samandarí, Mr Banání and Mr 'Alá'í who spoke no English. In writing about Faizi's role as translator for the Persian-speaking Hands of the Cause, Mr Furútan recalled that 'he never expressed any discomfort or tiredness'.[4] With the exception of Rúḥíyyih Khánum, whose home was the Master's house, the Hands of the Cause arriving at the World Centre for their Conclave were all accommodated in what were then the Eastern and Western Pilgrim Houses. Faizi and Hasan Balyuzi were so anxious to help Rúḥíyyih Khánum in her grief that she housed them in the building situated to the right of the outside gate of the Master's house in the room opposite the room that 'Abdu'l-Bahá had occupied so that they could be at hand in offering her comfort during those very difficult, lonely hours immediately after the departure of the Hands and the end of the first Conclave.

Some years later Faizi was asked at a summer school in Britain if there were any stories or experiences he could share of his years at the World Centre between the passing away of the Guardian and the election of the House of Justice by way of conveying the significance of that time. He replied that it was such a painful period that he did not want to talk about it and moved on to the next question.

THE HOLY LAND: A CHANGE OF DIRECTION

Rúḥíyyih Khánum, Amelia Collins, Leroy Ioas, Hasan Balyuzi, 'Alí-Akbar Furútan, Jalál Kházeh, Paul Haney, Adelbert Mühlschlegel and Mason Remey were the nine Hands of the Cause elected to remain at the World Centre. As Dr Mühlschlegel was not able to take up this post, Faizi was designated to replace him. The door to Faizi returning to, or even visiting Bahrain, was now completely closed.

The Exile

In his despondency Faizi wrote to his friends in Bahrain,

> I told myself that when I return and embrace you all and hug the children my grief may ease but it seems that fate has other plans for me and is going to deprive me of being with you. I have to stay here and I have no will of my own except to obey. In these days if there is anything one can do they must. Why was it that God the Bestower did not bring me here when the beloved Guardian was alive? . . . It is true that I am a pilgrim here on behalf of all of you . . . that I am the servant of Khánum, but I still pine in my separation from all of you. What stories I had gathered in my travels to share with you, what things I bought for the children . . . all has ended. It seems that a part of my life has died and I have entered another life where I will have no connection with you. A few nights ago Dr Ḥakím showed us the various things the beloved Guardian had given him at different times. We told him how lucky he was but he responded, 'I don't want any of these. I want him.' I too want you, I want the children. How much patience does a man have to have to be suddenly snatched, without any warning, from all he was attached to and his beloved ones? Although nothing is set or certain yet the thought of never returning, or if I can when it will be, makes me very despondent and sad. I pray that God grants me patience to endure and if I can do anything to do it well.

Some months later he wrote,

> It is seven months now that I am away from and forbidden to return to my nest in Bahrain. I travelled for some time in Europe and met with the youth and was thinking of travelling to other countries when the sudden passing away of the Guardian occurred . . . We endured a period of suffering . . . we were protected otherwise we would not have been able to take a single step forward because with every step there were a thousand difficulties . . . As soon as the sun goes down I start wandering in my mind from door to door; my belongings are all in Bahrain, my wife and children in Pakistan, my mother in Tehran and I myself here . . .

The volume of work placed on the shoulders of Hands was such that at one period Faizi had no time in 15 days to go to the Shrine of the Báb. Giving an indication of what state the Hands were in so soon after the loss of the Guardian, he wrote in one of his letters. 'God have mercy on us. Our condition these days is very bad. Some faint at work, some are so afflicted that they are not able to work'; and in his diary he wrote, 'O my Lord! Grant me the strength needed to begin this work. To me it is infinitely hard. I am like unto the one who is on the edge of a frozen lake and is invited to plunge in.' He then adds, 'This is a task that I have adopted for myself ever since I was 18 when, accompanied by Hasan Balyuzi, we were invited to enter the room of the beloved Guardian.' He felt there was no escape. Even so, his separation from Bahrain proved to be very difficult for him.

'No one believes that in this holy place I am constantly sad,' he wrote. 'This is a mystery which I may be able to explain when we meet in the afterlife. In brief, with the slightest excuse my burning heart flees to the desert of Arabia and Majnún-like searches for its Laylí and Laylá.'[5]

THE HOLY LAND: A CHANGE OF DIRECTION

Faizi's capacity to maintain his correspondence with hundreds around the world, regardless of all his other duties, was remarkable. His letters were written late at night after a full day's work and, if he was travelling, on buses, trains or aeroplanes. A Bahá'í youth at the time of one of Faizi's visits to Germany recalls Faizi giving him a bundle of letters to be posted every morning, ones that he must have sat up well into the early hours to write after an intensive day and evening of study with the friends. He loved receiving letters but complained about the ones written, for example, with 'pale blue ink on pale blue paper and envelope', which made deciphering the writing difficult, especially the address. This worried him because he had a strong sense of responsibility to answer every communication, even if it was a postcard. His letters were not just 'thank you' letters but contained words of encouragement, interesting news and many of the ones written in those early days after the passing away of the Guardian are an insight into the life of the Hands of the Cause based in the Holy Land as well as what they did in their rare free moments.

Amongst Faizi's correspondents were a number of children. His letters to them were very sweet, always on pretty paper and nearly always with one of his pieces of calligraphy enclosed. These letters would not be enclosed with the letter to their parents but rather posted to the children individually.

'It was almost the only post that I received as a young girl', recalled one recipient, 'and it was for me something very special.'

༄

Faizi had moved into rented accommodation once it was established that he was not returning to his homeland. There was an apple tree outside the bedroom window of the house he was living in during his first spring. He enjoyed looking at this tree when he lay down for a short rest in the afternoons, especially when little children from the neighbourhood crept up to it to pinch some of its blossoms. As soon as they were near the tree he would get up and tap on his window. The startled children would start running away but he would wave them back and let them know in sign language that they could come back and pick as many blossoms as they wanted.

To the Bahá'ís in Bahrain with whom he shared many of his innermost thoughts and feelings, he wrote,

> It seems that the wound is becoming more painful by the day . . . Khánum is not comforted, her eyes are tearful, her heart burning. She occupies herself during the day by working hard towards accomplishing the plans and wishes of the Guardian . . . she does not sleep much at night and is growing weaker by the day . . . Two nights ago Khánum asked to me to tell her about you. I felt so excited that I could not string two words together. Despite this I told her about the endurance of the friends, about the marriages between couples who had not seen or knew anything about each other and how all of them have been successful unions. It made Khánum happy.

One of the ways in which Faizi dealt with his heartache was to do everything he could to help Rúḥíyyih Khánum manage her grief. He and Mr Furútan were the only two Hands who did not return to their respective homelands after the Conclave and together they kept Rúḥíyyih Khánum occupied in the evenings and sometimes late into the night so that she would not dwell on her sorrow. Mr Furútan started giving her lessons in Persian writing and dictation, and Faizi played chess with her and helped her gain more experience in Persian calligraphy, an art Shoghi Effendi had introduced her to, and even wrote for her a line or so of what is known as '*mashq*' (calligraphic models) for her exercises. He wrote to Bahrain asking for his decorated papers – of which he always had a collection for his own calligraphy and letter writing – to be posted to him urgently, as he needed them for Rúḥíyyih Khánum. He believed she would 'work with more enthusiasm' if she had attractive paper to write on. He was astonished at the speed with which she mastered writing with reed pens and at the level of improvement in her calligraphy in a short time.

Rúḥíyyih Khánum spent much of the first summer after the passing of the Guardian in the Mansion of Bahjí with Milly Collins and Dr Alice Kidder, who was there to see to her needs. Faizi would often stay with them for a few days after their meetings. In the evenings when Rúḥíyyih Khánum and Milly Collins, and anyone else who was there, sat on the balcony of the Mansion looking down on the beautiful gardens below, he would chant the poems of famous ancient Persian poets for them.

'. . . what a marvellous voice he had,' Rúḥíyyih Khánum reminisced in a talk she gave in Canada shortly after Faizi's death. 'Really, he could have been a singer. He had a superb voice. Very deep, very velvety, very rich. What a pity they were never recorded . . . It was a unique and never-to-be-forgotten experience.'

When we were children in Bahrain Faizi often drummed out rhythms in the *zúrkhánih* style on a wooden chair for Naysán and his friends to exercise to. This was not something he did in public but he did it for Rúḥíyyih Khánum on an Arab drum she had and chanted the Sháh-Námih[6] for her. Rúḥíyyih Khánum recalled in the same talk,

> Well, if you could hear Faizi with that soft, glorious voice of his just gently tapping on this drum and singing the Sháh-Námih, I tell you, it was one of the experiences of a lifetime . . . But he was very shy about it, he didn't do it very often because it was not exactly the kind of occupation that the Bahá'ís were supposed to have, particularly a Hand of the Cause! It meant a great deal to me.

Rúḥíyyih Khánum always remembered what Mr Furútan and Faizi did for her and paid tribute to them in this extract from her talk:

> . . . I can't describe what condition I was in and really, so much

of my surviving this terrible thing that had happened to the Bahá'í world, and of course to me personally, the passing of Shoghi Effendi, was due to the love and kindness of these two to me . . . they did everything they could, with Milly Collins who lived with me and later with Dr Kidder, to try and take my mind off my burning condition. So that I owe these two Hands particularly a very, very great debt of gratitude for what they did for me personally.

Faizi became better acquainted with Rúḥíyyih Khánum during this period and described her in one of his letters to Bahrain:

It is impossible to find another like Khánum. I believe that this lady is not of human kind; she is an angel who was brought to earth for the Guardian to be his companion. She has no equal in speech, in writing, in wisdom, kindness and love.

He always wrote to Rúḥíyyih Khánum when he was travelling or when she was away, and she to him. In a letter to me in August 1969 she wrote, '. . . he says he wrote me 3 letters – I have only received *one* so far. Do tell him this and that there are 2 ties with Betty Reed for him (for his trip).' Faizi always felt very protective towards Rúḥíyyih Khánum and remained devoted to her to the end of his life.

As for his relationship with the Bahá'ís in the Gulf regions, particularly those in Bahrain, Faizi never stopped yearning for them. He kept in constant touch with them, even on his long travels around the world, and gave them news of all the places he had visited, in many instances describing the people and natural beauties of a particular country. He let them know in advance if he was going to be in a country where he thought they might be able to rendezvous with him. To one of the friends he wrote, '. . . you have no idea what is happening to me in my separation from all of you. I remember you on Friday mornings, especially the children who must have grown more and become more sweet and

THE HOLY LAND: A CHANGE OF DIRECTION

mischievous', and he eased his nostalgia by reminiscing about his life with them in his letters, recalling the evenings they gathered for a simple meal of bread, cheese, yogurt and herbs. He dreamt of them frequently years after he had left: he dreamt he was saying goodbye to them, that they were all gathered in the Mansion at Bahjí bidding each other farewell and saying they would not see each other again; that he was in Bahrain, walking in the back streets so that no one would see or recognize him. When he woke up he would worry, wondering if they were all right, if the children were well and happy. Once when he returned to his home in the Holy Land after a long period of travelling he fell on his bed in total exhaustion, looked around his room and was transported to our house in Bahrain, thousands of memories flooding back. He imagined embracing and kissing all the children, he 'heard their cries and their laughter and saw their sweet smiles'. A year before his death he wrote to them, 'No one knows the depth and strength of our relationship.'

Faizi held on to as many links as he could with Bahrain. For example, he continued to make donations to the funds of the Local Assembly of Bahrain and on one occasion wrote, 'I am sending you a sum of money in my mother's name. I'll send some more whenever I can . . . I hope you will accept it. Even if I contribute a thousandfold I will still not be able to repay my debt to that esteemed Assembly.' When, years later, he heard that the friends in Bahrain had hung a large photograph of him in a prominent position in their new Bahá'í Centre he became very upset. He wrote to them immediately and reminded them of their first Assembly meeting when they had made a pact to be nameless, 'to be together, one in heart and united as brothers' and begged them to remove the photograph.

On a more personal level, Faizi the family man found being separated from his family particularly difficult, especially as he had no idea whether we would ever be together again. My mother had left Bahrain with Naysán and me and moved to Murree, a hill-station in the lower ranges of the Himalayas in Pakistan, as it would have been impossible for us to continue living in Bahrain without my father.

A Brief Visit

In September 1958 Faizi participated in the International Conference in Djakarta. He then had to attend a summer school in Karachi, which my mother also attended, after which he was to come up to Murree (Dr Muhájir[7] came with him, but I cannot remember how long he stayed). Naysán's and my euphoria deflated somewhat when he arrived as we took in the change in our jovial, fun-loving father. Although he made every effort to be light-hearted it was evident that he was tired, exhausted and broken. The death of the Guardian had etched its pain in his heart and the expression in his eyes.

The threat of separation hung over our heads during my father's entire stay and nine year old Naysán constantly told him that he did not want him to go away again. Although he was in need of as much rest as he could get in the short time he was with us, my father decided to take the two of us away on our own for a weekend in Rawalpindi, the nearest town. We stayed in a hotel and he tried to cheer us up by taking us shopping; but his main aim was to talk to us at length about the sudden change in our lives, to explain why he had to leave us again and that until a decision was made by the Hands we would have to remain living apart (of the nine Hands of the Cause chosen to reside at the World Centre, my father and Hasan Balyuzi, and later John Ferraby, were the only ones with school-age children).

Although my father would himself show deference to anyone he held in high esteem, and at times drew attention to an individual related to a well-known Bahá'í, he did not like it if anyone expected to be treated differently from others on the basis that they were related to an eminent personality, be they from within or without the Faith, and would feel extremely uncomfortable if he himself was treated with exaggerated respect. On one occasion

THE HOLY LAND: A CHANGE OF DIRECTION

when a group of Bahá'ís on pilgrimage started praising him and the other Hands of the Cause and questioned him about their station, my father's response was, 'We must not think too much about "station"; we are all servants of the Blessed Beauty, working together for the Cause.' He then begged those present not to praise the Hands of the Cause, saying that hearing the praise of the friends was not good for them. He gave Naysán and me a word of warning that weekend: he told us that although he had been appointed a Hand of the Cause, which carried with it a heavy duty of responsibility, it had nothing to do with us and that if he ever heard or found out we had become boastful because we were the son or daughter of a Hand of the Cause he would be extremely upset and displeased with us.

Naysán's and my relationship and love for our father was deep and intense – even when he used to go out to teach every day while we were still in Bahrain we would greet him on his return home as if he had been away for months, so saying goodbye to him was always extremely difficult for him and for us, and it did not get any easier as we grew older. My father hoped that we 'would not be too tearful this time' when he left but on his return to the Holy Land he wrote to a friend, 'God knows with what tears I had to, once again, be separated from Gloria, May and Naysán. My heart still burns with the memory of it.'

My father, who was, of course, very aware of the distress of every goodbye, had mentioned his concern to Rúḥíyyih Khánum before coming to visit us in Murree. The evening after his arrival he handed me a letter from Khánum, addressed to me. I quote from it because it contains words of wisdom and comfort for anyone finding themselves in the same situation. It is dated 9 September 1958 and parts of it read as follows:

> Your dear father has been very much concerned over the fact that when he goes to see you and your brother and mother he will again have to part from you in order to return to his important services here as one of the Custodians of our beloved Faith.

He remembered how difficult for you the 'good bye' was last time and is afraid this next one will again make you suffer. That is why I want to write to you now to tell you something of my own life and feelings.

. . . you will increasingly have to bear the burdens of life which come to us all as we grow older. So much depends on how we meet these burdens mentally. When I was a child – and a girl – I was very often separated from my mother [May Maxwell], whom I adored, because she was a member of the N.S.A. and not in good health and she used to go to America for the sessions and be gone sometimes for many months – and I suffered and longed for her! I was an only child (you are lucky to have a brother) and this made it all the harder. But as I look back on life now I see it was much better, indeed a great blessing for me, to have a mother who put the Cause of God first and sacrificed even her beloved child for it. This was a true example for me, it made me not only realize how great and Holy our Faith is but it also made me proud of my mother as a Bahá'í and as a noble and high-minded human being. So many children can love their parents but don't have any reason to be truly proud of them. You, May, can be proud of your father because of his great devotion to the Faith and to our beloved Guardian which makes him put service above family, even above his love for you which is so deep and tender.

So dear, if you again suffer when you must say good bye to your father, suffer proudly, knowing this wonderful Faith of ours is worthy of any suffering, indeed of the sacrifice of our very lives, and be glad you have such devoted Bahá'í parents with whom our beloved Guardian was always pleased . . .

Family life is extremely important in the Bahá'í Faith and the cornerstone of any civilization. There should, therefore, be a sense of balance between bringing up children and serving the Faith as they are one and the same; so I doubt that Rúḥíyyih Khánum, who was not a lady of extremes, was advocating that parents should

THE HOLY LAND: A CHANGE OF DIRECTION

serve the Faith to the detriment of the emotional well-being of their children. What I believe she meant in her letter was that there are times when, for the greater good of others, sacrifices must be made. This is what the faithful Hands of the Cause did, particularly during the period after the loss of the Guardian and the election of the first Universal House of Justice.

Return to Work

Faizi returned to Haifa and was immediately admitted to hospital, close to death. The emotional stress and pressure in the wake of losing the Guardian had taken its toll and he was diagnosed with very high levels of glucose in his blood. However, hospital staff took such good care of him that when he was discharged after 20 days he had no need for insulin or medication but was told that he had to be very careful with his diet. He was to battle against diabetes for the rest of his life.

Now that he was no longer cocooned in his close-knit community Faizi felt as if he had 'died from that world'. He and his companions were at the helm of not only the Ten Year Crusade but also responsible for the protection of the Faith. What they achieved in the intervening five and a half years is recorded in detail elsewhere. Suffice it to say that their achievement was nothing short of a miracle and a living demonstration of the power of the Covenant of Bahá'u'lláh in keeping His followers, from backgrounds of every race and creed, united and focused on bringing the Plan their Guardian had left for them to a triumphant conclusion.

※

Despite the fact that most of the news and reports received at the World Centre were positive, Faizi could not understand why his sadness and sorrow did not leave his heart. He tried to hide his feelings once the Bahá'ís resumed coming on pilgrimage to the

Holy Land but some of them could detect the melancholy and questioned him about it.

'God knows what has happened to me in this period and in what fire I am burning,' he wrote to Bahrain.

> I have transformed and am sad that there is no remedy but to spend some time communing with you. I become more detached from the world day by day, second by second; I long to go to the next life; hour by hour I become more despondent and sad . . . What a difference there is between the magnificence of the Cause and our behaviour . . . Day by day the Guardian becomes clear to me and moment by moment I understand why that pure heart stopped and am surprised that it did not stop before . . . Khánum says think with what people the Guardian accomplished all he did and then you will be even more surprised. She says that one of the biggest characteristics of the Guardian was that he worked with great strength and determination and pursued the job in hand to the end. For instance, he would say the builder should come at six in the morning. At four in the afternoon he would ask if the man had been sent for and would be told yes. At seven in the evening he would ask what the man had said, is he going to come or not? He would be told that he had promised to come. At eleven at night he would say don't forget, he has to be here at six in the morning. This was one of a thousand duties he had on a daily basis but he paid attention to all the minor jobs. It was with this force that he pushed the work forward. How different this is to the way we do things: if something is not done today it can wait till tomorrow, if not this year then next year.

Resumption of Family Life

By 1960 work routines had been established at the World Centre and decisions about the family life of the Hands of the Cause could be made. Faizi was sent to the United Kingdom in the early part of the year and to Latin America from May to July. He was, of course, in constant correspondence with us (we were by now living in India, where my mother was the superintendent of the Bahá'í New Era School in Panchgani) and kept us abreast of where he was. He was back by the autumn and with great excitement began making preparations for our arrival as my mother, Naysán and I were going to join him.

Rúḥíyyih K͟hánum invited us for dinner the evening after our arrival. My father was very excited, not only about introducing his family to K͟hánum, but more so about taking us to 'Abdu'l-Bahá's house to meet the Guardian's wife. My recollections of that evening are hazy. I recall my father being anxious that Naysán and I should behave impeccably, that my mother was feeling quite emotional as it was the first time she was returning to the house of 'Abdu'l-Bahá since her childhood and that Naysán and I were feeling overawed by all that was happening to us. K͟hánum, with her own particular charm, immediately put us at our ease. Although we dined quite formally in the small dining room, the feel of the evening was relaxed and at one point K͟hánum remarked that my father was not saying much – he just sat there glowing, with a smile that did not leave his lips all evening.

Not wanting us to 'see everything at once', my father had drawn up an itinerary to take Naysán and me to each of the holy places at a slow pace. The first place we went to, of course, were the Shrines of the Báb and 'Abdu'l-Bahá. How different to our lives in Bahrain only a few years before and how we all remembered members of our spiritual family still there! We basked in the warmth of our father's company as he took us, mostly on Saturdays, to all the Bahá'í historic sites, giving us a brief history of each and telling us stories, while at the same time taking care not to overwhelm us. At no time did he tell Naysán or me to behave in any particular manner in the Shrines or any of the other holy places but rather left us to respond to the spirit of the Shrines in whatever way came naturally to us.

We lived in my father's two-bedroom third-floor apartment at the foot of Mount Carmel below the Shrine of the Báb for several months and Naysán and I started going to school. Like any father, my father was always proud of our achievements but he never spoke about them to others. When Naysán, who attended the local school, gave his first talk about the Faith a year after he started there, Faizi proudly recorded the event in his diary and asked God to protect him.

We were still in this apartment when the Bahá'í month of fasting arrived. My father woke me up every day before dawn by tickling my cheek with his moustache and by the time I rose and went into the tiny kitchen he had already made a pot of tea and put out a breakfast of bread, butter, jam, cheese and boiled eggs; he would close the kitchen door quietly so that we did not disturb Naysán and my mother (who was unwell and unable to fast). There was no need to look at the time because my father could tell from the light in the sky when the sun had risen. After finishing our breakfast he would quietly chant the long prayer for the Fast. It was magical looking out across the bay from the kitchen window in anticipation of the rising sun with the sound of that subdued, warm voice in my ears.

After some months my mother found more suitable accommodation and we moved to a house on top of Mount Carmel. Khánum always took an interest in our lives, as she did in the lives of all her friends, and I remember her going shopping with my mother for various essentials such as crockery and cutlery for our new home. She would often invite us to spend the evening with her, usually on Friday nights. John Ferraby, who initially came to the World Centre on his own, would join us after he became one of the nine Hands resident there and we would sit in the room in the Master's house which Khánum had made her own and where she kept her parrot and many of the interesting artefacts she had collected from around the world. It was a cosy, welcoming room and completely informal. Khurshid (one of the ladies working in the Master's house) would bring in various delicious dishes and we would eat sitting around two or three small coffee tables or balancing our plates on our knees. Often, as soon as we had finished eating and the dishes were cleared away, the scrabble board would come out and a competitive game ensued, with Naysán usually partnering my father and me siding with either my mother or Khánum. John Ferraby, who never took as much time as the rest of us putting his letters down, played very quietly and without fail won every round, hands down.

Among my mother's duties at this time were guiding at the Shrines of the Báb and 'Abdu'l-Bahá with Dr Luṭfu'lláh Ḥakím during the hours the Shrines were open to the public and changing the flowers in the two Shrines. She often replaced the flowers with wild ones in springtime which we would pick during the weekend. We did not have a car so it was Dr Kidder who drove Khánum and us to the countryside where we would have a picnic and then start picking flowers such as asphodels, boraginaceae, tall vetches, broom, sword lilies and crown daisies by the armful. I don't recall my father ever joining in; he just enjoyed the scene before his eyes and nine times out of ten took a nap. There were times, too, when Dr Kidder would drive Khánum up to our house to take us on an impromptu picnic or drive to the countryside. My father would unhesitatingly drop whatever he was doing – usually working at his desk – and join us without protesting that he had too much to do or that he had to finish a particular piece of work, so respectful was he of Khánum's every wish.

೮ఎ

During their custodianship the Hands of the Cause did not change any of the procedures established by the Guardian that they did not have to alter. The maximum number of pilgrims at the time were 18 (nine from the East and nine from the West) who were accommodated in the Eastern and Western Pilgrim Houses respectively during their nine days' pilgrimage. As well as having to diligently attend to everything pertaining to the administration, protection and propagation of the Bahá'í world community, the Hands met with the pilgrims in the evenings and a number of them took turns accompanying them on their three day pilgrimage to Bahjí. Meeting with the pilgrims was something they all always looked forward to, no matter how heavy their workload. Being in close contact with believers in the field of service rejuvenated them and they were, for a few hours, able to shed the heavy weight of their daily responsibilities and relax. For Faizi, who was essentially a very gregarious man, it was very important that he spend time with the pilgrims, listening to them and making their pilgrimage as memorable and enjoyable as possible by sharing with them stories and anecdotes about the Central Figures of the Faith and the early believers.

Even when it was not his turn to be with the pilgrims Faizi would invariably be either at the Western Pilgrim House in the evenings to translate for one of the Hands who needed translation into English or at the Eastern Pilgrim House to translate for the Hands who did not speak Persian; and when it was his turn to take the pilgrims to Bahjí he used to stay with them in the Mansion rather than return home for the night. Many a time when sleepless pilgrims wandered in the Mansion in the early hours they would find Faizi sitting under a small lamp, writing.

ஒ

Faizi was very sensitive to the needs of others and had a special gift of drawing people out, of pointing out the significance and importance of incidents that would normally pass others by. There was in one particular group of pilgrims a western pilgrim so drawn to the friends from Iran that he spent as much time as possible with them in the Eastern Pilgrim House where he communicated with them through Faizi when he was there to translate, or through smiles and gestures. One day an elderly Persian lady, who seemed not to be able to take her eyes off this man, offered him an orange. As he was peeling the orange Faizi approached him and said, 'I want to thank you for being here.' The young

THE HOLY LAND: A CHANGE OF DIRECTION

man, amazed that he was being thanked for being where he felt he was being an intruder, started to say that it was he who should be thankful when Faizi silenced him. Motioning towards the old lady, he explained to him that the woman was from a small village in Iran where it was impossible to speak about the Faith and that her main source of encouragement was what she read and heard about the teaching activities in other countries. He then said, 'To see you, a Bahá'í from Alaska! You have no idea what this means to her. It makes everything she has been reading and praying for become real!'

In another group of pilgrims there was an unsophisticated woman who lacked formal education named Rubábih. Rubábih had worked as a domestic servant for 20 years and saved her money to come on pilgrimage. She had only one change of clothing with her and was so quiet and unassuming that her fellow pilgrims, quite unintentionally, did not notice her much in the group. On the last night of this group's pilgrimage Rubábih suddenly burst into the Pilgrim House clutching an album to her breast and sobbing her heart out. Her concerned fellow pilgrims could neither get an explanation from her as to why she was so upset nor could they stop her sobbing. One of them gently took the album from her and opened it. It was full of the pictures of the Shrines, the gardens and all the Bahá'í holy places with an explanation and history written under each picture in Faizi's beautiful writing. He had made up the album specially for Rubábih and, as the time for her return to Iran drew near, he had given it to her 'as a token of his love and for her to keep in remembrance of her pilgrimage'.

Later when one of the pilgrims told Faizi what effect this kind gesture had had on Rubábih he told her with some sadness that the Guardian had once told him to 'be different', then added that noticing those with a vibrant personality and great achievements was easy but he always tried to seek out the Rubábihs of this world.

Another insight into Faizi's character involves the eight year old daughter of that Alaskan young man. She went on pilgrimage with her mother two years after her father. At the end of their visit to the Archives with Faizi, Faizi excused himself as he was in a hurry to get to another appointment. The little girl, however, was anxious to take a picture of him in front of the Archives building so he stood where she wanted him to and waited for her to take the photograph.

Looking into her viewfinder she exclaimed disappointedly, 'Oh, you don't fit!'

Faizi immediately squatted down and said, 'Now do I fit?' He did.

A Challenge to Unity

On 5 May 1960 my father came home unexpectedly early with an expression on his face that said something really, really dreadful had happened. All he told us was that he had to go to France the following day. We later found out that a number of the members of the National Assembly of France had accepted Mason Remey's claim to be the next Guardian of the Faith and that within a few hours of receiving this news the Hands had decided that, as he spoke French, Faizi should go to France to deal with the situation. He flew out the following afternoon.

As soon as he arrived in Paris Faizi sent a message to the National Assembly that he wanted to meet with them and a meeting was arranged for two o'clock on the following afternoon.

The next day Faizi entered the Bahá'í Centre at the appointed hour. When he and members of the National Assembly were about to sit together to start the meeting, the chairman, who was one of the detractors, told Faizi that the Assembly wanted to have a private discussion before meeting with him. Faizi's obedience to the institutions of the Faith was absolute but when it came to safeguarding the Faith he would reveal a facet of his character seldom seen by anyone. He would transform from the loving, gentle Faizi and become uncompromising and unyielding in his defence of the

THE HOLY LAND: A CHANGE OF DIRECTION

Covenant of Bahá'u'lláh, irrespective of who confronted him. His response to the chairman's statement was that they had promised to meet with him at two o'clock, that he had come as arranged and that if it were necessary for them to have a private meeting they should have had it before. As soon as some members started to vacillate he told them firmly to sit down. They all sat down.

Faizi's fellow Hands had given him copies of all the relevant correspondence and documentation which he might need. His objective was to ascertain from those who had decided to accept Mason Remey's claim the answers to two specific questions. At one point the responses so shook him that his 'whole body was trembling' and his 'mouth was frozen'. Eventually, he asked if there were other members of the Assembly who accepted Mason Remey's claim. Five members raised their hands. Faizi immediately rose from his seat and told the assembled members that his duty was ended and he had nothing more to do.

Before Faizi had left the Holy Land his colleagues had told him that if the majority of the National Assembly members had become followers of Mason Remey then the Assembly had to be disbanded and a new one elected. He spent a restless night thinking how he was going to resolve the problem and keep the dignity of the Faith but he was saved from his dilemma when early the next morning one of the four loyal members of the National Assembly arrived at his hotel with great joy and put five sheets of paper in front of him. All five followers of Mason Remey had, of their own accord, resigned from the National Assembly. Faizi felt as if the world had been given to him and immediately sent copies of the resignations to Haifa.

Faizi then visited every centre in France where Bahá'ís resided to meet with them, explain the situation and advise them to go ahead with the election of a new National Assembly.

In the midst of this very difficult mission Faizi kept up his correspondence. A recipient of one of his letters during this time commented that sometimes Faizi's letters were received 'just when they were most needed' and that a particular one arrived when the small community he was living in at the time was experiencing 'difficulties of ego' and 'being too concerned over the actions of others'. Faizi had written this to the believer:

> Yesterday a friend was talking to me about some very insignificant mistake of a member of one of the committees and he was so insistent that he was urging me to take his voting rights because of a very little mistake. We were crossing Paris in the underground Metro which are really wonders of speed, exact timing and practicability, when our friend emptied his heart. I told him: 'My dear brother, your statement resembles that of a person who puts aside all this exact, quick and regular movements of the Metro and how very useful it is for the people and spends his whole time on a stub of a cigarette which someone by mistake has left on the bench. You see hundreds of people come and go, and each one has a destination towards which he is hurrying and the Metros are taking them to different directions with wonderful rapidity and really miraculous exactitude. No one looks at the dead cigarette on the bench.
>
> Now the whole world is crying out of hunger that they have for their share of this bread of life. The banquet is spread by the mighty hands of Bahá'u'lláh and people are gathering round it. Some find the food delicious and they still want more. Some do not touch that table. Some do not even approach. Now, in the midst of all such great chances of service, sacrifice and winning victory for the Cause, do you want me to waste my time for some very insignificant matter which does not have any bearing on the main problem of the Cause?

Faizi found having to deal with Covenant-breakers extremely difficult but he did it because his fellow Hands asked him to. Referring to this particular task, which he was asked to undertake on more than one occasion, Rúḥíyyih Khánum remarked, '. . . he was never lacking; he never flagged in his devotion or in his desire to serve, his determination to do what he could do and what he should do.' In a talk he gave after Faizi's death 'Alí Nakhjavání said that what Faizi did in those few days was to 'save the Cause of God in France and in Europe' and that future historians 'will pay tribute to what he was able to accomplish'.

Another Change

A year after our arrival my parents decided that it was best for me to continue my education in England. I was upset and perplexed when a short while before my departure my father went on his own to Bahjí for two or three days. It was only after coming across the following extract from a letter written to one of his friends in Bahrain that I understood his reason for absenting himself.

> Today is two days that I have come to Bahjí because it is a quiet place and full of spirituality which has effect on one's heart. I come here from time to time and this time deliberately to be away from May for a few days so that when she leaves it will not be difficult for either her or me . . . I don't know when I'll next see her after she leaves . . . separation from her will now be added to my separation from all the children.

At least this time Gloria and Naysán were still with him, although he had hardly any time to spend with them. He wrote to one of his friends,

> I'll tell you about one day's work so that you will understand how much work there is. Early in the morning to the site of the House of Worship . . . then the Hands' meeting; two in the afternoon translation for one of the Hands who is talking to the western pilgrims; at half past three with the western pilgrims to the Archives; at six o'clock prayers at the Shrines of the Báb and 'Abdu'l-Bahá with the western and eastern pilgrims; at seven translation for another Hand of the Cause meeting with the pilgrims; I went to the Master's house at ten and returned

home at midnight. I see Gloria and Naysán for only ten minutes in the mornings; they have both resigned, one from being a wife, the other from being a son.

My parents, particularly my father, wrote to me regularly and frequently after I left for England, telling me what my brother was up to and giving me little bits of news. In one of his letters he wrote,

> One day Gol-jún was speaking to a large crowd outside the Shrine. The group's guide was standing at a distance and when I went closer he turned round to me and whispered, 'My! She is beautiful!' I didn't want to embarrass the man so quickly walked away from him.

Every now and again, if I had not written for a length of time, I would receive a letter such as this from my father: 'Dear Madam, I want to tell you that it is nearly three months that you have not written to your father. If I have offended you, you will of course forgive me; if you have exams you must still have some time to write a few words to your father. I am very, very sorry to be taking your time, but my patience has come to an end and I am extremely worried.' When I occasionally slackened in writing to him after my marriage he found an ally in my husband, Peter, and wrote to him saying, 'Please advise your respected spouse to write to her father more often than she deigns to write.' Many of his letters contained amusing sentences such as, 'I was delighted to read your letter, especially when I read you are not coming!' or when Peter and I got engaged, 'Gol-jún had four wisdom teeth and yet she married me! Just think of it! How many does Peter have?'

My father came on one of his visits to England very soon after Peter had asked me to marry him. He knew nothing about Peter and when I told him I wanted to marry him, he teasingly told me he would not give his blessings until he had spoken to Peter to make sure the poor man knew what he was doing. Peter fully expected my father to ask him a lot of questions about his circumstances, his future plans, etc., etc., before giving his consent (my mother, who was by then living in England, knew and loved Peter and had already made it clear that she had no objection) but in the private meeting they had my father asked him just one question: 'Do you love her?'

Peter's parents, who were very loving, and mine did not meet often but they always enquired about and sent each other greetings through us. When my father visited us after our first child's birth he noticed that we had only his picture in the baby's room (because he was the absent grandparent) but he was not happy about this at all and insisted that if we were going to have any pictures then it should be of all his grandparents so that he would not grow up thinking any of them was more favoured.

Milly

A few nights before she passed away Amelia (Milly) Collins asked to see Faizi. She suffered from severe arthritis, had been bedridden for some time and hardly received anyone, except, of course, Rúḥíyyih Khánum, with whom she lived in the Master's house. As Faizi entered her room quietly and sat by her bedside, she took his hand and caressed it while repeatedly saying, 'Faizi, Faizi, why? why?', meaning why was she alive in this state. She then embraced and kissed him and reminded him that he used to chant Tablets and prayers for her. He asked if she would like him to chant for her and then gently filled her room with the liquid gold of his voice chanting this Tablet of 'Abdu'l-Bahá:

> O thou who art turning thy face towards God! Close thine eyes to all things else, and open them to the realm of the All-Glorious. Ask whatsoever thou wishest of Him alone; seek whatsoever thou seekest from Him alone. With a look He granteth a hundred thousand hopes, with a glance He healeth a hundred thousand incurable ills, with a nod He layeth balm

on every wound, with a glimpse He freeth the hearts from the shackles of grief. He doeth as He doeth, and what recourse have we? He carrieth out His Will, He ordaineth what He pleaseth. Then better for thee to bow down thy head in submission, and put thy trust in the All-Merciful Lord.[8]

At the end of his chant Amelia Collins wanted to know the meaning of the Tablet and he told her it was in answer to her question, that 'He doeth as He doeth'. Once again she embraced and kissed him as his tears of sadness fell on her fragile face. She passed away a day or two later on 1 January 1962 in her eighty-eighth year.

Rúḥíyyih Khánum, who had now lost her closest companion, was so upset that she did not receive, as she always had, any of the pilgrims already there and their joyful pilgrimage became sad and restrained. On one of the evenings when they were gathered together in the Pilgrim House in a subdued mood Faizi arrived and started distributing beautiful cards with quotations from the writings written in his exquisite calligraphy. This unexpected distraction created some excitement in the group and lightened their hearts. As he distributed his token gifts he remarked, 'If these don't make the friends happy then of what use are they? Now that life is so unfaithful, I, too, want to give away all I have.'

Faizi did what he did for the pilgrims because he loved doing it. When some expressed their appreciation of the little gifts of calligraphy he gave them his response was, 'I never dared to think that the little I do for our dear pilgrims would be received with so much appreciation and understanding. I must really do more, but every time I find myself racing against every hour.'

Priorities

In May 1962 my parents and Naysán had a pocket of family time together when Mádar-jún went on pilgrimage. This was a precious time for them as they were on the threshold of yet another

THE HOLY LAND: A CHANGE OF DIRECTION

major change in their lives. My father was preparing for a long tour of South America soon after Mádar-jún returned to Iran and it became apparent that he would be undertaking many more such programmes of travel, which meant that he would be away from the World Centre for months at a time, sometimes for over a year. They decided that my mother and Naysán should move to England where my mother, who was anxious to lend her support to the final years of the Ten Year Crusade and future Plans, could be of some service to the progress of the Faith.

My father did not expect my mother to accompany him on his long and arduous travels but rather encouraged her to travel in her own capacity and was always supportive of her teaching projects. He had, some 20 or so years before, written to the National Assembly of Iran suggesting that Bahá'í women from Iran should, like their European counterparts, be sent on international teaching trips. The Assembly's response had been that Gloria was very suitable, but nothing was done until, as he commented, 'she herself came forward and set off'. When the National Assembly of India invited her to India to lecture about the Faith in several universities and colleges Faizi was anxious to see her before she started her journey. At the same time he wished that he, too, had the chance to do what she had been asked to undertake but, as he lamented, he could not because of 'the fourth dimension discovered by Einstein called TIME!' He sent my mother information about the communities she was going to visit to which he had been himself, asking her to make sure she met with specific people. For example, before she set off on a long trip to Malaysia, Singapore, Japan, New Zealand, Australia, Samoa, Hawaii and the United States he gave her a list of addresses and names of friends he felt she must see, with footnotes under each name: 'Hugh Blundell, the oldest Bahá'í in Auckland, who is very dear. I'm sure you will go and visit him.' 'Go to New Caledonia from New Zealand – it is where the Battricks are,' etc. When she travelled to Iran, he warned her that if she was not careful and did not have a definite programme which she stuck to, she would be swept off her feet.

South America

Faizi loved meeting all the Bahá'ís in South America but the ones he lost his heart to were the native Bolivian Indians living high up in the Andes. The way they came forward, embraced him with a welcoming 'Alláh-u-Abhá!', the way they asked for their greetings to be taken to their fellow believers in other parts of the world removed all the fatigue of a twelve-hour drive on precarious roads.

One of his most memorable meetings in Bolivia was by the side of the road. As he and Mas'úd <u>Kh</u>amsí[9] were on their way to yet another centre they saw in the distance a group of people sitting in a field by the roadside. In their curiosity they slowed down and as they drove closer, men, women and children rose to their feet, one by one, and came forward in greeting. They were Bahá'ís from a village which was very difficult to reach. The community, not wanting to miss meeting Faizi, had decided to walk down to the road on which they knew he would be travelling, sit by the roadside and wait for him. They had brought bread, potatoes and eggs with them for lunch, which they shared with Faizi and his companion. After saying prayers together and asking Faizi many questions they bade him farewell and returned to their village. Faizi was so delighted with this gathering that he felt its enjoyment for months.

Covenant-breakers

Just over two years after the defection of some members of the French National Assembly Faizi had to deal with another attempt to cause a schism within the Faith: in September 1962 a number of believers in Chile became followers of Mason Remey. Arriving for a National Assembly meeting the chairman (who had become a follower of Mason Remey) had announced to the members present that after a visit from a believer from France the Local Assembly of her community had decided to support the claims of

THE HOLY LAND: A CHANGE OF DIRECTION

Mason Remey and had written to the National Assembly requesting that they, too, support the claim. The 'agitation that seized some of the members present was indescribable'. One of the stunned members suggested that the situation should be reported immediately to the World Centre and that the chairman should be asked to leave the meeting to allow the rest of the Assembly to consult on what steps they should take. A cable was sent to the World Centre, to the Auxiliary Board Member in Bolivia and then to all the Local Assemblies in Chile asking them not to receive any followers of Mason Remey until further notice. It soon became clear that Mason Remey's followers in Chile had 'a concerted campaign'.

The National Assembly received a cable from Faizi in answer to the one they had sent to the World Centre giving them the date and time of his arrival in Chile. Faizi, who had already visited Argentina, Paraguay, Bolivia, Peru and Ecuador and was on his way to Central America from Colombia, had been asked by the Hands at the World Centre to immediately redirect his steps to Chile and deal with the situation there.

Faizi, who never dreamt that he would have to deal with such problems again, did not have any relevant documents with him and had to ask one of his colleagues at the World Centre to post copies to him. In the meantime, he met with those who had accepted Mason Remey's claim and 'spoke very frankly with them'. When a couple told him that they had been Bahá'ís for about nine years but had remained inactive and not even told their children that they were Bahá'ís, he was completely amazed and felt their 'cold attitude' killing him.

After meeting with one of the communities affected by the Covenant-breakers he wrote to a member of the National Assembly, 'Either these people must rise to serve or a new community must start over again; a community whose members are not ashamed of calling themselves Bahá'ís or of serving it with at least a little bit of their time and energy.' He felt it worthwhile spending as much time as was needed in this community until he achieved 'a certain definite result'.

'It is my nature,' he wrote. 'Either I will destroy the whole thing or will build it solidly. If the friends here do not come to their understanding and do not rise to serve, it is much better to say that we do not have an Assembly in this place.'

In the middle of the very disturbing situation in which he found himself, a situation which required his undivided attention, Faizi somehow remembered that when he was in Bolivia Mrs <u>Kh</u>amsí, an American lady, had mentioned how difficult it was for her to find shoes because the Bolivians were a small people with small feet. When her husband, Mas'úd <u>Kh</u>amsí, who had come to Chile to consult with Faizi about the situation, returned to Bolivia he had with him a pair of shoes that Faizi had bought for his wife.

Faizi remained in Chile for three months from September to the beginning of December. He met believers in Santiago and travelled to centres with Local Assemblies to help them in their understanding of the situation. He met alone with the followers of Mason Remey and finally, despite every effort to show them the way to remain faithful to the Covenant of Bahá'u'lláh, a total of nine were eventually declared Covenant-breakers by the Hands in the Holy Land. One of the communities which was affected but remained firm was Punta Arenas on the southern tip of Chile. Faizi stayed there for some time and boarded in Hotel Cabo de Hornos which overlooked the Straits of Magellan. It was here that he was inspired to write his *Meditations on the Eve of November 4th*, three meditations on pioneers and pioneering, on his love for the indigenous peoples of the world and on the loss of the Guardian, one of his most poignant pieces of writing.

13

The End of an Era

The Bahá'í world celebrated the end of the Ten Year Crusade and the election of the first Universal House of Justice with the World Congress held in the Royal Albert Hall in London in April 1963. Faizi missed this exciting Bahá'í gathering because the World Centre could not close down for the duration of the Congress and he was the Hand of the Cause chosen to remain but he flew to London for the last day of the Congress to give the closing address.

With controlled elation Faizi delved into 'story after story to illustrate deep spiritual truths', carried the audience to the summit of their achievements in the years since the passing of the Guardian and gave them a glimpse of the future. He drew his address to a close by voicing what was in the hearts of many, that 'although the Ten Year Crusade of the beloved Guardian has come to a victorious conclusion, we are always in his service, we live forever under his shadow, and we will carry in our hearts forever the memory of his beautiful face'.[1]

Filled with emotion mingled with their love for and gratitude towards all the Hands of the Cause who had for five and a half years steered the Crusade and kept it on course to its triumphant finale, the audience erupted in applause.

There is no more appropriate recognition of what the Hands of the Cause achieved in those significant five and a half years than the tribute paid by the newly-elected Universal House of Justice in its first message:

> The paeans of joy and gratitude, of love and adoration which we now raise to the throne of Bahá'u'lláh would be inadequate, and the celebrations of this Most Great Jubilee in which, as

promised by our beloved Guardian, we are now engaged would be marred were no tribute paid at this time to the Hands of the Cause of God. For they share the victory with their beloved commander, he who raised them up and appointed them. They kept the ship on its course and brought it safe to port. The Universal House of Justice, with pride and love, recalls on this supreme occasion its profound admiration for the heroic work which they have accomplished. We do not wish to dwell on the appalling dangers which faced the infant Cause when it was suddenly deprived of our beloved Shoghi Effendi, but rather to acknowledge with all the love and gratitude of our hearts the reality of the sacrifice, the labour, the self-discipline, the superb stewardship of the Hands of the Cause of God.[2]

༄

Faizi's love for the members of the Universal House of Justice and his devotion to that institution was immeasurable. He was so excited when the first Universal House of Justice was elected that he could barely contain himself and poured out his feelings in many of the letters he wrote during that period.

'Now that we have the House of Justice', he wrote in one, 'and every day I see these precious souls with so much love, energy, enthusiasm and devotion, I feel no more tired even though mountains of work and responsibilities are put on my shoulders; I feel happier, readier and more uplifted than ever.'

In another he wrote, 'Please pray that the friends will know in what day they are living! They will understand what the House stands for. They will sacrifice everything they have to help the House.'

And, 'If only you knew what a House of Justice we have. If the friends knew in truth all their sadness would be removed and they would sacrifice everything they have for it so that it gains strength day by day and add to its greatness. Each dear member works with such seriousness, purity, selflessness that I am at a loss to describe. Sometimes they work so hard that I become worried about their health.'

One of the most enjoyable days of the week for the Hands of the Cause was when they had their joint meetings with the House of Justice. 'One actually can clearly perceive', observed Faizi, 'how pure hearted and illumined souls can become the recipients of the will of God. It is most amazing and extremely enjoyable to observe.'

Travels Resume

From now on Faizi's travels were under the direction of the Universal House of Justice. He went on a tour of South America and the United States after the Congress in London and returned to the Holy Land via Iran, where he stayed for about 45 days. As he was by now very tired the friends had been asked not to arrange extensive programmes for him but it proved beyond his power or that of any committee 'to control the many demands of the dearly beloved of Tehran', as they were eager to benefit from having him in their midst. He soon had a daily programme that started early in the morning and ended at midnight. It was winter and heavy snow lay on all the roads. Having lived in a hot climate for nearly 15 years Faizi was no longer accustomed to such freezing weather and was never warm enough, but 'the waves of love and enthusiasm' which encircled him everywhere compensated for his physical chill. In all the gatherings he encouraged the friends to ask questions, as he felt that the questions they asked gave him an insight into 'the nature of the community, their difficulties, problems and shortcomings', and he in turn would give them news of Bahá'í activities from around the world. His daily routine after the morning meetings was to go to the houses of veteran teachers and the sick and poor who could not travel the long distances to meetings and sit with them to listen to their stories and experiences.

Faizi had special praise for the Bahá'í youth of Iran during this trip and was very impressed by their activities and achievements in public speaking, teacher training classes, publications, etc., despite the many difficulties with which they were continually confronted. He wrote an account of one of their classes to the House of Justice:

> Let me describe to you one of their classes. On a special day parents and friends were invited to observe the final examination of the Public Speaking class. There were two groups, each group consisting of more than 30 boys and girls under the supervision and guidance of three teachers. The members of each class had gone on many teaching tours from Tehran to many different parts of Persia, especially to villages. Each one had committed to memory more than 75 quotations from our Sacred writings . . . Each knew by heart at least five long Tablets in Persian or in Arabic. Though the means of transport are not adequately comfortable, available or cheap, scarcely any of the students had been late to any of the classes. When they made speeches or recited the Tablets or quoted the writings their pronunciation and delivery was clear and penetrating. At the end of the meeting we had the pleasure of looking at the many different books that the students had copied and the different books to which they had referred during the whole year. When they asked me to tell them something I was so thrilled that I could hardly talk. At the end of the day they promised to continue their studies to get ready for their future services. With tears in their eyes they expressed homage, respect and loyalty to this House of Justice and conveyed the message that they would be ready to participate in the new year's plan arranged by that exalted Body.

From Tehran Faizi went to Isfahan where he spent five nights, one of them in the nearby village of Najafábád where he had spent four and a half years before moving to Bahrain. A huge tent had been pitched in the large courtyard of one of the houses; the floor was covered with carpets on which more than a thousand Bahá'ís sat, eager to meet and listen to Faizi. Among these friends were those who had suffered the most during the 1955 wave of persecution. For months they had not been allowed to buy provisions from the market and errand boys were paid by their enemies to go on bicycles round the lanes to see if anyone dared help them; nor could they gather their own crops, most of which had been plundered by the angry mobs. They had managed to survive with what they had previously stored in their homes but many were eventually forced to leave for other places in search of ways to earn their living, some of them on foot because the buses and taxis refused to take them. Standing in the midst of these wonderful Bahá'ís Faizi 'could not utter a word'. As he looked at the faces of the gathered friends he recognized many who as children had sat on his lap. He felt 'immersed in the ocean of their love, care and consideration'. He struggled for words, received strength and inspiration from the expressions of love and devotion on their faces and started to tell them about the Bahá'ís of Bolivia, about the rapid progress of the Cause in India and Africa and related stories which he had gathered throughout his trips round the world. He then saw in the tearful emotions playing on their faces that 'if their feet are in fetters and can't take the torch of God freely round the countries, their brothers and sisters in other parts of the world with their sacrificial services take the light of the Cause even to the very dark and obscure corners of the world.'

ತಾ

Before going on to Shiraz, where he was to spend five nights, Faizi had sent a cable to the Hands at the World Centre asking them to appoint a day and hour when they would go to the Shrine of the Báb so that he could go the House of the Báb in Shiraz at the same time to join them in spirit, 'thus a spiritual magnetic chain would be stretched between the starting point and the final one: His House in Shiraz and His resting place on Mount Carmel.' Unfortunately, he did not receive a response to this request.

On one of his days in Shiraz Faizi was drawn, 'as if by a mysterious force', to the House of the Báb with a feeling which remained for him 'indescribable'. He entered the House reverently and was struck by its modest size, the smallness of the rooms and the little pond in the courtyard and compared it to 'the grandeur of the Message which covered the whole earth'. 'That very tiny room, by His decree and desire,' he wrote, 'became the fountainhead of all the blessings, the springtide of the spiritual revival of mankind and the Primal Point from which powers are constantly released for the spiritual conquest of the globe!' In a state of quickened cognizance he entered the room in all humility and bowed his head in devotion. On the same day and at the same hour his fellow Hands of the Cause gathered at the Shrine of the Báb to join him in prayer. They *had* responded to his cable but he received it only when he returned to Tehran.

Mádar-jún Passes Away

Faizi lost his beloved mother in July 1966. When a cable was received from the National Assembly of Iran saying that she was seriously ill in hospital Faizi was surrounded by the love and affection of everyone working at the World Centre but it was two of his closest friends, 'Alí Nakhjavání and Hushmand Fatheazam, who were the ones to give him the sad news when she died, and they did it so gently, with so much love.

On receiving the news that Mádar-jún had passed away the two friends drove to Faizi's flat. It was five in the afternoon and Faizi went into the kitchen to make tea. When he returned to the living room he saw an envelope had been placed on the table. He opened the envelope and found a sheet of paper with the picture of the Master under which his friends had written, 'I go to the paradise on high because I am a bird belonging to that garden.'[3] Faizi knew immediately what it meant. 'Drowned in the ocean of their love', he did not shed any tears at that point but later, in the privacy of his room, this tender-hearted son of Mádar-jún sobbed his heart out.

'I am not sad about her,' he wrote. 'I am happy because she passed away without very much pain. But I weep because I did not do anything for her. I hope I will do something by which she will be happy in the Abhá Kingdom.'

In Iran, on hearing of Mádar-jún's death, a very good family friend hastened to the hospital where she had been a patient for some time. In response to his offer of help my uncle, who was deep in sorrow, handed him an envelope from Rúḥíyyih Khánum. It was addressed to Mádar-jún and had arrived with the latest group returning from pilgrimage, two hours before Mádar-jún passed away. It contained a small folded card on which Rúḥíyyih Khánum had sewn a circle of nine white, sweet smelling jasmines and in the centre of these jasmines she had written, in Persian, 'For Mádar-jún'. Knowing how much this gesture of love would have meant to Mádar-jún, the friend asked my uncle if he could keep the card and think of an appropriate way to use it.

On the day of her funeral the friend requested to have a few moments on his own with Mádar-jún before her coffin was taken to the cemetery for prayers and then burial. Alone in the silence of the room he gently pulled the shroud back from her serene face, placed Rúḥíyyih Khánum's card on her heart, kissed her forehead in his final farewell, and tenderly drew the shroud back in place.

૭ૐ

Faizi's focus in 1967 was to complete the translation into Persian of Rúḥíyyih Khánum's biography of Shoghi Effendi, *The Priceless Pearl*. He spent every day in the Master's house, from early morning till night, going through his completed translation. He felt so honoured to have undertaken this project and worked on it with such zeal that the Persian translation was ready for publication before the original English.

Faizi loved writing but he was not possessive of his works and would seek guidance when he wrote anything for publication in English. This note he wrote to Ian Semple[4] at one o'clock in the morning regarding his booklet on Imám Ḥusayn explains the standard he set himself.

> I believe that whatever is written in the name of the Cause must have a high standard of literacy value. I know that I can't reach that, but I desire to keep my own style. Therefore that which I really need is your help in the use of correct words, prepositions, idioms and any other help which makes the sentences readable and understandable.

In another to a Bahá'í publishing committee he wrote,

> When I offer my works to the Bahá'í publishers I no more think of them as my works. I submit them to my dear co-workers and all together, depending upon the bounties of God, we will produce something which will be worthy of the beloved friends and their spiritual upliftment.

He was very pleased when he started receiving letters of appreciation for his *Meditations on the Eve of November 4th*.

'The language of the heart', he wrote in a letter, 'is something that we do not have.'

> We borrow the expressions of material existence and make moulds of them; then pour in each the surging waves of our feelings. We always feel that the love within the heart is not revealed. The same thing is true about letters I received from my dear friends who have read the little book *Meditations*. I know for sure that there are two causes which have made the book so liked by my dear ones: 1 – It is filled with the love of our beloved, the one whom we did not recognize sufficiently and whom we did not make happy as we really had to. 2 – It is

the love of the friends for him expressed after reading this little and humble tribute to him. I know myself. To write a simple letter proves difficult for me. English is not my language. The friends are trained by the beloved Master to encourage each other; and I receive such outpourings of love as the caresses of dear and encouraging friends and promise to do more and better.

When Faizi was in hospital in 1972 after having been taken ill in India, he started to write 'glimpses of the lives of the glorious early heroes of the Cause in India'. They were not complete stories, just short accounts 'for the present generation lest they would think that the Cause had started with them'. 'They must know', he wrote, 'that there are gigantic pieces of solid rocks in the foundations of this ever rising edifice.'

Faizi also wrote a number of romantic novels in Persian. The following extracts are from an article written by Dr Fereydoun Vahman about Faizi's writing:

> Writing requires enthusiasm and talent, which he had; it also requires time, freedom, seclusion and quiet, none of which he had. Most of his stories were written in a hotel room while he was travelling, or sitting at a café table in South America or India.
> ... In the 150 odd years of Bahá'í history we have not had anyone writing romantic novels or short stories, except for Faizi. He was the only one who led the way and showed certain bravery and foresight...
> Perhaps one cannot name Faizi as a master and successful writer in the field of story writing in the Persian language. He himself never made such a claim and never paid much attention to what happened to his books after they were published; but while being aware of all his shortcomings he continued writing stories to show the present and future generation of Bahá'ís that this is a path they can pursue.
> ... Faizi did not limit his reading only to Bahá'í writings and books. Furúgh Farrukhzádih, who unfortunately died young in

a car accident, faced much opposition in Iran with her poetry. She published a collection of her works in which she expressed with insight and beauty her innermost feelings – for example, the loneliness of women and their oppression in a male dominated society. Today, after 55 years, the people of Iran have recognized her worth and see her as an able poet. However, this is what Faizi wrote about her in the years when she was on her own and some of the newspapers insulted her writing and called her a loose woman:

> Poets suffer more than most people and write and speak on behalf of all about the pangs of love. Furúgh's poetry is a light from her innermost feelings. We all harbour within us the pain of sin and shortcoming but do not have the strength to write about it. Furúgh shines; she gives voice and speaks of the fire within her which is why hearts burn because we see the same within ourselves. Well done Furúgh, who suffered on behalf of all of us, opened the secret of kindness and, as the saying goes, scattered them on the tambourines and running and dancing hastened to the presence of the Friend.

> . . . Faizi's message in all his stories is about the high station of humanity, human virtues, friendship and honesty, seeking peace and reconciliation . . .

The First Bahá'í Oceanic Conference

The first Bahá'í Oceanic Conference was held in Palermo, Sicily, from 23 to 25 August 1968, to commemorate the centenary of Bahá'u'lláh's arrival in the Holy Land, sailing across the Mediterranean Sea from Turkey on His way to exile. Faizi was one of the Hands of the Cause present at this Conference during which he spoke to the 2,300 or more Bahá'ís present. He gave them an account of the circumstances surrounding Bahá'u'lláh's exile and took them through the arduous stages of His journey. He spoke of the journey made by the countless staunch believers from Iran to the Holy Land, many under very difficult and dangerous circumstances, just to have a glimpse of Bahá'u'lláh before 'returning to assist in raising the structure of a world Faith in the land of its birth'. He compared their sacrifices to the schemes and plans of the sovereigns who made every effort to quash the message of Bahá'u'lláh, their plans 'as painting on water'. He then reminded the audience of the effect of the Apostles of Christ scattering far and wide to spread His teachings and invited them to reflect on what they might achieve if they, too, rose to serve the Faith with the additional spiritual charge they would receive on their pilgrimage to the Holy Land.[5]

છે

At the invitation of the Universal House of Justice over two thousand Bahá'ís travelled to the World Centre at the end of the conference. It happened that on a Saturday evening in one of the hotels where some of the Bahá'ís were staying, the hotel management approached all the hotel guests and asked if there were any who would be willing to give up their room so that they could accommodate a group of Israelis who had arrived for a special gathering in Haifa. A number of guests agreed. One of them, a young man, left with his suitcase and went to the gardens surrounding the Shrine of the Báb, where he came across Faizi. When Faizi learned that he was without a place to stay that night he invited him to share his apartment. The young man felt this would be an imposition and politely turned down his offer but Faizi, 'like a loving brother, warmly insisted'. Faizi had, in fact, gathered another three under his wing and taken them to his sparsely furnished flat for the night.

It was during this historic gathering at the World Centre that Mr Samandarí became very ill and slipped towards the end of his life. For his own protection the House of Justice had asked that his whereabouts not be made known to the gathered Bahá'ís. Faizi, however, who loved Mr Samandarí very much and was in awe of his drive and the fact that even at the age of 92 he was so active, visited him in hospital as often as he could. His admiration for Mr Samandarí was such that he tried to follow his example in many ways. For instance, 'Abdu'l-Bahá had asked Mr Samandarí to correspond with the friends, which he did to the very end of his life – Faizi wrote letters to hundreds around the world. Mr Samandarí travelled extensively for the Cause, as did Faizi. Faizi felt deeply honoured when, realizing that Mr Samandarí was not going to be well enough to chant the Tablet of Visitation on the day of commemoration, the House of Justice asked him to replace his revered Hand of the Cause.

Faizi was of the view that we must educate ourselves and fine tune our senses 'to see harvests in a grain and in a drop an ocean'. He would at times be so alive and sensitive to the world of nature that a wave of exhilaration would wash over him. One such occasion happened while he was standing outside the Shrine of Bahá'u'lláh on one of these historic days. With head bent in reverie and listening to a chant, he 'felt that all objects in creation were talking' to him; his eyes searched the pebbles he was standing on and it was as if they were whispering to him that they were from the shores of Lake Tiberias, that they remembered the time of Christ.

Observations of His Fellow Workers

Faizi's relationship with his fellow Hands was that of deep respect and love. He felt humbled by a number of them and interesting pen-pictures of a few of them have emerged from his letters.

Agnes Alexander:

> ... Everyone thinks that because she is elderly she is incapable of doing anything and has no thoughts whereas she is like a mountain. Just think of a person remaining in one place

for 50 years or more and on the face of it nothing to show for it[6] . . . She does not delegate any work to anyone, she does everything herself. You have no idea with what difficulty she accepted to let me take her shoes to her . . . She related a story to me which made me so sad. Many prisoners in the Philippines became Bahá'ís and they built themselves a Bahá'í Centre in the prison. When Agnes visited them for the first time she gave some of them photographs of 'Abdu'l-Bahá and the Greatest Name. The second time she met with them a young man came forward and showed her his photograph of 'Abdu'l-Bahá and with great sadness told her that he had killed someone before becoming a Bahá'í, that his trial had finished on that day and that he was going to be executed the following day. Agnes said she became so very sad, then thought to herself that, thank God, he is going to meet his Lord tomorrow . . . Her life is full of amazing events. She was one of the closest friends of Khánum's mother and understands Khánum's pain. God knows what love she feels towards Khánum . . .

Bill Sears:

Dearest Bill Sears is here now and being with him is a constant source of joy and happiness . . . the friends must be very happy and grateful that they have such a great and gifted writer among them. When Bahá'u'lláh was singled out for God's Message in this Age He promised that the treasures of the world would rise to serve Him. Now Bill is one of these.

Paul Haney:

. . . As to Paul's mother: I always tell Paul, 'I congratulate your mother. Usually when a mother has one and only one son she spoils that child. But I see that your dear mother had been very strict and educated you so beautifully that you are an example of a Bahá'í.' Paul is a perfect Bahá'í. He has consecrated his life to permanent service to the Cause. One should work with Paul, then one knows what an unusual soul he is. He is indefatigable, pure in thoughts and feelings. He stands firm in consultation, but never obstinate. His method of life and service is so pure that it must be emulated by all the young believers. He is very strict with himself, so much that he reminds us of the hermits who denied themselves all the luxuries of life. It is a joy to converse with him, to exchange jokes with him and to serve with him.

Faizi and Paul Haney had an ongoing debate with one another about exactitude and richness of languages: Paul Haney maintained English was the language and Faizi was firm in his belief that it was Arabic. He once sent Paul Haney the following with a note asking him if he was still going to argue that English was the most precise language:

A telephone conversation:

'Who is calling?'
'Watt.'
'What is your name?'
'Watt is my name.'
'That is what I asked you. What is your name?'
'That is what I told you. Watt is my name.'
A long pause, then Watt asks, 'Is that James Brown?'
'No. This is Knott.'
'Please, what is your name?'
'Will Knott.'
Whereupon they hung up.

༄

The Hands in the Holy Land and around the world continued to shoulder their responsibilities of propagating and protecting the Faith, which increased in proportion to the growth of the Faith around the world. Faizi rose at five in the morning and worked 'like a whirlwind till midnight'. He returned home for lunch and ate whatever was at hand, worked for about two hours until five then returned to the Hands' office where he continued working till ten or eleven at night and it was only because of his fear of falling ill that he slept at all. Furthermore, his travels to summer and winter schools and visiting various Bahá'í communities around the world increased by the year.

Among the many duties of the Hands residing in the Holy Land was reading the reports that arrived on a daily basis from the National Assemblies around the world. Reports from the National Assemblies in the Gulf states (by now expanded to more than the one original National Assembly) were among those allocated to Faizi. He perused these with great enthusiasm and, it has to be said, a certain degree of pride when he read with what speed they responded to the goals given them by the Universal House of Justice. They made him 'extremely happy, to such an extent that I want to cry'.

Faizi's knowledge of history, particularly Bahá'í history, was profound, as was his knowledge of the Qur'án and the Old and New Testaments, and he always had an insatiable desire to delve deeper into these fields of study. He was, however, careful not to relate anything, be it about an event or the early believers, before making sure that it was not hearsay. He always thoroughly researched answers to the many questions he was continually being asked and his lectures, lessons and deepenings were all rooted in the writings and a lifetime of study, all of which needed 'a bit of rest and non-disturbance, patience and diligent work'. The 'rest' and 'non-disturbance' he seldom had; nevertheless, he believed that this was his mission and that he should fulfil it. When he prepared for his travels he wrote all his lesson plans in one book 'to reduce weight'. He truly enjoyed meeting the friends on his travels, having deepening sessions with them, talking to them and listening to them and learning from them. But when he returned home after months of travelling he would be 'utterly exhausted' and 'sapped of every ounce of energy'. Yet he continued with his project of 'putting together many of the inexhaustible historical documents to form a chain by which events will be clearly understood'. He loved this work and felt 'an inner urge' to continue with it.

✧

When Faizi was not travelling the Bahá'ís at the World Centre, despite their very heavy workload, took care of him in Gloria's absence and made sure he had some relief from the burden of work he and his fellow Hands carried. A group would frequently telephone to tell him that they were going to come over to his flat for a potluck meal. Faizi provided the tea and they the food. They would spend an enjoyable evening together, wash up the dishes and tidy his kitchen before leaving. When he moved house in January 1965 Rúḥíyyih Khánum wrote, 'Today the Nakhjavánís, the Fatheazams, the Salímís, the Gibsons and I will go to your father's new apartment for a surprise dinner. Everyone will take something and we will have a "house warming" for him. He does not know so he had no chance to protest about it all.'

When he was on his own, especially in wintertime, Faizi liked to settle in bed after a hot bath to read all the documents he had to go through. One day as he walked home from the Hands' office in the Master's house he thought to himself that he would really like to have some pitta bread with cottage cheese after his bath, so he went into the small grocery near his flat. Like the rest of those working at the World Centre he did not read Hebrew but buying pitta bread and picking up a tub of cottage cheese was easy. He returned home, made a pot of tea and left it to brew on a tray which he placed in readiness by his bedside with the pita bread and cottage cheese. He had a quick, hot bath, wrapped up and settled himself in bed then eagerly tore off a piece of bread and, scooping a mouthful of cottage cheese with it, put the morsel in his mouth. To his shock his mouth immediately felt as if it was on fire! Jumping out of bed, he spat the mouthful out, flung his window open and called down to Faḍíl. Faḍíl, who for years was one of the Arab workers at the World Centre, had now been housed with his family in a flat below Faizi's so that he would be at hand should Faizi need his help with anything. He was known for his laid-back, nonchalant approach to life in general and for his languid, high tone of voice. Taking his time and slip-slopping in his slippered feet up the stairs to Faizi's flat, he eventually entered and stood in front of Faizi, showing no reaction to poor Faizi's discomfort.

'Faḍíl!' cried Faizi. 'Take a look at this cheese and tell me if it has gone off because it has set my mouth on fire!'

Taking the tub of cottage cheese from Faizi's hand in his usual impassive manner Faḍíl looked at it and lethargically gave his verdict. 'This isn't cottage cheese; it's cream soap for washing dishes.'

The containers for cottage cheese and this soap were identical and Faizi, in his haste, had picked the wrong one! Shafíqih Fatheazam, to whom Faizi related this incident, on the one hand laughed at Faizi's description of Faḍíl's typical response and on the other found her eyes welling up with tears at what had happened to her dear Faizi.

ಆ

A few years after the election of the House of Justice Faizi started a class on *The Book of Certitude* with a number of the friends working at the World Centre. These classes were held in the house of Amoz[7] and Mary Gibson. They lived next door to the Fatheazams and their three sons who had a dog called Ráj.

Ráj had replaced the boys' pet boxers they had had to leave behind in India when their father was elected to the Universal House of Justice. When the three boys were going to meet Rúḥíyyih Khánum for the first time after their arrival at the World Centre their mother told them not to speak until they were spoken to and to mind their manners. They all sat quietly and the two older brothers, when asked by Khánum, replied that they were happy being there. To his mother's consternation the youngest, six year old Shafíq, replied that no, he was not happy. Rúḥíyyih <u>Kh</u>ánum asked him why and he told her it was because he was really missing their pet boxers. A few evenings later there was a knock on the door of the Western Pilgrim House where they were staying at the time and a little boxer was delivered for the boys. Rúḥíyyih <u>Kh</u>ánum had gone to Tel Aviv and bought them the puppy.

To return to Faizi's classes on *The Book of Certitude*, Ráj would always be the first to arrive and sit by the Gibsons' door and he would go down the few steps to his home at the end of the class. The study group celebrated the completion of their book by having an enjoyable evening sharing the food each had brought for the occasion. During the evening Faizi told his students that he had brought prizes for the students who had been the best at listening and answering questions in class but that the first and best prize was for Ráj, who had not missed a single class!

ೞ

Faizi's diabetes was not always under control and he eventually had to use insulin. He had to constantly watch what he ate – which he did to some extent when not travelling but not always while on his travels – and the pressure of work together with moving from one country to another, from one hotel room to another, did not help matters. If he felt unwell he would keep quiet about it and not say anything to his colleagues because, as he told a friend, there was 'a lot of work to be done and no room for putting on airs and graces'.

Faizi was essentially undisciplined in watching his diet and his health. Rúḥíyyih <u>Kh</u>ánum once wrote, 'He does not pay enough attention to diet – unscientific minded, which lots of people are!' It was not that he did not think it important to take care of one's body but it was not one of his priorities, and if it came in the way of serving the Faith by having to sit or stand for hours in meetings giving talks and answering questions, or hurting someone's feelings by not taking a cake or sweet offered to him,

THE END OF AN ERA

then he would ride roughshod over his own needs. On the rare occasions Gloria was with him she would keep an eagle eye on his diet but even then he ignored her pleas at times. Rúḥíyyih Khánum personally thought that Faizi might have lived longer 'if he had been more careful about his health and less careful about the Bahá'ís'. She used to beg him whenever he embarked on one of his long trips, 'Faizi, there is one word you have not learned. Please learn it, it's very short. N - O. No. This is something that you don't understand. You've got to protect your health. You've got to learn to say no to the Bahá'ís' because they would 'storm him wherever he went'. He never heeded this good advice and always put the needs of others before his own.

༄

During a visit to India in February 1969 Faizi looked unwell on arrival and tired easily. He was persuaded to see a doctor whose diagnosis was that he had had a heart attack in the previous few days. He was immediately ordered to have complete bed rest in his hotel. The friends, however, in their love and affection for him and in their eagerness to benefit from having him in their midst, continued to visit him in his hotel room. Faizi being Faizi would never turn anyone away, certainly not because he was told he had to rest, so the doctor was obliged to move him to the hospital where visiting hours were restricted. The hospital was by the sea in quiet surroundings where he was not only obliged to take it easy but also had the chance to write. His doctor was quite surprised at the speed of his recovery and remarked that it seemed to have come about 'by some other power apart from the medicines'. He was not aware that the House of Justice was praying for Faizi at the Shrines and it may have been difficult to make this man of science understand the power of prayer.

Faizi recovered sufficiently to continue on his tour and reached Tehran in April 1969 where he stayed with his much-loved niece Qudsiyyih Faizi-Mahjúr and her family. He ignored the continued feeling of fatigue in his heart and threw himself into activity but in less than a month he found himself, once again, hospitalized. The pattern repeated itself: he was not left alone and visitors to his bedside were so many that a separate room was set aside for them. He would go to the room for an hour or so, greet everyone then say, 'Now you talk and I will listen.' Some spoke of teaching activities, some spoke of their problems and he listened with patience, briefly answering their questions and encouraging them in what they were doing.

In one such gathering an individual started complaining about the Local Assembly of her area. Her remarks were personal, inappropriate and accusatory. Faizi suddenly stood up and walked calmly to the door, saying bluntly, 'I cannot bear anyone speaking about Spiritual Assemblies in such a manner!'

When he left the room one of the friends broke the ensuing silence by saying, 'We mistake the patience and tolerance of that rock of endurance and forget that when it comes to the affairs of the Faith he is like an iron hand in a velvet glove.'

Staying in hospital proved to be useless as far as any rest was concerned so Faizi was taken to a house in north Tehran. This time his telephone number was not given to anyone and no one, but a select few, knew where he was. He was very disappointed that he could not continue with the classes he had prepared on 'Knowledge', 'Value in Life' and 'Standards', all based on his research into the writings of Bahá'u'lláh and 'Abdu'l-Bahá. The forced rest, however, gave him a chance to supervise the publication of his translation of *The Priceless Pearl*.

By June Faizi was feeling better but commented in a letter to a friend that 'Tehran and its atmosphere needs iron, nay steel, nerves'. While in Tehran he went to a Bahá'í tailor and asked him to measure him for a suit which he then sent to a friend in the United States he was very fond of and he knew would deeply appreciate what he was receiving. His accompanying letter explained that he was not sending the suit because he felt his friend needed one but rather that it came from Bahá'u'lláh's birthplace.

'I made it to my own measure', he wrote, 'as I believe yours is the same as mine. Two hearts palpitating with the same love must be in two bodies of the same measure. I hope and pray that you will like and accept it from your humble brother.'

༺༻

Returning to the World Centre in July 1969 after travelling for six months Faizi was immediately ordered absolute rest before starting on another tour in August. One of the countries he visited on this tour was Luxembourg where he made friends with a Bahá'í child with Down's Syndrome.

When Faizi met the boy he treated him as he would any other child. One day he asked the lad's parents' permission to take him out. He took his young friend to a restaurant, ordered two large ice creams and then told him that they were going to have a race with one another to see which one of them would finish their ice cream first. Faizi's new-found friend won. Thereon every time Faizi arrived in Luxembourg he would telephone his friend from the airport. Faizi's friendship with this young boy and the way he behaved towards him helped his parents change their relationship with their son as they, too, started treating him as an equal so that he grew into a calm adult.

One of the Bahá'ís in Luxembourg related that one day, after Faizi had passed away, the same young person asked him, 'Do you want to see my friend's picture?' He took this Bahá'í to his room and showed him Faizi's photograph which he had stuck onto his wall together with pictures of other people.

The friend asked, 'Who is this?'

The boy replied, 'He is my friend. I love him very much.'

His parents had not had the heart to tell him that his friend had died.

༺༻

Faizi's correspondence was not only with Bahá'ís but with everyone he knew. For example, Ralph Elberg, the manager of Peltours travel agency from whom he bought all his airline tickets, was devoted to Faizi and Faizi always sent him letters when he was on one of his long world tours, giving him information about the country he was in and conveying to him the spirit of the Faith. From Bolivia he wrote to Elberg:

> To many of my friends I have spoken of you particularly and your wonderful spirit of love and friendship . . . In one of the meetings when after a long speech I opened the meeting to friendly discussion and questions, someone immediately sprang up and said, 'What have you brought from the East?'
>
> I said to him, 'Do you ever ask the sun, "What have you brought from the East?" I have brought you the light of knowledge and the warmth of divine love so that you will love all the people of the world without discrimination of race, colour and politics.'

After Faizi's death Elberg wrote to Gloria, 'He was a man full of love, understanding, respect and feelings towards everyone he met. He brought with him a ray of light that always left whoever met him with the impression of having known someone special. I was privileged to be called by him "friend" and "brother". I shall never forget him.'

❧

The Hands of the Cause continually received letters from Bahá'ís around the world seeking their advice on personal problems and numerous other matters, or wanting answers to various questions. Many of the letters Faizi received were of this nature, which he would answer as promptly as he could, often referring them to his own source of information, the writings. At times, owing to pressure of work and lack of time, his answers would be very brief but to the point. For example, when he received a long list of questions from one of the believers, he responded that as he had just returned from a long tour in the Pacific and had only five weeks to get ready for another tour in Africa and Europe, he was going to be 'brief, but sufficient' in his replies. And he really was.

Q: Is the one thousand years before the appearance of a new Prophet from 1844, 1853 or 1863?
A: Our calendar starts from 1844.

Q: Why did Bahá'u'lláh say, 'My tongue reciteth what no ear can bear to hear!' (People were with Him in the prison.)
A: When you went to the prison cell in the Citadel of 'Akká, did you hear that He was all alone by Himself there?

Q: Why so many references to wine ('unseal the choice wine') when we cannot drink?
A: Figurative way of speech is an art in literature. As wine gives intoxication, so do the words of God. Our spiritual experiences should be expressed in the words which pertain to our physical experiences. There is no other way.

Q: Is it true that you are not allowed to eat after dinner, according to the Aqdas?
A: Absolutely wrong.

Q: Did Shoghi Effendi ever speak about Lourdes, France or Theresa Neuman of Germany?
A: No! Why should he spend his time on such matters?

Q: What happens if you die aboard a plane or boat in mid-ocean?
A: Ask the House.

Q: Is contributing to the Fund in someone's memory emulating

the masses?
A: You may contribute in memory of people. It is a praiseworthy deed. But the phrase, 'emulating the masses' makes the question ambiguous.

Q: Did Bahá'u'lláh say why we should fast if our energy is less in the afternoon and our work is service to God and we [therefore] do less efficient work?
A: We fast, pray, contribute to the funds, etc., because we love Him.

☙

When Faizi once again fell ill during one of his heavy schedules of travel, doctors told him that because of his many years of playing football and tennis and weight lifting his body was strong enough to withstand the pressures he was under. However, they asked him, 'What mental distress do you have?'
Faizi smiled and said nothing.
During this relapse in his health he received petals from the Shrines with signatures from those serving at the World Centre. He responded, 'Rising and falling I tread the path of His love; please pray that the last fall will be at His feet holding His hem and receiving the smile of forgiveness.'
Faizi was in Haifa for about one and a half months in February 1970 after his tour of the Pacific before proceeding to Africa for about three months and then to Britain to visit his family. Notwithstanding his exhaustion and the little turnaround time he had between his travels, he conscientiously responded to the mountain of letters, writing in one, 'I hasten to note down these lines lest you would think I have forgotten you and I am discourteous.'

☙

Naysán and I went to my father for our summer holidays, if he was not travelling, while my mother went on travel teaching trips. These were always very special times for us and for him.

'I feel different from the day they arrived,' he wrote during one of our visits. 'I feel excited and even in the meetings feel I'm in a trance, but because they all know why I am forgiven'.

He would excitedly prepare for our arrival. When Naysán and Zohreh were going to spend a month with him he wrote, 'You have no idea what state I'm in at the news of your arrival. I have already started hiding the books, papers and beautiful things here and there because as soon as Naysán arrives he will, like a mouse, begin opening all the boxes!'

No one could make my father laugh like Naysán did. Naysán was relentless with his jokes and mimicking, to such an extent that my father would beg him to stop because his laughter would reach such a pitch that he felt his ribs would break and that it was dangerous for his health. When they left he wrote to Peter and me, 'You can't imagine how intensely I miss them. Every night I light the lamps of the room and look everywhere to find them.'

Grandfathering

When Peter and I sent a telegram to my father to tell him that I was expecting his first grandchild his excitement was such that he could hardly contain himself; but he was in Africa when our child was born and had to wait five months before he could hold his grandson, Paul-Faizi, in his arms.

'I can't wait! I want to know what he looks like,' he wrote to us. 'I can't think of him very much. I go crazy. I practise patience.'

When Naysán and Zohreh were expecting their first child, Chehreh, my father's delight at the prospect of having two grandchildren rose even higher and he wrote to tell them that he had already started talking to their baby. And when his third and fourth grandchildren, Thomas and Árám, arrived he was well and truly the proudest of grandfathers.

Our son was only six months old and not yet very mobile when my father left after a month's stay with us but in his first letter after that visit he wrote,

> I think that by now he has started moving around and his little blanket is not enough for him. He will start going into every room. Please secure the stairs both from the top and bottom and write and tell me you have done so that I don't worry. It is now ten o'clock at night and I know he is asleep but I am worried about him because you mentioned that he is going to have his injection this week. You can't imagine how intensely I miss him. If someone hears me talking to myself and him in my room and kitchen they will think many screws are loose!

Paul-Faizi and I spent nearly four wonderful months in Haifa with my father in the spring of 1971, with my mother joining us half way through. My son and I returned to England a few hours before my father had to fly to Iran. Going back to the hotel near the airport where the three of us had stayed the night before, my father wrote to Peter, 'I looked everywhere for them. I smelled his little blanket . . . Then I slept and covered myself with it. I could smell him. Therefore I started to talk to him and sang for him and kissed his quilt. No one was here.'

୪୬

My mother had many fine qualities. Letter writing was not one of them. My father once wrote and told us that she had written only two letters to him while she had been recently in Beirut and that in her second letter she had asked him if he had received *all* her letters. He wrote back to her saying that 'grammatically it is wrong to use "all" for "two"!'

Notwithstanding the fact that he was now seldom with us, my father played his role as the head of our family from a distance. As he was anxious that our mother's mind should be at rest about us and our children, he asked us to write our letters to them both which he would then forward to my mother and thus ensure that she was always informed of how we were and what her grandchildren were up to while she was on her teaching trips. He himself would, of course, write his own letters to her. After one visit to him by Naysán, Zohreh and their two year old daughter Chehreh, he wrote to her,

> Her honour, Chehreh, comes to my room every day to 'frighten' me and I have to pretend to jump from my sleep so that madam can laugh. She then wriggles in my bed for some time and then we go to table together. But yesterday, the day of their departure, she did not come and she would not even say goodbye to me . . .
>
> Naysán is so neat and tidy in his work . . . in ten minutes he sorted out and tidied my library so that everyone knew it was not my doing . . .
>
> The children's place is so empty and I have no patience or energy to do any work. I walk in the rooms, sit in a corner and remember them. What a dream it was. Whatever it was has gone.

My father would with great delight record the antics, of which there were many, our mischievous children got up to, and loved receiving our detailed accounts of what they had been doing. He once wrote, 'I am delighted to know that Paul-Faizi is so naughty and independent. This indicates that he is healthy. I am also very happy to understand that Chehreh talks very much. This indicates that she is really a lady.' He would write little letters to them and tell them something of the country he was in. When in Brazil he wrote to Chehreh,

> There are two important things in Brazil: one is football and the other carnival. The carnivals are fantastic, thousands of men and women dress up in special clothes and play music and dance for several days and nights. They dance the samba, which is a difficult but wonderful dance.

In another letter, when Paul-Faizi and Chehreh were together, he wrote, 'I am very happy that you are together and have a very good time in Cyprus. I wish my arms were long enough to be able to embrace you both. Many hugs to both of you devils! Little devils! I love small devils.'

Despite finding separation from his grandchildren painful and longing to be with them, when he pondered the situation of some parents whose children were pioneering in far-off lands and who had no hope of seeing them again in their lifetime, my father would not complain.

෴

The Protective Arm

It was during one of his tours in 1972 that Faizi, while addressing an overflowing audience of Bahá'ís in a hall in Poona, India, suddenly collapsed. He was rushed to hospital where the doctors' diagnosis was that he had suffered a heart attack. Complete rest in the intensive care unit was ordered and no visitors allowed.

The National Assembly of India immediately notified the Universal House of Justice of Faizi's collapse and the House responded with a cable:

> ASSURE HAND CAUSE FAIZI FERVENT PRAYERS HOLY SHRINES RESTORATION COMPLETE HEALTH EARLY RESUMPTION DEEPLY VALUED SERVICES URGE HIM POSTPONE TRAVELS FOLLOW MEDICAL ADVICE CONVEY DEEPEST AFFECTION STOP KEEP HOUSE REGULARLY INFORMED CONDITION HIS HEALTH ADVICE DOCTOR.

Faizi himself also sent the House of Justice a cable, 'lest other exaggerated news' reached them, and in his anxiety to carry on with his duties informed them that he was better and would soon resume his responsibilities. The House of Justice, of course, valued very highly the unique services of the Hands of the Cause, and while making full use of their expertise and deep knowledge of the Faith, was also always very protective of them and, if necessary, stepped in to safeguard them. Their answer to Faizi's cable was:

> GRATEFUL YOUR CABLE STOP STRONGLY FEEL YOU MUST CONSIDER RESTORATION HEALTH FIRST OBLIGATION MODIFY OR DELAY SCHEDULE ACCORDINGLY STOP YOU MAY ALSO CONSIDER ADVISABILITY FLY WHENEVER POSSIBLE TO UNITED STATES FOR MEDICAL ATTENTION GETTING READY PARTICIPATION SUMMER SCHOOLS AS PLANNED STOP PLEASE KEEP US INFORMED BE ASSURED FERVENT PRAYERS LOVE.

Faizi flew to a sanatorium in Germany where the situation and atmosphere was completely different to his normal life of meetings, giving talks, listening to and answering questions and having little rest or sleep. He wrote to a friend that there was 'no sound of footsteps, nor aroma of stew, no laughter of friends'; no one spoke English and he did not speak German so he had no alternative but to rest. As he was told by the doctors that he had to lose five kilos he was put on a diet of vegetable soup and boiled meat, a far cry from the food he had been eating in recent months, so that he felt he was going to 'wither away' if kept on the diet long enough! He wistfully wrote that the doctors had not given him much hope of regaining good health but that he would 'never abandon the Lyre of Hope' and would play on 'even if all the strings are cut'. As his health improved he started to get 'thoroughly tired' of the place and looked upon the sanatorium as a prison. He became tired of writing and hoped that the doctors would soon discharge him so that he could resume his travels to Europe and the United States. He found the problems he was having with his heart 'bitter and disappointing' but concluded that in essence it was a bounty which drew him closer to God to seek more help and assistance. He prayed that Bahá'u'lláh would give him a chance so that he could be 'of some little service' to the friends to whom he had given his life, each of whom was 'a breeze of mercy'; but at the same time he felt that if Bahá'u'lláh desired he should retire then he would accept His Will with all his heart and soul.

One of the many letters he wrote while in the sanatorium was in answer to one he had received from a couple who had lost a child and felt that this was their punishment because they had not remained in their pioneering post. He wrote to them:

... I don't want you to be sad because it is against the wishes of Bahá'u'lláh. I don't want you to be afraid of Him because He came for love and not fear; and I don't want the friends to spend their time in discussing calamities because we are here to remove them.

Do you remember when I was in Hawaii and the friends asked me about the pending calamity I almost lost my temper? It is like someone who shivers in the middle of the summer because a very freezing winter is coming. Bahá'u'lláh has said about this calamity but it is a source of joy to the friends because: 1st – He says to the friends and recommends them to be deeply engaged in teaching so that when it comes it passes away without hurting us. 2nd – He says that immediately after that the world will be awakened to the glory of the Cause of God. Therefore why should we feel afraid of the advent of something which is ordained for the proclamation of a glorious morning in the life of man?

... There are two different things which the friends often mix one with the other. One is the commandment of Bahá'u'lláh and the other is encouragement. If we break His commandments of course punishment will be the result; and the punishment is not the events which take place in life and we say that this is the punishment ... These are very wrong conclusions and usually are made by the friends without having any authority in the writings. Bahá'u'lláh ordains prayer, fasting, etc. Now suppose a Bahá'í does not pray nor does he fast. We must not think a certain calamity will befall him. Suppose his house falls down.

If someone says that this event took place in his life because he did not say his prayers this is absolutely wrong. There is no relation between the two. The punishment of the one who does not pray is his deprivation and loss of confidence and assurance. This is the result of such disobedience to this rule. Punishment is of the same nature of the act that we do.

Now, there are things which we are encouraged to do in the Faith, such as pioneering, etc. If someone does not go pioneering to some place he is not a sinner. He has not broken the laws of Bahá'u'lláh. It is encouraged that the pioneers remain in their posts. If someone returns he is not considered a sinner. He will never be the subject of God's anger and there is no punishment ordained for him.

There are more than 50,000 Bahá'ís in Tehran. Are they all sinners because they are not pioneers? There are more than one thousand who, because of many circumstances, returned from their pioneering posts. Shall we call them sinners and subjects of the wrath of God and His punishments?

These are the wrong conclusions made by the friends and often they become the cause of disappointments, dismay and even withdrawal from the Cause of God.

Our Faith is that of joy and moderation . . . There are so many doors open for us to enter and do that which is in our capacities. To be a member of a committee, on a LSA, NSA, or to hold a very small fireside, to go and visit patients in the hospitals, etc., are all the same. They are chances given to each individual to be joyful and happy. 'Abdu'l-Bahá used to ask the friends, 'Are you happy? If not now, when will you be happy!'

In no religion do we have so much about the glory, majesty and the endless joys of life after death. Therefore to say because we returned from our post God carried away our dear one to my mind is equivalent to believing in a wrathful and revengeful God. We are as a tiny worm in an apple, the apple on a tree, in a garden, in a village, near a town, in a state of a country, in a large continent, on this planet, a part of the solar system – one of the innumerable solar systems of the universe – and we tiny worms desire to grasp and comprehend all the indispensable relationships of all the events! Is it possible? Never. What shall we then do? Be happy with whatever happens, thinking of it as a part of the immense plan of God. Please my sweet darlings, never think that God is angry at you. If He was He would not give you the best of all the gifts: His Faith. I am sure it is sad to bear the loss of one's own sweet darling! I still lament the loss of our twins . . . but will never say that they were punishments; we always think that soon we will join them and be with them throughout eternity. Be happy and contented my sweet friends.

14

'I Do It Because I Must'

Faizi was very conscientious with his lessons and talks and would prepare his lesson plans before setting off on his journeys – not word for word but rather in note form, giving a logical sequence to what he wanted to convey on a particular subject. He would worry when he had to give lessons and talks in French, which was his fourth language, and although he gave inspiring talks and wrote movingly in English he would always say that it was not his language. Persian and Arabic were his languages. Nonetheless, it was in the English language that he delivered most of his lessons and talks around the world, with his particular way of conveying deep thoughts in a clear, uncomplicated way using appropriate analogies and examples. His audience 'listened raptly for hours as he spoke about the history of the Faith' and 'his scholarly answers to complex questions on religion were superb'. Many of his analogies were drawn from the world of nature and from objects around him. Speaking on one occasion about the human heart he compared it to the vase on his table: he remarked on its beauty, smoothness and delicate form, noting that the glass had no colour of its own and when empty allowed everything to be seen through it; but as soon as it was filled it took on the colour of whatever was poured into it, it lost its clarity, it became like a mirror of self-admiration, seeing no one.

Faizi travelled lightly. He had one small suitcase in which he had the minimum change of clothing and his briefcase in which he carried all the papers he needed for his lectures. He washed his clothes himself in his hotel room when he had time. Once when a couple bought him a few shirts he told them he really did not need any more than he had. On their insistence he chose one of the shirts they had bought for him then gave them one he already had to give to a needy person. He would always bring us presents when he visited – nothing expensive, just small gifts – a little Grecian vase, a silk head scarf, a tie from Thailand.

Faizi hardly ever accepted gifts and certainly never when individuals or communities felt moved to contribute towards his expenses. When a Local Assembly sent him a cheque after he had visited their community, he wrote to them:

> As to your cheque. Please remember that wherever we [Hands of the Cause] go we pay our own expenses. We accept no gift, no support and no financial help. 'Abdu'l-Bahá has set an example. When they gave Him a cheque He held it in His hands and then gave the same back. Therefore the beloved friends should not be distressed if I send back the cheque with all my love and devotion. I beg you to explain the same to your beloved LSA and request them to accept this and do not allow me to consider an exception. Many, many heartfelt thanks for the beautiful thoughts, love and devotion which prompted your LSA to send the cheque. This joy can never be gained by the treasures of the world.

༄

Faizi's tour of Africa in 1970 moved him deeply. 'Nothing in this world is worth paying attention to except the waves of love – true divine love which penetrates, rejuvenates, heals and recreates,' he wrote from Kinshasa.

> The more I travel and the more I see people, countries and nations the more I am convinced that nothing except true love will ever save humanity from the depths of miseries and follies created by his own hands.
> . . . Never should the pioneers enter human society with the slightest sense of superiority or, God forbid, with a feeling that they are there to 'civilize' or to 'westernize' these people. Such

an approach is doomed to eternal failure. We must go to find the lost members of our own families, our own brothers and sisters, and learn humility and patience from them.

We need hundreds of teachers, speakers, tourists, writers, actors, musicians, etc., so that they can one and all spread throughout the vast barren soils and by their God-given talents, gifts and capacities cleanse the hearts of nations, peoples and races. The whole planet is ours if we just get a glimpse of this glorious victory.

How I regret that I am in Africa at this age when I have reached the downward march of my life during which one loses all and gains nothing. I could go, in my youth, to their cottages, sit with them, have their darling children on my lap, embrace them, hug them, play with them and let them feel with their hearts and souls that I am part and parcel of them. Now all these are dreams, empty dreams and when I awake I find my heart more aching than before.

From Dahomey (Benin):

... The depths of poverty and the abyss of ignorance are such as can never be measured or described. One must see the little innocent children, all naked and swimming in the dust of the streets! One should enter the very narrow black painted room called 'Bahá'í Centre'! The false pride and the animosities – one does not know which country is at war with another – prevailing in these poverty-stricken and God-forsaken countries. How often I repeat the words of our beloved Guardian where he explains three voices raised: one of war which is loud, forceful, fear inspiring; one of peace which is raised by the Bahá'ís and it is indeed weak; but the third one is from the very depths of the heart of humanity which is the strongest. Masses of the people cry havoc and search for a way out of all such unfortunate circumstances. But alas! Such voices are suffocated and man remains in dust, poverty and immorality as

I see them everywhere. Except for the hours I spend with the friends I am often in my room and pray and pray. I hope that the Almighty will turn His face towards this continent and turn some screws above to bring closer the hour of their redemption.

Our beloved pioneers in these parts of the world are the very embodiment of self sacrifice . . . Such souls are plenty and in front of every one of them I prostrate in salutations and praise.

From Gabon:

One of the many incidents that happened on his tour of Africa made a deep impression on Faizi. One day an old soldier walked into one of the meetings and sat down listening. He attended the meetings for three days and on the third day he stood up and said, 'Please accept me as one of yourselves.' When Faizi asked him what it was that had brought about this change of heart the old soldier replied, 'We must search for God. God does not search for us.'

༄

As the years went by Faizi found travelling for any length of time increasingly tiring. He wrote to a friend, 'When I am invited to give a lecture or a lesson you can't imagine how strongly I cling to His Hem and ask Him, "Confirm me. Guide me. Inspire me", and when the talk is over I feel released and happy.' When in 1973 he embarked on another long journey to Europe, Latin America and North America he dreaded that his health would fail him and started his trip depending totally on the prayers of his family and friends, in full confidence that they would support him.

Faizi's tour of Latin America was described in reports as being 'like a bright meteor, arising in the north, flaming across the central skies, passing on to the southern horizon and disappearing from our sight in Argentina, but leaving behind a brilliant streak of light'.[1] To an audience of youth in São Paulo he spoke of the influence of the world around them and cautioned them, saying,

'I DO IT BECAUSE I MUST'

'You can reach down one hand to a drowning man to pull him up, but if you give him two hands he will pull you in. Be careful of your companions and their influence.' In a ten day study course he traced the Plans given by Shoghi Effendi and the Universal House of Justice, all based on 'Abdu'l-Bahá's Tablets of the Divine Plan, and drew the audience's attention to the fact that the underlying purpose and goal of all these Plans was the establishment of the Kingdom of God on earth.[2]

During his first visit to Bolivia Faizi had seen what beautiful and colourful clothes the Bolivian Indians wore. When he returned to the country in 1974 he wore a jacket he had had made especially for this trip from a similarly colourful Persian material, *tirmih*, and the Bolivian friends loved it. On the eve of his departure from these dear people he wrote to a friend,

> . . . separation from them is very difficult for me. I have one heart and a thousand lovers; I cut it into pieces and give it to everyone; I'm afraid by the time I reach the Holy Land nothing of it will be left.

Someone once asked him which people of all he had been in contact with did he find the most civilized. Faizi's reply was, 'The Bolivians, next to them the Japanese and after them the Indians.'

From South America Faizi went to the United States where he spoke on a diverse number of topics from prayer to the education of children to living the Bahá'í life, continually emphasizing how important it is for Bahá'ís to integrate the Bahá'í teachings into their everyday lives.

Faizi next went to Canada where, again, 'the depth of his knowledge of both the teachings and history of the Faith, the sense of intimacy which he created in even the largest gatherings, and his never-failing patience, love and tact, all contributed to produce an atmosphere that captivated both hearts and minds'.

There were two points that Faizi consistently referred to on this trip: consolidation and the relationship between the individual believer and the Bahá'í community. When asked what 'consolidation' really meant his reply was that a community can be regarded as being consolidated 'when the decisions of its Spiritual Assembly are obeyed by the believers'. As for the individual's relationship to the Bahá'í community, he referred to 'Abdu'l-Bahá, who had said that Bahá'í life is like water is to fish. The moment we decide that we are tired of being on an Assembly, tired of going to 19 Day Feasts, tired of everything and think of removing ourselves from the activities of a Bahá'í community, our 'retirement will grow in measure and intensity' until such time as we will no longer consider ourselves to be a Bahá'í. At this stage of our development there may well be a clash of personalities and other problems in the community which muddy the water but, as 'Abdu'l-Bahá had said, no matter how muddy the water, if the fish falls out, it will die.

Faizi also went to Alaska during this trip. One night, as he was having dinner with a group of friends, they asked him how on earth he kept going the way he did. He had paused for a moment and then in a reflective tone replied, 'I do it because I must.'

15

No Time for Rest

When Faizi returned to the Holy Land after his trips it was not to take a rest but, as he himself put it, 'I am like an automobile that after a race has to remain in the garage for some time for repairs.' For example in May 1975 he had one month in Haifa, during which time he also had to finish an 80 page pamphlet in Persian about the Covenant of God in all ages, before going to Europe to attend nine summer schools, after which, in October, he returned to his home to prepare for a trip to Iran the following month. To give the reader some insight into the travels he undertook I have copied below a sample of one of his schedules as drawn up by the World Centre:

Schedule of the Hand of the Cause Abu'l-Qásim Faizi: November 1976 to May 1977

To	Arrival	Departure
Cyprus	1st November	14th November for Turkey
Turkey	14th November	19th November for India
India: [New Delhi]	19th November	23rd November for Bombay
[Bombay]	23rd November	6th December for Singapore
Singapore	6th December	10th December for Papua New Guinea
Papua New Guinea: [Port Moresby]	10th December	15th December for Goroka [PNG]
[Goroka]	15th December	20th December for Lae [PNG]
[Lae]	20th December	24th December for Rabaul [PNG]
[Rabaul]	24th December	31st December for Solomon Islands

To	Arrival	Departure
Solomon Islands [Honiara]	31st December	4th January for New Hebrides
New Hebrides [Port Vila]	4th January	10th January for New Caledonia
New Caledonia	10th January	17th January for New Zealand
New Zealand [Auckland]	17th January	1st February for American Samoa

(International Bahá'í Conference 19/22 January)

To	Arrival	Departure
Samoa [Pago Pago]	1st February	8th February for Western Samoa
Samoa [Apia]	8th February	14th February for Tonga
Tonga	14th February	21st February for Fiji
Fiji [Suva]	21st February	1st March for Gilbert Islands
Gilbert Islands [Tarawa]	1st March	7th March for Marshall Islands *(cancelled)*
Marshall Islands [Majuro]	7th March	14th March for New Hebrides *(cancelled)*
New Hebrides [Port Vila]	14th March	19th March for New Caledonia
New Caledonia	19th March	24th March for Australia
Australia [Brisbane]	24th March	9th April for New Hebrides *(Rest period)*
New Hebrides [Port Vila]	9th April	25th or 26th April to Australia

(First Convention of NSA of the New Hebrides 23/24 April)

To	Arrival	Departure
Australia [Sydney]	26th April	2nd May to Melbourne
[Melbourne]	2nd May	9th May to Adelaide
[Adelaide]	9th May	16th May to Perth
[Perth]	16th May	24th May to Mauritius
Mauritius	24th May	1st June to Madagascar

(Subsequent travels planned for African continent from 1st June onwards)

In August 1976 he began putting together more than 20 deepening lessons in preparation for the long tour of the Pacific, which included representing the House of Justice at the International Conference in New Zealand in January 1977. Although he felt that his health might not hold up he was 'absolutely sure that the Concourse on High' would keep him 'on the straight path'. Faizi himself would never tell anyone that he needed to rest at regular intervals but would place himself at the disposal of the friends in whatever country he had travelled to and give his all to the needs of the community. The Universal House of Justice, however, ever mindful of all the Hands of the Cause, would, in their letters to National Assemblies notifying them of Faizi's visit to their country, give them instructions to ensure that he was not over burdened. This, for example, is an extract from its letter to the National Spiritual Assembly of the Bahá'ís of New Zealand (dated 1 November 1976) confirming his travel schedule to the International Conference:

> It is important that your Assembly understand its obligation to shield the beloved Mr Faizi from the importunities of the friends and the pressures of too demanding a schedule. Apart from your privilege of meeting and transporting him as may be called for, Mr Faizi should have nothing scheduled for his mornings unless he himself takes the initiative to change this pattern . . . do not schedule Mr Faizi for any event whatever either on the day of his arrival or that of his departure. Please do not place Mr Faizi in a private home, however comfortable, rather he must be assured the privacy of a hotel where he can have needed rest periods, and can pursue his studies and correspondence.

After the International Conference in Auckland where over 1,200 attended, Faizi wrote to a friend,

> I was singing only one song in my heart and soul: O God, Where is Síyáh-<u>Ch</u>ál and where is New Zealand?! How is it possible that the Prisoner of that pit has brought Himself here? With

what strength have the waves of the Heart of Tehran reached the heart of the Pacific Ocean and created such excitement that the friends laugh and sigh together, pray together, embrace one another and are still loath to be parted?

With the increasing problems he was having with his health, Faizi wondered, 'With this troublesome heart, this ailing body, this burning breast how can I travel so far? It is only strength from God which is moving me forward.' He was feeling very tired, lost his balance occasionally, could not walk properly and had to climb steps one at a time but he concealed his pain and proceeded with his plan to visit many of the island Bahá'í communities before attending the inaugural Convention of the New Hebrides at Riḍván 1977, after which he travelled to India and Iran. He became quite ill and weak during his tour of the Pacific and spent some time in Samoa with Gloria's cousin Suhayl 'Alá'í and his wife Lilian.

Suhayl had asked one of the young Bahá'ís to come to the house when Faizi was on his own with strict instructions that he should keep Faizi in bed so that he could rest. However, this young man had no power over his charge. An hour after Suhayl left the house Faizi would get up and go into the living room to keep the company of his young carer. On one of these days, much to the youth's alarm, Faizi fell but as he helped him to his room Faizi turned to him with a conspiratorial smile and said, 'Don't say anything about this to Mr 'Alá'í!'

While he was in Samoa arrangements were made for Faizi to pay his respects to His Highness Susuga Malietoa Tanumafili II of Samoa, who he described as 'a very dear, pure and kind man'.

As soon as he was well enough to travel Faizi resumed his journey. His visit to Fiji was 'timely, inspiring, galvanizing and unforgettable' and 'gave rise to a surge of unprecedented activity with attendant publicity'. He imbued the community 'with a deep and solemn determination to live the life, to proclaim the Faith and to spread far and wide the teachings of Bahá'u'lláh'.[1]

Hand of the Cause Enoch Olinga, Faizi and Hand of the Cause Adelbert Mühlschlegel, Plön Youth Conference, 1972

Faizi and May, Famagusta, Cyprus, 1973

Members of the National Spiritual Assembly of Peru greeting Faizi as he steps down from the plane, July 1974

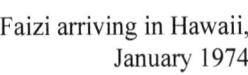

Faizi arriving in Hawaii, January 1974

Written on back of the photograph: 'This is a nice photograph of your dear father and me and I thought you would like to have a copy. Much love Rúḥíyyih', January 1974

Faizi in front of the Bahá'í House of Worship, Wilmette, 1974

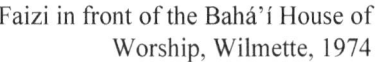

Faizi wanted this picture taken, Norway, 24 October 1974

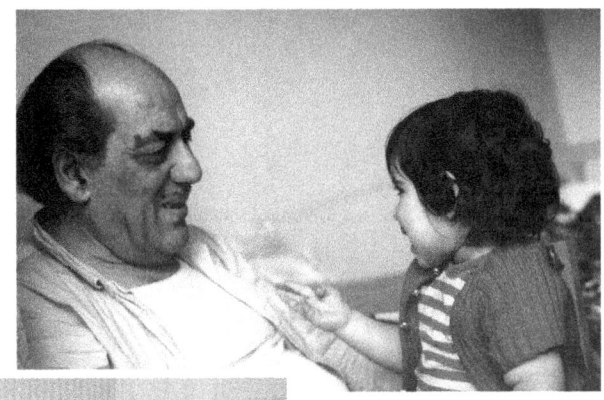

Faizi listening to his granddaughter, Chehreh, holding forth, 1974

Faizi with friends in Vienna, September 1975

Faizi addressing the International Teaching Conference in Auckland, New Zealand, 1977

Faizi's meeting with His Highness Susuga Malietoa Tanumafili II of Samoa, *second from left*. Suhayl 'Alá'í, *right*, Samoa 1977

Faizi taking a deepening class in Samoa, 1977

Faizi with grandsons Paul-Faizi and Thomas, Cyprus 1977

A tired and unwell Faizi, Papua New Guinea, April 1977

Faizi meets the friends, 1970s

Faizi and youngest grandson, Árám, London, 1978

Faizi in a pensive mood, London, 1978

Faizi and Gloria during Faizi's last time with Zohreh, Naysán, Chehreh and Árám, London 1978

Rúḥíyyih Khánum and Faizi in conversation

Faizi and Gloria in their home with Paul-Faizi, Peter and Thomas, Haifa, summer 1979

Faizi and Gloria at an exhibition of Faizi's calligraphy, Haifa early 1980

Sample of Faizi's calligraphy

Faizi's funeral cortege, Haifa, 23 November 1980

Faizi's resting place in the Bahá'í cemetery, Haifa

Throughout his travels Faizi was interested not only in the Bahá'í communities of the countries he visited but also in the country itself – not its politics but rather its people, natural phenomena and beauty and its arts and crafts. For example, in his view Fiji was one of the most beautiful islands of the Pacific. 'Every plant and flower', he wrote, 'is so great and ever in bloom that one thinks nature has overworked here and brought all things to exaggerated size and beauty.' This island in particular received him 'as one of them' when he arrived and there is a story behind this close spiritual bond between Faizi and that community.

One evening in the 1940s, when the few Bahá'ís who had settled in Bahrain used to meet at night, Faizi brought to their meeting a letter given to him by a young man who was a member of a correspondence club. The letter was from a woman in Fiji and it said:

> A certain American lady came to Fiji, stayed one night, gave a lecture about a certain religion totally unknown to us in this area and unfortunately she left and did not give us any book or even an address. The only thing that I remember is that this religion is called Bahá'í and it originated in Arabia. As you are living in Arabia could you help me to find and send me some books about this religion. I am very much touched by what that American tourist told us.

The small group were astounded by this letter and by the chance that had been given them to give some expression to their deep desire to teach the Faith. They prayed and consulted and agreed to ask the young man to give them the lady's address so that they themselves could send books to her. The man asked if he, too, could have some books on the Bahá'í Faith to study. However, owing to the instruction they had from Shoghi Effendi, Faizi told him kindly but firmly that he could not and he went home happy and content that his letter was being dealt with.

The small group of Bahá'ís in Bahrain sent a parcel of books to the enquirer in Fiji and for six long months their gaze 'was fixed on the hands of the postman in the most unbearable test of patience'. Then one day in January they received the letter they had been waiting for with such eagerness. The lady, Zaynab, had received the books, studied them carefully for six months and become a Bahá'í. Her husband, however, was not at all interested in reading anything to do with religion. Around Naw-Rúz of the same year the group received another letter from Zaynab: Fiji had a Bahá'í group, she was the secretary and her husband the treasurer!

Nearly 30 years later, sitting in the Bahá'í Centre of Suva in Fiji among the spiritual children of Arabia, Faizi, who always drew parallels from his vast knowledge of history, recalled the story of one of the Persian kings who ordered the payment of the salaries of his soldiers based in the far eastern states of his empire (Russian Turkistan of today). The grand treasurer ordered the governor of Asia Minor to immediately pay the salaries.

'Why send the order to Asia Minor?' asked the king.

'To show the extent of your empire, my lord,' replied the chief treasurer, 'so that in future historians will know that your orders were obeyed from Asia Minor to the heart of Asia.'

Now the friends of Arabia, who felt the deprivation of not being able to speak openly as much as a word about their Faith, were indirectly responsible for giving the gift of faith to souls in the Pacific Ocean.

೧౧

Of his visit to Papua New Guinea Faizi wrote to a friend:

> I have had the great honour to visit the poorest followers of Bahá'u'lláh. They are so beautiful, so gentle, satisfied and contented. Even the children, though naked, show the greatest amount of nobility. In other places though the children are well taken care of, well dressed, well fed, they are mostly greedy,

impolite, with no manners and insatiable. The children with their large black eyes, smiling faces, their cheeks always ready for a kiss and an embrace, they may be hungry, but they do not confiscate the tables like the children of other parts; they wait; and when they are given their tiny share they are happy and satisfied. The people here have a certain dignity which may be the fruit of too much persecution. Bare headed, bare foot, with one set of underwear and a pair of shorts they take the hard road of the jungles and go to teach the Faith of Bahá'u'lláh. When I see them, or think of them, I cry within my soul and repeatedly rebuke myself and say, 'Who are you? What are you? Can you go on these dangerous paths?'

☙

As much as Faizi loved meeting the Bahá'ís in all the countries he visited, the trips sapped him of all energy and he once wrote that when he got back to his home he intended to 'sleep and sleep and sleep'. Returning home, 'pummelled and broken', he was so exhausted that he wanted to flee from even looking at his desk. But then he believed that, 'Everything in this transient life is doomed to vanish except the humble efforts which we exert with the sole aim and purpose of elevating the beloved Faith that we have embraced. This is eternal. This will be our password to the presence of our beloved Master,' and so he willed himself to carry on.

16

Anecdotes and Insights

After the conference in Palermo in 1968 Faizi was, more or less, travelling from one continent to another for nearly ten years, until 1978. He spent the summer of 1978 teaching at summer schools in Europe. This is another example of his schedule:

To	Arrival	Departure
Cyprus	1st July	7th July
	(Visit Peter, May & children)	
London	7th July	15th July
	(Visit Naysán, Zohreh & children)	
Norway	15th July	24th July
	(Summer School 18/23 July)	
Finland	24th July	31st July
	(Summer School 26/30 July)	
Sweden	31st July	7th August
	(Summer School 1/6 August)	
Denmark	7th August	17th August
	(Summer School 8/17 August)	
Luxembourg	17th August	19th August
	(Summer School 18/19 August)	
Iceland	19th August	25th August
	(Summer School 20/24 August)	
England	25th August	17th September
	(Summer School 29 August/2 September)	
Germany	17th September	2nd October
	(Cancelled because of illness)	
Greece	2nd October	7th October
	(Cancelled because of illness)	
Cyprus	Late October	Early November
	(Visit Peter, May & children)	– return to Haifa

ANECDOTES AND INSIGHTS

This chapter contains a string of anecdotes and extracts from letters Faizi wrote during this period, not necessarily in any particular date order but giving some further insights into the man he was, his thoughts on the teachings of Bahá'u'lláh and his personal views on how to put them into practice. He was of the opinion that the success of Bahá'ís depended solely on the confirmations of Bahá'u'lláh and that if we relied entirely on our own capacity we would fail. He believed that when teaching the Faith we must create in the hearts of the listener a realization that 'they are missing something of urgent importance to their growth, tranquillity and spiritual development'. 'The ideal life of the Bahá'í community', he wrote, 'is to make people see, know, understand and believe that we are all brothers and sisters in a world community, flowers of one world garden, drops of one wave, waves of one sea and seas of one ocean. What greatness, power and immensity is decreed by God for us and yet we find people bogged down in the layers of dust and mud!'

ა

Prayer and Thinking Globally

On one of his visits to Ireland Faizi told a Bahá'í, 'When we pray we must pray to be subservient to God's Will. He always answers our prayers. Sometimes He answers them in the negative. We cannot expect personal guidance but sometimes it comes.'

He also spoke about what, in his experience, was one of the main reasons for problems in communities.

> In communities where problems of personality exist the work suffers . . . In all communities where someone starts to dominate the work suffers . . . When any community has been established wrongly the problems that existed there in the beginning seem to continue for many years. We must try to think universally not

locally. Instead of spending too much money on local needs we must think of international needs.

Faizi had a firm and deep belief in the power of prayer and was in the habit of chanting quietly to himself during the day. When he moved to live in the Holy Land he started keeping a list of those he wanted to pray for in the Shrines. He would start from Punta Arenas (on the southern tip of South America) and go round the world in his mind's eye, 'remembering my dear ones and praying for them and their children'.

૭୬

Although my father was an ardent believer in the power of prayer, he also believed that prayer alone was not always enough and that one had to be pragmatic. When a believer wrote to tell him that he was ill but would continue serving where he was and keep praying, Faizi told him that praying alone was not enough, that he should arrange to go to Tehran or somewhere else for treatment, adding 'otherwise if you are not well, how can you serve?'

A month before leaving to go to Cyprus in 1972 my husband, Peter, became very ill. My father wrote to him that he had to take care of his health, to rest before going because he would need all his strength when he reached his pioneering post, adding, 'I firmly believe in the blessings and confirmation which will be showered upon every group of pioneers, but I also believe that we must do our share too.'

Peter's resignation from the Bahá'í Faith soon after we settled in Cyprus upset my father deeply but he never tried to make him change his mind or pressurize him to talk to him about it. He kept a special place in his heart for Peter and always regarded him as his loving son-in-law.

૭୬

When a friend wrote to Faizi about the difficulty he occasionally had praying, Faizi shared his thoughts on the subject with him. He told him he should not worry if he sometimes could not pray and that this happened to many. He then added, 'The demand for prayer is like thirst. It should come at its own opportune moment. If sometimes it is delayed we must not make this as a great source of our chagrin. At the same time we will try to woo our prayer, just like unto the poets who woo their muse.'

༺༻

Once at a meeting during a visit to Germany a Bahá'í woman asked Faizi about obligatory prayers. She explained her dilemma and told him that while she always had a prayer book near at hand which she would open and read from whenever she felt moved to commune with God, she could not understand why she could not say the obligatory prayers in the same way, whenever she wanted, and asked why ablutions were attached to them and why they had to be recited at specific times.

In reply Faizi asked the lady what she would do if she received a letter from the general manager of the place she worked in asking her to attend a private meeting with him on a set date and time as he wanted to discuss a matter of importance with her. The lady responded that she would make sure she was suitably dressed and well-groomed then arrive at the general manager's office a few minutes before the appointed time to make sure she was not late for her appointment. Faizi then asked the lady what she would do if instead of an invitation to meet with him she had received a letter from the general manager wanting her opinion on a particular matter. The lady said that in that case she would just read the letter carefully before sending a reply.

The essence of what Faizi then explained to the lady was that, in his opinion, obligatory prayers have the status of being summoned to a private meeting, on our own, with the general manager: we are given a personal invitation at an appointed time when the doors of mercy are open wide for us to enter and we prepare ourselves in readiness for this special time of communion with our Creator with our ablutions. Other prayers, he said, have the same status as correspondence which requires only concentration of heart and mind.

༼༽

The Smoking Beggar

A close friend of Faizi recalled that on one of his visits to Tehran Faizi came to his house one night and asked him what he had for supper. He told Faizi that his wife was out and there was nothing in the house to eat but that they could go and buy something. So they got in the car and drove to the city centre where the friend parked his car and went into a shop to buy pickles and salami to make sandwiches. When he returned to the car he saw Faizi, who was not a smoker, standing in front of a shop with a cigarette in his hand, talking to a beggar. Going up to him, he looked at him in astonishment and asked, 'Faizi! What is this?! What's with the cigarette?!'

Turning calmly to his friend Faizi explained: 'This man came up to me and asked me for five *qiráns*. I told him I didn't have any. He then asked for four *qiráns*, and then three, two and one. I repeatedly told him that I had no money on me. He then said, "In that case give me a match to light my cigarette," which again I had to say I didn't have. So the man said, "Well then, let me give you a cigarette" and I said all right. Now he has begged a match off a passer-by and lit both our cigarettes!'

༼༽

Supporting New Publications

Faizi had an ability to draw people out, especially young people, and encourage them to use their talents. He supported the development of a number of enterprises for youth and children such as the magazines *Glory* and *Varqá*.

In dedicating the tenth volume of the magazine to Faizi's memory, *Glory* opened its pages with these words:

> With fond memories of our founder-father, beloved Hand of the Cause of God Mr AQ Faizi, whose loving guidance and interest was a constant source of inspiration to us. It was he who first visualized a youth deepening magazine and entrusted it to the youth of India. With characteristic zeal and unfailing determination he saw it through its setbacks and was a light of confidence beckoning *Glory* to greater and greater heights. And now, so close to the triumphant conclusion of *Glory's* tenth volume, he is no longer with us. We can only offer our undying gratitude and rededicate ourselves to realize the goal of *Glory* as our thoughts reach out to him in the Abhá Kingdom.

Another example of how he encouraged the young occurred when he was en route to the Bahá'í school in Panchgani during one of his visits to India. All of a sudden he turned to Shirin, the musical young teenage daughter of his friend who was driving him to Panchgani, and spoke to her about composing a song about Hiroshima, telling her that what happened there was very important in the history of the world. Shirin did not at the time quite understand the value of what he said. On their way back to Bombay Faizi was taken ill and rushed to hospital where complete rest in the intensive care unit was ordered and no visitors allowed.

Shirin, who loved Faizi and looked upon him as an uncle, was so distressed by what had happened that all she wanted to do was to make him happy. She remembered his suggestion and immediately set to writing the song 'Hiroshima!'. In the time it took her to complete her song Faizi was permitted a few visitors, provided he did not speak. Begging her way to his bedside she held her song in front of him to read. Faizi read the words, smiled and nodded his head. Neither one spoke but Shirin could tell from the expression on his face that he was very pleased. To her delight she received a letter from him months later telling her that he had sent her poem to the Austrian Dawn-Breakers, who were going to set it to music and perform it. Several years later she herself became a musician performing with the same group.

Writing to two young Bahá'ís in Turkey who had started a Bahá'í journal for the youth, Faizi encouraged them to, for instance, write sometimes about friends in Turkey who had risen to go pioneering, but 'in a way that does not go beyond the bounds of moderation', meaning that they should 'not write like Persians who raise an individual higher than an angel and then release him between earth and heaven'. He advised them to 'Write in such a way that the person does not become the cause of anyone's envy. For example, if a Bahá'í youth has finished his doctorate and written a good thesis write a few sentences about it; if some have enthusiasm for writing poetry publish their poems; if they are good writers ask them to write. Write about the early believers. The youth will then feel that the magazine belongs to them.'

Faizi's involvement with the children's magazine *Varqá* was significant. Fariborz Sahba, who started the magazine, recalled in a talk he gave at Landegg Academy in Switzerland some years ago that on one of his trips to Tehran Faizi invited a group of Bahá'í authors and educationalists to meet with him. During this meeting Faizi stressed the importance of starting magazines and books for children. For some time after there was much discussion among those who had been at that gathering but nothing actually happened. Fariborz, who was at the time engaged to be married to Gulnár Rafí'í, was troubled that Faizi's suggestion had not been taken up. He discussed his concern with his fiancée. Together they decided to approach a number of Bahá'í youth and, without publicizing what they were doing, the group gathered material, produced a magazine and presented it to the National Assembly for approval. Thus *Varqá* came into being. As soon as the first edition was distributed the small group started receiving support from the institutions. Having received the first copy, Faizi wrote his heartfelt congratulations, saying how delighted he was that after much hardship and difficulty 'the child is born', adding that this birth needed a gift and assistance. Together with his words of encouragement he sent the magazine the sum of five hundred dollars. The funds available to the newborn venture were limited so Faizi's contribution gave the group an added incentive to continue with their project.

Thereon Faizi's stream of letters to Fariborz and Gulnár, who had a major involvement in the production of *Varqá*, continued on a regular basis from wherever he was in the world. He gave them support and careful guidance. He advised them always to set a high benchmark, not to copy the fleeting modern trends in the Persian language but rather to familiarize the children with the language of the writings by emulating their style. He told them not to become disheartened by people's indifference, even if it was from within the Bahá'í community, because the angels on high assist those who persevere, and he assured them that *Varqá* would go from strength to strength so that in time its value would be appreciated to such an extent that even adults would start reading it.

When Fariborz took a model of the Indian Bahá'í House of Worship to the Holy Land, Faizi, although he was unwell at the time, wanted to see it before it was presented to the Universal House of Justice, so Hushmand Fatheazam took him to view it. Having seen the model Faizi quietly told Fariborz, 'I want to tell you that Bahá'u'lláh has given you this Ma<u>sh</u>riqu'l-A<u>dh</u>kár [House of Worship] as a prize for the magazine *Varqá*.'

☙

After attending a summer school in France in 1975, Faizi wrote the following letter about the youth in the community to the National Assembly of France, comments which are relevant to every Bahá'í community:

> . . . it is incumbent upon us to free this fire of enthusiasm by preparing sufficient and suitable Bahá'í literature on the fundamental verities of our stupendous Faith and make it available for their youthful, eager and hungry souls.
>
> Deepened in the world order and the universal principles of our Faith they will never fear any challenge in the teaching field. Well armed with the divine knowledge, adorned with the living of a Bahá'í life, and embellished with the garment of the Covenant, they will earn honour in the world as pioneers, teachers, and champions and protectors of the Cause they love so tenderly and so courageously.

ல

So Many Mistakes!

On one of his many visits to Germany Faizi once told one of the young Bahá'ís that he had heard there was a white ink for correcting written mistakes and asked him to buy him some of this fluid. The young man, who was delighted to be asked to do something for Faizi, found the largest container of correcting fluid in the shops, took it to Faizi and proudly said, 'I bought the largest I could find.' Faizi took a look at the size of the container, then at the youth, and laughingly responded, 'My son, do you think that I make that many mistakes?'

ல

A Focused Aim

After speaking to my brother on the telephone one evening my father wrote to him saying that he detected disappointment in his voice. He reminded Naysán of the first time he had mentioned his plans to pioneer, when my father had told him that 'there would be much disappointments and tests on this path'. He encouraged Naysán to 'Stand firm. Never doubt. The harder the place, the more will be the help and assistance of God.'

Although Naysán did not physically have our father with him from a young age, my father was standing behind him with his hand on his shoulder throughout his life with his steady stream of letters pouring out his love for him and giving him encouragement.

He once wrote to Naysán, 'It seems that you do not know the Persian proverb which says, "One can shut the gates of towns but no one is able to shut the mouths of people." You should never expect very much from people. You must always concentrate on your love for the Cause which you sacrifice everything for.' He then gave him examples from his own life, such as the false rumours that were spread about his intentions when he left Tehran to serve the Faith in Najafábád.

'. . . I persisted on my own path,' he wrote to him.

. . . I went on ahead with my mission, concentrating on the joy which had been created in the heart of the Beloved of all hearts. People, having no programme in life, no special aim except to satisfy some ambitious goals in life, cannot control their tongues; therefore a man of determination should never, never think of such matters even for one second. Have your goal in front of you and march on towards that. The beloved Guardian, who expects such exalted services as you render the Cause, will surely place his generous hand on your shoulders and in the sweetest terms express his joy and pleasure. This is worth the bounties of the two worlds. I deeply feel your worries, share your unrest, but at the same time feel extremely proud of you.

༄

One day Faizi was reading the pilgrim notes of Dr Youness Afroukhteh, who had lived close to 'Abdu'l-Bahá for many years. The account was set during the time of the troubles in Palestine, when everyone, except 'Abdu'l-Bahá, was in fear of the Commission of Enquiry. While the believers knew that nothing would ever harm 'Abdu'l-Bahá, they were, nevertheless, very worried and begged Him to take care. Faizi came across a passage in the pilgrim notes telling of 'Abdu'l-Bahá's serenity during this time. He found the passage so beautiful that he shared his provisional translation of it in a letter to one of his many correspondents:

> I make the sails very strong, the ropes tight and firm and everything in perfect order and then have my aim visibly in front of me and drive towards it. No tempest will ever cause me to deviate. Should I change my path at every wave, there would be no success. Look at the rays of the sun, spread everywhere. Have them pass through a lens and concentrate on a point, then conflagration takes place. Look at the steam coming out from the boiling water. Concentrate it in one place then the same weak and feeble steam will move trains and ships.[1]

Taking 'Abdu'l-Bahá's total focus on the progress of the Cause as an example, Faizi contemplated what wonders could be performed if Bahá'ís concentrated 'their material, mental and spiritual powers to one end, aim or purpose', adding that we fortunately have Plans at every stage to concentrate on, 'win its goals and then start another more glorious Plan'.

To the same individual he gave the following reply in answer to one of her letters. Reflecting the needs of the Faith at the time, he wrote:

As to your pioneering possibilities, I would like to mention the following points. I hope that these will serve as stepping stones for your future move forward.

1. I always pray that the pioneers will have the means to stay in their pioneering posts. During the many years, they learn about habits, customs, rituals, backgrounds and the history of the inhabitants of a certain country. They learn their language, then they come to know the people, find friends and contacts and people come to know them. When all these are gained they must go to another place and start the same spiritual exercises over again. This is indeed a loss of money, time and energy. Meanwhile, the pioneers grow in age and do not have the enthusiasm, energy and patience of their first years of experience.

2. The pioneers must have patience and remain sure that the seeds they sow will surely sprout and grow in due time.

3. The pioneers must know that the response of people of the world is not the same throughout the world. For example when we hear that some thousands have embraced the Faith in India we must not expect the same should happen in Germany. Sometimes the poor pioneers are judged on this basis. They are even told, 'Look, 1000s in India and only 15 in your pioneering post!' This darkens the vision of our pioneers and deadens their souls. Some have returned home because of such wrong approach.

Whatever happens I believe that the pioneers must stick to their posts.

These are my personal opinions and express the same in general to anyone who asks me.

And in another letter some years later:

But all the pioneers who have very often asked me as to the changing of their posts I have invariably said, 'No' and here are my humble reasons:

1. You are in Argentina about five or six years during which you have learned the language, contacted many people, have made yourselves known to the people, have established a business, etc.

2. You are just starting to have an Assembly.

3. Your new enrolled believers are not yet very strong to uphold the burden.

4. The contacts who are just ready to declare may stop.

5. Should you go to utterly a new place, you must start the language over again, make contacts, make yourselves known, find people to enrol, etc. What do these mean? It means that you will lose the years you have spent in Argentina and God knows whether you will gain them in Africa.

6. Bahá'u'lláh had always recommended patience. It is in the pioneering post that we must have patience. Therefore remain in your post, try your utmost to do more, establish some Assemblies and when you have enough, spend some months in travelling in South America so much in need of inspiration, encouragement and upliftment . . .

შ

When someone wanted to drop everything and go pioneering he advised him that 'going pioneering with no income is not right', that he should bide his time, work with patience and draw up a proper plan of where he wanted to go and then go, adding that, 'When God does not want something to happen we should not ask it of Him with force and insistence . . . Pray, but don't insist. Your plans will, sooner or later, work out with the will of God. As the saying goes, "Make haste slowly".'

છત

Faizi's response to a young man bemoaning the fact that he was forced to move to London instead of one of the goal towns was this:

> As to your transfer to London, I do not want you to have a guilty conscience and say that you have failed. Our Faith is the Faith of reason and moderation. We do and must do our best, but when something goes contrary to our plan, a force which we can't fight and extricate, we should never think or take this as a 'failure' . . . We are like pieces with which God plays chess. He moves us wherever He finds best. The condition is that we surrender ourselves into His hands.

છત

Faizi believed that the most important factor in wanting to serve the Cause is one's motive. He explained this point to a friend to whom he wrote:

> There were people who never physically accompanied Bahá'u'lláh on His exile and yet He called them the sole companion of His journeys. There were also people who were not killed but were called martyrs. The beloved Master named two doors of the Shrine of the Báb after two people who had not participated in the actual construction of the Shrine, but, as He has put it, they had 'spiritual affiliations' with that edifice.

છત

When a new centre was opened to the Faith Faizi wrote to the lone pioneer, 'Events such as this, though to the undiscerning eyes of the people of the world are small, to us are peepholes to eternity.'

To another he wrote,

> The harder the tasks the more abundant the results will be. Rest assured dearest that Bahá'u'lláh will never leave you alone and will surely take both of you under His wings of protection and love. No matter how hard the stones of people's hearts are, how hard the horizons of their souls and how bitter and heedless their attitudes are, they will eventually give way. This I tell you with all the love of a brother to his pioneering sister and out of the experience of a lifetime of pioneering. When the pioneers go to a goal they invariably are confronted with many bitter tests. Sometimes they lose children, health, all their money and eventually all hope. At this time two things may happen: 1) either they will leave their posts for their original home or 2) they will show resistance and steadfastness. In the first case nothing happens. They will be again one of the individual Bahá'ís. In the second case they will surely find success. All doors will be open. Jobs will be available. Homes will be prepared. Arms will be opened to receive them. They even go farther than this and each individual becomes the sole refuge of the people. They will come to the pioneer for advice, comfort, guidance and consolation. It is only at these moments that the Bahá'ís will see themselves really surrounded by the grace of God and His bounty. In the Qur'án it is said that the people should not think that they would be left untested by God.
>
> . . . This also I must tell you out of my experience. Please try your utmost to win the confidence of the people first and do not directly tell them first about the Faith . . . Every spirit has its own time of spiritual ripening. Like unto fruits the response of populations of different localities will come at different periods. Should all the fruits ripen at the same time then mankind will not witness the glory of summer and the beauty of autumn.

Faizi was saddened when Bahá'ís brought problems for him to resolve and would invariably encourage them to turn to their Local Assembly regarding such concerns. Referring to this he wrote in one of his letters, 'sometimes I become very tired and that happens when people bring their marital problems to me. There is nothing I can do and I never interfere in such matters . . .'

During his long stay in London in 1972 for treatment an individual came to see him to complain about another person who had misused his money. Faizi sat quietly and listened to the man. When the man was finished, Faizi explained that he was not a merchant and he did not know about such matters then suggested to the man that it would be of benefit if he instead turned to his Local Assembly for advice.

Fatherly Advice

Although he was always interested in our lives, my father did not interfere but would express his views when we asked for it. There were a few occasions when he gave us some fatherly advice. To my brother and his wife, Zohreh, soon after their marriage he wrote, 'As long as you love each other and make sacrifices for each other, material means are worth nothing.' And then he added, 'By the way, did you acknowledge the receipt of cables, letters, messages and gifts? Be sure to do this in due time, even if it will be gradual.'

Naysán and Zohreh were very young and still studying when they married. They would often seek both their parents' guidance before coming to major decisions in their lives and many of my father's letters to them contain his views and advice on various aspects of their lives, ones which can apply to anyone. When they had their first child Zohreh wrote to him asking him for his views on what to do about her studies. He replied,

> Your problem can be solved by yourselves after prayerful consultations. I do not allow myself to interfere in your life, I mean your joint life together. Nor do I ever desire anyone else to

dictate to you or Naysán. It is true that he is my son, but when I signed my consent to your marriage it meant that he is mature enough to live in perfect peace, love and harmony with the girl whom he adores. Therefore what I write to you I do never mean that both of you should obey. My suggestions will be in the form of questions. You study them together and then come to a peaceful settlement. Both of you say, 'Let us ask ourselves what is the central aim of our life together?' When you fix that pivot of your life then all other things will take shape and form accordingly. I presume both of you have the sole aim of consecrating your precious lives to the service of the Cause of God, which is the most exalted aim of all.

He then posed a few questions for them to consider: What was their responsibility towards their baby daughter? Did she need someone to feed her on time and change her nappies? Or did she have other needs? He believed firmly that children 'need the touch of their parents, their caresses, their bosoms and even their perfume'. He advised them,

> Please keep the love and harmony that you have now. Never do anything one-sided. One word, one deed, even one gesture which lacks love will prove detrimental even after twenty years. One of you may win a point, but it must be based on absolute harmony, mutual understanding and complete love and attachment to each other. This will make your life together very fruitful. Your children will grow in an atmosphere of love and unity and all their talents will be awakened to learning . . .
>
> Never approach anything which, God forbid, will keep you away from each other, even if it is one metre. This one metre will become the distance of East and West in future and even God will not be able to bring you back together.
>
> Therefore I beg both of you to study the situation and come to an absolutely loving determination accepted, approved and loved by both of you . . . As I said before, I do not allow anyone

to plan for you, to dictate and urge you to do this or that. It is your life. You must arrange it yourselves. The beloved Guardian has said that there is no difficulty in the whole world which cannot be solved by love and wisdom.

☙

Contrary to many people's perception of my father, he was quite worldly wise. When Naysán was selling his house he told him to be careful the agents did not cheat him. And this is what he wrote to him when he was thinking of going into business with another person:

> As to your office and your relations with owners . . . remember this: put everything on paper above your signature and others concerned. Do not say 'Oh, we are Bahá'ís!'

He cited a simple example. It so happened that once when he and Paul Haney were out buying stationery for the Hands' office my father did not have enough money on him so he borrowed some from Paul Haney. However, before taking the money he wrote out a receipt and gave it to his colleague, which Mr Haney kept until my father repaid the borrowed money, after which Mr Haney gave his receipt back to him.

'On this basis', he told Naysán, 'we are always on safe ground. No misunderstandings, no suspicion and no skirmishes.'

Writing to Naysán in the same vein he told him that he believed in helping others and being hospitable to people, but if he was going to leave the door of his office open to everyone to come and ask for his help in purchasing goods, getting visas, etc. then there would be no end to it and the situation would put him and Zohreh under so much strain 'that it will eventually become unbearable'. 'Moderation', he told him, 'is the law of our Faith and we must consider it in all aspects of our life.'

☙

'The Morning of Your Lives'

Attending the Hawaiian Youth Conference in August 1974 Faizi based his talk on a quote from Louis XIV of France. This is part of what he told them:

> The title comes from a letter of Louis XIV to his young daughter. She had decided to become a nun and wanted her father's permission and blessing. He wrote to say 'I am very glad that you are consecrating your life for the service of Christ. Even more glad because it is in the morning of your life. I'm in the evening of mine and can do nothing.'
>
> A story in the Qur'án . . . Muhammad says when God created the universe, He found it perfect and decided to have a representative on earth. He chose Adam, to whom He taught divine knowledge and asked the angels of heaven to bow down before him. All obeyed, except Satan, who said, 'Adam is created from earth and I am from fire.' Please consider this point . . . ever since mankind has had a divided nature, earth and fire. The beloved Master describes the difference. Earth has the characteristics of being faithful, patient, generous. Faithful: as thousands of treasures are deposited there for all eternity. Patient: although you tear it into pieces it accepts seeds and gives back so much. Generous: give it a piece of stick and it will change it into a growing tree. Fire has the characteristics of being angry, devastating and insatiable. It reaches everywhere in its thirst for danger and will devastate. All of us should adopt the characteristics of the earth. Servitude is the only path of success we can ever tread – the only path where every step is illumined by the Tablets and example of 'Abdu'l-Bahá. Every other path becomes an egotistical path which is doomed to failure.
>
> A new age is dawning upon the world. We are in the twilight of that age. Man has invented instruments to fight against nature but has also destroyed himself too. The path of servitude gives

us a way to explore our own hearts and souls without which we will never be anything. We must reach the rank destined for us. The youth must be careful about the current movements in the world today. All around us is a failing and dying civilization – the dead body of which gives rise to many new movements and thoughts. We must be taken by 'Abdu'l-Bahá on the path of servitude. We must realize the exalted position and destiny of man. He is the symbol of the whole universe – a miniature universe. He must explore himself, his talents, potency and powers to use in the path of God.

Youth is the greatest opportunity given man, to prepare himself for his life, every moment of every day. In the age of achievement, manhood, he will reap the preparation of his youth. A moment of these days (that is the dawning of a new age) is worth one hundred years of the future. Please do not transfer such moments to low aims and desires – be grateful that you were born in this day. People will come in flocks for remedy and healing . . . prepare yourselves from ten years previous. Follow the Dawn-Breakers and 'Abdu'l-Bahá . . . can a moth ever be separated from the candle? Walk in the shoes of the Master – that is the only way for us!

∞

To a young Bahá'í who had had several tragedies in her life he wrote, 'Stand on the summit. Never worry about the people who prefer to live in the depths of the valley of misery. Look for that beautiful morning and yours will be a life full of confirmation, progress, joy and great spiritual achievements.'

∞

Mysteries and Opti-mystics

The following are extracts from a letter Faizi wrote to Alexander Reid in Chile, which would be of interest to many.

As to your question about my stories in the Cause and the mystic side of which we must be conscious, I fully agree with your point of view. We have mystics in the Cause and at the same time we are practical and opti-mystics too.

As you said, no one, however long the list of degrees after his name or whatever position he holds in the Faith, is in a position to create a system of thoughts or in the slightest degree influence the opinion of friends by his own erudition or interpretation. We are free to express our thoughts, understanding and even elucidations; but the moment we start to ask others, or to force others to believe in the same way as we do, this will be utterly against the spirit of our Faith.

I believe that we must educate the believers to always turn to the texts and follow the institutions and not the individuals. Thus they will grow in the sunshine of the writings and remain protected under the shadow of our institutions.

Those who claim that there are no mysteries in the Cause and there is no mystic path to approach reality perhaps do not know that by mysticism we do not mean the life of the hermit who takes the path of the mendicants and adopts a secluded life and always prays and never enters the arena of service. Such a life is condemned in the Cause. But if we think of it as problems which challenge man to struggle, explore, meditate, pray and draw closer to the threshold of Truth, this, of course, exists in our Faith. From a practical point of view, as we travel round the world we find people who have embraced the Faith through visions, dreams, sudden awakening and other mysterious forces. 'Abdu'l-Bahá says that when we look at a candle we know that there is light in it but it needs someone to ignite it. But He also says that there are souls who are ignited by themselves.

This is the point. This is what is called by the true psychiatrists 'clairvoyance' through which many people recognize the Manifestation of God and which is obtained by prayers, meditations and true, sincere and honest approach to our Lord. Should we ignore all such bounties then we would question why to pray? This gives a perfect balance to our Cause. From one point of view we see that each individual believer is encouraged to become teacher, travel teacher, member of committees, LSAs, NSAs and other institutions of the Faith through which all the God-given capacities are streamed forth; and from the other point of view we find in an epistle written by the UHJ on the problems of the Guardian where they clearly state that there are mysteries in the Cause of God. It is the beauty, the perfection and the equilibrium of the Faith which keeps the two wings with the same importance and significance.

༄

The following extract is from a letter my father wrote to Naysán in answer to some questions Naysán had asked of him about The Seven Valleys:

The Seven Valleys should indeed be studied in the original language because, as Bahá'u'lláh has revealed the sentences, at the same time He has beautified each one by one or more words from the Qur'án. He has decorated the whole composition with the jewels of Persian poetry. It is so natural and so influential that the reader does not feel that there are jewels studded here and there. To understand the particular points you have referred to I believe we must start from the beginning.

The first valley is that of search. Why should a man search? Someone is living in a very luxurious mansion, is well equipped with everything. His hunger, thirst and all physical needs are well fed. Therefore such a man has no urge to start a path of search. In his own mansion he has wealth, servants and comfort; he will never face a thirst for something.

But the moment the same man experiences pain in his head, this pain will be the starting point of search. He will call his steward, or secretary, or one of the servants and command him to go and find a physician. This is the starting point of the spiritual journey to go through the Seven Valleys. You want explanation about Valley of Poverty and The Valley of Nothingness.

As one goes through the valleys, one after the other, the success, the overwhelming ecstasy may deter man from the straight path. I mean that man becomes proud. The moment one enters the realm of pride and arrogance, the downfall will start. Here Bahá'u'lláh advises the wayfarer to enter the Valley of Poverty.

To understand this, let us suppose that I become thirsty. I am dying for a cupful of sweet, translucent and appeasing water. I am dying of thirst, but I have a cup full of dust. What shall I do first? I must wash and wash the cup and make it absolutely crystal clean. Then the water will quench my thirst, otherwise water absorbs all the dust; I swallow and then I will be afflicted with some kind of illness. Having reached the end of this valley we will realize that we are nothing, absolute nothingness. If deeply convinced that we are nothing, then the Lord of creation will confirm us to render valuable services. Ponder upon the words of Bahá'u'lláh about the time when God raised Him. He says to the King of Iran, 'I was asleep on my bed. There passed over me the breeze of the grace of God and taught me all the knowledge' (it is not exact translation. I have just written this to you from memory). In another place He says, 'I am just like a dead corpse in the hands of the washer. He turns me whichever way he pleases.' There are many such references in the writings of the Báb, Bahá'u'lláh and particularly in the Tablets written by the beloved Master and more particularly the prayers of the Guardian.

☙

Firm Foundations – Stepping into a New Age

Faizi himself steered away from telling stories about the Faith which he had not first researched, and nipped in the bud any that were just hearsay. He explained in a letter that in this Dispensation we have the divine, authentic teachings of Bahá'u'lláh; we also have the early history of the Cause such as *Nabíl's Narrative*, Tablets in which some accounts of the lives of the three Central Figures are given and *Memorials of the Faithful*, which are some recollections recounted by 'Abdu'l-Bahá. What concerned him was relating unsubstantiated stories about the Faith which, although amusing or interesting to the listener, were 'bare bone and no flesh'. Such stories he felt 'will surely become unworthy of the Bahá'ís, dangerous for their children and disrespectful to our awe-inspiring history'.

On the subject of writing stories for children about the history of the Faith he felt that to dwell only on the lives of the martyrs was not wise. 'We have many heroes,' he wrote:

> Let us write about them, use our tenderest styles and beautify their stories with the anecdotes of their many sacrificial deeds. Stories about the first man or woman who embraced the faith in a country. Who was the first believer in Switzerland? In Germany? etc. They are fascinating stories and the children can read and digest. We have saints and heroes in the past religions and as we believe in all religions we must let the children taste the spiritual beauties of all Faiths.

For years Faizi sought the company of early believers still alive to record their stories and he always encouraged as many as would listen to him to do the same and to 'start now while many are still living who remember vividly all the early believers'. He used to cite 'Abdu'l-Bahá who, despite His busy life full of hardships and difficulties, 'spent many a night in giving sketches of the lives of early believers, especially those who accompanied Bahá'u'lláh into exile' and was certain that 'in future the people of the world will prove thirsty to read books and recollections about the Founders of the Bahá'í Faith in all the lands'.

'Bahá'ís should gradually do away with the habits of other religions which they have brought into the Faith with them, change their ways and model every detail of their daily lives on the teachings of the Faith,' was Faizi's advice.

'This is the beginning of the Faith,' he wrote in a letter,

> . . . and if certain habits are established it will be very difficult to get rid of them in the future so they must be stopped now. When I enter a meeting or gathering the chairperson rises from his seat and with his hands asks the audience to rise. I cannot describe how uncomfortable this is for me. It brings to my mind the gatherings of the clergy and mullás in Qum and Isfahan and what protests there would be if a person did not rise up when one of them entered . . . O God, grant some moderation! If they want to show love and respect how much better it would be if they listened to what is being said.

୧୬

Out of Obscurity

When Faizi resigned from the oil company in Tehran to teach the Bahá'í children in Najafábád his manager, like many others, could not understand why he wanted to give up such a lucrative job and disappear into obscurity by teaching village children and he tried to discourage him from doing so.

Many years later on one of his trips to Iran Faizi flew into Shiraz where a very large group of Bahá'ís had come to the airport to greet him. The same manager happened to be at the airport and saw him.

After the two greeted each other warmly the man remarked, 'I don't know who this crowd is waiting for. I have never seen so many people at the airport!'

Whereupon Faizi, giving him one of his special smiles, said with self-effacement, 'Mr [. . .] they are the Bahá'ís of Shiraz who have come to greet me.'

He hoped his former manager remembered that he had tried to discourage Faizi from going to Najafábád and disappearing into obscurity.

17

The Indomitable Spirit

My mother returned to live in Haifa in August 1977 and immediately set about tidying their flat. In a jovial mood my father wrote to Naysán and Zohreh that his books, papers and pens now all had their own assigned place which he dared not disturb. In another letter he referred to a friend in New Zealand who was helping my mother with tapes she was making for a radio broadcast: 'Gol-jún doesn't talk to me but speaks every day to someone in New Zealand and I have to pay the bill, but I pretend not to have noticed . . .'

By 1978 Faizi's health had deteriorated to such an extent that he could no longer travel as much as he used to. He wrote to a friend, 'When it rains we open an umbrella, when it snows and the weather is freezing we put on an overcoat to protect ourselves from the cold but when old age descends upon us there is no way one can stop the onslaught of that rain and snow.'

With a sense of urgency he spent most of his time gathering together the notes and stories he had written in the course of his life because he did not want to 'leave things undone or half finished' before his time came. However, he found this a demanding task. He would say that like the simpleton who, when asked by a mullá if he had memorized the daily prayer, replied that he had but could not put the words in the right sequence, he, too, found it an effort to put his papers in order. He also admitted that he could not be neat and tidy, that even his army training had not made him any more orderly and that in fact he was becoming 'more chaotic with every day that goes by'. I remember, however, that no matter how untidy his desk and bookshelves were, he always knew exactly where every letter, document and book was and would simply move a paper here or a file there and say, 'Here it is!'

Although his diabetes and problems with his heart were taking their toll on his health, the one activity Faizi persevered with was his correspondence, saying, 'What can I do, I am in the claws of the eagle of love for my friends.' He wrote to a group of his friends, 'You are always (I mean all of you) with me, present in my prayers, near me in the precincts of the Shrines; so much so that I often feel the touch of your hands on my shoulder, pushing me to go on, though the burden is too heavy!'

Faizi was very excited on 21 February 1978 because his brother was arriving in the Holy Land. The two brothers had a close bond but had spent all their adult lives living away from one another in their respective pioneering posts so that the short periods of time they were able to be together every now and again were very precious to them.

One problem Faizi had during this time was that he could not bend two fingers on his left hand and the doctor told him that he needed an operation to release the fingers. Faizi remembered that when he was in Tarbíyat School one of his teachers, Jináb-i Fáḍil Shírází, constantly rolled a ball of wax in his hand during his lessons. The day after being told he would need an operation Faizi bought himself some wax and willed his two fingers to move by rolling the wax in the palm of his hand. He was so pleased with himself when after about a week the doctor told him that there was now no need for an operation.

Under Gloria's care Faizi's health gradually improved somewhat and towards the beginning of summer his doctor told him that he was fit to travel. Gloria went on an assignment to Tehran and he travelled on his own during the summer months attending three summer schools in Europe and visiting seven other countries to meet with the Bahá'í communities. He particularly enjoyed a ten-day stay in Austria where the spirit of the friends and their eagerness to learn made him extremely happy. He also really enjoyed the classes he taught in Norway, Sweden, Finland, Iceland and Denmark and commented that all the schools were very well organized. By September and while in Denmark he was forced to discontinue his travels and seek treatment. He spent almost an entire day being examined and having various tests. The end result was that the specialist told him there was no sign of diabetes and that the pain in his shoulders would gradually go away. He was then offered coffee and cake, which he thoroughly enjoyed after the strict regime Gloria had kept him on. Despite this encouraging news, Faizi did not really feel well but so engrossed was he in the activities of every country he visited and so overjoyed with the meetings he had with the youth during these months that he, once again, neglected his health to such an extent that by the time he reached Naysán and Zohreh in London in October he had no energy left and arrived in their home totally worn out and seriously ill. He had not informed the World Centre that his health was failing him and soon after his arrival Naysán received the following cable from the House of Justice:

> INFORM DEAR FATHER OUR CONCERN LACK NEWS ABOUT HIS HEALTH WHEREABOUTS REQUEST HIM CONTACT US.

Once again the protective arm of the House of Justice embraced and lifted this valiant warrior and, in response to Naysán's reply, sent another cable:

> FOLLOWING CABLE SENT YOUR FATHER QUOTE DEEPLY CONCERNED RECENT RECURRENCE AILMENT URGE YOU RECONSIDER PROJECTED TRAVELS EUROPE FOLLOW DOCTORS ADVICE FERVENTLY PRAYING SHRINES UNQUOTE URGE YOU IMPRESS UPON FATHER NEED GIVE HIS HEALTH FIRST PRIORITY STOP AMONG POSSIBILITIES YOU MAY CONSIDER KEEP HIM LONDON OR RETURN HAIFA STOP UNDERSTAND MOTHER STILL TEHERAN STOP ASSURE YOU PRAYERS GUIDANCE ARRIVE RIGHT SOLUTION

Naysán, who, despite the unfortunate reasons, was jubilant at the prospect of having his father with him for some time, took my father in hand and became his assistant, his organizer and his shield; he drew up a strict timetable of treatment and rest and ruled over him with a rod of iron while Zohreh took care of his daily needs and seven year old Chehreh and baby Árám gave him constant joy. He started feeling a little better and was able to conduct some classes and occasionally accepted invitations to have a meal with friends but was by no means a well man.

One evening after dinner at a friend's house when the guests were sitting round and socializing, the host's little daughter came up to Faizi and with eagerness held a box of chocolates in front of him to take one. Totally ignoring Naysán's frantic gestures from across the room telling him to not even think of taking one, Faizi leaned over, kissed the little girl and put a chocolate in his mouth – which in effect was poison to his diabetes. On the way home when he was being reprimanded for ignoring his strict regime he said he would rather die than disappoint a child.

For years Faizi would put his hand on his heart in moments of extreme fatigue and say, 'My heart feels tired', so Naysán took him to see a heart specialist while he was in London. The specialist's diagnosis was that one of Faizi's heart chambers was partially closed and that to operate was risky; he gave him an estimate of how much longer he could expect to live. He advised him to be moderate in his activities and arranged for him to be treated for the pain in his back and shoulders.

My father did not tell any of us that he had only a few more years of life left. In researching for this biography I found this entry in his diary:

> O Bahá'u'lláh! May my life be a sacrifice to Thee! . . . My heart is so worn out that I have only four or five years of life left to me which means that, at most, I will breath my last breath in 1983.

18

A Quiet Year

As soon as he had regained some strength and was able to travel, Faizi flew to Cyprus to spend some time with Peter and me and our two sons before returning to Haifa. Although he put on a brave face and tried not to make much of his poor health, it was clear to us that he was drained of any energy. The years of travelling, giving his all from early morning to late night and into the early hours of the following morning, of not taking care of his increasingly ailing self, had racked his body. He arrived in Haifa 'fallen and aimless', feeling that he 'cannot be of any service' as he was no longer able to spend as much time as he wanted with the pilgrims.

Faizi had always used public transport in Israel but as he became more frail he had to be driven to his appointments. One of the friends would drive him to the Pilgrim House every day and then take him back home after his meeting with the pilgrims. In an effort to regain some strength and energy he started taking vitamins which a trusted friend and medical doctor, Dr Enáyatí, sent him from Germany but the damage to his system was already such that he was never to enjoy any degree of good health again. He was 'forced to leave the arena of service' and his active life of travel, teaching, lecturing, meetings and being with people most of his waking hours was gradually coming to a close. From now on he spent most of his time at home 'burning' in his own company, looking back on his life, remembering friends, longing to see them and regretting his separation from them.

'How is it that it has been my luck to be separated?' he lamented to one of the friends in Arabia. 'Although I see all of you in my mind's eye the outer eye has some rights too.'

My mother had by now returned from her travels to devote her entire time to caring for my father. Months went by in which my father became 'weak and despondent by the day'. The tinnitus from which he had suffered for many years made him dizzy and sleep came to him with great difficulty. Added to this he developed extreme pain in his back which eased only when my mother heated a bath towel and put it around his neck. He was acutely aware that his photographic memory and that retentive power of his brain which was always razor sharp were rapidly failing him.

I remember many years before, in the mid-1960s, he arrived at a youth winter school in York and sat at the back of the room during a talk being given by a new young Bahá'í. He sat relaxed, resting with his eyes closed and looked as if he were sleeping when the speaker, who seemed a little put out by this, suddenly called out and asked him if he knew where a particular passage he was referring to in his talk came from. I became angry within myself and felt that my father had deliberately been put in an embarrassing situation. My father, however, who had been listening attentively to the talk, calmly opened his eyes and in a very awake tone of voice gave the speaker the title of the book, the page number and the approximate place on the page he would find the passage!

'I have become rebellious,' Faizi wrote in a letter, 'and have supplicated and prayed so much that it seems I have tired God and I don't know what to do in my predicament.'

Nonetheless, the lessons he had learned from others and his own inner strength made him content with his lot. He remembered someone he knew whose brilliant son had developed mental health problems, telling him that from the day his son started having his problems he was content with the little brain he had. Faizi knew that although the man made this remark jokingly, it was evident that he had surrendered to the Will of God. On another occasion he saw the same person sheltering from a downpour, and while wiping his head and neck with a large kerchief, thanking God. Faizi asked him why he was thanking God?

'If it had been the Will of God', replied the man, 'to give us a downpour of vinegar and molasses from the sky, what would we have done? We must therefore thank Him!'

Despite his constant physical discomfort Faizi, without fail, worked at his desk and wrote letters every day. He asked a friend to send him stickers of flowers to decorate his letters to children 'to make them happy'. To a young woman who had written to tell him that she wanted to pioneer to Portugal he answered that her plan was noble and would receive blessings and recalled 'the joy and spiritual upliftment' of the many years he himself had spent pioneering. In this letter was one example of his many hundreds of pure, sweet gestures: a tiny picture of three bunches of flowers he had cut out from a magazine with a footnote reading, 'I wish I had fresh flowers to send you. Please accept this as a token of my best wishes.' These gestures of my dear father were made with such sincerity that the recipient felt their warmth and love in equal measure.

Faizi was no longer able to attend the meetings with the Hands, especially as he would have had to climb a flight of steps to their meeting room, but they regularly sent him some work and reports from National Assemblies to read. News of the progress of the Faith throughout the world rejuvenated him and gave him enough energy to send his response to his fellow Hands. When he felt better after some months, his ever kind and considerate colleagues held their meeting once a week in the Master's house so that he could attend by walking in from the back of the house where there were only a few steps to negotiate.

Faizi always found practising his calligraphy relaxing as he penned quotations from the writings or lines of poetry while quietly whistling a plaintive melody to himself. He also always had his radio on to negate the ringing in his ears, which he found very testing.

To a friend who had taken up calligraphy he wrote, 'When I am tired I take up my reed pen and start writing poetry or from the writings to relieve me of melancholy . . . my calligraphy is not matured.' He then gave him this advice: '. . . sharpening the reed pens is very important, as is holding the pen properly. If the pen is held correctly when it is placed on the paper the movement of the hand will form the letters well ... You should also have good ink so that you will gain mastery in this art, which truly gets rid of tiredness and brings calmness to one's heart.'

1979 was 'a miserable year' for Faizi. 'At the end of my life', he wrote to a friend, 'I have to pray and supplicate so much for just a little strength. These things that I'm telling you are not complaints, they are about my circumstances.'

In a letter to Peter he said, 'I am very tired. It is about three days that I am composing an introduction to a book and God knows how many times I have changed papers, pens, outlines, etc., because it is their fault and not my tired mind and fingers.'

❧

Peter and nine year old Paul-Faizi went to stay with my parents during Riḍván 1979. My father was so happy to have them in the house with him. He wrote to tell me that he and Paul-Faizi exercised together every morning and then they wrestled together, after which they would say some prayers and have breakfast.

In June of the same year our younger son and I went to Haifa for two weeks. My father was still enjoying the memory of the time he had spent with Paul-Faizi when two year old Tom arrived. They spent the mornings playing together in the living room and in the afternoons my father would go to his room and sleep. Tom would be told to keep quiet to allow his grandfather to rest but he would quite often creep into the forbidden room after a while, quietly climb onto the bed and lie down beside my father where I would find both of them fast asleep.

By July Faizi was able to pace himself to work at his desk for 15 minutes and lie down for 15 minutes. He hoped that his vanishing strength would return so that he could continue holding 'the thin thread of service' in his hands. He wanted to write articles about the Faith for the youth but simply did not have enough strength to do so. In despondency he wrote, 'If I cannot do this small service then my life is wasted.'

With the kind permission of the House of Justice, Peter and I returned to Haifa the same summer with our sons to spend one month with my parents. As their flat was not large enough to accommodate all of us, Shafíqih Fatheazam (who was like a daughter to my father and for whom he had a deep, tender love) very kindly arranged for us to use one of the vacant flats used by Bahá'í personnel at the World Centre. We would find my father waiting anxiously to greet his grandsons as we climbed up the steps to their flat every morning. Whereas he used to tease, laugh and play with the boys *ad infinitum*, he was now no longer able to get involved in the rough and tumble of their games and we had to be careful they did not tire him out. It was sad to see the grandfather who could not tear himself away from his grandchildren, even when they were asleep, slowly get up from his armchair in the living room at frequent intervals to go and lie down for a rest.

My father hardly spoke the day we were to sail back to Cyprus. He was very quiet and pensive. Having said our goodbyes and gone down to the waiting car taking us to the port, I ran back up to the flat to see him one more time. He was sitting in his armchair with his head slightly bent forward. He did not look up. I hugged him from behind and kissed the top of his head but he did not move. Deep in my heart I knew that that was probably the last time I would be seeing him.

19

Twilight

By August 1979 Faizi started to feel better and his extreme fatigue and pains subsided somewhat. He occupied himself by saying prayers for all the pioneers and his friends, reading their letters and answering them. It was generally during the quiet hours after midnight when he would begin his 'heart to heart exchange of love, feelings and prayers'. He was now physically unable to serve the Cause but he could pray and regarded remembering and praying for the pioneers around the world as one of his duties, a duty he performed in all sincerity and with all the love in his heart. He had a deep belief that we Bahá'ís need extra doses of the 'divine wine of His love', that it was this love that purified our hearts, 'gave flow to dormant feelings which must be manifested by tongue or pen'. It was in these early hours too that he would gaze on the photographs of his grandchildren, 'converse' with them and pray not only for them but also for all the children of the world. It was in his nature to pray for others, particularly pioneers and children. 'Closing my eyes,' he had written to some friends a number of years before, 'with the sight of heart I encircle the world and go to the friends' houses and even visualize the little darlings in their beds, kiss their angelic faces and give them as much as my feeble and humble power allows me the fragrances of these Holy Spots.'

୧୬

A deep love for Bahíyyih Khánum[1] had settled in Faizi's heart on first meeting her when in his youth Shoghi Effendi had asked him to go and chant for her. He now felt an urge to write a tribute to her, first in English and then in Persian, but was 'stuck as if on a mound, as if her pure heart did not want anyone to write about her'. Every time he started to write he would be gripped with such tiredness and sadness after about half a page that he had to escape to his bed with a severe headache. He eventually succeeded in writing much of the booklet which my mother completed for him after his death.

To give both of them some respite, my parents spent a few days in Bahjí. Resting in those peaceful and hallowed surroundings, Faizi felt his soul dilate to the beauty of nature around him. He delighted in watching the play of sunlight on a wall, the vastness of the sky above his head and the passion with which the sun sprayed its fiery colours across the horizon as it slipped away for the day.

℘

It now seemed a very long time ago that he had taken voyages around the world and he really missed his friends scattered around the globe.

'I wish I would go to the next world sooner,' he wrote to a friend, 'so that I would not suffer so much separation – wherever I go the friends are so kind and generous that I miss all of them.' He would place the letters he received from them in date order on his desk and answered each one in turn.

In the last year of his life Faizi felt that he had 'to say so many prayers for even a little strength'. Even though he found writing increasingly difficult, and was aware that it showed in his handwriting, he never gave up penning letters of love and encouragement.

There were several people with whom Faizi had a strong bond of affection. One of them was Amoz Gibson, as revealed in this missive:

O my dear brother, Faizi,
Alláh-u-Abhá!
May the blessings of Bahá'u'lláh
Surround you and your dear ones.

May He guide your steps, assist
You in your efforts to serve Him,
May His light shine upon your
Dear eyes and face
And may His all encompassing
Love continue to fill your heart
So that
All who meet you may
Feel what I feel for
You
Purest love!

Dear Brother
This paper is an expression of thanks for the beautiful paper you gave to me some years ago on which I should write to my sons. So precious was it to me that I only used it for special letters. The last five sheets are for even more special occasions.
Much, much love, Amoz

In his last few months of life Faizi complained that 'Life isn't worth it if it is to be spent being separated'. He was acutely aware that his time was running out and Hasan Balyuzi's death in February 1980 dealt a painful blow to his tender heart. 'Wherever I seek consolation to ease my mind it is impossible,' he wrote. He recalled past memories of their student days in Beirut and in a very poetic, sad and touching letter of commiseration to one of Mr Balyuzi's cousins he wrote, 'Now what can I do? It is impossible for me to deal with this thin, delicate veil of separation.' He would decide to write a letter to his friend every week and then suddenly remember that his friend was no longer in the same realm. Whenever he came across a beautiful sentence in English, Persian or Arabic he would automatically want to copy it and send it to him and never quite accepted that he was gone.

೧೨

In February 1980 my parents, at the invitation of Dr Daryush Haghighi, a heart specialist and a Bahá'í, flew to the United States for my father to receive treatment to help alleviate his condition. As my father was not feeling well they decided to fly directly to their destination without stopping over in London to see Naysán and his family. Had it not been for a fellow passenger who was a Bahá'í lady working for TWA and who did all the necessary running around, my mother could not have managed on her own. My parents stayed in the home of the doctor and his family and tests started from the moment they arrived. My father had every faith in his doctor and said that he had 'healed each pain'. Although Faizi could not be completely cured of his heart problem, Dr Haghighi gave him medication which helped calm it. The cataract in his right eye was also removed, which he was very pleased about, but nothing could be done about his gradual loss of memory, which became worse if he went somewhere new and had different people around him. Despite this, the trip rejuvenated him somewhat, particularly as my uncle, who was by now living with his eldest daughter in the United States, was able to visit him. Faizi's letters from the United States reflected an improvement in his mood and were a change from his, at times, despondent letters and there was a touch of humour in some of them.

'Gol-jún has won every heart,' he wrote in one, 'and everyone who sees me asks after her and it is apparent that they come to see her and not me.'

౸

The lift in my father's mood continued after their return home and his letters gave us an insight into the life he and my mother were leading.

'I can hear Gol-jún in the kitchen. She has tied a silk scarf around her head . . . thank God she has no expectations of me except to keep my desk tidy. She will bring coffee for me at ten o'clock.'

'I will improve with all the delicious food that Gol-jún is cooking for me . . .'

'Gol-jún and I are completely alone tonight, we have no guests, no meeting. We spend our time thinking and praying for you.'

'It is nearly morning. We have both woken up and come to the room where all our books have been placed in bookcases. I will swallow my morning pills and I'll then return to bed.'

'Gol-jún is all right. She sings and cooks. Her voice is good and loud, but the food is totally burnt.'

After some time his letters once again started reflecting his state of mind and the physical difficulties he was facing.

'I went to bed at eight o'clock but no matter how many prayers I said I could not sleep,' he wrote to Naysán and Zohreh.

The distance between my bed and desk is about one metre so I have come to my desk and started writing this letter to you so that you know I am constantly thinking of you . . . I am now fallen because I am at home every day, all day and incapable of achieving anything. My thoughts are with you, my heart encircles you; when I am busy thinking of you I feel happiness in my life but at other times I don't know what I have to do . . . Chehreh's and Árám's pictures are on my desk, they are my companions, I talk to them . . .

As if he knew he would not see us in this life again he wrote to me in January 1980, 'I want to embrace dear Peter one more time and to kiss you and the children . . .'

In almost all his letters he would write sentiments such as, 'In the dark of night I chant all the prayers I know and think of you, Peter and the dear children. I hope the warmth of my prayers surround you'; and to Naysán, 'All my concentration and thoughts are gathered in yours and May's house.' In July he wrote, 'I am well but my heart becomes joyful with difficulty.' In September,

It is weeks I have not been out of the house. All the work is on

Gol-jún's shoulders. Thank God the amount of work has not made her sick. They say that during the war in Europe the children prayed and said, 'O God! Protect yourself because if you are in danger all of us will be destroyed.' Now you pray so that Gol-jún does not fall.

☙

When he felt he had some strength Faizi would spend some time with the pilgrims, which he enjoyed immensely. He would share with them wonderful accounts of the history of the Faith, ancient poetry about the Mansion of Bahjí foretelling the coming of Bahá'u'lláh and explain the quotations from the writings he had prepared for them and was, as always, very sensitive to their needs. One afternoon when he detected that the group were tired he told them he would like to share many more stories with them but thought that as they were tired from so much travel perhaps they should have a prayer and then tea and thanked them for letting him spend some time with them.

Towards the end of his life 'Atiyyih Haghighi, who worked at the World Centre and was a good friend of my parents, would come to the house every Tuesday afternoon to go for a walk with Faizi. They would walk to the end of the road my parents lived on, sit and rest on a bench for a while and walk back, but even this was sometimes difficult for him.

Faizi appeared to gradually be preparing himself to take leave of this world and spent more and more of his time in prayer and meditation and writing to friends, which in retrospect were letters of farewell. In his last letter to one of his dearest friends, Salim Noonoo, he reminisced about their mutual profound love for the Guardian and ended by telling him, 'Be always happy, uplifted, joyful and remain assured in heart, because he is not separate from you.'

'Alí Nakhjavání was one of my father's closest friends. Notwithstanding his own heavy responsibilities as a member of the

House of Justice, he was in constant communication with my parents during my father's last months. On one of his visits, my father sat relaxed on the sofa and told Mr Nakhjavání that when as a young boy he attended Tarbíyat School he dreamt of 'Abdu'l-Bahá. 'Abdu'l-Bahá told him, 'Come here', and he went to Him. 'Abdu'l-Bahá then rubbed his chest and as He rubbed my father started feeling a warmth in his chest and heart. Speaking about my father after his death 'Alí Nakhjavání remarked,

> . . . this warm-heartedness of Mr Faizi that we all have felt was something really special, very special. This warmth you could feel in his voice, you could feel in his look, in his words, in his letters . . . when he chanted. He must have received this from this source of spiritual heat and love from the Master.

༄

Towards the end of October my father's health appeared to be deteriorating at a rapid rate. My mother, who was devoting her entire time to caring for him, asked Mr Nakhjavání to write to Naysán and me to give us information about their situation.

'I am writing this joint letter to you', he wrote, 'with all the love that my heart can contain to share with you news about your dear parents . . .

> Although the main purpose of the letter is to familiarize you with the condition of your distinguished father's health, I must begin by telling you that your mother has radiantly accepted the responsibility of looking after Abu-joon [Gloria's nickname for my father] with a degree of self-abnegation, nobility and courage which is truly worthy of everyone's commendation and praise. It is a well-known fact that her efforts in giving attention to and caring for dear Abu are offered not only on a twenty-four hour basis, but all the time with utmost dedication and loving patience.
>   But as to our dear Faizi-joon, his health has sharply

deteriorated during the past year. The trip to the United States proved to be helpful to him generally, but it soon became apparent that the lapses of memory which had already commenced prior to that trip were becoming more noticeable.

During the past several weeks, the deterioration in his health has become more visible. He has lost weight because of his depressed metabolism, his heart irregularities are more recurrent, and his lapses of memory more frequent. On certain days he feels such fatigue and weakness that he finds it difficult to climb steps, and even walk in the house, without help.

The doctors who attend to him are sure they are doing all they can to slow down this visible deteriorative process in his general condition, but they can give no assurance to what extent they will succeed in their treatment.

... Should Abu-joon's health worsen in the weeks ahead, she or I will notify you at once by cable or by phone ...

It is with deep sorrow and profound concern that I am penning these words ... Our prayers are regularly offered at the Holy Shrines for both of your distinguished parents, whose lives are nothing but a string of bejewelled gems in selfless service to His glorious and precious Cause.

Circumstances overtook him before he could post the letter to us.

స్

My father had a bath on the afternoon of 19 November. His back was hurting so he asked my mother if she could massage it for him. He then laid back, took her cold hands and placed them on his chest to warm them.

That afternoon Mr Nakhjavání was meeting with the Custodians of the House of 'Abbúd in 'Akká and had been invited to have dinner with them after their meeting. Their meeting finished at five o'clock and Mr Nakhjavání suggested that they have an early meal as he had to visit the Faizis; he drove back to Haifa as soon as they finished their meal. The road from 'Akká to Haifa has so many traffic lights that a good part of the journey is spent waiting for them to turn green, and from the outskirts of the city of Haifa to my parents' home there were at the time some 25 traffic lights. Something very strange happened that evening, and in relating the events Mr Nakhjavání wrote,

> These lights on that evening seemed to be under the control of some angelic forces of the Concourse on High. Every single one of these lights – and this is not an exaggeration – was either green, or just turning green, as my small Peugeot was due to cross. I was stunned! Was this really true? Was I in a dream world, or was this a miracle of some kind?

As soon as he reached my parents' flat he hurriedly climbed the steps to the front door and knocked. The door was instantly opened by my mother who was in a very agitated state.

'Abu is slipping away. Run to the bedroom,' she told him as she herself hastened to telephone the doctor. My father was sitting in bed with his eyes closed and was having difficulty breathing. His friend sat by his side and tenderly held him in his arms and 'in almost a second, it was a gentle heaving, and his last breath'.

༄

Among the last papers Faizi left on his desk were letters to be posted, a few gifts he had prepared to give away – quotations from the writings in his own calligraphy. At the bottom of each he had written, 'For the dear pilgrims.'

The Universal House of Justice sent the following message to the Bahá'í world:

HEARTS FILLED WITH SORROW PASSING INDEFATIGABLE SELF-SACRIFIC-
ING DEARLY LOVED HAND CAUSE GOD ABUL-QASIM FAIZI. ENTIRE BAHAI
WORLD MOURNS HIS LOSS. HIS EARLY OUTSTANDING ACHIEVEMENTS IN

CRADLE FAITH THROUGH EDUCATION CHILDREN YOUTH STIMULATION FRIENDS PROMOTION TEACHING WORK PROMPTED BELOVED GUARDIAN DESCRIBE HIM AS LUMINOUS DISTINGUISHED ACTIVE YOUTH. HIS SUBSEQUENT PIONEERING WORK IN LANDS BORDERING IRAN WON HIM APPELLATION SPIRITUAL CONQUEROR THOSE LANDS. FOLLOWING HIS APPOINTMENT HAND CAUSE HE PLAYED INVALUABLE PART WORK HANDS HOLY LAND TRAVELLED WIDELY PENNED HIS LITERARY WORKS CONTINUED HIS EXTENSIVE INSPIRING CORRESPONDENCE WITH HIGH AND LOW YOUNG AND OLD UNTIL AFTER LONG ILLNESS HIS SOUL WAS RELEASED AND WINGED ITS FLIGHT ABHA KINGDOM. CALL ON FRIENDS EVERYWHERE HOLD BEFITTING MEMORIAL GATHERINGS HIS HONOUR, INCLUDING SPECIAL COMMEMORATIVE MEETINGS HIS NAME IN HOUSES WORSHIP ALL CONTINENTS. MAY HIS SHINING EXAMPLE CONSECRATION CONTINUE INSPIRE HIS ADMIRERS EVERY LAND. PRAYING HOLY SHRINES HIS NOBLE RADIANT SOUL MAY BE IMMERSED IN OCEAN DIVINE MERCY CONTINUE ITS UNINTERRUPTED PROGRESS IN INFINITE WORLDS BEYOND.

UNIVERSAL HOUSE OF JUSTICE[2]

Hundreds of telegrams and letters of condolence from National Assemblies and individuals began pouring in as soon as news of Faizi's death reached the Bahá'í world. One of the most poignant was from his friend Bill Sears, which read: 'A SPECIAL SWEETNESS HAS GONE OUT OF THE WORLD AND OUT OF MY HEART.'

༄

Three days before he passed away my father wrote a long letter in strong, black ink to Mr and Mrs Zahrá'í (Zohreh's parents), Naysán and Zohreh. On the reverse of the last page, in green ink, he had added two lines to his darling daughter-in-law: 'My dear Zohreh, I am fortunate because this time both my letter and I will together be with you.'

༄

Peter, our two sons and I flew in from Cyprus the following day and a day after that Naysán arrived from London. Our father's funeral had been prepared with such love and reverence by the World Centre. The service was held in the then Seat of the House of Justice in the presence of his fellow Hands of the Cause residing in the Holy Land, Mr Furútan and Mr Haney, members of the Universal House of Justice, Counsellor members of the International Teaching Centre and staff serving at the World Centre, as well as close family members. His coffin was covered by a green (his favourite colour) silk cloth with beautiful gold embroidery. At its head was placed a wreath of flowers from Rúḥíyyih Khánum, who was in Canada at the time, at its foot another from his fellow Hands of the Cause and the rest of the floral tributes from all over the world were placed on the floor around his coffin. There was no sobbing and all sat in silence wrapped in their own thoughts listening to the prayers; but it was a prayer for children read by Faizi's eldest grandson that brought tears to the eyes of many who remembered his abounding love for children.

Ten children, each carrying a wreath, slowly and silently led the way out of the hall, followed by representative members of the House of Justice, the International Teaching Centre and Naysán and Peter carrying the coffin to the hearse waiting in front of the gates of the Master's house. During all the years he served in the Holy Land, Faizi would, without fail, embark on his travels from the Master's house. He would go to the Master's room and spend some time there beseeching help, guidance and protection and then walk out to the waiting car taking him to the airport. And so it was arranged that on this journey he would, once again and for the final time, leave from the Master's house.

૭૩

There was a hushed silence in the cemetery as the subdued cortège wended its way to the prepared resting place. I think it had rained the night before because all the trees, bushes, plants and flowers were fresh and revived and the distant bay sparkled, mirroring the clear blue sky above. The children carefully laid their wreaths around the coffin and then knelt for a few moments to bid their farewell to one who had loved them so tenderly. Listening to the occasional distant call of a bird, my thoughts turned to his friends in Bahrain and I wondered if my father in his freedom was, at last, able to return to them.

We walked away reluctantly, in ones and twos, and left the dear earthly remains of that loving, warm-hearted servant of Bahá'u'lláh to rest under the shadow of the Shrine of the Báb.

༄

'We were living in the filthy city, Qum', my father wrote to Naysán in the last year of his life,

> when, as in the prayer where He says 'I was in the ocean of negligence Your Voice called me . . .' I was summoned by Bahá'u'lláh and then saved from drowning. This is the same boy from Qum whom He saved then sent around the world to talk in meetings and gatherings. I am always in a constant state of amazement and constantly give my thanks and say, 'O Bahá'u'lláh! Grant Thy same favours unto my loved ones so that in their lives they will want no other pleasure except service to Your Cause.'

20

Vignettes

I can remember the first time that I knew he existed . . . Shoghi Effendi had received some communication from him or about him . . . and I said, 'Who is Faizi, Shoghi Effendi?' 'Oh,' he said, 'Faizi is a wonderful man.'

Wherever he went, from morning till after midnight, literally, the Bahá'ís were there: one of them or ten of them; or a meeting or three or four meetings in a day, or whatever it was. Finally, as he got older and much frailer and his heart began to give him trouble then he had to have a little bit more protection and during the course of his travels there would be self-appointed Bahá'í bulldogs who would take care of Mr Faizi . . . Faizi gave unceasingly from himself. He gave till the last drop, until the last breath, till the last kindness in that great, big, loving heart of his. It was like a furnace and he emanated love and encouragement and kindness, along with, of course, the great knowledge of the teachings, a scholarship in the Bahá'í Faith, and his gift as a speaker and his gift as a calligraphist . . .

When I was travelling in South America a number of years ago a Bahá'í in Bolivia came up to me and she said, 'You know, when you go back will you please give Mr Faizi a message from me? Tell him that in the hardest year of my whole life it was his letters that sustained me. He was the one who carried me through.'

. . . what a terrific correspondence Mr Faizi had. Till the very end of his life there would be a pile of letters to be mailed all over the world. He did this even though he was failing in strength, although the last two years he had quite a lot of pain . . . With *all* of this condition, physically, which was very hard for him . . . all of these things did not prevent Faizi from going on with his correspondence and I think that we underestimate what an act of

that kind can *mean* in the lives of dozens and hundreds of people.
. . . Faizi helped people to raise their quality as Bahá'ís. He contributed to polishing their characters, to enlarging their understanding of the Faith, to fanning their devotion, to increasing their craving to go out and serve in the pioneer field and serve Bahá'u'lláh and, if necessary, give their lives to Bahá'u'lláh.

He had, as I say, these warm, endearing qualities. He was just like a fireplace, you could get nice and warm by the spirit of Faizi. And children just adored this. I only know two people in the Bahá'í world that have this tremendous affection for children. One is Faizi, and one is his great friend 'Alí Nakhjavání. And these two men, whenever they saw anything that came under the heading of a child – in a street, in a Bahá'í meeting, anywhere – would just melt like butterballs . . . They had this characteristic that was so sweet and the way that Faizi would do things for children was really a very, very wonderful thing.

I think that we all miss Faizi. Certainly the world to me is a chillier place when a soul like that, who is so warm and loving, passes away; it's a colder place now that Faizi isn't here.

Rúḥíyyih Khánum (extracts from a talk given in Canada in 1980)

Faizi did not like anyone talking about his qualities, which is why we have spent our life keeping quiet; but now is the time to speak out.

He never saw bad in anyone; he used to say every flower has a different colour, shape and scent, but they are all flowers. It would be egotistical if one of them wanted the rest to be like it. We must love everyone for the way they are, not because they are the way we want them to be; otherwise the person would be you, which would mean that you love yourself. This is selfishness.

I remember the Christian missionaries had an orphanage. Whenever these children saw Faizi they would shout out 'Uncle Faizi! Uncle Faizi!' They would ask whatever they wanted from him as if they had found their father and Faizi was all generous . . . He made no distinction between friend and stranger . . . 20 years after he left Bahrain those who knew him would still ask about him, wanting to see him.

<u>Dh</u>abíbu'lláh Gulmuḥammadí

Faizi had a special relationship with three Hands of the Cause . . . One was Balyuzi . . . the other one was Mr Banání . . . Faizi was in love with Mr Banání . . . because Mr Banání was pure-hearted, very open, very frank, full of candour, and he loved these qualities. And humility . . . There were two Hands that did not like to be called Hands. One of them was Mr Banání and one of them was Faizi. Faizi was embarrassed every time someone would try to introduce him as a big figure in the Cause. He didn't like it.

I remember when the letters of Mr Faizi came to Mr Banání it was a feast for him. Faizi's letter had come! There are two Hands again here that had a special relationship with Mr Banání as far as his correspondence was concerned. One was Mr Faizi and the other was Mr Samandarí. When these two Hands wrote to Mr Banání that was something. He would put everything aside and ask his dear wife to read these letters and they were so beautiful. He would say, 'Read them again – and again.' He would immerse himself and his soul in the love and affection that these letters radiated.

'Alí Na<u>kh</u>javání (extracts from a talk given in 1980)

Your father was unique in many ways. Among them was the way he exemplified in his daily life the spirit of genuine, love-inspired humility, of true detachment, of radiant purity of motive and of utter self-effacement. Bahá'í audiences in the East and the West would sit spellbound as he spoke, with such dignity and affection to the friends. They willingly allowed every word uttered by him to sink in their hearts. This was because they knew that his outward behaviour and his inner reality were one and the same, and if he was giving any exhortation, he was the very embodiment of that exhortation. Undoubtedly anyone who crossed his path was favourably impressed, perhaps for a lifetime, by the influence of his heart-warming personality and presence.

'Alí Na<u>kh</u>javání (in a letter to Naysán and May)

None among the multitude of Bahá'ís that I have met in my 25 years as a Bahá'í have so much impressed me and indeed influenced in the deepening of my Bahá'í life as Hand of the Cause Mr Faizi . . . manifesting such qualities of love and pardon, patience and longsuffering, ever present attention to the smallest details to see that everyone was happy, able to withstand unperturbed the most violent storms of human emotions blowing around his person. He was able to discern and rectify at once any grievous injustice thanks to the calm and serenity expressed by the whole of his person.

Jacques André Schweitzer

My outstanding initial impression of Mr Faizi was his incredible way with the children at the school[1] (I at that time knew nothing of his immense experience with and understanding of young people). During question times his way of drawing out the shy ones who tried to hide from his gaze, his communication with them was a sheer joy to behold! Never have I seen (with the exception perhaps of Mr Furútan) anyone with such a winning way with children.

. . . When his fellow Hand Bill Sears was paying a tribute on one occasion . . . he recalled how (when sharing a platform with Mr A. Q. Faizi) he sometimes diverted questions to AQF saying that as well as standing for Abu'l-Qásim these initials meant 'Answers Questions'.

Alan Bell

I remember going to visit my two cousins who were pioneers in Bahrain and had come to Iran to visit the family, when the telephone rang and their mother announced that Mr Faizi was in Tehran. My cousins, like lightning, got up and with great excitement left us all behind in their haste to go to Mr Faizi. I had not met Mr Faizi and was very put out by this. Years later in 1961 when I was on pilgrimage I met Mr Faizi for the first time. Like my cousins I fell under his spell and understood their behaviour and knew that I would have done the same myself.

. . . When I returned from my pilgrimage I wrote to all those I had met and who had shown kindness. The only one who replied to my letter was Faizi – of course I did not expect any replies because I knew how busy they all were – and this correspondence continued until towards the end of his life.

On his first visit to Austria we went to the airport to greet him and I took my two year old son with me. My son was so influenced by Faizi's kindness that he would not leave his side. He never forgot 'Faizi-joon', to such an extent that every night before going to sleep he would ask me to relate the story of Faizi arriving at the airport, from the point when his aeroplane landed to the end.

He would ask me to buy things he needed but would never accept that I should pay for them and always insisted on reimbursing me. He never accepted any gifts; if he ever did he would give the gift away to someone else. The only things he would not give away directly were paper and envelopes of which I would always try and find ones with flowers and decorations on for his correspondence. One day, after my repeated insistence he agreed to tell me what he needed and I, with great joy, set out to buy what he had asked for. In the first letter I received from him after his return to Haifa was a receipt of a donation he had made to the Universal House of Justice in my name.

Faramarz Farid

When Hushmand Fatheazam moved to the World Centre with his family after being elected to the first Universal House of Justice, his wife, Shafíqih, wanted to make their three children's first Naw-Rúz in the Holy Land a memorable one. The clothes and shoes sold in shops in Haifa in those days were simple and basic so she decided to go to Tel Aviv to buy something more upmarket; but she was new to the country and nervous about driving on the roads which were at the time unmarked, without name or direction. Anyone going to the airport, for instance, had to rely on landmarks for the correct turnings – for example, at the large plane tree by the crossroad turn right and after the wooden bridge turn left, etc. 'Don't be afraid,' exclaimed Faizi the evening this discussion took place, 'I'll go with you!'

It was during the Fast so they set off early the following morning. In her anxiety not to get lost Mrs Fatheazam turned to Faizi as they drove out of Haifa and asked him to look out for landmarks so that their return journey would be easier. Faizi, in calm confidence, replied with a twinkle in his eye, 'Don't worry. I am on the lookout. There was an old man with a white beard standing on the corner of the crossroad we just passed!'

From an account by Shafiqih Fatheazam

One of Faizi's stories: A ruler had a beautiful daughter who had many suitors. The ruler eventually announced that all those who wanted his daughter's hand should bring her a gift; his daughter would marry the giver of the gift she chose. Gifts from all corners of the land began arriving at the palace: beautiful horses, white camels, expensive jewellery. After some time the ruler announced that his daughter had become ill and had died. Perforce all the men who had sent gifts came and collected what they had sent, with the exception of one man who said that the gift he had given was for love of the ruler's daughter, not because it was a condition of marriage. It became evident that announcing his daughter had died was a test. He was the one she married.

Maḥmúd 'Aṭṭár

As a pilgrim to the holy places in the year 1964 it was my great privilege that AQ Faizi accompanied us on our visits to the most holy places. How patient, what humour and courtesy; it will always be an exquisite experience and example for all my life.

... such a busy man and yet he had time to reply to a casual request, apparently filling in flying time whilst commuting from country to country ... the very fact that he had time to write to me endeared his memory.

E. Dekker

AQ Faizi was one who inspired my children in a way no other human being could. All three of my sons had the privilege of partaking of his love and affection ...

There was the time when I asked your beloved husband if he would want to chant a prayer in the German House of Worship – we were at that time rather formal in Germany and expected the readers to be at the lectern. Faizi chose to chant with his warm and loving voice remaining seated in the midst of the audience and under the Most Great Name. During German National Conventions and in summer schools he was a towering figure ...

I still carry the ring which came from his hands one morning in Rimini after he had heard that mine had been either stolen or lost in the ocean. And the many beautiful cards and flowers, the ever present thoughtfulness ...

Rene Steiner

Mr Faizi made a great impression on me every time he spoke at a conference or summer school. His words linger in my mind even to this day, maybe because he never tried to make too many points and then illustrated so beautifully what he said with quotations from the writings that they stuck in one's mind.

Katherine Villiers-Stuart

I shall always remember Hand of the Cause Mr Faizi because once you met him the imprint of his love and personality could never be erased.

Blanche Rudnick

It was during my pilgrimage in 1965 that I decided to go pioneering to Belize and it was Faizi who encouraged me to go. Indeed it was he who first mentioned to me Central America and suggested Belize . . . It is interesting that everyone else was encouraging me to first get married and pioneer later. Faizi was amongst a very few friends I had who said 'Go'. He wasn't concerned that I was a Persian girl 25 years old and not yet married.

. . . every letter which I received from him was like a healing medicine to all the ills of loneliness and suffering which pioneering to a remote and foreign land is bound to bring. It was he who encouraged me to stay, to persevere and it was he who later when I had met John after seven years of separation and had decided to marry him poured his love and support. Not for one moment did he admonish me for wanting to marry a non-Bahá'í or to leave Belize, which marrying John would inevitably mean doing.

Rouhi Huddleston

I found he had a special place in his heart for the pioneers. I had observed him with different people and he was kind to all but had a special interest in the pioneers. When he went to Manila in 1970 he said he went just so he could embrace the Persian students there and tell their parents in Iran that he had done so . . .

Occasionally I saw him greatly annoyed. I recall one time when he tossed down a letter and said, 'Why do they write me such things. This is not my business' (it was from one of the Bahá'ís in [. . .] with a problem in his local area – something for a National Assembly, not a Hand of the Cause).

Yes, Mr Faizi was a very special person who had a great impact on those who knew him. I don't know why; but one time I asked him why and he replied, 'It's the love.'

Barbara Sims

VIGNETTES

On receiving news of Faizi's death:

... This is a sorrow that is shared in whatever city or village visited by Mr Faizi. Eyes that have only seen him once cry for him, nor was it necessary for the friends to spend much time with him in order to love him; his spiritual attraction was such that a glance or a few words captivated the heart of friend and stranger, and those who remained in his presence felt more and more humble before the greatness of his spirit, his detachment and his deep love for all.

In the writings of 'Abdu'l-Bahá there is a clear affirmation that if the Bahá'ís would put into practice but one of the teachings of Bahá'u'lláh they would conquer the world. Mr Faizi was a Bahá'í who was able to put into practice one of these teachings in all of its perfection: the law of love. His love for the Bahá'ís and non-Bahá'ís alike was so deep and so universal that at times it seemed almost impossible that a human being could attain this degree of love. He would not tolerate any criticism about a Bahá'í, even if justified. If anyone dared to speak ill about another person, the sweet smile of Mr Faizi disappeared from his countenance, and as if that person spoken of were his dearest friend, his eyes would sadden. He would remain silent for a few moments and then with a very serious look would describe some good quality of that person. He never failed to find something good in anyone – and he would praise that person. In this way he would silence the criticizer or change the subject. He was a true father and brother to all the believers. His overflowing love did not permit him to see defects or faults in others.

... There were hundreds of persons who received letters from Faizi in all corners of the world. His constancy in this correspondence was another of the incredible facets of Faizi that was like springtime showers giving life to thirsty souls. If the friends didn't write to him because they didn't want to disturb him he would send letters to them and send them gifts.

... Beloved Mr Faizi was like a candle that is consumed drop by drop in order to illuminate a multitude of hearts.

R. Mehrábkhání

In looking back on my contact with your late husband, contact which has been more significant for me, perhaps, than any other personal encounters I have had with anyone, I realize with a kind of shock that I had almost no *personal* contact with him at all. And yet every word and gesture of his I was able to perceive sank intimately into my soul. Hence this poem . . .

> An Anecdote
> (In Memory of Mr AQ Faizi)
>
> If I have no anecdote to send
> Of the gentle doings of the Hand,
> I do not hesitate to stand
> A witness to that wondrous friend.
>
> If I cannot think of things he said
> That are not known by all,
> Having stood so far and small
> From that kindly light that shed.
>
> Illumination all around,
> Do not think I did not hear
> His voice, or was not near.
> I stirred to every tone and sound.
>
> I was a child upon his knee
> Staring widely at his face,
> Imbibing of his loving grace,
> And swimming in his knowing sea.
>
> Does it matter that I have no news
> Of glorious word and deed
> If word and action all were seed
> Of blooms my fate could not but choose?

I have no anecdotes to send
Save this love I bear that friend.

Brett Breneman

Here is the story of my dream I had of Mr Faizi on 5 July 1981:

I was a little girl of five or six and I was dressed in a white, long nightgown that a child wears, I even had thick white stockings. I awoke at dawn in a Bahá'í Pilgrim House in the Holy Land. I got out of bed and quietly ran downstairs across a courtyard and up another set of stairs. I remember that the banisters were a beautiful dark wood with carpets on the stairs. The dawn was still, peaceful and fresh with nice smells and a wonderful atmosphere of expectation. I wanted to see the sun rise over the Shrine of the Báb from the highest point I could get to. I crept over to the window at the top of the stairs where I bumped into this man in a dark suit. I was caught! This grandfatherly man just looked at me and laughed and laughed the way someone does when a child had just done something precious and wonderful. There was such love and joy in the laughter. It appeared that he was out of bed at that hour for the same reason and perhaps I had also caught him. Then he took my hand and we went out to the gardens together to see the dawn.

It is hard to describe my feelings during the dream; wonder at the dawn, a sense of adventure and then such love and warmth and companionship for this man. I felt really loved and accepted because of that love.

This dream was two weeks before I came on my first pilgrimage in July of 1981. I had no conception of the Shrines and the gardens but my dream seems to have been in Bahjí, at least with the feelings of the gardens.

I had the dream the night before I was scheduled to take an important exam which was the culmination of four years of university studies. I would think of my dream and feel the beauty of dawn and love of that man and was calm and relaxed amidst the confusion of two thousand people also taking the same exam. (I passed.)

I did not know who the man was until I was at Mary Ann Gorski's after my pilgrimage and she showed slides of the World Centre staff and members. One of the slides was the man in my dream, the same smile, the same suit – everything. It was Mr Faizi.

I have been a Bahá'í for six years and I am ashamed to say had never read anything by Mr Faizi or seen his picture. I knew he was a Hand of the Cause, but I had no associations with him.

Catherine Thompson

Mr Faizi had just received a letter from Mr Frank Khan and then very soon afterwards one from his son, Dr Peter Khan. In his reply to Dr Peter Khan Mr Faizi wrote: (approx) 'I have received a letter from the father and from the son and now I am waiting for the Holy Ghost!'

Vahid Tehrani

Even when he gathered us to spend time together he would devise games through which a lesson would be learned. One of the games was whoever was asked a question that individual did not have the right to answer the question but rather the person sitting next to him. This was an entertaining pastime and also a good lesson in not interfering in something that was none of our business and that when one is not asked a question directly one should not express an opinion.

He was the one who generated happiness and joy in every gathering. No matter what difficulty or worry he had, the moment he met with someone or stepped into a gathering the first thing he would do would be to bring joy rather than burden anyone with his own problems.

Ruḥu'lláh Náṭiq

He never forgot his friends and in matters of love made no separation between those he knew or not. If he saw good in anyone he would praise this trait; I never heard him say anything negative about anyone.

If he entered a place of worship with idols he would admire the craftsmanship of the idols; if he heard the call to prayer in a good voice he would delight in it to the core of his being; if he passed a beautiful mosque he appreciated the tile work and mosaics.

He was invited to an official's house one night during one of his visits to Bombay and asked me to accompany him. I told him that my garment was unironed and that in any case one needed to have a suit and tie on for such an occasion. He responded that his clothes were not ironed either and took out a crumpled jacket from his suitcase and put it on so that I would not feel embarrassed.

Hishmatu'lláh Rayḥání

Qatar in the 1950s had no greenery and the few Persian pioneer families sometimes longed to see just a blade of grass. One Naw-Rúz the community received a parcel from Bahrain. When they opened it at their gathering they found that Faizi had sent them fresh chives, one bunch for each family. The small group sat in silence and stared at the verdant chives, the first greenery they had seen for a long time, and immersed themselves in the love each little bunch had come with.

From an account by Púrán Muqarrabín

Mr Faizi encouraged the positive qualities in everyone. I have yet to meet another individual with such great love and affection. I often heard beloved William Sears say, 'Wait until you meet Mr Faizi, he is 200 pounds of love.'

. . . His explanations of the writings of the Bahá'í Faith, his knowledge of the Qur'án and of the Bible were exquisite. We never wanted him to stop. The more he spoke the more we wanted to listen. He spoke with all his heart and it penetrated into our souls . . . His keen sense of humour invariably made its way into every talk he gave. He often left his audience in a state of enraptured bliss. Although a native of Qum, he would jokingly implore, 'Please don't introduce me as being from Qum.' Anyone familiar with Qum would appreciate this humour . . .

Although he held a great station as Hand of the Cause of God, he never put himself above anyone else or expected any reward for his services to the Cause. He said that the ultimate lesson for man is to realize that he is nothing in comparison to God's might, wisdom and will and that His Cause is the supreme obligation of every age. We must realize that no matter who we are or what position we have in the Cause we are *nothing* except chosen by His will to serve Him.

Mohi Sobhani

I don't know how I can explain the great human quality of this great man. He always tried to remember and find occasions to say something good about people and praise them, no matter how small their achievements.

Farhang 'Alá'í

Bahrám Ṣádeqí, one of the famous writers of Iran, was much loved and respected by university students. No one knew that he used to be a Bahá'í and as he was involved in politics would not himself make any mention of the Faith. I had a friendship with him in those days and would occasionally consult with him about the children's magazine *Varqá*; he would express his opinion but he would never make mention of the fact that he used to be a Bahá'í. I had heard that he had been in Najafábád during Mr Faizi's time there and always wished that I could in some way bring him closer to the Faith.

It was during this time of my friendship with Bahrám that Mr Faizi came to Tehran, but unfortunately he was ill and his doctor would not allow anyone to visit him. However, one day Mr Faizi asked me to come and see him. During our conversation I mentioned Bahrám Sádeghi to him, that he was a prominent man who held a high position in academic circles and was much loved and popular but that he never met anyone [Bahá'ís]. I told Mr Faizi that I was aware Bahrám knew him from his Najafábád days and that with his permission I would like to bring him for a visit. Mr Faizi could not remember Bahrám but said that he would be happy to meet him and, although it was against his doctor's permission, told me to definitely bring my friend.

I told Bahrám I had heard he knew Mr Faizi from his days in Najafábád and he said, 'Yes, I have much admiration for him.' I told him Mr Faizi was in Tehran, that I had spoken to him and that if he wanted we could go and visit him together. He responded that he would come with great pleasure. This surprised me as I did not think he would agree to a meeting.

Mr Faizi was alone and sitting on his bed in his dressing gown. He greeted Bahrám with great kindness and courtesy. I said nothing and remained silent. Mr Faizi paid Bahrám such respect, as if it was he who had sought to meet with Bahrám. He told Bahrám that he had heard he had achieved great fame, that he was very happy for him and that he would pray for him. They spoke for about one hour. It was evident from the start of their conversation that Bahrám was a famous writer whose company and opportunity to converse with was longed for by all the undergraduates. However, I felt that he gradually, as if with the heat of Mr Faizi's kindness, started to thaw and melt till he reached a point of silence.

Bahrám said nothing when we left and I drove him to his house. With a lump in his throat he said, 'This meeting has completely changed my being. I feel I have wasted my life. It has passed me by . . .' Years later I heard that Bahrám was hosting 19 Day Feasts and had had a Bahá'í marriage. He died just before the revolution.

My point is that in this short visit with Mr Faizi this man's spirit was so revolutionized that it changed his entire life.

During the time we lived in England one of the pioneers to India became ill and came to London to see a heart specialist. When the doctor found out that his patient was originally from Iran he told him that he had had another patient from Iran some time ago but that that patient was not human: he was an angel whose wings were invisible. The patient asked the doctor what the man's name was, but he could not immediately remember so he called out to his nurse and asked her to look through their records for the name of the man who had come to the practice some time ago and who, after he had left the surgery, he had told her he was an angel. The nurse returned after a few minutes and said, 'Abu'l-Qásim Faizi.'

In the course of a short visit, while sick and feeling unwell, Mr Faizi had touched the heart of this doctor who knew nothing about the Bahá'í Faith or about Mr Faizi's status within the Bahá'í community.

Fariborz Sahba

Faizi would endure good naturedly any criticism directed to himself; but at the slightest thing which he felt was an attack on the majesty of the Cause he would roar like a lion and would not hold back in any way from defending the Faith.

Reza Jahangiri

He was very humble. I never felt embarrassed or overawed by his personality. I felt I could talk to him without thinking what I said, at complete ease and at peace. I do not remember him ever correcting me. He had a way of explaining spiritual truths in a simple way, never appearing to be fanatical or making other people feel he knew more than others.

Mansur Shah

He was pure and sincere . . . His kindness and behaviour to everyone was the same . . . I never saw him sad, he was always smiling . . . he never complained about anyone, he spoke about their service and accomplishments in such a manner that the individual concerned would involuntarily long to be of some service.

He never told anyone to pay attention and do as they were told but rather would find out what their talent was and then help them strengthen that talent. He never paid any attention to anyone's weaknesses and I can say with confidence that he never even saw them because all his concentration was on deep feelings, kindness and joy.

The enthusiasm both Bahá'ís and non-Bahá'ís had for Faizi was such that I seldom saw him alone . . . It sometimes happened that we would drop in without letting them know beforehand and every time Faizi would greet us in such a way as if he had been waiting for us for hours. Seldom did anyone have to wait for him, he was always in the room waiting or at the top of the stairs ready to greet one.

When we were all together there was never any talk of rank; we all associated with one another as members of one family, relaxed and in complete comfort. He was always full of stories and would always say from whom he had heard the anecdote . . . but most of all he enjoyed listening to other people's stories. In all the time I knew him I never heard him say he had done this or that, or that it was his idea. He would always refer to the writings and to the early believers and their achievements.

Manouchehr Ágáhi

I was a new Bahá'í when Mr Faizi came to Cyprus and one of the first questions I put to him was 'Why do we have to pray?' His answer was simple and one that I remember to this day: You are in a dark place and you want light to see where you are going. Praying helps you find the light switch.

Another of Mr Faizi's simple, but profound, analogies was given when I asked him about tests. He said that when he was visiting the friends in Africa the same question was raised at meetings. One of the believers gave an answer that he liked very much: A fine string instrument maker spends a lot of time to make an instrument. When he finally strings and finishes it, the first thing he does is to pluck the strings to test if his 'creation' can really give good melodies.

Mehmet Niyazi

One day a friend and I were travelling with Faizi from Qazvín to Tehran. We were talking about various subjects when Faizi suddenly turned round to face both of us and said, 'A woman is the queen of the household. This queen must have the door of her home open to all and she must entertain all, with the exception of one uninvited guest, and that uninvited guest is backbiting.'

  On an unforgettable day when a meeting had been arranged for Faizi the chairman, by way of introduction, opened the meeting by speaking about Faizi and all his accomplishments. Faizi rose with tears in his eyes and with a voice full of wretchedness said, 'Dear friends, Mason Remey lost his hold on the hem of the Faith because of all these praises. I beg you don't throw me in the midst of such a big test.'

  . . . I remember taking my four year old son to one of Mr Faizi's meetings and feeling very proud of myself for making him sit quietly. During the break Mr Faizi embraced my son, turned to me and said, 'This child is innocent and sweet but, my dear, you should not force children of this age to sit in formal meetings when they should be running around and playing, otherwise, God forbid, they will be fed up with such meetings when they are grown up.'

Mahnaz Afshin

Ten year old Mark Benatar, who was on pilgrimage to the Holy Land in January 1967 with his parents, started having severe pains in his abdomen and was eventually diagnosed with a burst appendix and rushed to hospital. Half an hour after he was admitted Faizi arrived by his bedside to support him and his parents. Mark and Faizi exchanged stories and jokes until the nurse came in to prepare the lad for his operation; but Faizi returned to his bedside and continued telling him stories about a character from a funny western cowboy film. Mark remembered looking down the corridor as he was wheeled into the operating theatre and seeing Faizi, Violette Nakhjavání and his parents sitting on a bench to begin the wait. He was told later that Faizi had not left the hospital until he was brought out of the theatre and he was assured that all was well.

  Faizi remembered that Mark had told him he collected stamps and would send him small packets of used stamps long after he and his parents returned home.

From an account by Mark Benatar

VIGNETTES

Naysán and his young family spent a year in Tehran in 1975 trying to get his exemption from the army as Faizi's only natural son. He refused to pay the customary bribes, which resulted in a two-week process becoming a nine-month ordeal of being sent from pillar to post, from one department to another, from one official to another and getting nowhere.

Six months passed and every document and every request had now been completed and met, leaving no room for a refusal to grant Naysán his exemption. At this last stage, having queued for hours to submit the completed four-inch thick document to a desk sergeant, the sergeant insisted that he wanted to witness his father actually signing an affidavit that Naysán was indeed his only son. This resulted in Faizi travelling to Iran to help Naysán.

By the time Faizi got to Iran the rules had again changed. This time the army insisted that Faizi go for an interview before a military panel. One of the Bahá'ís who had some know-how in these matters offered to help Naysán and in due course a day was arranged for Faizi to appear before the military panel.

Rank and hierarchy carry a lot of weight in Iran, especially in the army, who look down on all civilians and even more so on those seeking exemption from military service. Added to this, the panel had heard that Naysán was a Bahá'í and his father a leading figure in the Bahá'í community.

One of the lackeys who was in the room before the interview later told the friend the five high ranking interviewing officers had decided that when Faizi came in they would be as cautiously disrespectful as possible. The only chairs in the room were the ones the interviewing officers were sitting on.

Faizi, who was expecting trouble, pulled his shoulders back and was the first to walk into the room in his naturally regal, dignified manner. As soon as he entered all five officers, involuntarily, stood up and while offering one of their own chairs to him, called out to the lackey to go and bring in a more comfortable one for Faizi!

The interview became a formality and no questions were asked of Faizi. He signed the necessary papers and when he stood up to leave the five officers, once again, respectfully stood up to usher him out. Naysán's exemption was granted the same day.

From an account by Naysán Faizi

There were some rare occasions when a few immature Bahá'ís who had not grasped the spirit of the Faith approached Faizi seeking his help. Faizi found these encounters very testing, as reflected in the account below.

On one of his many visits to Iran a father and mother brought their son to Faizi and asked him to persuade the son to marry a Muslim girl without abiding by the Bahá'í law on marriage. Suddenly, this calm, patient Faizi, as like an angry bullet, raised his voice and shouted, 'Madam! Bahá'í institutions see to such matters, not Hands of the Cause; secondly, how can you allow yourself to consider such a thing? Who can give permission to act against the laws of the Faith? What marriage is this that for its sake your son should act contrary to the laws?' I tried to get the couple out of the room. Faizi's kindly face was in pain and he was despondent . . .

'Ináyat A<u>kh</u>aván

One night, during a break after a talk he [Faizi] gave in our local Bahá'í Centre, two young men came up to him wanting him to settle an argument between them. One of them believed that, compared to other religions, Islam is less important and has a lower status and waited for Faizi to agree with him. His friend believed that Islam has the same status as other religions. Faizi put his arms around the shoulders of both young men and with a smile told them that our standard is the teachings of Bahá'u'lláh. 'Study the *Book of Certitude*', he told them, 'and you will find the answer there.' He deflected their insistence on getting an answer from him there and then and before leaving, laughingly and with great kindness, told them again to study the book and to let him know the answer the next day.

In this way Faizi not only brought the youths' attention as to where they should seek their answers but also avoided embarrassing the one who was of the view that Islam was lower in rank to other religions in front of his friend and Faizi himself.

Dr Fereydoun Vahman (*Payám-i Bahá'í,* no. 132, November 1990)

I joined my parents in Haifa having finished the first years of schooling in Iran and speaking only Persian. I was registered to attend the Convent of Nazareth, a school just below the Shrine of the Báb, where the main language was Arabic . . . Mr Faizi was my first Arabic teacher who kindly put together a course for me and I used to see him on most Wednesdays after school. As I am writing these lines I can see myself walking up the stairs to his flat and being really excited. He would ask me to translate passages and at times sections of the writings, which were written in Persian (relatively easy ones) into Arabic, English and French. Incidentally, Mrs Faizi was my first English teacher.

Mr Faizi also kindly used to hold gatherings at the pilgrimage house in Haifa every other week (Mr Furútan continued to do this at times as well and particularly when Mr Faizi was away travelling) where parents and friends who spoke Persian used to attend and children (some of us by then would have been junior youth age group) would stand up and either read a piece that we had prepared or give a talk on a subject. We all knew that we had to prepare something and were ready to deliver it on the day. Mr Faizi very much believed that children should be given the opportunity to stand up and practise giving speeches, to build their confidence, knowledge, etc., and was always keen to provide opportunities to help us develop these skills. He truly loved children and showered us with love and care. I can still hear his voice expressing his pleasure and proudly praising and encouraging us.

Being in the presence of Mr Faizi was always like attending a Bahá'í class or life coaching, not tiring at all. It was a joy. One felt at ease and picked up things just by listening or watching Mr Faizi and how he interacted with others, particularly with the children.

He had an inner warmth and was truly a fountain of love. I so miss him.

I have letters from Mr Faizi written when he was travelling, or when I was in England studying, and some are so touching. One in particular made me cry as I could feel he was unwell and tired but was still sitting and writing to me rather than resting. He used to normally send me a postcard if he attended a big conference with a picture of the building that the conference was held at.

. . . I owe everything to the likes of Mr Faizi (of course my parents as well). He taught me with his actions. Through his actions I understood what was meant by 'actions speak louder than words'. If in this earthly world I can ever come close to appreciate or see a glimpse of 'sacrifice', I believe it is because of Mr Faizi and a few others. His face used to glow with love and warmth. When he entered a room he made every single one in that room feel that they were special . . . He had such a majestic build and yet was extremely humble. Full of knowledge, and yet the way he used to impart his knowledge one felt that one already knew that subject. This was because he was so good at teaching – he used to be able to take the lines that normally one sees between a learned and a student away. He was always full of praise. One could never get tired of being with Mr Faizi. If I am honest I used to feel like a butterfly wanting to fly around him and in my small way protect him, because he did not look after himself at all. He used to give away everything he had. Sometimes friends used to bring him a present, say a shirt, and he immediately afterwards used to say to my father, 'Mr Youssefpour, I have so many shirts, take this and give it to someone who needs it.' But what really used to hurt me a lot was that he used to give himself away as well, work too hard, and not look after himself. Although he had so much to do, he never complained, and kept paying attention to everyone including little nobody me.

Mr Faizi basically taught me that whatever one does in life has to have a purpose and at the core of this has to be the Faith. And serving the Faith does not stop because it is 5 pm or whatever;

service to the Faith is an ongoing endeavour. He also brought me closer to Shoghi Effendi and made me fall in love with Shoghi Effendi by talking about his eyes and how warm, beautiful and penetrating they were. Whenever he spoke about Shoghi Effendi you could see his eyes light up, but there was a hint of sadness as well, because physically he was no longer with us.

Mitra Murray's recollections of living at the World Centre as a young person

From a letter sent to Gloria Faizi:

I had walked into the kitchen (in the House of 'Abbúd while on pilgrimage) to return some dishes and found your husband sitting in the corner talking to some children. On the table was a fruit which, as I recall, was yellow and when it was cut open the inside was filled with black seeds. I couldn't seem to find one which was ripe enough to eat and I wanted to taste it. Mr Faizi came to the table and picked up one of these fruits and cut it open. He cut it into bite-size pieces and placed one of these into my mouth. He seemed to be so happy to see that I was satisfied by the ripe and sweet flavour of this fruit which was new to me. He proceeded to cut up the fruit and feed me from his own hand until I was quite satisfied. I do not recall what the fruit was or even remember the taste, but the memory of Hand of the Cause Faizi feeding me with his own hand will be with me for the rest of my life. As I think back on that precious moment I remember feeling how wonderful, humble and loving was this Servant of Bahá'u'lláh. Each Hand of the Cause of God has a special quality and to Mr Faizi was given the qualities of humbleness, showing forth an unlimited love to all he came in contact with and patience in teaching us the Faith of Bahá'u'lláh whether in story form or through his own example.

Isobel Wilson

Pilgrimage in 1977 was blessed with several meetings with Hands of the Cause Paul Haney and Abu'l-Qásim Faizi. Every evening one of the Hands, a UHJ member or a Counsellor would come and talk to us. Each evening I wanted to ask if I should apply to work at the World Centre but I felt too shy to ask a question. On the last evening we had Mr Faizi with us and I had resolved to ask him if I should apply to work in Haifa. Again I missed the opportunity through feelings of inadequacy, and when Mr Faizi stood up and headed for the door of the Pilgrim House I was so annoyed that I had missed my last chance to get his advice. Suddenly, he stopped in the open doorway, turned to face the pilgrims and said, 'Service at the World Centre is better than serving anywhere else, but teaching is better than this.' I had my answer, and in such a dramatic way!

Paul Bellamy

I can still hear his words as he explained to us the meaning of various themes. It was not so much the explanations – although these were brilliant in their simplicity – but the spirit in which they were spoken which so deeply affected the heart; and there was such an atmosphere of peace as he spoke – he was so gentle and mild, so charming and loving – that he melted all hearts! One almost wanted to weep at the beauty of his devotion to the Faith!'

Edna Warren

. . . his selfless love and affection touched the depths of one's being . . . Mr Faizi had that marvellous quality of talking with you or greeting you as if you were the most important person in the room. He treated all with such humility and love and his eyes were the mirror of a noble soul.

Iain McDonald

Appendix I
Passion Plays

From Faizi's own account (translated by Gloria Faizi):

Apart from the events which took place on the day of the martyrdom of Imám Ḥusayn, much mourning went on during the whole month of Muḥarram. Preparation for mourning began a few weeks before Muḥarram. The mosques were covered with black cloth and large tents were set up in them and in some private residences where people would be gathering to grieve over the death of Imám Ḥusayn.

Everyone started wearing black – all except those who had made vows for the martyred Ábbás[1] and went about in white clothing. Cloth merchants displayed a variety of black material to their customers, and salesmen went from house to house selling black clothes. By the time Muḥarram arrived it seemed as though a black cloud had descended on the whole town.

During the days of mourning, huge crowds of people gathered in the tents to hear about the events that had taken place on the battlefield of Karbilá. The clergy were experts at telling the story. They recounted the tragic events which culminated in the martyrdom of Imám Ḥusayn in such a heart-rending way as to induce the greatest sorrow in the hearts of their audiences. Many hours were spent in commemorating those days, in weeping and bewailing the sufferings of Imám Ḥusayn and his family. Impressive passion plays were performed, depicting the various tragic scenes of the battle; and those same youths who beat themselves with chains and cut their heads with swords in the processions on the streets now came forward to serve tea and sherbet to those who gathered for mourning. Some of the civil servants, too, who had great prestige in those days, would go about serving the crowds in bare feet.

One of the greatest excitements we had in life was to watch the passion plays. Crowds of people made their way to the tents from early in the morning, taking food and refreshments with them . . . There were different groups that went round performing pageants but there was one group of professionals whose only job was to enact the events of each day of the battle. They earned so much money during Muḥarram that it was enough for them to live comfortably for the rest of the year.

These professional actors were such experts in the roles they took on that even in their private lives they showed some of the traits of the various characters they represented on stage. People knew them by the names of those who had fought in Karbilá, and whenever I thought of his blessed Holiness, Imám Ḥusayn, it was the wonderfully radiant and impressive face of Ḥáj Áqá Javád that appeared to me with his blue eyes, dyed beard and green turban. Ḥáj Áqá Javád was an exceptionally good actor and people who made vows and supplications to Imám Ḥusayn threw so much money, gold and jewellery on his bed in the centre of the stage that he had become an extremely wealthy man.

The person who took on the role of Shimr[2] was a huge man with thick beard and moustache and a loud terrifying voice. He wore a red outfit, long boots, heavy armour and a helmet with a peacock feather. His appearance struck terror in every heart as he wielded his sword and galloped round the stage on his steed performing extraordinary feats of horsemanship. When he struck 'Alí Akbar[3] on the head and the blood-red dye spilled on the ground, the lamentation of Imám Ḥusayn was raised from another side of the battlefield. This scene was so tragic, and the chants of the father for his dying son so sad, that it could break any heart. The audience wept bitterly in uncontrollable sorrow.

'Alí Akbar's role was played by a young, handsome man with a heavenly voice, and the loud expressions of grief reached a climax when he chanted his last lament before he died . . .

Another handsome man with a very fine voice who made a profound impression on the audience was Áqá Qulám 'Alí, a strong,

APPENDIX I: PASSION PLAYS

well-built person who took on the role of the martyred 'Abbás.[4]

Áqá Qulám 'Alí was a sportsman and would come to the *zúrkhánih* at times. He would sit by the *gawd*[5] and add to the fervour of the men who were doing their exercises by chanting inspiring verses in his rich voice and in keeping with the beat of the leader's drum.

Some of the actors of the passion play made a lasting impression on me and I remember how sad I would become, particularly on the ninth day of Muḥarram, when I thought of how everyone had been killed[6] and Imám Ḥusayn was left alone, and that he, too, would be martyred the next day.

The tragedy of Karbilá continued to haunt me, and the grief I felt in my heart remained with me for a long time to come.

Appendix II

Zúrkhánih

This is what Faizi himself wrote about the zúrkhánih *(translated by Gloria Faizi)*:

The *zúrkhánih* near our house had a low entrance door[1] which opened onto a large stable where many horses were kept . . . The leader of the *zúrkhánih* was an elderly man with a pleasing, smiling face. He had long hair and a thick moustache. His back was slightly bent and I particularly remember that he had long fingers. He would come to the *zúrkhánih* very early each morning to clean and prepare the place for the men who arrived for their exercises after the call to prayer at dawn.

Pahlaván Ḥusayn, the most well known of all the *pahlaváns* in Qum, would be the first one to enter the *zúrkhánih*. He was more than six feet tall, had blue eyes and blond hair, and wore a big moustache . . . After him came the rest of the men, who would all change their clothes in the left side corner of the place. Only Pahlaván Ḥusayn would change close to where the leader sat with a bell hanging in front of him and a charcoal fire burning in a small brazier by his side.[2]

When they were ready to start, the men would step into the *gawd* one by one and kiss the floor.[3] They would also raise to their lips the apparatus they used in their exercises which were handed out by a young man in charge of the things. The beat of the leader's drum would then begin, very slowly at first, and his full, warm voice, chanting inspiring verses, would spur the men on to courage and bravery. One could feel the effect of his words and the enthusiasm it created in his hearers. Then, at the right moment, there would be a single loud beat on the drum and all hands would be placed on the board used for the swimming exercise. The men followed the lead of Pahlaván Ḥusayn in their exercises, and Áqá 'Alí demonstrated his extraordinary skills. While continuing with the swimming exercise, he would make a complete round of the men by sliding under their lifted bodies in imitation of a fish swimming under water. Then he would somersault on the Pahlaván's shoulders while the Pahlaván continued with his exercise.

After the swimming exercise came the one in which Indian clubs were used.[4] The Pahlaván would swing round with his clubs singing verses of poetry in a rich, manly voice to enthuse and spur the men on to excel in performing difficult stunts . . . He himself would then stand in the middle and perform such incredible feats as to astonish everyone. He would throw his heavy clubs right up to the ceiling and catch them, even with closed eyes; he would throw them up, turn around himself and catch them; he would throw them from behind, from over his head, from under his feet . . . None of the others ever used the Pahlaván's clubs, not only because they were too heavy but also out of respect for their mentor.

When the time came for the windmill exercise, Áqá 'Alí would again show his special skill. He would place both hands on the floor, bring his legs out from between his arms, then start whirling in the air while resting on only one hand. The movement was slow at first but the whirling gradually became so fast that it took on the appearance of a windmill.

During the windmill exercise some of the moral rules practised by true *pahlaváns* could be observed. As the most revered among them would be the last to perform this exercise, when one of them stepped forward to be the first to start, another would take him aside and start whirling himself, to show respect towards his comrade. I found this ritual, which was intended to teach the lesson of humility, very pleasing to watch.

When the time came for the Pahlaván to start whirling, everyone else left the *gawd*. He would turn around himself so fast towards the end of the exercise that anyone coming in contact with his fingers would be flung to the floor, yet he never showed any sign of dizziness when he stopped.

After that the men got ready for wrestling. The two rivals stood opposite each other, slightly bent and, at a sign from the Pahlaván, they started wrestling. The Pahlaván taught them the different forms of wrestling and constantly encouraged them to excel in their performances. If they showed signs of tiredness, he would spur them on with encouraging words but if the two opponents engaged in a heated confrontation, he would motion the leader of the *zúrkhánih*, who would throw down a cloth and say, 'Honour the cloth.' Both men would then instantly stop . . .[5]

When all the various exercises were over, there would be a short prayer session with the recitation of certain set verses. The Pahlaván and another person would then hold the two sides of a long cloth and go round, while the men threw coins into it.

Appendix III
Record of Faizi's Travels

Where no specific date is provided, the entries are in date order of travel.

**Before 1958,
while still living in Bahrain**
Dubai
Germany
Iran
Iraq
Kuwait
Masqat
Qatar

1958
September
Indonesia
Singapore
Pakistan

1960
May – July
France
Germany

June 1962 – March 1963
United States
Argentina
Chile
Bolivia
Paraguay
Brazil
Uruguay
Colombia
Costa Rica
Panama
Dominican Republic
Ecuador
Peru
El Salvador
Guatemala
Haiti
Venezuela
Honduras
Nicaragua
Mexico

1965 [dates from letters]
02.07.65   Finland

1966
Visited centres in Europe
Philippines
Taiwan
Korea
Japan
Hawaii
United States

1967, November – December
New Delhi, India: Intercontinental Conference
Malaysia
Thailand
Vietnam
Indonesia
Philippines
Taiwan

Korea
Japan
Hawaii
United States
Canada
British Isles

1968 [dates from letters]
February 1968   UK; Holland;
  Denmark; Italy; Greece
23.05.68   Finished 'From
  Adrianople to 'Akká'
August 1968   Plön Conference
05.12.68   Sri Lanka; India
19.12.68   Malaysia
21.12.68   Thailand; Singapore;
  Hong Kong; Iran

December 1968 – February 1969
India
Sri Lanka
Malaysia
Burma
Hong Kong
Cambodia
Laos
Thailand
India
Tehran

1969 [dates from letters]
01.01.69   Thailand
05.01.69   Laos
16.01.69   Hong Kong; Philippines;
  Macau
21.01.69   Singapore
28.01.69   Thailand
19.02.69   New Delhi
11.03.69   Bombay
14.04.69   Tehran
16.09.69   Holland
25.09.69   Luxembourg; Paris;
  Geneva

01.10.69   Milan
13.10.69   Genoa; Rimini; Naples;
  Haifa
24.10.69   Tel Aviv for visas to India,
  Singapore, Australia,
  New Zealand, New
  Caledonia, Fiji, Samoa,
  Tahiti, Honolulu, Japan,
  Guam, Philippines
05.11.69   Singapore
26.11.69   Melbourne
30.11.69   Sydney
03.12.69   Mara (Pacific)
05.12.69   New Caledonia
15.12.69   Fiji
16.12.69   Tonga
25.12.69   Samoa

January [1969]
Hong Kong
Philippines
Singapore
Thailand
Laos

February [1969]
India

April [1969]
Iran

June – July [1969]
Philippines
Singapore
India
Tehran

August – September [1969]
England
Holland
Denmark
Luxembourg
Switzerland

APPENDIX III: RECORD OF FAIZI'S TRAVELS

Italy
Greece

November – December [1969]
Malaysia
Tonga
Auckland: Continental Board of
   Counsellors Conference
Melbourne: Continental Board of
   Counsellors Conference
New Caledonia
Fiji
Western Samoa: Youth Conference
   (29.12.69 – 02.01.70)

1970 [dates from letters]
26.01.70 Singapore
16.02.70 Haifa
10.04.70 Kampala to see Mr Banání
04.05.70 Bangui, Central African
           Republic; Zaïre
17.05.70 Gabon
27.06.70 Senegal
06.07.70 Paris
16.07.70 Switzerland and Germany
           while waiting for visa to
           England
10.08.70 Chelmsford, UK
19.09.70 France
02.10.70 Cologne; Luxembourg
07.10.70 Bonn; Frankfurt; Cologne
12.10.70 Frankfurt; Athens
13.10.70 Athens
15.10.70 Haifa
15.10.70 Athens
18.10.70 Haifa
20.12.70 Naysán and Zohreh in
           Haifa

January [1970]
Hawaii
Japan
Guam
Philippines
Singapore
Hong Kong
India

February [1970]
World Centre

March – September [1970]
Kenya
Tanzania
Uganda
Burundi
Congo (Kinshasa): Convention of the
   new NSA
Bangui: Convention of the new NSA
   of Central Africa
Gabon
Congo (Brazzaville)
Chad
Cameroon
Nigeria
Togo
Dahomey
Ivory Coast
Ghana
Liberia
Gambia
Senegal
Canary Islands
Madeira

March – September [1970]
Portugal
Spain
Southern France
Switzerland
United Kingdom: Summer Schools
Western France
Germany
Greece

383

October [1970]
World Centre

1971 [dates from letters]
05.04.71 Dar es Salaam
16.04.71 Haifa
28.04.71 Congo
13.06.71 Tehran
20.06.71 Tehran
12.07.71 Najafábád; Isfáhán; Shiraz
15.08.71 Haifa
29.08.71 Italy
31.08.71 Rome; Rimini
09.09.71 Kampala (for Banání's funeral) then Athens
25.09.71 Geneva
03.10.71 UK
10.11.71 Holland; Denmark
14.11.71 Germany
22.11.71 Nuremberg
29.11.71 Austria
07.12.71 Istanbul; Ankara
21.12.71 Haifa
? Germany

1971
Italy
Switzerland
England
Holland
Denmark
Germany
Austria
Turkey
Tanzania
Iran

1972 [dates from letters]
02.01.72 Copenhagen; Holland; Germany; Greece
01.02.72 Cyprus
15.02.72 India
14.03.72 Poona
15.04.72 Bombay
02.06.72 Germany (Sanitorium) – Frankfurt
23.06.72 Sanitorium in Germany
July 1972 Munich; Nuremberg; Stuttgart; Hamburg
12.07.72 Cologne
25.07.72 German Summer School
02.08.72 Padua Conference
02.09.72 London
07.11.72 Ipswich
22.12.72 Amsterdam; Denmark; Hamburg; Frankfurt; Athens
31.12.72 Copenhagen

1972
British Isles
Denmark
Germany
Austria
Italy: Padua Conference (31.07.72 – 07.08.72)
Turkey
Greece
Cyprus
India
Australia
New Zealand
New Caledonia
Hawaii
United States
Alaska
Canada
Holland

1973 [dates from letters]
12.01.73 Hamburg
15.01.73 Frankfurt
16.01.73 Cologne
30.01.73 Athens
01.02.73 Famagusta
08.04.73 Haifa

APPENDIX III: RECORD OF FAIZI'S TRAVELS

22.08.73	Haifa – completed *Delight of Hearts*	

1973
Germany
Greece
Cyprus

1974 [dates from letters]
21.01.74	Haifa preparing for travels starting in May: Spain; South America; Hawaii; UK; Europe
22.05.74	Spain
23.04.74	On way to Sanitorium in Germany ?
27.05.74	Sanitorium in Germany
29.05.74	Brazil
31.05.74	Brazil
10.06.74	Brazil
26.06.74	Argentina
03.07.74	Peru
10.07.74	El Salvador: San Salvador International Conference 12 – 14 July
11.07.74	Panama
17.07.74	United States: San Francisco; St Louis Conference
03.08.74	Hawaii: Hilo Conference
August 1974	Canada
10.08.74	Alaska (Summer School 10 – 14 August)
September 1974	United Kingdom ?
03.12.74	Luxembourg; Greece
04.12.74	Luxembourg
07.12.74	Geneva
08.12.74	Geneva
21.12.74	Milan

1974
Turkey
Germany
Spain
Portugal
Brazil
San Salvador: International Conference (12 – 14 July)
United States: St Louis Conference
Hawaii: Hilo International Youth Conference (03.08.74)
Canada
Alaska : Summer School (10.08.74 – 14.08.74)
British Isles
Norway
Luxembourg
Greece
Switzerland
Italy

1975 [dates from letters]
06.01.75	Vienna; Turkey; Haifa
January	Tehran [with Naysán, Zohreh and Chehreh]
22.01.75	Haifa
14.02.75	Haifa
20.03.75	Solomon Islands
03.06.75	Preparing for ten Summer Schools
05.07.75	Summer School in Holland
10.07.75	Holland; Denmark; Belgium
11.07.75	Summer School in Denmark
19.07.75	Summer School in Belgium
01.08.75	Summer School in Leicester
09.08.75	Summer School in Devon
16.08.75	Summer School in France
20.08.75	France
23.08.75	Summer School in Normandy

385

27.08.75	Summer School in Luxembourg	15.12.76	Goroka, Papua New Guinea
31.08.75	Summer School in Italy	15.12.76	Malaysia
04.09.75	Summer School in Austria	16.12.76	Melbourne
01.10.75	Haifa	20.12.76	Lae, Papua New Guinea
08.11.75	Tehran	24.12.76	Rabaul, Papua New Guinea
		29.12.76	Adelaide; Perth
		31.12.76	Honiara, Solomon Islands

1975
British Isles
Austria
Italy
Turkey
Holland
Denmark
Belgium
France
Solomon Islands
Cyprus
India
Singapore
Australia

1976
Denmark
Belgium
British Isles
Summer School in the Netherlands
Summer School in Luxembourg
French Summer School in Normandy
Summer School in Italy
Summer School in Austria
Greece
Turkey
India
Malaysia
Australia
Singapore

1976 [dates from letters]

06.02.76	Shiraz; Isfáhán; Yazd; Kirmán; Rafsanján; Záhidán; Bandar 'Abbás
March	Greece
24.04.76	Turkey
25.05.76	Haifa
June/July	Preparing for Pacific tour
01.11.76	Cyprus
14.11.76	Turkey
17.11.76	Athens
19.11.76	New Delhi
20.11.76	Turkey; India
23.11.76	Bombay
01.12.76	Panchgani, India
06.12.76	India
06.12.76	Singapore
07.12.76	Singapore
10.12.76	Port Moresby, Papua New Guinea

1977 [dates from letters]

01.01.77	Canberra
04.01.77	Port Vila, New Hebrides
10.01.77	New Caledonia
14.01.77	Sydney
17.01.77	Auckland: International Bahá'í Conference (19 – 22 January)
24.01.77	New Zealand
25.01.77	New Zealand with Hooshang
01.02.77	Pago Pago (Samoa)
06.02.77	Australia
08.02.77	Apia, Western Samoa
14.02.77	Tonga
14.02.77	Samoa

APPENDIX III: RECORD OF FAIZI'S TRAVELS

21.02.77 Suva, Fiji
25.02.77 Apia, Samoa: met Malietoa Tanumafili II
01.03.77 Tarawa, Gilbert Islands
07.03.77 Majuro, Marshall Islands
14.03.77 Port Vila, New Hebrides
19.03.77 New Caledonia
??.03.77 Fiji; Tonga
24.03.77 Brisbane, Australia: rest period
28.03.77 Solomon Islands
06.04.77 New Genoa
07.04.77 New Guinea
09.04.77 Port Vila: First Convention NSA of New Hebrides
26.04.77 Sydney: Annual Convention NSA of Australia
28.04.77 New Caledonia
02.05.77 Melbourne
05.05.77 Singapore
09.05.77 Adelaide
15.05.77 Istanbul
16.05.77 Perth
May/June Cyprus
16.06.77 Haifa
July Cyprus
(Subsequent travels planned for African continent from 1st June onward)

January 1977
New Zealand – Representative of the UHJ at Auckland International Conference
Malaysia
Samoa

March 1977
Tonga
Papua New Guinea
Solomon Islands

April 1977
New Hebrides – Inaugural Convention of NSA of New Hebrides
Fiji
Samoa
India
Iran
Singapore
Cyprus

1978 [dates from letters]
21.02.78 Amoo-joon to Haifa from Cyprus
01.07.78 Cyprus
07.07.78 England
15.07.78 Norway
24.07.78 Finland
31.07.78 Sweden
07.08.78 Denmark
17.08.78 Luxembourg
18.08.78 Iceland; Denmark
19.08.78 Iceland
20.08.78 Norway; Finland
25.08.78 England
27.08.78 Denmark; UK [became ill]; Germany
17.09.78 Germany
02.10.78 Greece
07.10.78 Cyprus
16.10.78 Holy Land
05.11.78 Cyprus

July – September 1978
Summer School in Denmark
Summer School in Belgium
Summer School in France
Summer School in Luxembourg
Summer School in Italy
Summer School in British Isles
Iceland
Cyprus

Appendix IV
Major Publications

The publications are listed in date order.

Books in Persian

Ranj-i-Pisar (A Son's Suffering). A novel. Published in Iran (1933).

Chahár Sál va Ním dar Najafábád (Four and a Half Years in Najafábád). Published in Iran (1942).

Diyári-yi-Janún (Land of the Insane). A novel.

Zunnár (The Girdle). A collection of three stories. Published in Iran (1958).

Cárt-pustál (Postcard). A novel. Published in Iran (1960).

Khánum-i-Malakút (The Heavenly Lady). Amelia Collins's Life and Services. Published in Iran (1963).

Zamánih (Times/Fortunes). A collection of 20 previously published articles. Published in Iran (1964).

Payám-i-Dúst va Bahár-i-120 (The Friend's Message and the Spring of 120). Diary of Faizi's travels to South America, an account of the first Convention held in the Holy Land and of the World Congress held in London in 1963. Published in Iran (1964).

Dástán-i-Dústán (The Friends' Narrative). An account of the services of ten pioneers and well-known figures of the Bahá'í Faith. Published in Iran (1965).

Qand-i-Pársí (Persian Sugar-Cone). An account of Rúḥíyyih Khánum's travel to India and the Intercontinental Conference in New Delhi. Published in Iran (1965).

Nadhr (The Vow). A novel. Published in Iran (1970).

Ṭabl-i-Saḥar (Drumroll at Dawn). A novel. Published in Iran (1971).

Buzurg. The life and services of Buzurgmihr Himmatí. Published in Germany (1972).

APPENDIX IV: MAJOR PUBLICATIONS

Qáfili-yi-Sálár-i-Bandigí (Caravan of the Commander of Servitude). Essay on the Covenant of Bahá'u'lláh. Published in Iran (1976).

Imrúz Rúz-i-Sitáyish ast na Áláyish (This is the Day of Praise, Not Corruption). Essay on the Bahá'ís' first duties in serving the Faith. Published in Iran (1978).

Asfár-i-Bahr-i-Muhít (Travels in the Pacific). Diary of eight months of travel in the Pacific region. Published in Iran (1979).

Muhibbat-i-Hijrat (The Love of Pioneering). Essay on the importance of pioneering, requested by the National Overseas Pioneering Committee of Iran. Published in Pakistan (1980).

Books Translated into Persian

Tawqí'át Hadrat-i-Valí Amru'lláh Khitáb bih Ahibbá-yi-Imríká va Kánádá (1930–1) Shoghi Effendi's Letters to the Bahá'ís of the United States and Canada (1930–1).

Shálúdi-yi-Sulh (*Anatomy of Peace* by Emery Reeves, abridged translation). Published in Iran (1947).

'Azimat-i-Muslimín dar Ispániyá (*The Splendour of Moorish Spain* by Joseph MacCabe). Published in Iran (1948).

Dargah-i-Dúst (*Portals to Freedom* by Howard Colby Ives). Published in Iran (1969).

Gawhar-i-Yiktá (*The Priceless Pearl* by Rúhíyyih Rabbaní) (1969).

Works in English

'A Village Scriptorium: Isfahan'. Photocopy (1939).

A Flame of Fire. The story of the Tablet of Ahmad. Published in India (1969).

Bahá'í Lessons. Published in Australia (1969).

From Adrianople to 'Akká. Published in the United Kingdom (1974).

Longing. One act play in three parts. Photocopy.

Narcissus to 'Akká. Published in India (1970).

Three Meditations on the Eve of 4th November. Published in the United Kingdom (1970).

Thy Heavenly Army. Published in Canada (1971).

Our Precious Trust. Published in India (1973).

The Wonder Lamp. A play. Published in India (1975).

The Prince of Martyrs. Published in the United Kingdom (1977).

Milly. A tribute to Hand of the Cause of God Amelia E. Collins. Published in the United Kingdom (1977).

Stories from the Delight of Hearts. Published in the United States (1980).

A Gift of Love. A collection of writings on the Greatest Holy Leaf, collated and published posthumously by his wife (1982).

Commentary on the Kitáb-i-Aqdas. Published in India (1987).

Articles

'Explanation of the Symbol of the Greatest Name'. Published in India (1968).

'Equality of Men and Women'. Published in Puerto Rico (1975).

Faizi wrote countless articles about the early believers and various aspects of the Faith which were published in the Bahá'í newsletters of several countries.

Bibliography

All references to letters/cables from Shoghi Effendi are from copies of originals in my mother's papers. Those in Persian have the English translation in 'Alí Nakhjavání's handwriting in the margin.

'Abdu'l-Bahá. *Selections from the Writings of 'Abdu'l-Bahá.* Haifa: Bahá'í World Centre, 1978.

Afroukhteh, Dr Youness. *Memories of Nine Years in 'Akká.* Oxford: George Ronald, 2003.

Amatu'l-Bahá Rúḥíyyih Khánum. 'The Passing of Shoghi Effendi', in *Bahá'í World*, vol. 13, pp. 223–5.

Bahá'í International News Service, 4 September 1968.

Bahá'í International News Service, 1 September 1974.

The Bahá'í World. vol. 13. Haifa: The Universal House of Justice, 1970.

The Bahá'í World. vol. 14. Haifa: The Universal House of Justice, 1974.

The Bahá'í World. vol. 18. Haifa: Bahá'í World Centre, 1986.

Bahá'u'lláh. *The Kitáb-i-Aqdas.* Haifa: Bahá'í World Centre, 1992.

Emerson, Ralph Waldo. 'Voluntaries'. Various editions.

Faizi, A.Q. 'Explanation of the Symbol of the Greatest Name'. New Delhi: Bahá'í Publishing Trust, 1968.

— Letter written to a believer, 3 December 1964.

— *Meditations on the Eve of November 4th.* London: Bahá'í Publishing Trust, 1970.

'Hands of the Cause', in *Bahá'í World*, vol. 13, p. 378.

Ḥuqúqu'lláh: The Right of God. London: Bahá'í Books UK, 2007.

Let Thy Breeze Refresh Them: Bahá'í Prayers and Tablets for Children. Oakham: Bahá'í Publishing Trust, 1976.

'The Most Great Jubilee', in *The Bahá'í World*. vol. 14. Haifa: The Universal House of Justice, 1974.

National Spiritual Assembly of Fiji. Report, April 1977.

Payám-i Bahá'í, no. 132, November 1990.

Payám-i Bahá'í, no. 316, March 2006.

'Proclamation by the Hands of the Cause to the Bahá'ís of East and West', in *Bahá'í World*, vol. 13, p. 342.

Shoghi Effendi. Cable of Shoghi Effendi to A.Q. Faizi, 25 May 1944.

— Letter written on behalf of Shoghi Effendi to the National Spiritual Assembly of Iran, 23 December 1935.

— Letter of Shoghi Effendi, 4 December 1938.

— Letter written on behalf of Shoghi Effendi, 29 July 1942.

— Letter written on behalf of Shoghi Effendi to A.Q. Faizi, 12 April 1946.

— Letter of Shoghi Effendi to Mádar-jún, 16 July 1946.

Universal House of Justice. Letter to the National Spiritual Assembly of the Bahá'ís of New Zealand, 1 November 1976

References and Notes

Chapter 1: Childhood

1. 14th-century Persian Sufi poet.
2. Siyyids, or descendants of the Prophet Muhammad, claim one fifth of the wealth of every Muslim.
3. Strongman; body-building athlete in the ancient Persian tradition.
4. *Mádar* is mother in Persian and *jún* is a term of endearment.
5. A richly embroidered and expensive material.
6. A head-to-foot cloth covering worn by women for modesty.
7. Used for smoking hashish.
8. A large urn in which water is boiled for tea.
9. Opium was used in Persia, the Middle East, Europe and Asia as a medicine as well as for recreational purposes. In the 19th century, opium trading was one of the most profitable businesses of the British Empire.
10. A large, square, low table with a brazier of hot embers underneath and covered with a huge quilt. People entering a room with a *korsí* during the winter months would remove their shoes by the door and sit round the table, stretching their legs under the quilt and table for warmth.
11. Plucked stringed instrument resembling a long necked lute.
12. Minced lamb kebab with rice.
13. A one-class old-fashioned primary school.
14. Large parts of this section were translated by Gloria Faizi.
15. A mode of punishment whereby the victim is laid on his back on the floor, his ankles tied to a pole which is then lifted by two people, one on either side, while a third person beats the soles of his feet with a cane.
16. Faizi was not a Siyyid.
17. The smallest denomination of money in those days – a few pence in today's money.
18. Faizi's grandfather was a famous calligrapher and what Faizi had taken to the school was probably much more precious than anything the others had brought.
19. Shí'as mourn the martyrdom of several Imáms, the most important of them being Imám Ḥusayn, who was martyred on the 10th of Muḥarram. On this day groups of men come out onto the streets to

beat their breasts and inflict bodily harm on themselves in different ways.
20. The more important a clergyman was, the higher he climbed up the steps to the pulpit.
21. People in Persia continued to refer to the Bahá'ís as Bábís for many years, and many still do.
22. Shí'í Islam disapproves the use of all musical instruments.

Chapter 2: Tehran – Tarbíyat School – Youth
1. A respectful form of address in Persian.
2. 'Abdu'l-Bahá, in *Let Thy Breeze Refresh Them*, no. 35.
3. Mr Fatheazam's eldest son was to become one of Faizi's closest friends and a member of the first elected Universal House of Justice.
4. Appointed by 'Abdu'l-Bahá as Guardian of the Bahá'í Faith and head of the Bahá'í world community in 1921. He passed away in 1957.
5. Edison 'Edson' Arantes do Nascimento.

Chapter 3: Beirut
1. The family had been living in Beirut since the time of Bahá'u'lláh's imprisonment in 'Akká.
2. Bahá'u'lláh's daughter.
3. Those who claimed to be Bahá'ís but turned against Bahá'u'lláh, 'Abdu'l-Bahá or Shoghi Effendi. In this case, these Covenant-breakers were members of Bahá'u'lláh's family who did not accept 'Abdu'l-Bahá's Will and Testament appointing Shoghi Effendi Guardian of the Faith after 'Abdu'l-Bahá's death.
4. Appointed a Hand of the Cause posthumously and regarded as the first American martyr of the Faith.

Chapter 4: Return Home
1. Mírzá Muḥammad Ḥusayn and Mírzá Muḥammad Ḥasan, two rich and successful merchant brothers who were natives of Isfahan and well known for their uprightness, selflessness and kindliness. They were tortured and beheaded in 1879 for refusing to recant their faith. The titles 'Beloved of Martyrs' and 'King of Martyrs' were given to them by Bahá'u'lláh after their deaths.
2. Appointed Hand of the Cause in 1951.
3. The King.
4. *Payám-i Bahá'í*, no. 316, March 2006.
5. Forty-four Bahá'í schools throughout Iran were closed. *Payám-i Bahá'í*, no 316, March 2006.

REFERENCES AND NOTES

6. Letter written on behalf of Shoghi Effendi to the National Spiritual Assembly of Iran, 23 December 1935.

Chapter 5: Najafábád

1. The *túmán* is the highest denomination of money in Iran.
2. 'The "Right of God". Instituted in the Kitáb-i-Aqdas, it is an offering made by the Bahá'ís through the Head of the Faith for the purposes specified in the Bahá'í Writings' (Kitáb-i-Aqdas, p. 253). The sum to be offered is 19 per cent of the net value of one's possessions after the deduction of needful expenses and exempt items such as one's home, 'and on subsequent annual increases to this net property arising from surplus income after the payment of necessary expenses' (*Ḥuqúqu'lláh*, no. 110).
3. Traditional Persian shoes worn by village people.
4. Bahá'u'lláh's book of laws.
5. Smallest denomination of money.
6. Keith Ransom Kehler.
7. Músá Banání was appointed a Hand of the Cause in 1952.
8. Letter of Shoghi Effendi, 4 December 1938.

Chapter 6: Qazvín

1. Jalál Khádih, appointed Hand of the Cause of God in 1953.
2. Ḥakím Áqá Ján, a physician who was the first Jew to become a Bahá'í in Hamadán.

Chapter 8: Baghdad

1. Places of pilgrimage for Shí'í Muslims.
2. Letter written on behalf of Shoghi Effendi, 29 July 1942.
3. An Islamic scholar whose belief in the imminence of a new revelation from God prompted him to prepare his students for the coming of the Báb.

Chapter 9: Bahrain: The Lonely Years

1. Traditional Arab vessel.
2. Information provided by the Research Department of the Universal House of Justice.
3. Simple huts made of dry palm branches.
4. Cable received 25 May 1944.
5. The Guardian's wife.
6. A well-known Persian poet.
7. Indian laundrymen.
8. Letter dated 12 April 1946.

Chapter 10: Bahrain: Beginnings of a Community
1. Letter of Shoghi Effendi, 16 July 1946.
2. Believers and poets at the time of Bahá'u'lláh.
3. Manúchihr Salmánpúr.
4. Leader of the *zúrkhánih*.
5. Appointed Hand of the Cause of God in 1951.
6. An assistant to the Hands of the Cause.

Chapter 11: The Road of No Return
1. Amatu'l-Bahá Rúḥíyyih Khánum, 'The Passing of Shoghi Effendi', in *Bahá'í World*, vol. 13, pp. 223–5.

Chapter 12: The Holy Land: A Change of Direction
1. 'Proclamation by the Hands of the Cause to the Bahá'ís of East and West', in *Bahá'í World*, vol. 13, p. 342.
2. ibid. p. 345.
3. ibid. p. 342.
4. *Payám-i Bahá'í*, no. 132, November 1990.
5. A poignant love story in ancient Arabic and Persian literature with spiritual allegories.
6. Persian *Book of Kings* composed by Ferdowsi, one of Iran's foremost 10th-century poets.
7. Appointed Hand of the Cause in 1957.
8. 'Abdu'l-Bahá, *Selections*, p. 51.
9. Auxiliary Board Member at the time.

Chapter 13: The End of an Era
1. 'The Most Great Jubilee', *Bahá'í World*, vol. 14, p. 78.
2. 'Hands of the Cause', *Bahá'í World*, vol. 13, p. 378.
3. A famous line from one of the poems of Háfiz.
4. Member of the Universal House of Justice from 1963 to 2005.
5. *Bahá'í International News Service*, 4 September 1968.
6. A native of Hawaii, she was the first Bahá'í there; she pioneered to Japan in 1914.
7. Member of the Universal House of Justice from 1963 to 1982.

Chapter 14: 'I Do It Because I Must'
1. Excerpt from a report from South America, 1974.
2. *Bahá'í International News Service*, 1 September 1974.

Chapter 15: No Time for Rest
1. From a report by the National Spiritual Assembly of Fiji, April 1977.

REFERENCES AND NOTES

Chapter 16: Anecdotes and Insights
1. Words of 'Abdu'l-Bahá, provisionally translated by Faizi in a letter written to a believer, 3 December 1964. See also Afroukhteh, *Memories*, pp. 186–7 for another provisional translation of this passage.

Chapter 19: Twilight
1. Bahá'u'lláh's daughter.
2. *Bahá'í World*, vol. 18, p. 659.

Chapter 20: Vignettes
1. Bahá'í summer school in Tiverton, Devon, 1975.

Appendix I: Passion Plays
1. A younger brother of Imám Ḥusayn.
2. The man who killed Imám Ḥusayn.
3. The 19 year old son of Imám Ḥusayn.
4. 'Abbás, a younger brother of Imám Ḥusayn, went to fetch water when everyone was suffering from thirst. On his way back, the enemy struck off the arm that carried the skin of precious water. 'Abbás hung the skin on his neck and struggled on, but he was decapitated before he could reach his comrades.
5. The *gawd* or pit was where the men did their exercises. It was lower than the rest of the floor of the *zúrkhánih* by a little more than a metre. The size of the *gawd* was 6 x 6 metres or more, depending on the size of the *zúrkhánih* itself.
6. The 72 followers of Imám Ḥusayn who fought with him were all killed during the battle.

Appendix II: *Zúrkhánih*
1. The entrance door of a *zúrkhánih* was always built low so that those who came in would bow their heads in humility.
2. The fire was to warm the drum.
3. As a sign of reverence for the *zúrkhánih*.
4. The leader of the *zúrkhánih* regulated the timings of all the exercises with the instructions he chanted, and he kept the pace with the beat of his drum.
5. Wrestling was considered an art, not a fight between two individuals, and anger was not tolerated.

Index

This index is alphabetized letter by letter. Articles, prepositions, conjunctions, spaces, hyphens, apostrophes and the connecting letter -i- in entries are ignored.

'Abdu'l-Bahá, ix, x, xii–xiii, 190, 267, 270, 289, 292, 296, 303, 314, 317, 322, 323, 324, 327–8, 394
  Faizi's dream of, 345
  house of, 57, 58, 62–3, 230, 243, 244, 253, 336, 349
  Shrine of, 243, 245, 251
  Tablets of the Divine Plan, 295
  wife of, 63
'Abdu'l Ḥusayn Khán (Faizi's father), 3, 4–6, 40–1, 51, 52, 69
Áb-i Mangul, 49
Abu'l-Faḍl, Mírzá, 78, 116
acting/actors, 27, 60, 293, 375–7
Administrative Order, ix–x
  see also Auxiliary Board Members, Counsellors, Hands of the Cause, Local Spiritual Assemblies, National Spiritual Assemblies *and* Universal House of Justice
Africa, 292–4
Afroukhteh, Dr Youness, 314
Afshin, Mahnaz, 367–8
Ágáhí, Manouchehr, 366–7
Aḥmad-i-Ahsá'í, Shaykh, 138, 140, 142
Ahsá, 138, 141
Akhaván, 'Ináyat, xvii, 160, 179, 370
'Alá'í, Behjat, 72
'Alá'í, Farhang, 364
'Alá'í, Lilian, 300
'Alá'í, Manúchihr and Manúshán, 117, 133, 193
'Alá'í, Najmiyyih Lámi' (Faizi's mother-in-law), 109, 193
'Alá'í, Ni 'mat, 134–5
'Alá'í, Núrí, 216
'Alá'í, Raḥmat (Faizi's father-in-law), 55–6, 76, 106, 107–9, 137
'Alá'í, Shu 'á 'u'lláh, 205
'Alá'í, Suhayl, 193, 300

Al Arrayed, Ibráhím, 154
Alaska, 347, 296, 384, 385
alcohol, 6
Alexander, Agnes, 180–1, 270–1, 396
'Alí Akbar, 376
'Alí Asghar, 113–14
American College, Tehran, 51
Arabia, 140, 174, 224, 301–2
Arabic
  language, 59, 142, 162, 179, 199, 200, 215, 272, 291, 371
  literature, 210, 396
  music, 191
  poetry, 67
Argentina, 257, 294, 316, 381, 385
arts, the, 27, 50, 67, 211, 301
Asadu'lláh Iṣfahání, Mírzá, 113
Ashraf, Fu'ád, xvii, 51
Ashraf, Qudsíyyih, 51, 52
'Aṭṭár, Maḥmúd, 356
Auckland, International Conference, 299–300
Australasia, 206–8, 209
Australia, 206–8
Austria, 331, 355, 384, 386
authors/writing, 266–8, 309–11
Auxiliary Board Members, xi, xii, 227, 396
  Faizi appointed, 199
the Báb, viii, ix, x, xii, xiii, 84, 140, 395
  commemoration of the martyrdom of, xii, 71, 187
  house of, in Shiraz, 106, 111
  remains of, 113
  Shrine of, *see* Shrine of the Báb
Bábís, viii, 9
  Bahá'ís called, 28, 394
  superstitions about, 28
backbiting, 367

life in, 142–5, 150–6, 161
literacy course taught by, 175
teaches school in, 192
travel to, 141–2
wearing of veil in, 147–8
brothers of, 117
childhood of, 55–7, 62, 71–2
children of, 144, 149, 161, 164, 194–5
twins, 157–8, 161, 290
see also Faizi (Mosaed), Hooshang; Faizi, Naysán; *and* Faizi-Moore, May
driving lessons of, 202
in England, 253, 255
in Haifa, 243–5, 251–2, 330, 334–5
and Hooshang, 117, 193
ill health of, 190, 195, 212–13, 244
in India, 243
introduction written by, vii
leaving Iran, 129–31, 132–5
marriage of, 105–9
married life of, in Najafábád, 109–12
music enjoyed by, 191
in Pakistan, 232, 237–8
in Qazvin, 120, 125, 129–31
relationship with Faizi, 56–7, 71–2, 77, 212, 239, 251–2, 277, 284–5, 331
relationship with Mádar-jún, 110–11
tends Faizi during his illness, 334–5, 342–4, 345–7
travel teaching of, 255, 282, 331
Faizi (Mosaed), Hooshang (Faizi's adopted son), xix, 77, 119, 120, 125, 193
relationship with Mádar-jún, 83, 116–17
Faizi, Muḥammad 'Alí (Faizi's elder brother), 1, 41, 48, 51–2, 64–5, 68–9, 133, 223–4, 265, 331, 342
attends Bahá'í school, 5–6
Faizi, Naysán (Faizi's son), 7, 35, 144, 181, 190, 206, 304, 330, 342, 343–4, 383, 385
account of Faizi, 368–9
advice to, from Faizi, 138–9, 239, 313–14, 319–21
birth of, 164
childhood of, 165–8, 176–7, 192, 194–5, 199–200, 202, 211–16, 235, 237–8, 282–3
children of, 283, 285
exemption from military service, 368–9
Faizi's explanation of The Seven Valleys to, 325–6
Faizi's letters to, 138–9, 283, 313, 319–20, 321, 325–6, 330, 343–4, 348, 350
and Faizi's ill health, 332–3
and Faizi's passing, 345–6, 348–9
in Haifa, 243–5, 251–2, 254
letters from 'Alí Na<u>kh</u>javání, 345–6, 353–4
marriage of, 319–20
moves to England, 254–5
relationship with father, xix, 239, 283, 313
wrestles with father, 167
Faizi, Zohreh, (Faizi's daughter-in-law) 283, 285, 304, 319–21, 330, 342, 343, 348, 383, 385
Faizi-Mahjúr, Qudsiyyih (Faizi's niece), 277–8
Faizi-Moore, May (Faizi's daughter), vii–viii, xix, 181, 190
advice to, from Faizi, 239
birth of, 149
childhood of, 165–8, 175–7, 192–3, 195, 199, 202, 211–16, 237–8, 282–3
Faizi's letters to, 252, 343–4
and Faizi's passing, 345–6, 349
in Haifa, 243–5
letter from Rúḥíyyih <u>Kh</u>ánum, 239–40
letters from 'Alí Na<u>kh</u>javání, 345–6, 353–4
relationship with father, xix, 239
Falsafí, 213–14
family life, 240–1
Farid, Faramarz, 354–5
Farru<u>kh</u>zádih, Furú<u>gh</u>, 267–8
fast, Bahá'í, 48, 124–5, 177, 198, 213, 244, 282, 288
Fatheazam, Hushmand, 264, 311, 355, 394
Fatheazam, Shafiq, 276
Fatheazam, Shafiqih, 274–6, 338, 355–6

INDEX

Fatheazam family, 274–6, 355–6
Fatḥ-i-A'ẓam, Núru'd-Dín, 44, 94
Fayḍiyyih, the, 3
Feast, 19 Day, xii, 196, 365
   in Bahrain, 181, 184, 194
   in Najafábád, 86, 91–2
Featherstone, Collis, 225
Ferdowsi Club, 157
Ferraby, John, 223, 225, 238, 244, 245
Fiji, 198, 300–2, 382, 383, 386, 387
Finland, 304, 331, 381, 387
fire carriage, 32–3
football, 52, 90, 282, 285
France, 251, 281, 312, 381, 383, 385, 386, 387
   National Spiritual Assembly of, 248–9, 312
'The Fridge', 177–8
funds, Bahá'í, 86, 89, 98–9, 100, 146, 158, 237, 305
Furútan, 'Alí-Akbar (Hand of the Cause), 72, 205, 224, 230, 349, 354, 371
   Hand of the Cause residing in the Holy Land, 231
   and Rúḥíyyih Khánum, 234, 235–6
   at Tarbíyat School, 74
   travels to Australia with Faizi, 206–7

Gabon, 294
Germany, 327, 357
   Faizi's travels in, 224, 225, 233, 287, 304, 307, 312, 381, 383, 384, 385, 387
   National Spiritual Assembly of Germany, 226
Giachery, Dr Ugo, 199, 205
Gibson, Amoz and Mary, 274, 275–6, 340–1
Giddings, Captain Brian, 203
Glory magazine, 309
God, Will of, 335–6
Gorski, Mary Ann, 361
Guardian of the Bahá'í Faith, *see* Shoghi Effendi
Gulf states, 130, 273
Gulmuḥammadí, Dhabíbu'lláh, 32–3
gymnastics, *see* sports and exercise *and* zúrkhánih

Haghighi, 'Atiyyih, 344

Haghighi, Dr Daryush, 352
Ḥakím, Dr Luṭfu'lláh, 231, 245
Ḥakím Áqá Ján, 127
Hamadán, 5
   visit of Jalál Kházeh, 124–6
Hands of the Cause, x, xi, xii, xiii, 72, 358, 373, 394, 395, 396, 239, 241, 251, 242, 263–4, 287, 292, 299, 336
   appointment of, 225
   attend conference in New Delhi, 205
   and Charles Mason Remey, 248–51, 258
   Conclaves of, 230, 234
   correspondence of, 280–2
   custodianship of, 229–31, 239, 245–6, 259
   Faizi appointed, xix, 225, 239
   and Faizi's funeral, 349
   Faizi's relationship with, 270–2, 353
   letters from, to Bahá'ís, 217
   meeting with the Universal House of Justice, 261
   and passing of Shoghi Effendi, 226–7, 229–31, 233, 235, 238
   residing in the Holy Land, 229–31, 233, 272–3, 348, 349
   role of, 206, 274, 370
   tribute to, by the Universal House of Justice, 259–60
   workload of, 272–3
   see also individual Hands of the Cause
Haney, Paul, 231, 271–2, 321, 349, 373
Harrison, Dr, 144–5
hashish, 6, 393
Hawaiian Youth Conference, 322–3, 385
Ḥaydar 'Alí, Ḥájí Mírzá, 78
Henry, O., 210
The Hidden Words, 194
Hiroshima, 309
'Hiroshima', 309–10
Hishmat, 162–4
history
   Faizi's interest in, 27, 59, 118, 137, 146, 200, 210–11, 243, 273–4, 291, 302, 309, 327, 344
Holley, Horace, 205
Holy Land, 78, 82
   commemoration of Bahá'u'lláh's arrival in, 268–9
   Faizi's life in, 229–58, 272–6, 306,

348, 349, 387
Faizi's visits to, 61–5, 69–70, 103, 261
Hands residing in the, 229–30, 233, 272–3, 348, 349
transportation of the remains of the Báb to, 113
House of Worship, Germany, 357
Huddleston, Rouhi, 357–8
Ḥusayn, Imám, 26–7, 79, 397
Faizi's booklet on, 27, 266
passion plays about, 375–7, 393–4
Ḥusayn, Pahlaván, 3, 34, 35, 378–80
Húshyár, Dr, 72

Iceland, 304, 331, 387
India, 267, 286
National Spiritual Assembly of, 206, 255, 256, 286
Indians, Bolivian, 256, 295
Ioas, Leroy, 231
Iqbal family, 57
Iran
Bahá'í youth of, 261–2
Faizis leave, 132–5
Faizi's travels around, 118, 147, 261
National Spiritual Assembly of, see National Spiritual Assembly of Iran
persecution of Bábís in, viii
persecution of Bahá'ís in, ix, 78–80, 92–3, 213–14, 263
Iraq, 130, 135, 136–9
Ireland, 305
Isfahan, 85, 93–4, 119–20, 127, 262–3, 328
Bahá'ís killed in, 92–3, 394
grave of Keith Ransom Kehler in, 70–1, 103
Ishráq-Khávari, 'Abdu'l-Ḥamíd, 94, 127, 128

Jahangiri, Reza, 366
Javád, Ḥáj Áqá, 376
Jews, 45, 169, 395

Karbilá, 377
Karím Khán-i-Zand, 3
Keats, John, 67
Kehler, Keith Ransom, 70, 71, 103, 395
Khadem-Missagh, Bijan, 191
Khádim, Dhikru'lláh, 205, 225

Khamsí, Mas 'úd, xvii, 256, 258
Khamsí, Mrs, 258
Khan, Frank, 362
Khan, Peter, 362
Kházeh, Col. Jalál, 124–6, 134–5, 231
Khurramshahr, 135, 136
Khurshid, 244
Khushábi, 'Abdu'l-Karím, 157
Kidder, Dr Alice, 235, 236, 245
kindness, 97
King of Martyrs, 71, 394
Kinshasa, 292, 383
Kitáb-i-Aqdas, xiii, 85, 89, 94, 121, 281, 395
Kitáb-i-Íqán (Book of Certitude), 85, 93, 114, 194, 275–6, 370
korsí, 8, 9, 393
Kúchih-Bághí, 63

Landegg Academy, 310
Latin America, 256, 294–5
Lebanon, see Beirut
library, Bahá'í
of Najafábád, 112–16
of Qazvín, 127–8
literacy, 91, 173, 175
literature, 27, 59, 210, 267
Bahá'í, banned in Iran, 87
Local Spiritual Assembly/Assemblies, 278, 296, 319
first, of Bahrain, 183–4
election of, x, xi
women on, 222
London, 317
Faizi in, 304, 319, 332–3, 342, 384
first World Congress in, 47, 259
Shoghi Effendi's passing and funeral in, 225–8
Louis XIV, 322
love, 68–9, 320–1, 339, 358
Luxembourg, 279, 304, 382, 383, 385, 386, 387

Mádar-jún (Siddíqih Khánum, Faizi's mother), 1, 3–4, 84, 132–3
attitude to Bahá'í Faith, 44, 47–8, 53
journey to Tehran, 40
letter from Shoghi Effendi, 160–1
in Najafábád, 77, 110–12, 119, 134
passing of, 264–5

INDEX

pilgrimage of, 254–5
  in Qazvin, 120, 134
  relationship with Faizi, 3–4, 44, 77, 83, 100, 134, 223
  relationship with Gloria, 110–11
  takes Hooshang under her wing, 83, 116–17, 193
  words of Faizi about, 132–3
maktab, Faizi's, 12–27, 41, 43
Maláyir, 5
Mammad Ganúkh, 185
Manama, 142, 151
  see also Bahrain
Manama College, 139, 142, 152, 155–6
Manifestation of God, 325
Marie, Queen, of Romania, 61
martyrs, 82, 92–3, 218, 317 327
  'Abbás, 375, 377, 397
  the Báb, *see* Báb, the
  Imám Ḥusayn, *see* Ḥusayn, Imám
  Keith Ransom Kehler (first American martyr), *see* Kehler, Keith Ransom
  King and Beloved of Martyrs, 71, 394
Master, the, *see* 'Abdu'l-Bahá
Ma'ṣúmih, shrine of, 2
Mavadat, Naṣru'lláh, xvii, 48–9, 51
Maxwell, May, 240
Mázandárání, Fáḍil, 94
McDonald, Iain, 374
Meditations on the Eve of November 4th (Faizi), 258, 266–7
Mehrábkhání, R., 358–9
Memorials of the Faithful ('Abdu'l-Bahá), 327
Michelangelo, 211
military service
  Faizi, 51, 71, 74, 75
  Naysán, 368–9
Mírzá, Íraj, 48
Miṣbáḥ, 'Azíz, 41, 46–7, 51, 74, 129
Miṣbáḥ, Fayḍu'lláh, 72
missionaries, 144–5
moderation, 321
money, 2, 10, 55, 64, 104, 172, 186–7, 319, 376, 393, 395
  for the Bahá'í funds, 86, 89, 98–9, 100, 146, 158, 237, 305
  communal money box, 171
  Faizi and, 15, 16–17, 29, 35, 60, 70, 86, 109, 113, 114, 119, 133, 139, 146, 152–5, 158, 163, 201, 237, 321
  pioneers and, 315, 316
Moore, Paul-Faizi (Faizi's grandson), 283–4, 285, 286, 337, 338, 343, 349
Moore, Peter (Faizi's son-in-law), 252–3, 283, 284, 304, 306, 334, 337–8, 343, 349
Moore, Thomas (Faizi's grandson), 283, 337, 338, 343, 349
Mosaed, Hooshang, *see* Faizi, Hooshang (Mosaed)
Mount Carmel, viii, 62, 65, 69–70, 244, 264
Muhájir, Raḥmatu'lláh, 225, 238
Muḥammad, from Shiraz, 171–2
Muḥammad Fayḍ, Mullá (Áyatu'lláh Fayḍ, maternal uncle), 3, 34, 41, 103–4
Muḥammad Háshim, 83
Muharraq, 220
Mühlschlegel, Adelbert, 231
Muhsin-i-Fayz-i-Káshání, Mullá, 3
mulberry tree, in Qum, 7–8, 37
Muqarrabín, Púrán, 363
Murray, Mitra, 371–3
music/musicians, 9, 63, 285, 293, 309–10, 394
  Faizi's interest in, 31, 149, 191–2, 309
Muslims, 2, 45, 78, 92, 97, 101, 151, 213–14, 393, 395
mysticism, 324–5

Nabíl's Narrative (*The Dawn-Breakers*), 91, 106, 118, 124, 128, 129, 327
Najafábád, 78–119
  Bahá'í cemetery in, 83, 92–3
  Bahá'í library of, 112–16
  description of, 80–1
  Faizi teaches school in, 75–7, 84–90, 120
  Feasts in, 86, 91–2
  first Bahá'í school in, 78–80
  first summer school in, 93
  history of, 78
  Mádar-jún in, 77, 110–12, 119, 134
  public showers in, 98–101, 102, 104–5
  youth in, 47, 83, 84, 86, 87, 89, 90–1, 113, 119
Nakhjavání, 'Alí, 251, 264, 274, 345–6, 352, 353–4, 391

403

Nakhjavání, Violette, 368
National Education Committee, 72
National Geographic, 211
National Spiritual Assembly/Assemblies,
   x, xi, 219, 226, 230, 273, 358
   election of first, in region, 220–23, 224
   first, of Iran, 74
   women on, 222
   see also individual National Spiritual
     Assemblies
National Spiritual Assembly of the
   British Isles, 226
National Spiritual Assembly of Chile,
   256–7
National Spiritual Assembly of France,
   248–9, 312
National Spiritual Assembly of Germany,
   226
National Spiritual Assembly of India,
   206, 255, 256, 286
National Spiritual Assembly of Iran, 77,
   80, 127, 158, 220, 311
   flowers for grave of Keith Ransom
     Kehler, 103
   formation of, 74,
   and Faizi, 76, 118, 120, 129–30, 154,
     223–4, 225, 255, 264
Náṭiq, Ruḥu'lláh, 362
Naw-Rúz, 9, 113–14, 148, 184, 355, 363
Nehru, Jawaharlal, 206
New Delhi, Bahá'í conference in, 203–6
New Era School, Panchgani, 243
New Hebrides, 300
New Zealand, 206–8, 209, 255, 198,
   299–300, 330, 382, 384, 386, 387
Niyazi, Mehmet, 367
Noonoo, Salim, 344
North America, 294
Norway, 304, 331, 385, 387
novels, romantic, 267
Núshábádí, Mr, 94

Oceanic Conference, 268–9
oil, 140
oil companies, 75–6, 150–1, 178, 200,
   328
Olinga, Enoch, 225

Pacific, the, 299
pahlaváns (athletes, body-builders), 3,
   27, 34–5, 39, 192, 378–80
Palermo, Sicily, 268–9, 304
paper, Faizi's love of beautiful, 15–16,
   29, 233, 234
Papua New Guinea, 297, 302–3, 386, 387
Paraguay, 257, 381
parenting, 319–21
passion plays, 27, 375–7
Peltours, 280
pencil, story of blue and red, 16–17
Persian language, viii, 59, 192, 267, 291
Peru, 257, 381, 385
Peter, Joseph, 178–82
photographs/photographers, 86, 114, 116,
   169–71, 211–12, 271, 339
   Faizi's, 20–2, 77, 109, 137, 201, 237,
     248, 279
picnics, in Bahrain, 196–8
pilgrimage/pilgrims, 245–8, 344
   Bahá'í, ix
   Faizi's to Haifa, 58–9
   to the shrine of Ma'ṣúmih, 2
pioneer/pioneering, xiii, xix 218, 258,
   286, 288–9, 292–3, 306, 336, 352,
   357–8, 363, 396
   and money, 315, 316
   prayers for, 339
   qualities of, 315–18
   sacrifice of, 173–4, 294
   youth, 199
Plans, Bahá'í teaching, ix–x, 295
plays/playwriting, 59–60, 65–6, 68, 293
   passion plays, 27, 375–7
poetry/poets
   Faizi and, viii, 66, 67, 107, 235,
     267–8, 336–7
   poem about Faizi, 360
poverty, 293–4
prayer/s, xiii, 42–3, 48–9, 62, 86, 118,
   253–4, 288–9, 325, 326, 339, 340,
   343, 344, 349, 350
   at the House and Shrine of the Báb,
     263–4
   power of, 305–8
'Prayer for the Dead', 228
The Priceless Pearl (Rúḥíyyih Rabbaní),
   265
public speaking lessons, 57, 61, 262

Qatar, 169, 363, 381

INDEX

Qazvín, 120–31
  Bahá'í library in, 127–8
  Bahá'í youth in, 120–31
    prepare for service, 128–9
  Faizi's classes in, 120–2
  Gloria in, 120, 125, 129–31
  Mádar-jún in, 120, 134
  troublemakers in, 123
  visit of Jalál Kházeh, 124
Qulám 'Alí, 376–7
Qulúm, 185–6
Qum, 83, 84, 103, 104, 350, 363
  childhood of Faizi in, 1–39
  Faizi's home in, 7–9
  Faizi's last months in, 36–9
  Faizi's school experience in, 12–27, 41, 43
  modern technology in, 31–3
  neighbourhood in, 9–11
  zúrkhánih in, 34–5, 378–80

radio, 31, 191, 192, 210, 213–14, 336
Rafi 'í, Gulnár, 310–11
Rawshan, Dr, 72
Rayhání, Hishmatu'lláh, 362–3
record/record player, 31, 149, 164, 186, 191
Reed, Betty, 236
Reid, Alexander, 324–5
Remey, Charles Mason, 205, 231
  claim to be second Guardian and its effect, 248–51, 256–8, 368
Remover of Difficulties, xiii
Reza Shah, 74, 80
Robarts, John, 225
Romeo and Juliet, 68
Royal Albert Hall, 47, 259
Rubábih, 247
Rudnick, Blanche, 357
Rúhíyyih Khánum, 243, 253, 254, 275–6
  card for Mádar-jún, 265
  and Faizi, 234–6, 239, 250–1, 265, 274, 276–7, 349
  letter to Faizis, 156
  letter to May Faizi, 239–40
  and the passing of Shoghi Effendi, 226, 227, 228, 230, 231, 234–5
  talk about Faizi, 351–2

Sádeqí, Bahrám, 363–6

Sahba, Fariborz, xviii, 310, 363–6
Salímís, 274
Samandarí, Tarázu'lláh, 205, 208, 217–18, 220–1, 222, 230, 269–70, 353
Samímí, Mihdí, 72
Samoa, 298, 300, 382, 383, 386, 387
São Paulo, 29405
Saudi Arabia, 140, 174, 224
schools
  Bahá'í
    closure of, 74–5, 80
    in Hamadan, 5
    in Najafábád, 75–80, 84–90
    Tarbíyat School, *see* Tarbíyat School
  in Bahrain, 142
  summer and winter, *see* summer schools/winter schools
  in Qum, 12–27, 41, 43
Schweitzer, Jacques André, 354
Sears, William, 225, 271, 348, 354, 363
service
  to the Bahá'í Faith, 57, 61, 62, 72, 76, 125, 139, 148, 157, 159, 161, 173, 212, 216, 219, 240, 246, 255, 259, 262–3, 272, 313, 317, 320, 346, 350, 372, 374
  to humanity, 42, 75, 88, 322–3
  youth in Qazvín prepare for, 128–9, 131
The Seven Valleys (Bahá'u'lláh), 325–6
Shah, Mansur, 366
Sháh Abbás the Great (Faizi), 60
Sháh-Námih, 235
Shakespeare, William, 68, 210
Shanghai Express, 68
Shápur, 162–4, 169
Shelley, Percy, 67
Shimr, 376–7
Shiraz, 263–4, 329
Shírází, Fádil, 51, 331
Shírkhudá, 192
Shoghi Effendi, ix, x, 64, 71
  accomplishments of, 242
  appointed Guardian of the Bahá'í Faith, xiii
  encouraged Bahá'ís to study in Beirut, 52
  and Faizi, 61, 218–19
  first meeting, 58–9

405

letters and cables to Faizi, 139, 148, 149, 159
letters about Faizi, 76, 138
letters and cables
 from Bahrain, 148
 to Mádar-jún, 16–1
passing and funeral of, 225–8, 238, 258
photograph of, 84
and Raḥmat 'Alá'í, 56, 108
showers, 184
public, in Najafábád, 98–101, 102, 104–5
Shrine of 'Abdu'l-Bahá, 243, 245, 251
Shrine of the Báb, viii, 58, 62, 65, 69, 199, 243, 244, 245, 251, 263–4, 317, 350, 361
Shrine of Bahá'u'lláh, 58, 229
Siddíqih Khánum (Faizi's mother), see Mádar-jún
Sims, Barbara, 358
Síyáh-Chál, xiii, 299
Skelton, Red, 211
smallpox vaccinations, 221–2
smoking, 308
 in Iran, 6, 11, 40, 136, 393
 smoking beggar, 308
Sobhani, Mohi, 363–4
Some Answered Questions, 194
South America, 256, 294–5
'Spiritual Conqueror of Arabia', 224
sports and exercise, 15, 34–5, 45, 90–1, 124, 157, 192, 235, 337, 377, 378–80, 397
Steinbeck, John, 210
Steiner, Rene, 357
stories, 137, 187, 327
 for children, 327
 of early believers, 60, 91, 118
 told by Faizi, 94, 118, 161, 165, 167, 207, 243, 246, 263, 301–2, 324, 327, 356, 357, 368
 see also Faizi, anecdotes
 written by Faizi, 267–8, 327, 330
students, Bahá'í, in Beirut, 57–8
summer schools/winter schools, 202, 212, 238, 273, 287, 331, 357, 385
 in Europe, 224, 230, 297, 304, 312, 331, 383, 384, 385–7, 397
 in Najafábád, 93
 in Tehran, 118, 129, 223–4

Yerrinbool, 207
Sweden, 304, 331, 387
Szweig, Stefan, 210

Tablets of the Divine Plan, 295
Tablets to the Kings, 194
Tanumafili II of Samoa, Highness Susuga Malietoa, 300, 386
Tarbíyat School, 41–7, 50–1, 88, 331, 345
 closure of, 74–5
 Faizi's intention to teach at, 52, 71, 74
 teachers at, 50–1
 technology, in Qum, 31–3
Tehran, 2, 63, 118, 382, 384, 385, 386
 American College in, 51
 Faizi and Gloria leave, 132–4, 146
 Faizi's mission to, on behalf of Shoghi Effendi, 103–4
 Faizi's move to, 36–9, 41
 Faizi's return to, 71–7, 120, 261–2
 Faizi's visit to, in 1969, 278
 Naysán and family in, 368–9
 Tarbíyat School in, *see* Tarbíyat School
Tehrani, Vahid, 362
Ten Year Crusade, x, 229–30, 241, 255, 259–60
 launch of, 203–5
Thábit, 'Atá'u'lláh and 'Ináyat, xviii, 48–9
Thompson, Catherine, 361–2
Toynbee, Arnold, 210
translations, 61, 265
travel teaching
 Faizi, *see* Faizi, Abu'l-Qásim, teaching trips
 Gloria, 255, 282, 331
 youth, 93, 124–6
True, Corinne, 229
Turkey, 216, 268, 297, 310, 384, 385, 386

United States, 261, 287, 295, 342, 346, 381, 382, 384, 385
Universal House of Justice
 election of, x, xi, xiii, 230, 259
 tribute to Faizi on his passing, 347–8
 tribute to Hands of the Cause, 125–60

INDEX

Vaḥdat, Ḥusayn 'Alí, 72
Vahman, Dr Fereydoun, 267–8, 370
Varqá, Jináb–i, 78
Varqá, Valíyu'lláh, 205
Varqá magazine, 309–11, 364
Vienna, 208
vignettes of Faizi's life, 351–74
Villiers-Stuart, Katherine, 357

Waklin, F. J., 141, 147, 151, 155–6
Waklin, Mrs, 141, 147
Warren, Edna, 374
weddings, 33, 214–15
  Faizi and Gloria, 108–9
West Side Story, 139
Will and Testament of 'Abdu'l-Bahá, ix, xii–xiii
Wilson, Isobel, 373
wine, 281
Wolseley car, 201–2
women, 157, 222, 254, 367
  equality of, with men, xi, 91, 161
  literacy of, 91, 173, 175
World Centre, Bahá'í, ix, xiii
World Congress, 47, 259–60, 261
wrestling, 167, 337, 380, 397
writing/authors, 266–8, 309–11
writings, Bahá'í, x

Yerrinbool Summer School, 207
York youth winter school, 335
youth, Bahá'í, 47, 93–4, 118, 137, 147, 182, 224, 225, 294–5, 309, 312, 322–3, 337–8, 348
  in Baghdad, 136
  in Bahrain, 157, 162–4, 173
  Faizi as a, 40–53, 339
  in France, 312
  Hawaiian Youth Conference, 322–3, 385
  in Iran, 261–2
  in Najafábád, 47, 83, 84, 86, 87, 89, 90–1, 113, 119
  pioneers, 199
  publications for, 309–11
  in Qazvín, 120–31
  and travel teaching, 93, 124–6
  York youth winter school, 335
yoyo, 67

Zahrá'í, Mr and Mrs, 348
Zaynu'l-Muqarrabín, 78, 114, 115, 116
Zoroastrians, 45
zúrkhánih, in Qum, 34–5, 377, 378–80

www.ingramcontent.com/pod-product-compliance
Lightning Source LLC
Chambersburg PA
CBHW040746020526
44116CB00035B/2953